Inside the Ropes

SPORTSWRITERS GET THEIR GAME ON

EDITED AND WITH AN INTRODUCTION BY
ZACHARY MICHAEL JACK | UNIVERSITY
OF NEBRASKA PRESS | LINCOLN & LONDON

Acknowledgments for previously
published material appear on
pp. 46–67, which constitute an
extension of the copyright page.

Library of Congress Cataloging-
in-Publication Data
Inside the ropes : sportswriters get
their game on / edited and with an
introduction by Zachary Michael Jack.
p.   cm.
Includes bibliographical references.
ISBN 978-0-8032-5997-3 (pbk. : alk. paper)
1. Sportswriters—Anecdotes.
2. Sports—Anecdotes. I. Jack,
Zachary Michael, 1973–
GV742.4.I57 2008
070.4'49796—dc22
2008020376

Set in Quadraat by Bob Reitz.

CONTENTS

PREFACE

Good readers want to know: Am I, the reader, cut out for this book? Is this book *me*? Will this book make for good company at Starbucks? Will it look good under the Xmas tree? Will it accessorize well with a fire-engine red Ipod? Just who, Mister Big Shot Editor, should read this book, anyhow?

Who? Everyone. Everyone who loves sports well played and writing well crafted—amateur and professional athletes, extreme sports enthusiasts, coaches and athletic directors, writers, recreators, travelers, and adventurers par excellence.

For aspiring athletes and their parents and coaches, here's a book of world-class inspiration. For sportswatchers, pundits, and bloggers, here's a book of the best, richest fodder, of unadulterated, unmitigated sportive pleasure. For journalists in general and sportswriters in particular, here's a book that demonstrates the vivacities and verities of participatory journalism, of the discoveries implicit in practicing what's preached.

Most especially, this book is for those brave souls nearing or firmly entrenched in middle age—that frighteningly broad, often- divotted, always-fraught playing field spanning the ages of thirty to sixty. The world's best experiential sportswriters huddle up between these covers with us middle relievers firmly in mind: those of us whose heads hit the pillow each night doubting whether we've really lived out Thoreau's charge to live deeply and suck the marrow out of life, that we not arrive at the end only to discover that we have not lived.

Here, then, is a once-in-a-generation collection of readings that are notable for their energy-giving capacity, for their sweet call to engage—not in the haughty, in-your-face, sportier-than-thou sense, but in the way watching people play the sports they love, or watching their first attempts at playing the sports they will come to love, has the power to move us, quite literally, from our chairs. The way witnessing first love can move us, or the way knowing that a favorite team is reporting to spring training somewhere in the great, sunshiny beyond. For me the moment always comes on Master's weekend in April, when I fill myself to brimming with azaleas and Amen Corner. Weather be damned, I launch myself out into the cold midwestern spring to take my first ecstatic, erratic swings of the year. By that point I've read about golf, heard about golf, dreamed about golf. Now I must *do golf*.

For the love of sport, then, dear reader. For taking that first swing. For filling yourself up.

ACKNOWLEDGMENTS

A collection as rich and broad as *Inside the Ropes* would not have been possible without the generosity and goodwill of its many contributors and their representatives, to whom I would like to express my profound gratitude. In particular I am indebted to Karen Hustoft at *Outside* and the many fine writers that have graced the pages of that venerable magazine and whose work appears in this collection. Cathy Henkel, at *The Seattle Times*, and Joli Sandoz, at Evergreen State College, provided invaluable referrals in the early stages of this project. Thanks to Robert J. Taylor and the University of Nebraska Press for bringing these athletic voices to readers nationwide. A raise of the glass and a doff of the cap to George Plimpton and Paul Gallico, who trailblazed. As always, my deepest appreciation belongs to my family, who understood that this farm kid needed to play as much as he needed to work. And to the many teams, organized and not, that granted me the pleasure of playing ball—I tell you I have never been happier.

INTRODUCTION

Full-Court Journalism

"It is fairly obvious that a man who has been tapped on the chin with five fingers wrapped up in a leather boxing glove and propelled by the arm of an expert knows more about that particular sensation than one who has not, always provided he has the gift of expressing himself."—Paul Gallico, "The Feel"

So what's it like to scale Everest, parachute out of a Cessna, stunt with the Blue Angels, tend goal for the Boston Bruins, burn rubber on a NASCAR track, marathon one hundred miles in twenty-four hours, quarterback the Detroit Lions, sail the ocean blue between Los Angeles and Honolulu on an all-woman crew? What's it like to receive John McEnroe's slice serve, paddle Jack London's Alaskan river route, take a punch from Muhammad Ali, coach the Phoenix Suns' Steve Nash, or call "fair" or "foul" to a Manny Ramirez line drive and suffer the consequences?

If you're a good little sports reader, you know already—because you've skipped the dry stuff, the bunny hill of prefaces and intros, the bookish yadda yadda yadda—and headed straight for the slopes: the forty eye-popping accounts that follow from the world's top participatory sportswriters.

In a July 2007 interview with National Public Radio, veteran sportswriter Frank Deford claimed sports were "the easiest thing to write about, and I guess the most fun to write about. . . . Every day there are winners and losers and there's drama and there's joy and there's glamour." As a former newspaper sports editor, I can vouch for the second part, the part about sportswriting being a whole lot of fun. But some would beg to differ with the "easiest thing" thing, as the rigorous brand of sportswriting that fills this book is the antithesis of a walk in the park and one reason why the sportswriting milquetoast must sit this one out: that person isn't willing to lace up the sneakers or strap on the jock to experience the world of the athlete from the inside out.

Sportswriting great Paul Gallico had the empathy principle figured out way back in 1937, circa his seminal sportswriting memoir, *Farewell to Sport*. When a *mere sportswriter* gets knocked out by the likes of Jack Dempsey, as Gallico did, or by Archie Moore, as George Plimpton did, or by Muhammad Ali, as Davis Miller did, he's indisputably been "touched." His hard-won knowledge makes him special—in a sense, shamanic. And, if you believe in the six degrees of separation, you are, through the accounts written by Gallico, Plimpton, and Miller as they appear in this collection, one degree removed from those famous fists. By the same token, if you've received McEnroe's serve, as James Kaplan did, you're just two steps removed from Bjorn Borg, Jimmy Connors, and Boris Becker, and only one step from Jimmy Mac himself, whether you consider him the tennis Christ, the tennis Antichrist, or somewhere in between. The religious analogy, fanciful as it may seem, serves here: participatory sportswriters assist, witness, and testify, Magi-like, one hand filled with frankincense, the other with smelling salts.

Insofar as this collection is concerned, a reporter hasn't really begun to report—or become real like the Velveteen Rabbit—until he or she follows a star, leaving behind a desk calendar, a faux leather chair, and a half-eaten jelly roll to take part in the minor miracle that is big-time sports. Sports-hungry television audiences are rapidly reaching the same conclusion, which is one reason why it seems that every immaculately enunciating, moderately interesting, mildly amusing host playing emcee in the broadcast booth is joined by two ex-pro athletes doing the heavy lifting alongside. Put another way, the on-camera sports vets constitute the real life of the party. Still, who better to sort through the vainglorious athlete's whopping fish tales or those larger-than-life battlefield blow-by-blows than the retiring writer standing next to the punchbowl, jotting it all down on a well-worn notepad?

The fact is, it takes two to do the sports coverage tango: a skilled communicator—light of foot, deft of pen—and an amateur or ex-athlete still close enough to the "thrill of victory and the agony of defeat." And sometimes, rarely, when the beast in question—half-sportswriter, half-participant—puts it all together, a perfect centaur sings.

Athlete-journalist-visionary Walt Whitman sums up the esprit de corps of the participatory sports journalist in "Song of Myself," where the old wrestler-vagabond avows: "I am the teacher of athletes / He that by me speaks a wider breast than my own proves the width of my own." In a bear-hug of all things participatory, Old Walt reminds us that it's "first-rate to ride, to fight, to hit the bull's eye, to sail a skiff." Another fine poet-athlete, Theodore Roethke, who, incidentally, once worked as a tennis coach, puts an equally fine point on it in his great poem "The Waking," wherein he writes, "I feel my fate in what I cannot fear / I learn by going where I have to go."

Roethke and Whitman have it right: the most athletic writers in any genre are those who choose the unadulterated, unmediated experience and, through it, achieve a natural high, a moment of clairvoyance, of clear seeing, to share with their readers. There's a palpable youthfulness about the work of the participatory journalist. The thirty-something-year-old narrator of Chuck Palahniuk's blockbuster novel, *Fight Club*, for example, speaks volumes for participatory sportswriters everywhere when he muses, "Love and life belongs to great risk."

Like the existential characters in *Fight Club*, participatory journalists often get spooked by their own complacencies and domesticities and rubberband into a competitive world, into a fight club real or imagined. Hunter S. Thompson, whose oblique gonzo accounts of gambling and racing make a gesture at participatory sports journalism without fully becoming it, posed the crucial rhetorical question in his 1955 essay, "Security," penned at the ripe old age of seventeen: "We shall let the reader answer this question for himself: who is the happier man, he who has braved the storm of life and lived or he who has stayed securely on shore and merely existed?"

The journey of the participatory sportswriter is thus a hero's and a heroine's journey, as mythologist Joseph Campbell sketched it—the writer hears the call to adventure, initially resists it as pure folly, and finally relents when the voices (e.g., *If you build it, they will come*) become too loud to ignore. The man or woman who accepts the participatory challenge undertakes the hero's journey, in fact doubly so: each faces the epic self-doubts implicit in both sport *and* writing. These folks are not just facing a blank screen, a blinking cursor, or a screaming editor. No sirree, as these pages attest, they are about to get hit by a two-hundred-and-forty-pound lineman or mauled by a thousand-pound bull. Playing out the Joseph Campbell storyline, then, participatory sportswriters face threshold guardians and gatekeepers (in the guise of micromanaging owners, dubious editors, and dismissive athletes) yet fully immerse themselves in the alluring athlete's world (typically disguised, having donned the chosen sport's uniform) to face the supreme ordeal (the game, the race, the contest) and return home safely, often regretfully, to their humdrum cubicles, bearing fantastical dispatches from another world. As Palahniuk writes, "After a night in a fight club, everything in the real world gets the volume turned down."

There is, it's fair to say, something of the wild child's willfulness and acting out in the sportswriter who demands to *see* and *feel* for himself or for herself, to go inside the ropes and beyond the call. Whether participatory sports journalism may be considered an offshoot of Tom Wolfe's New Journalism or not, what's distinct about the next-generation work in this compendium is what editor Robert Boynton claims, in his anthology, *The New New Journalism: Conversations with America's Best Nonfiction Writers on Their Craft*, characterizes the journalistic new age: namely, "innovative immersion strategies" forever changing "the *way* one gets the story." In Boynton's book and others, Tom Wolfe gets more than his fair share of credit for pioneering, or at least defining, New Journalism. In his definitive 1973 book, *The New Journalism*, Wolfe famously declares nonfiction, and journalism especially, "literature's main event." Easily lost in such creation myths, however, is the fact that a *mere sportswriter*, George Plimpton, had already published his bestselling participatory, New Journalism account of exhibition pitching in the Major Leagues, *Out of My League* (1961), a half dozen years before Wolfe's breakthrough *The Electric Kool-Aid Acid Test.* While Wolfe postulated in a 1966 interview with *Vogue* that the key to every journalistic article worth its salt should be "discovering and defining a new status," Plimpton was living that nugget as he entered the lion's den, quite literally, by suiting up as a Detroit Lions quarterback for the 1963 NFL preseason, a tale he relayed in his second participatory book splash and eventual major motion picture, *Paper Lion.*

More than forty years after the publication of *Paper Lion,* Plimpton's brand of shape-shifting, disguise-making, boundary-crossing New Journalism remains front and center in the participatory writer's bag of tricks. Non-sport immersion journalist Ted Conover—whose books have featured an undercover Conover hoboing his way across the United States—working as a prison guard at Sing Sing, and smuggling himself across the U.S.-Mexico border—told Boynton in an interview, "I am fascinated by the wearing of different hats, of how one's outlook changes depending on one's position in the world, by the whole question of *identity.*" The use of personality as both costumery and journalistic strategy may be traced, in part, to Plimpton. Hence the real father of New Journalism may not be the Ph.D.-wielding, white linen–clad Wolfe after all, but a regular ol' sports guy, forsooth.

If George Plimpton is the godfather of experiential sportswriting, in the way that James Brown is the Godfather of Soul, the genre's grandfather is certainly Paul Gallico, who Plimpton himself describes as a "crack sportswriter" of the 1930s. Gallico, Plimpton reports in his introductory tribute to his mentor in *The Best of Plimpton,* gave himself what was then a novel assignment: "To find out firsthand about athletic skills at their very best—catching Herb Pennock's curveball, playing tennis with Vinnie Richards and golf with Bobby Jones, sparring with Jack Dempsey and getting knocked down."

Granted, Gallico was not the first American writer to make his niche by attempting sport and writing about it—pitching and telling—but it is fair to say that he was the first to make a journalistic calling card of it, the first to gain consistent, playful access to professional athletes in a Golden Age when sportsmen and sportswomen first became media superstars. Likewise, Gallico's was probably the first sustained practice of the *journalism* aspect of *participatory sports journalism*, complete with the hallmarks that today define the field as a discipline, a pursuit, and a methodology rolled into one. Before Gallico, accounts of first-person adventure and sport were often penned by those who otherwise earned their livings as naturalists, adventurers, and literary luminaries—men and women like Walt Whitman, John Muir, Frances Elizabeth Willard, Jack London, Zane Grey, and Ernest Hemingway, to name a few—but history doesn't remember these folks primarily for their journalism. Appropriately, it was the ever-eclectic, rough-riding hunter-naturalist-writer-politician Teddy Roosevelt who, in speaking to Chicago's Hamilton Club in 1899, first used the presidential platform to advocate the strenuous life of the sportsman that so appealed to Gallico. In a forerunner to Nike's "Just Do It" sloganeering, the Bull Moose roared, "I preach to you, then, my countrymen, that our country calls not for the life of ease but for the life of strenuous endeavor. The twentieth century looms before us big with the fate of many nations. If we stand idly by, if we seek merely swollen, slothful ease and ignoble peace, if we shrink from the hard contests where men must win at hazard of their lives and at the risk of all they hold dear, then the bolder and stronger peoples will pass us by, and will win for themselves the domination of the world." Though Plimpton was a thoroughgoing ironist by comparison with the more literal-minded, dogmatic Bull Moose, both men demonstrated for their respective generations that a man of letters could also be a man of action.

Gallico's influence on Plimpton was more immediate than Roosevelt's, and it hit closer to home, too: Plimpton, born in 1927, grew up in New York City in the era when Big Apple–native Gallico enjoyed his heyday as the sports editor at the *New York Daily News*. Both men, in addition to being gifted writers, were natural athletes: Plimpton, a lithe six-foot-four with a quarterback's hands, and Gallico, a boxer and the inventor-organizer of the Golden Gloves amateur boxing competition. After reading Gallico's memoir, *Farewell to Sport*, it came as a revelation to Plimpton that he could, as he put it, "undertake the same kind of research . . . and expand it somewhat—to find out not only about athletic skills at their best, but

INTRODUCTION: FULL-COURT JOURNALISM

also something about the society of athletes, to join the team as a kind of 'amateur professional.'" To conceive of Plimpton's joyous, participatory romps through the NFL, NHL, MLB, and PGA as "research" stretches the moth-eaten definition of scholarship wonderfully, and leads us back squarely to Frank Deford's shot-across-the-bow proposition. Maybe sportswriting *is* the most fun, and doubly so when the journalist doesn't have to hold someone else's jock.

Still, in an age of professionalism, when many Olympic athletes have gone pro, the question remains: What does the amateur know that the professional doesn't? What did Bobby Jones, the quintessential amateur of Gallico's era, understand that Tiger Woods can't fathom? Humility? Honor? Heritage? The best participatory sportswriting, like the best, most noble amateurism, resurrects long-lost virtues America preserves in purposeful, Jeffersonian hybridity: the citizen-legislator, the farmer-teacher, or, in the case of Bobby Jones, the lawyer-scholar-engineer-writer-golfer. In a phrase, *inside the ropes* suggests fortuitous, anomalous access, existential manna, and perspective-giving centaurism: it tells the feel-good Cinderella story of a housemaid guesting as a princess for an evening, the tale of a beggar permitted, for a day, to be king.

Literature and myth are, of course, chock-full of command sports performances in which the heir apparent must come to the fore, must transform from backstage hand to leading man. In Homer's *Odyssey*, the sporting prince Telemachus laments, "Ah! Shall I ever be a coward and a weakling. . . . Come, you who are stronger men than I, come try the bow and end the contest." Staying with the Greeks, there was, of course, Heracles (Hercules)—not much of a writer but one helluva wrestler. A couple of millennia after Heracles whopped Achelous, hard-pressed amateur and celebrated folk hero Willy Tell, taking a page from Odysseus's playbook, had to draw the crossbow under duress to save both son and homeland. The modern day sportsperson-writer seeks such Herculean labors while simultaneously scribbling them down for posterity, à la Plato.

While folk legends abound with tales of inspired athletic amateurism, science-fiction narratives project the role of the amateur-cum-athlete-cum-protagonist ages hence, most notably Brian M. Stableford's 1976 sci-fi sports classic, *The Mind-Riders*. In *The Mind Riders* athletes have become extinct, in much the same way drones figure to replace flesh and blood soldiers in a future War on Terror.

The editorial description of Stableford's *The Mind-Riders* nicely distills the work of today's participatory sportswriter: "If millions pay today just to watch two men fight for a champion's crown, tens of millions will pay for the additional thrill of being actually within the mind and body of the boxers themselves, to experience, *in person* the tension and combat, to throw themselves into punch and counter-punch *without having to feel the pain.*" Published in 1976—the year Ali escaped Norton in the Bronx, his world heavyweight title still intact—Stableford's sci-fi title bouts prove eerily prescient as, in the futuristic world of the novel, experience-hungry spectators, otherwise known as "vamps" and "mind-riders," psychically merge or "e-link" with sim-athletes who duke it out cathartically in the ring.

Similarly, the 1975 sci-fi film *Rollerball* lends to action sports and their narratives the dreadful centrality typically reserved for war. The film, set in 2018, follows the trials of Jonathan E., an athlete-hero-everyman seeking authentic individual sports experiences in a world dominated by corporations. Ring any bells? Apropos to the contemporary ascendancy of participatory sport as political and cultural *primum mobile*, the tagline for the Hugo-nominated *Rollerball* read, "The next war will not be fought, it will be played."

In an era when surveys show young people, young men especially, are demonstrating less interest in the armed services than ever before, and when the Army, in particular, struggles to meet quarterly recruitment goals, the sci-fi logic implicit in *Rollerball* and *The Mind-Riders* makes alarming sense. Sports have become the surrogate battlefield, the new-old sociopolitical arena. In this sense, and in others, ESPN's highly rated broadcasts of the X Games were only the beginning of an alt-engagement strategy for young men, as NBC, USA, FOX, and the Outdoor Life Network have at various times jumped on the bandwagon to carry popular spinoffs such as the Gravity Games and the Dew Action Sports Tour. More recently, extreme sports have launched entire networks the way Helen launched a thousand ships. One of the latest is Fuel, a Fox cable venture peddling round-the-clock "action sports television."

Traditional network television, too, has stepped to the plate, seeing stars and bars as well as dollar signs in the marriage of unscripted reality TV with sports programming. Such cross-pollination has produced programs such as NBC's 2005 boxing reality show, "The Contender," and Fox's "The Next Great Champ." More recently, ABC and NASCAR's reality offering, "Fast Cars and Superstars," and Spike TV's "Reality Racing: The Rookie Challenge" seek to translate NASCAR's cross-demographic popularity into cross-media synergy. In a phrase, participatory sports ventures have seen their stock rise to the level of "sure bet."

In such a multimedia age, for-print participatory sports journalists—the real McCoy—do invaluable, hands-on fieldwork on behalf of their readers. Characteristically humble, the participatory sportswriter seeks equity and integrity via unrestricted, pull-back-the-curtain access. Perhaps because of their *Rollerball*-styled corporate culture, today's professional sports leagues are less than open to such in-person, touch-it-taste-it-feel-it journalistic intrusion, and are more hostile to true, gold-standard participation of the kind celebrated in this book. Flies in the corporate sports ointment, experiential sportswriters fight the good fight, push back, seek a level playing field by way of subversive, subjective participation, much like investigative and undercover reporters do. They're our ultimate free agents.

If you've ever worked in a newsroom, you know there's something different about sportswriters to begin with. Let's start with their offices, which are invariably trashy. Where their colleagues in news and op-ed display something journalistically indispensable—a desk calendar or plat map—or at least personally meaningful—a picture of the better half or the kids—sportswriters glory in their inglorious trade's flotsam and jetsam: candy wrappers, cigarette butts (in the old days), and decades-old floppy disks. It is the sportswriter, the ungrateful imp, who typically is the first to provoke a water cooler dispute and the last to do the breakroom dishes. He's the last to arrive in the morning and the last to leave in the evening. He haunts the paste-up room, an untidy, flatulent ghost.

Sportswriters, especially if they're fond of close encounters of the participatory kind, often play without a full deck or, as Hunter S. Thompson put in his author's note to *Fear and Loathing in America*, "These letters are not the work of a wise man, but only a player with a dangerous gambling habit. . . . That is a risky mix that will sooner or later lead you to cross the wrong wires and get shocked, or even burned to a cinder." Garret Soden's recent book, *Falling: How Our Greatest Fear Became Our Greatest Thrill—A History*, verifies Thompson's brand of journalistic self-immolation: Soden's fascinating study concludes that the freaks who jump off cliffs and go over Niagara Falls in barrels aren't "necessarily brave" but more likely "mentally unbalanced." It makes sense, no? The sport shoe seems to fit. And yet, in a Reagan-Bush Era conspicuously short on such unpremeditated zaniness, it seemed for a while that the Thompsons and Plimptons of sportswriting days of yore were dying off, and their heirs were more likely to day trade in wingtips than crawl naked into barrels.

In the years between George Plimpton's apparent waning and the waxing of Tom Verducci, Rick Reilly, and Jack McCallum as his rightful heirs at *Sports Illustrated*—just as participatory sports journalism's future remained in doubt—a cultural revolution took place, carried out by canny media moguls such as ESPN's John Semiao, who was then programming director for ESPN2 and later became senior vice president at ESPN. The extreme sports X Games, created by Semiao in 1995, were an instant, industry-changing success and, more than that, a crucial epistemological, phenomenological moment for sport. If skateboarding could rightly be classified as a sport rather than an exercise in punk rebellion, what, then, defined "sport"? More to the point, *who* defined sport? If the all-important 17-to-24-year-old, television-consuming American male believed bungee jumping, street lugeing, sky surfing, sport climbing, and kite skiing counted as sport, well, then maybe they did. In America, shouldn't the market, the "invisible hand," decide, in the form of ad revenues and Nielsen ratings?

Emboldened by their newfound audience, a whole team of cliff-diving, barrel-wearing, next-generation gonzo sportswriters stepped out of the shadows to assume the Plimpton mantle. Davis Miller, included in this collection under his earlier nom de plume of Davis Lee, was one of the first to find a mass-market audience post-Plimpton, with his popular participatory memoirs, *The Tao of Muhammad Ali* and *The Tao of Bruce Lee*. But there were others, too. As in *Field of Dreams*: it turns out there existed a whole crew cooling their heels, waiting for the right field, the right audience, the right invite.

In the mid 1990s, newer, cheekier sporting traditions materialized, seemingly out of nowhere—extreme extreme sports with low-budget, often postmodern twists: the Great Bathtub Race in Nome, Alaska, the World Championship Rotary Tiller Races in Emerson, Arkansas, and the World Black-Pudding Tossing Championship in Lancashire, England, to name just a few. Tongue firmly in check, humorist Franz Lidz, writing for *Sports Illustrated* at the height of the extreme sports craze in 2002, remarked, "Once upon a time there were things called extreme sports, in which boys and girls did cute little tricks on skateboards and rode bikes down hillsides. How quaint." For young sportswriters on staff at major newspapers—a demographic represented in this collection by Greg Bishop, Corey Levitan, and Dan Washburn, among others—the opportunity to cover the rise of alternative sports was a once-in-a-lifetime chance to be present at the creation, to be a young man or woman covering a youthful movement rooted in "fierce individualism, alienation, and defiance," as Harvey Lauer, president of American Sports Data, Inc., put it in his 2002 interview with *American Demographics*. For the participatory journalist, dedicated to the proposition that all sports are created equal, these were, and still are, heady days.

In assembling this collection of the world's best contemporary practitioners of a time-tested and truly popular genre, *Inside the Ropes* functions as a kind of tribute album to George Plimpton and Paul Gallico written by the generations they inspired. It pencils in a line-up featuring the best, most dynamic participatory work from the last fifteen to twenty years, with an emphasis on work published in the new millennium. As befits George Plimpton, *Inside the Ropes* provides space to only the best and most established sportswriters. Fly-by-night dabblers, posers, and wannabes were turned away at the gate. Unlike the Best American Sports Writing series, where, in any given volume, many of the writers are not bread-

and-butter sportswriters, as Plimpton himself admitted in editing the 1997 series volume, the writers in *Inside the Ropes* identify themselves as sports scribblers.

What, then, qualifies as *sport*? In answer to this question, several layers of exclusivity were contemplated, from most to least inclusive. The most restrictive, implementable, and, if you will, enforceable definition of sport would probably permit only those games widely played in public and private high schools across the country: swimming, golf, baseball, softball, volleyball, football, basketball, soccer, tennis, track, cross country, and so forth. Right off the bat, though, this listing proved unsatisfactory, as it begged still further questions: Whose high school? What about club sports? More troubling still was the notion that a rigid definition would eliminate a new generation of extreme sports, a move that would run contrary to the anthology as conceived.

Okay, so if extreme sports, which extreme sports? After all, even the notoriously easygoing extreme sport gurus have begun to draw lines. Case in point: X Games progenitor Semiao found himself positively swamped with calls from marketers once he opened the anything-goes Pandora's box of the Winter X Games in 1997. By 1998 even Semiao had, by necessity, begun to reign in his criteria, telling the *New York Times*'s Bill Donahue that he favored sports with "a whole culture attached to them, a specific attitude, and a group of people who live and die by the sport." Indeed, by the time Semiao held forth on the same topic in the same newspaper in 2006, he had abandoned some of the more fanciful "sports" of earlier X Games, including bungee jumping, which he dismissed as, "in essence, an amusement park activity" without the requisite participant base or industry. By 2006 the initial giddiness surrounding alternative sports had given way to circumspection broad enough to reevaluate "extreme sports" as an appellation. Skateboarding icon Tony Hawk admitted to the *New York Times* that he preferred the moniker "action sports," saying, "The term to me means constant action, as opposed to ball sports, where you wait for the action. It's better than 'extreme,' which just sounds cheesy."

Consideration was given to limiting the forty selections presented here to only those sports that keep official records and involve contests of skill among or between athletes measured in terms of wins and losses. At least some sports—or are they merely "activities" or "recreational pursuits"?—such as hiking meet neither of the above criterion. And yet eliminating a "sport" like hiking from potential consideration would both rule out the freshly minted sport of speed hiking and deny the broader physical fitness aspects of sport implicit in the wider-ranging European conception of sport, especially the Norwegian *kropskultur*.

After much consternation, a working definition arose that seemed appropriately inclusive without degenerating into an anything-goes Unitarianism, metaphorically speaking. Any sport, broadly defined, that boasts a recognized national or international governing body or association made muster. This definition, easily justifiable, opened the gates to deserving yet still lesser-known sports that are given space here: shuffleboard, rafting, ski mountaineering, canyoning, highpointing, ultra marathoning, and the like.

And while demographers point to double-digit declines in participation levels in so-called traditional team sports (according to the Superstudy of Sports Participation published in the 2002 edition of *American Demographics*, baseball is down 28 percent since 1987, and softball and volleyball are down 37 and 36 percent, respectively), tradition, for most sports fans, rules the day. Hence, basketball, football, baseball, and other team sports are well-represented in these pages—in spite of a sports paradigm shift whereby skateboarding, to take just one example, appears poised to debut at the 2012 London Olympics, and skateboarder Hawk was, as of 2004, the third most popular athlete among teens twelve to nineteen, a level of clout that gave him license to declare the Olympics badly in a need of what he called a "cool factor." And despite the fact that traditional sports fans are growing older (the median age of PGA tour viewers is fifty-five; Major League Baseball, forty-eight), or maybe because of that fact, some reverence must be given to the old ball games.

Once resolved to using an appropriately eclectic view of sport that includes the new alongside the old, there remained the debate over the parameters of the terms *participation* and *participatory*. To earn his or her stripes, a sportswriter had to take part in the activity he or she was covering or investigating, such that the resulting reportage was appropriately compound—a simultaneous focus on self and others, theory and practice. Practitioners had to go behind the scenes, in the manner of George Plimpton, to offer an immediate, present-tense journalistic take not otherwise available in interview-driven, secondhand reporting. And, while the inclusivities of "sportswriting" as an appellation were chosen in lieu of the vagaries of "journalism," and "verity" was preferred to "fact," the selections reflect, in spirit if not in letter, Bill Kovach and Tom Rosenthiel's edict (in *The Elements of Journalism: What Newspeople Should Know and the Public Should Expect*) that the journalist's first duty is to "verification." The fact of athletic experience—in a word, its *realness*—defines this freewheeling gonzo anthology.

Applying the participatory, present-tense sportswriting filter alone eliminated from consideration a number of pieces best described as sports memoir: older men and women waxing nostalgic about their playing or coaching days. In this category were several excellent but nonetheless nostalgic sports recollections by such great athlete-writers as Pat Conroy, Rick Telander, and James McKean. A second round of scrutiny filtered out the typically ghostwritten "as told to" accounts of sports stars or other tracts "written" by sports glitterati who, while past or present participants on the pro level, had not pursued the training, formal or informal, requisite of a sportswriter. More often than not, participatory journalists were at their best when documenting a first, awkward attempt at a sport that was to them previously unknown, long ignored, or easily overlooked—the way one's powers of description suddenly soar upon a first kiss. Often contributors to this book tackle a new subsport, as is the case when savvy climber-adventurer Mark Jenkins tackles canyoning for the first time, or experienced angler Bob Shacochis gets his feet wet in an elusive Russian salmon run, or otherwise tried-and-true sailor Betsy Crowfoot attempts the Transpacific Yacht Race but with a difference: an all-woman crew.

Sometimes, too, the experiential sportswriter casts himself or herself in a supporting role; in gonzo parlance they are "on the bus," if not exactly behind the wheel. Where the participant-writer's mind is relatively free to wander, the "possibility of absurdity lurks alongside the possibility of athletic excellence," as writer Richard Ford once put it. Several humorous sports participations receive at-bats in these pages, including Tom Verducci's comedy-of-errors stint as an umpire described in "My Trip to the Show (Part II)"; Corey Levitan's pathos-rich batboying in "Now on Deck: Ruffians in the Diamond"; Ron Judd's wry America's Cup ballasting in "Race a Memorable First for 17th Man"; and Jack McCallum's sometimes red-faced chronicling of "assistant coaching" for the Phoenix Suns in "The Backstory." In any case, participatory journalists, if they're doing their job, put themselves outside their comfort zone, experimenting on themselves and those closest to them by virtue of proximity—nearness to the heart of the matter—the way psycho-gonzo Sigmund Freud experimented on his children, God help them, or the way Hunter S. Thompson experimented on himself and his attorney whilst racing, drug-addled, through the Vegas desert. As first-person journalism veteran Walt Harrington puts it in his introduction to *The Beholder's Eye*, "Along with the characters in my stories, I, too, had become a character."

A very few muy macho sportswriters aside, this collection acknowledges, in its better-than-expected-but-still-not-high-enough percentage of female contributors, that no other genre in contemporary letters is more stereotypically, needlessly male than sportswriting. Thus, in showcasing the work of contemporary women sports chroniclers, this collection goes one better than other contemporary anthologies, including the venerable Best American Sports Writing series. Sweeter still is the fact that these accomplished women sports journalists are living, not just writing, the strenuous life.

By rights, an introduction—always so eager to be useful—should foreshadow the book's organization and its big, redeeming themes. Thankfully, the organizational scheme used herein is simple: readings grouped seasonally according to the month of the participation, the calendar date of the article's first appearance, or, failing that, the traditional time of year for the featured sport; such a grouping is both logical and appropriately symbolic, as the sports fan lives and dies by the seasons. As for the Big

Themes, suffice it to say that there are many, too many, to name here: sports participation as romance, as mid-life crisis, as familial bond, as exposé, as intercultural exchange, as comic absurdity, as gender discovery, as physical and emotional redemption. But what say we leave the interpreting to the literary folks and get on with the show?

INSIDE THE ROPES

PAUL GALLICO, FOUNTAINHEAD

The Feel

Paul Gallico

A child wandering through a department store with its mother, is admonished over and over again not to touch things. Mother is convinced that the child only does it to annoy or because it is a child, and usually hasn't the vaguest inkling of the fact that Junior is "touching" because he is a little blotter soaking up information and knowledge and "feel" is an important adjunct to seeing. Adults are exactly the same, in a measure, as you may ascertain when some new gadget or article is produced for inspection. The average person says: "Here, let me see that," and holds out his hand. He doesn't mean "see," because he is already seeing it. What he means is that he wants to get it into his hands and feel it so as to become better acquainted.

As suggested in the foregoing chapter ["Young Men of Manhattan"], I do not insist that a curiosity and capacity for feeling sports is necessary to be a successful writer, but it is fairly obvious that a man who has been tapped on the chin with five fingers wrapped up in a leather boxing glove and propelled by the arm of an expert knows more about that particular sensation than one who has not, always provided he has the gift of expressing himself. I once inquired of a heavyweight prizefighter by the name of King Levinsky, in a radio interview, what it felt like to be hit on the chin by Joe Louis, the King having just acquired that experience with rather disastrous results. Levinsky considered the matter for a moment and then reported: "It don't feel like nuttin'," but added that for a long while afterwards he felt as though he were "in a transom."

I was always a child who touched things and I have always had a tremendous curiosity with regard to sensation. If I knew what playing a game felt like, particularly against or in the company of experts, I was better equipped to write about the playing of it and the problems of the men and women who took part in it. And so, at one time or another, I have tried them all; football, baseball, boxing, riding, shooting, swimming, squash, handball, fencing, diving, flying, both land and sea planes, rowing, canoeing, skiing, riding a bicycle, ice-skating, roller-skating, tennis, golf, archery, basketball, running, both the hundred-yard dash and the mile, the high jump and shot put, badminton, angling, deep-sea, stream-, and surf-casting, billiards and bowling, motorboating and wrestling, besides riding as a passenger with the fastest men on land and water and in the air, to see what it felt like. Most of them I dabbled in as a youngster going through school and college, and others, like piloting a plane, squash, fencing, and skiing, I took up after I was old enough to know better, purely to get the feeling of what they were like.

None of these things can I do well, but I never cared about becoming an expert, and besides, there wasn't time. But there is only one way to find out accurately human sensations in a ship two to three-thousand feet up when the motor quits, and that is actually to experience that gone feeling at the pit of the stomach and the sharp tingling of the skin from head to foot, followed by a sudden amazing sharpness of vision, clear-sightedness, and coolness that you never knew you possessed as you find the question of life or death completely in your own hands. It is not the "you" that you know, but somebody else, a stranger, who noses the ship down, circles, fastens upon the one best spot to sit down, pushes or pulls buttons to try to get her started again, and finally drops her in, safe and sound. And it is only by such experience that you learn likewise of the sudden weakness that hits you right at the back of the knees after you have climbed out and started to walk around her and that comes close to knocking you flat as for the first time since the engine quit its soothing drone you think of destruction and sudden death.

PAUL GALLICO

Often my courage has failed me and I have flunked completely, such as the time I went up to the top of the thirty-foot Olympic diving-tower at Jones Beach, Long Island, during the competitions, to see what it was like to dive from that height, and wound up crawling away from the edge on hands and knees, dizzy, scared, and a little sick, but with a wholesome respect for the boys and girls who hurled themselves through the air and down through the tough skin of the water from that awful height. At other times sheer ignorance of what I was getting into has led me into tight spots such as the time I came down the Olympic ski run from the top of the Kreuzeck, 6,000 feet above Garmisch-Partenkirchen, after having been on skis but once before in snow and for the rest had no more than a dozen lessons on an indoor artificial slide in a New York department store. At one point my legs, untrained, got so tired I couldn't stem (brake) any more, and I lost control and went full tilt and all out, down a three-foot twisting patch cut out of the side of the mountain, with a two-thousand-foot abyss on the left and the mountain itself on the right. That was probably the most scared I have ever been, and I scare fast and often. I remember giving myself up for lost and wondering how long it would take them to retrieve my body and whether I should still be alive. In the meantime the speed of the descent was increasing. Somehow I was keeping my feet and negotiating turns, how I will never know, until suddenly the narrow patch opened out into a wide, steep stretch of slope with a rise at the other end, and that part of the journey was over.

By some miracle I got to the bottom of the run uninjured, having made most of the trip down the icy, perpendicular slopes on the flat of my back. It was the thrill and scare of a lifetime, and to date no one has been able to persuade me to try a jump. I know when to stop. After all, I am entitled to rely upon my imagination for something. But when it was all over and I found myself still whole, it was also distinctly worthwhile to have learned what is required of a ski runner in the breakneck *Abfahrt* or downhill race, or the difficult slalom. Five days later, when I climbed laboriously (still on skis) half-way up that Alp and watched the Olympic downhill racers hurtling down the perilous, ice-covered, and nearly perpendicular *Steilhang*, I knew that I was looking at a great group of athletes who, for one thing, did not know the meaning of the word "fear." The slope was studded with small pine trees and rocks, but half of the field gained precious seconds by hitting that slope all out, with complete contempt for disaster rushing up at them at a speed often better than 60 miles an hour. And when an unfortunate Czech skidded off the course at the bottom of the slope and into a pile of rope and got himself snarled up as helpless as a fly in a spider's web, it was a story that I could write from the heart. I had spent ten minutes getting myself untangled after a fall, without any rope to add to the difficulties. It seems that I couldn't find where my left leg ended and one more ski than I had originally donned seemed to be involved somehow. Only a person who has been on those fiendish runners knows the sensation.

It all began back in 1922 when I was a cub sportswriter and consumed with more curiosity than was good for my health. I had seen my first professional prizefights and wondered at the curious behavior of men under the stress of blows, the sudden checking and the beginning of a little fall forward after a hard punch, the glazing of the eyes and the loss of locomotor control, the strange actions of men on the canvas after a knockdown as they struggled to regain their senses and arise on legs that seemed to have turned to rubber. I had never been in any bad fist fights as a youngster, though I had taken a little physical punishment in football, but it was not enough to complete the picture. Could one think under those conditions?

I had been assigned to my first training camp coverage, Dempsey's at Saratoga Springs, where he was preparing for his famous fight with Luis Firpo. For days I watched him sag a spar boy with what seemed to be no more than a light cuff on the neck, or pat his face with what looked like no more than a caressing stroke of his arm, and the fellow would come all apart at the seams and collapse in a useless heap, grinning vacuously or twitching strangely. My burning curiosity got the better of prudence and a certain reluctance to expose myself to physical pain. I asked Dempsey to permit me to box a round with him. I had never boxed before but I was in good physical shape, having just completed a four-year stretch as a galley slave in the Columbia eight-oared shell.

When it was over and I escaped through the ropes, shaking, bleeding a little from the mouth, with rosin dust on my pants and a vicious throbbing in my head, I knew all that there was to know about being hit in the prize-ring. It seems that I had gone to an expert for tuition. I knew the sensation of being stalked and pursued by a relentless, truculent professional destroyer whose trade and business it was to injure men. I saw the quick flash of the brown forearm that precedes the stunning shock as a bony, leather-bound fist lands on cheek or mouth. I learned more (partly from photographs of the lesson, viewed afterwards, one of which shows me ducked under a vicious left hook, an act of which I never had the slightest recollection) about instinctive ducking and blocking than I could have in ten years of looking at prizefights and I learned, too, that as the soldier never hears the bullet that kills him, so does the fighter rarely, if ever, see the punch that tumbles blackness over him like a mantle, with a tearing rip as though the roof of his skull were exploding, and robs him of his senses.

There was just that—a ripping in my head and then sudden blackness, and the next thing I knew, I was sitting on the canvas covering of the ring floor with my legs collapsed under me, grinning idiotically. How often since have I seen that same silly, goofy look on the faces of dropped fighters—and understood it. I held onto the floor with both hands, because the ring and the audience outside were making a complete clockwise revolution, came to stop, and then went back again counterclockwise. When I struggled to my feet, Jack Kearns, Dempsey's manager, was counting over me, but I neither saw nor heard him and was only conscious that I was in a ridiculous position and that the thing to do was to get up and try to fight back. The floor swayed and rocked beneath me like a fishing dory in an offshore swell, and it was a welcome respite when Dempsey rushed into a clinch, held me up and whispered into my ear: "Wrestle around a bit, son, until your head clears." And then it was that I learned what those little love-taps to the back of the neck and the short digs to the ribs can mean to the groggy pugilist more than half knocked out. It is a murderous game, and the fighter who can escape after having been felled by a lethal blow has my admiration. And there, too, I learned that there can be no sweeter sound than the bell that calls a halt to hostilities.

From that afternoon on, also, dated my antipathy for the spectator at prizefights who yells: "Come on, you bum, get up and fight! Oh, you big quitter! Yah yellow, yah yellow!" Yellow, eh? It is all a man can do to get up after being stunned by a blow, much less fight back. But they do it. And how a man is able to muster any further interest in a combat after being floored with a blow to the pit of the stomach will always remain to me a miracle of what the human animal is capable of under stress.

Further experiments were less painful, but equally illuminating. A couple of sets of tennis with Vinnie Richards taught me more about what is required of a topflight tournament tennis player than I could have got out of a dozen books or year of reporting tennis matches. It is one thing to sit in a press box and write caustically that Brown played uninspired tennis, or Black's court covering was faulty and that his frequent errors cost him the set. It is quite another to stand across the net at the back of a service court and try to get your racket on a service that is so fast that the ear can hardly detect the interval between the sound of the server's bat hitting the ball and the ball striking the court. Tournament tennis is a different game from weekend tennis. For one thing, in average tennis, after the first hard service has gone into the net or out, you breathe a sigh of relief, move up closer and wait for the cripple to come floating over. In big-time tennis second service is practically as hard as the first, with an additional twist on the ball.

It is impossible to judge or know anything about the speed of a forehand drive hit by a champion until you have had one fired at you or, rather, away from you, and you have made an attempt to return it. It is then that you first realize that tennis is played more with the head than with the arms and the legs. The fastest player in the world cannot get to a drive to return it if he hasn't thought correctly, guessed its direction, and anticipated it by a fraction of a second.

There was golf with Bob Jones and Gene Sarazen and Tommy Armour, little Cruickshank, and Johnny Farrell, and Diegel and other professionals; and experiments at trying to keep up in the water with Johnny Weissmuller, Helene Madison, and Eleanor Holm, attempts to catch football passes thrown by Benny Friedman. Nobody actually plays golf until he has acquired the technical perfection to be able to hit the ball accurately, high, low, hooked or faded and placed. And nobody knows what real golf is like until he has played around with a professional and seen him play, not the ball, but the course, the roll of the land, the hazards, the wind, and the texture of the greens and the fairways. It looks like showmanship when a topflight golfer plucks a handful of grass and lets it flutter in the air, or abandons his drive to march two hundred yards down the fairway to and look over the situation It isn't. It's golf. The average player never knows or cares whether he is putting with or across the grain of the green. The professional *always* knows. The same average player standing on the tee is concentrated on getting the ball somewhere on the fairway, two hundred yards out. The professional when preparing to drive is actually to all intents and purposes playing his *second* shot. He means to place his drive so as to open up the green for his approach. But you don't find that out until you have played around with them when they are relaxed and not competing, and listen to them talk and plan attacks on holes.

Major League Baseball is one of the most difficult and precise of all games, but you would never know it unless you went down on the field and got close to it and tried it yourself. For instance, the distance between the pitcher and catcher is a matter of twenty paces, but it doesn't seem like enough when you don a catcher's mitt and try to hold a pitcher with the speed of Dizzy Dean or Dazzy Vance. Not even the sponge that catchers wear in the palm of the hand when working with fastball pitchers, and the bulky mitt are sufficient to rob the ball of shock and sting that lames your hand unless you know how to ride with the throw and kill some of its speed. The pitcher, standing on his little elevated mound, looms up enormously over you at that short distance, and when he ties himself into a coiled spring preparatory to letting fly, it requires all your self-control not to break and run for safety. And as for the things they can do with a baseball, those Major League pitchers . . . ! One way of finding out is to wander down on the field an hour or so before game time when there is no pressure on them, pull on the catcher's glove, and try to hold them.

I still remember my complete surprise the first time I tried catching for a real curveball pitcher. He was a slim, spidery left-hander for the

New York Yankees, many years ago, by the name of Herb Pennock. He called that he was going to throw a fast breaking curve and warned me to expect the ball at least 2 feet outside the plate. Then he wound up and let it go, and that ball came whistling right down the groove for the center of the plate. A novice, I chose to believe what I saw and not what I heard, and prepared to catch it where it was headed for a spot which of course it never reached, because just in front of the rubber, it swerved sharply to the right and passed nearly a yard from my glove. I never had a chance to catch it. That way, you learn about the mysterious drop, the ball that sails down the alley chest high but which you must be prepared to catch around your ankles because of the sudden dip it takes at the end of its passage as though someone were pulling it down with a string. Also you find out about the queer fadeaway, the slow curve, the fast in-and out-shoots that seem to be timed almost as delicately as shrapnel, to burst, or rather break, just when they will do the most harm—namely, at the moment when the batter is swinging.

Facing a big-league pitcher with a bat on your shoulder and trying to hit his delivery is another vital experience in gaining an understanding of the game about which you are trying to write vividly. It is one thing to sit in the stands and scream at a batsman: "Oh, you bum!" for striking out in a pinch, and another to stand twenty yards from that big pitcher and try to make up your mind in a hundredth of a second whether to hit at the offering or not, where to swing and when, not to mention worrying about protecting yourself from the consequences of being struck by the ball that seems to be heading straight for your skull at an appalling rate of speed. Because, if you are a big-league player, you cannot very well afford to be gun-shy and duck away in panic from a ball that swerves in the last moment and breaks perfectly over the plate, while the umpire calls: "Strike!" and the fans jeer. Nor can you afford to take a crack on the temple from the ball. Men have died from that. It calls for undreamed-of niceties of nerve and judgment, but you don't find that out until you have stepped to the plate cold a few times during batting practice or in training quarters, with nothing at stake but the acquisition of experience, and see what a fine case of the jumping jitters you get. Later on, when you are writing your story, your imagination, backed by the experience, will be able to supply a picture of what the batter is going through as he stands at the plate in the closing innings of an important game, with two or three men on base, two out, and his team behind in the scoring, and fifty thousand people screaming at him.

The catching and the holding of a forward pass for a winning touchdown on a cold, wet day always makes a good yarn, but you might get an even better one out of it if you happen to know from experience about the elusive qualities of a hard, soggy, mud-slimed football rifled through the air, as well as something about the exquisite timing, speed and courage it takes to catch it on a dead run, with two or three 190-pound men reaching for it at the same time or waiting to crash you as soon as your fingers touch it.

Any football coach during a light practice will let you go down the field and try to catch punts, the long, fifty-yard spirals and the tricky, tumbling end-over-enders. Unless you have had some previous experience, you won't hang on to one out of ten, besides knocking your fingers out of joint. But if you have any imagination, thereafter you will know that it calls for more than negligible nerve to judge and hold that ball and even plan to run with it, when there are two husky ends bearing down at full speed, preparing for a head-on tackle.

In 1932 I covered my first set of National Air Races, in Cleveland, and immediately decided that I had to learn how to fly to find out what it felt like. Riding as a passenger isn't flying. Being up there all alone at the controls of a ship is. And at the same time began a series of investigations into the "feel" of the mechanized sports to see what they were all about and the qualities of mentality, nerve, and physique they called for from their participants. These included a ride with Gar Wood in his latest and fastest speedboat, Miss America X, in which for the first time he pulled the throttle wide open on the Detroit River straightaway; a trip with the Indianapolis Speedway driver Cliff Bergere, around the famous brick raceway; and a flip with Lieutenant Al Williams, one time U.S. Schneider Cup race pilot.

I was scared with Wood, who drove me at 127 miles an hour, jounced, shaken, vibrated, choked with fumes from the exhausts, behind which I sat hanging on desperately to the throttle bar, which after a while got too hot to hold. I was on plank between Wood and his mechanic, Johnson, and thought that my last moment had come. I was still more scared when Cliff Bergere hit 126 on the Indianapolis straightaways in the tiny racing car in which I was hopelessly wedged, and after the first couple of rounds quite resigned to die and convinced that I should. But I think the most scared I have ever been while moving fast was during a ride I took in the cab of a locomotive on the straight, level stretch between Fort Wayne, Indiana, and Chicago, where for the first time we hit 90 miles per hour, which of course is no speed at all. But nobody who rides in the comfortable Pullman coaches has any idea of the didoes cut up by a locomotive in a hurry, or the thrill of pelting through a small town, all out and wide open, including the crossing of some thirty or forty frogs and switches, all of which must be set right. But that wasn't sport. That was just plain excitement.

I have never regretted these researches. Now that they are over, there isn't enough money to make me do them again. But they paid me dividends, I figured. During the great Thompson Speed Trophy race for land planes at Cleveland in 1935, Captain Roscoe Turner was some eight or nine miles in the lead in his big golden, low-wing, speed monoplane. Suddenly, coming into the straightaway in front of the grandstands, buzzing along at 280 miles per hour like an angry hornet, a streamer of thick, black smoke burst from the engine cowling and trailed back behind the ship. Turner pulled up immediately, using his forward speed to gain all the altitude possible, turned and got back to the edge of the field, still pouring out that evil black smoke. Then he cut his switch dipped her nose down, landed with a bounce and a bump, and rolled up to the line in a perfect stop. The crowd gave him a great cheer as he climbed out of the oil-spattered machine, but it was a cheer of sympathy because he had lost the race after having been so far in the lead that had he continued he could not possibly have been overtaken.

There was that story, but there was a better one too. Only the pilots on the field, all of them white around the lips and wiping from their faces a sweat not due to the oppressive summer heat, knew that they were looking at a man who from that time on, to use their own expression, was living on borrowed time. It isn't often when a Thompson Trophy racer with a landing speed of around 80 to 90 miles an hour goes haywire in the air, that the pilot is able to climb out of the cockpit and walk away from his machine. From the time of that first burst of smoke until the wheels touched the ground and stayed there, he was a hundred-to-one shot to live. To the initiated, those dreadful moments were laden with suspense and horror. Inside that contraption was a human being who any moment might be burned to horrible, twisted cinder, or smashed into the ground beyond all recognition, a human being who was cool, gallant, and fighting desperately. Every man and woman on the field who had ever been in trouble in the air was living those awful seconds with him in terror and suspense. I, too, was able to experience it. That is what makes getting the "feel" of things distinctly worthwhile.

WINTER

The Hans Brinker Complex

Donald Katz

Hours before dawn we were arranged into long lines, and now 16,000 of us waited with sharp steel blades clutched in our hands like sabers.

We stood together in a great, bright hall that smelled of cattle and long winters. Vendors offered to sell us flashlights, since we would be skating in the dark for several hours. Some of the skaters looked young and lean in their racing suits, built like the best marathon runners, but just as many of the Dutchmen waiting in the Frieslandhal in the city of Leeuwarden that morning looked like they were heading off to work in the background of an old Dutch landscape painting, people grown thick and tough through years of work on land their ancestors stole from the sea.

For each of the last twenty-two winters, the legendarily skilled skaters of Holland had waited for the Elfstedentocht, the ice race of all races. The last "Eleven Towns" tour, a 124-mile-long circuit of the province of Friesland over frozen canals and inland lakes, had occurred so long ago that many of the skaters now waiting to begin the race grew up never seeing their national sporting event. The race had been held only twelve times during this century; the northern winters no longer seemed capable of producing a tract of solidified ice sufficiently hard and uninterrupted that thousands of people could travel it from darkness to darkness for all of a day. But each winter an entire nation of skaters still wiped the animal fat from their long touring blades and trained for an event that never came.

The Elfstedentocht had become less a race than a mythic component of the Dutch national unconscious, and as I stood in the great hall, trying to stay loose, I felt like an explorer who happened upon a native rite so private and strange and entwined in the secrets of history that all he could do was stand quietly aside and try to understand.

But for my choice of ice skates, I might have been anthropologically concealed in the crowd along with the handful of Swedes and Finns who'd been allowed to trespass on the hallowed ice for the first time in the history of the race. People kept coming up to me and staring at my hockey skates.

"You're the American," said a man with a long beard that already looked frozen. "I saw your picture in the paper." He had thick grease smeared on his face and wore bedroom slippers on his feet; his goggles wrapped around a wool skating cap that had clearly been knit at home. Like every other participant in the hall, his pants bulged out 7 or 8 inches around the knees from a lump of padding. I didn't fully understand the padding, though it had been suggested that some of the bridges along the course were so low that a skater would have to fall to his knees and slide through.

The man continued to stare at my short-bladed skates. "You are very courageous," he said, shaking his head.

"I think you are very stupid," said an older man behind him.

"Yes, well this is also possible," said the first man upon consideration.

Word passed through the long lines that a million Dutch citizens were waiting outside the hall and along the banks of the route to cheer us on, and as the moment approached for the first group of skaters to run to the ice, the Frieslandhal seemed to rumble with a terrible thunder. Ninety percent of the Dutch population was expected to watch the Elfstedentocht from start to finish on television, leaving, I assumed, only the blind or comatose to miss the event. Offices and factories were shuttered throughout the country, and Queen Beatrix had rushed back from abroad when she heard the ice had thickened.

Groups of 1,000 skaters were released from the hall in half-hour intervals, starting at 5:30 a.m. At 6:30, my group tore the bottom stubs off our *controlekaarten* and handed them to a race official as we rushed past him into the dark. The part we kept had blank spots next to the name of each of the eleven villages, to be stamped as we passed through.

Outside the hall, a slender chute divided the massive crowd. We began a tentative run over lightly iced ground that glistened under arc lights strung overhead. The violent light made silhouettes of the looming walls of faces and occasionally lit our skate blades bright as long, thin flames. The crowd was so close on either side that they warmed the wintry morning and filled the chute with amazing noise made of screams and bugle calls and cheers that fell into a rhythmic "Hey! Hey! Hey!" The sound pummeled us from side to side like gusts of wind across a slick road.

Three-quarters of a mile later, at the edge of the van Harinxma Canal, I could see tugboats and flat-bottomed barges frozen into the ice up to their hulls. A thousand skaters piled down the dirt banks of the canal and sat side by side to put on skates. No one said a word, and it had become so quiet that I could hear the complaint of cold leather being stretched by strong laces.

As they set off, most skaters simply tossed their bedroom slippers, running shoes, and heavy wooden shoes behind them. In light of the possibility of finding oneself a province away with no shoes to wear, the gesture seemed to tempt fate. I slipped my shoes into my pack.

I skated slowly down to the base of the canal and watched others disappear into the blackness to the south. The ice was even blacker than the lightless morning and felt strange underfoot. The skates of the others made an unusually deep, roaring sound against the ice as they disappeared into the dark, like hundreds of coal cars falling fast into a mine.

I tested my laces, skated back and forth in a mild panic, and jumped up and down on the marble-hard ice in what I'm sure a psychologist would call a test of reality. I waited beneath a grain elevator that rose above the base of the canal until I saw the next group of 1,000 skaters running through the sonic gauntlet of spectators toward the ice. As the first of them appeared on the rise at the edge of the canal, I took a breath and began to take long strides into the dense mist of an old dream.

As constant and unresolved as my Hans Brinker complex obviously was, my childhood fantasies of skating the canals of Holland had never included images of myself pitted in competition against 16,122 of the most powerful ice skaters in the world. For Hans it was the silver skates at the end of the race, but all I wanted were the glorious windmills I would pass along the banks of the canals.

I'd known about the famed tour through the eleven ancient villages of the northern province of Friesland in the Netherlands for a long time, and for years I'd badgered various Dutch government officials and journalists about calling me if the race were ever scheduled to take place. But along with 14 million *Nederlanders*, I'd finally given up the wait. Winter teased me and the people of the lowlands unmercifully for years. In 1975, the ice was so hard that skaters began to congregate in Friesland only to be informed that the ice was melting. The winter of 1984 was particularly cold, and in December the Elfstedentocht was scheduled, only to be canceled a few hours later. The ice was ready again in mid-January, but the temperature rose at the last minute. The latest the race had even been held was on a February 14, back in 1956, and that was considered a meteorological freak. So by mid-February of 1985, all hope was lost, and the depression that attends spring along the canals had settled in.

Then on February 18, the nation was electrified by the announcement that the race was to be held in three days, on the 21st. Four busloads of Dutch skaters on their way to an alternative race in Poland turned around, and thousands of skaters stood in lines to register. For the first time, the race committee announced, a limited number of foreigners would be allowed to enter this thirteenth Elfstedentocht.

There was a great commotion at the KLM Airlines ticket counter when somebody noticed my skates. "It won't happen," one woman said. "It never does." But four hours after I got the phone call about the race, I was on a plane to Amsterdam, and eight hours after that, I boarded a packed train headed north to Leeuwarden.

Most of the people holding skates on the train looked as tired as I did because they'd spent up to 12 hours in the cold waiting to register. As the

DONALD KATZ

younger skaters sat together and talked strategy, the older men—I didn't see women with skates on the train but just under 300 did enter—sat together and talked of past races. Many of them already had an Elfstedentocht Cross, a decoration as valued by a Dutchman as any badge of courage earned in war. They talked about old Karst Leemburg, who won the 1929 race, but lost his toes to the cold—he still keeps them in a jar by his bed—and they remembered the last race, held in 1963 during a blizzard so cold that only 200 of the thousands of entrants finished. There is a famous photograph of that year's winner crossing the finish line, looking for all the world like a man frozen solid; Dutch schoolchildren wear that image emblazoned in their memories.

Everyone on the train pored over newspapers given over entirely to news of the race. There was much conjecture about whether the thirty-year-old record of 7 hours, 35 minutes, would be broken, and most people agreed it would probably fall. Since the last Elfstedentocht, an entire semiprofessional sport called marathon skating had developed, replete with hundreds of world-class, full-time participants who regularly competed in races of more than 60 miles. These athletes were capable of skating at almost 20 miles an hour for much of a day. The favorite on the train was clearly the legendary Jan Roelof Kruithof. Known throughout northern Europe as "J.R.," Kruithof had won eight of the last nine annual alternative races held in northern Finland. He had spent every summer since the last Elfstedentocht working out in a meat locker, and he was quoted in the paper as believing that his entire career had been little more than training for the Eleven Towns race.

Another character named Hans Homme echoed Kruithof's praise of training in a freezer. The plainly mad-looking Mr. Homme made someone in his family lock him into a deep freeze, where he pedaled a stationary bicycle in front of a fan blowing a minus-6-degree wind in his face. "If you stop, you freeze and die," Homme contended in one article, "so it makes you pretty tough in the body and mind."

There were numerous bits about "Crazy Dries" van Wijhe, who abandoned all sophisticated strategies in favor of skating as fast as he could go until he dropped. Crazy Dries often won marathon races; he refused to skate on Sundays, however, because of his devout Calvinist convictions.

The newspapers universally described the course of the Elfstedentocht as "tortuous," and several groups on the train had large maps of the province of Friesland spread out on the floor. Though the official roots of the race extend back to 1909, the tour is descended from a two-hundred-year-old practice among off-season *friese* farmers of skating to all of the eleven towns in one day in order to stop in each town and have a drink.

Friesland is home to descendants of one of the fiercest tribes in the ancient world. The Friezen were one of the three original groups of marsh dwellers who settled the lowlands that became the Netherlands, and the modern Friezen still speak an ancient language called Fries, which sounds more like Middle English than Dutch. The locals are further distinguished by their propensity toward skating like the wind, and by a rather straightforward, stiff demeanor that causes them to be the butt of a great deal of national humor. In the main square of the capital city of Leeuwarden, atop the pedestal usually occupied by a founding father or a war hero, sits a huge bronze statue of a cow that during the nineteenth century produced 6,620 pounds of milk in one year. People from more sophisticated regions of the Netherlands think this "perfect cow" of Leeuwarden is pretty funny stuff, but as the train finally arrived in Leeuwarden, and we hiked across the town to the staging center at the Frieslandhal, it was clear that everyone was Friezen—except me.

"Do you know you are the only American ever to enter the race?" one of the circle of reporters asked.

"No," I said. "I guess I was the only one who could get here."

"You're not representing America?"

"No, I just had a childhood fantasy . . . "

"Are you in training?"

"Well, not really."

"Do you know you will have to leave the ice and run on your skates several times?"

"No."

"Sir," said another from the back of the crowd. "Do you have any idea at all what it means to skate 200 kilometers on natural ice?"

"I guess I'll find out," I said.

DONALD KATZ

"Yes," he said with a snicker, "I guess you will."

It seemed like only minutes later that I was being shaken from one dream into another. It was 4:00 in the morning, and I was in the home of a local insurance agent named Fokke (pronounced "fah-cur") de Boer. ("Ja, I know ze jokes about ze name.") As the full extent of the invasion of the town had become clear, the mayor of Leeuwarden asked the citizenry to open their homes to skaters, and more than five thousand families had offered free beds to strangers.

Fokke and Elshe de Boer and their two teenage daughters were waiting down in the parlor. Elshe put several bars of chocolate into my pack, and the five of us went out the back door to get the family bicycles.

We rode very slowly through a fog that hung wet as a downpour, over cobblestones that were slick with a thin patina of ice. From the dark, I could see into the windows of parlor after parlor of small, ivy-covered houses. Inside, skaters rose like shadows from pallets on the floor, and in the orange light cast by paraffin fires or in the glow of televisions already broadcasting news of the race, I could see figures sitting and rubbing skate stones along their blades. People emerged from the houses and ran alongside the growing sea of bicycles, moving to the ice through a wet, long night.

I'd been skating in darkness for more than an hour before dawn finally lit the mist. I knew I was passing through farmland from the odors along the way, but it wasn't until the light rose that I saw sheep and cows and farmers standing motionless at the edges of their wet fields. I saw flat pastureland stretching back, deep green and endless, and as the mist began to hold a bit more light, I was presented with the sight of my first windmill. It was a simple one, with a small thatched base and four delicate canvas-covered blades, but it was there.

"Windmill," I breathed as a tall skater who'd come up alongside me.

He looked up at the windmill for quite a while as we drew even with it. "Ja, a windmill," he said. He clasped his hands high behind his back and leaned forward. Then he moved 15 yards ahead of me with one deep, formalistic stride.

All around me skaters seemed to be moving to the same cadent dirge. There were long, snaking lines of skaters from the same village or town, all of them skating in a careful, even rhythm, their bodies so close behind one another that they could have rested their chins on each other's backs.

I watched hundreds of the finest skaters I'd ever seen pass me by, and their steady strides now seemed particularly amazing. In the soft light, I could see why I'd had to keep my knees bent like a skier traversing a mogul field during the hour in the dark. The surface of the ice was deeply rutted with cracks two and three inches wide, and with every lateral movement across the width of the canal, the ice seemed to be of completely different consistencies. There were places where small ice floes had risen and frozen, leaving a two-inch-high ridge along the surface, and there were deep holes.

Through conversations with several racers, I learned that the blackest ice would be the smoothest for another hour or so; then the rising temperature would make it slow. The alternative was white ice, which was full of snow and frozen pockets where a misplaced blade could crash through up to the boot. I was told to pay particular attention to the broad central crack zigzagging the length of the canal because many people break their ankles wedging a skate in the crack and having their bodies continue past it.

By the time we passed the cheering, singing crowds in the little village of Scharnegoutum, my pace had fallen off considerably. Eventually a barrel-chested, middle-aged man skated up next to me, and when we realized we were moving at a similar pace, we began to chat. His name was Hans Christian Schwenck, and he'd come up from The Hague for the event.

"What wonderful ice," he said. "A hint of spring in the air and wonderful ice."

I asked him if he wasn't soaked to the bone from the heavy fog, as I was.

"Of course," he said, glancing at me quizzically.

As we skated under bridges and across small lakes, he began to recall past races. In 1940, he said, the five leaders of the race clasped hands at the finish line and came across together, an act since banned from the competition.

We passed a group of farmers standing silently near a tractor, and Hans said, "Standing there so still like that, it reminds me of the race in '42. The German troops stood along the banks and just stared at us. The ice was good that year too—stone hard and black as pitch. Almost everyone in the race registered under a false name. It was quite a reunion for the underground."

"You skated in '42?"

"Ja. And '41."

"How old are you?"

"I'm sixty-three," Hans answered, then excused himself and picked up his pace.

Unlike almost every sport that involves strength and coordination, the best long-distance skaters are not young. A few weeks before I arrived in Holland, a sixty-year-old marathon skater had placed third in a 150-kilometer race. The man who'd won the 1933 Elfstedentocht had gone on to set a world record for 200 kilometers while in his mid-sixties and held it for several years. Jan Kruithof is forty-eight years old, Crazy Dries is about to turn forty, and all but a few of the best marathoners are over thirty-five. Kruithof said he felt he'd peaked at forty-three—after forty years on ice. The idea of some nineteen-year-old sprinter having the endurance and will to win a 200-kilometer event amused even the mature skaters.

At the outskirts of the medieval, brownstone village of Sneek (pronounced "Snake"), I began to see people pointing at my skates and calling out my name. I had apparently become a minor celebrity in Holland, not so much because I was the first American, but because I was the first skater foolish enough to try the race on *ijshockey-schaaten*. A photograph of the American wearing an inane grin and holding his hockey skates in the air appeared on the front page of the sports section of the country's biggest newspaper the morning of the race and hit the stands by the time I hit Sneek.

I was a skating fool in Sneek. I could dance over the widening puddles and do sidesteps and crossovers around the great gulfs in the ice as only a wearer of short blades can. I was particularly skilled at the dreaded *klunen* that began in Sneek, those places where we had to climb off the canal, run through town over rugs and hay bales, and then climb back down to the ice. Compared to the 16,122 others who had to shuffle along on their long touring blades, I flew through these portages.

The caption under my photograph in the morning paper contended that I "had every confidence in my ice hockey skates," but a few miles past the beautiful seven-hundred-year-old village of Ijlst, the statement began to strike me as one of the least intelligent assertions ever offered in print. My skates were clearly designed for something other than skating across the Netherlands. They were made for dodging puddles and body checks, for controlled, short bursts of speed, and neat, quick turns. As I observed another thousand or so skaters passing me, I became aware that I was taking at least three strides to every one of theirs. The blades of the skates flying by me were even longer than the speed skates worn by sprinters, the boots low to the blade to facilitate the classic skater's pose: head low, hands fixed behind the back. The Dutchmen couldn't have made the most obtuse turns if their lives depended on it, but they could go straight like nothing I'd ever seen. I felt as if I were riding a tricycle among 10-speed racers.

My lower back was completely tied in knots, and my knees were so battered from absorbing the constant shock of rough ice that I felt as if I'd been kneecapped. My layers of clothes had been wet and partially frozen since long before dawn, but now they felt as heavy as chain mail, and I longed for one of those nifty polypropylene skating suits.

I'd also discovered why everyone else in the race looked as if they were wearing catcher's mitts on their knees. Despite the long skate blades, all around me people were taking painful falls; some of them looked as if they'd just skated off a ski jump, bodies arching through the damp air and landing in heaps. Others fell from the hay bales during the klunen and those behind piled on top. Twice, I saw skaters go down and take a whole club along with them. The fallen would crawl to the reeds at the edge of the canal and try to suck some air back into their lungs, but no matter how badly they seemed to be hurt, they always got up and continued.

I considered the knifelike projections protruding from the ice and decided that I simply would not fall down. So in my constant effort to yank

DONALD KATZ

my skates out of holes and maintain my balance, I'd managed to pull most of the muscles along my upper back by the time I skated onto the huge, dreaded inland lake called Slotenmeer.

A white cloud had descended onto the lake, and it was so dense that after a few strides the shoreline disappeared. With huge stumps and treetops rising through the ice, Slotenmeer looked like the proverbial haunted forest of no return. The surface of the windswept ice was as pocked as the surface of the moon, and it was all I could do to keep my balance. At one point I completely lost the *schaatsroute* and came face to face with a stream of skaters who had already rounded the village of Sloten on the other side of the lake and were heading back the other way.

By the time I found the route again, I had seen my eventual fate. I was certain I would lose strength, take one of the terrifying falls occurring all around me, and die. There would be no story in America about my race, but I would probably make the Dutch papers for the second day in a row.

At the far end of the lake, the mist broke briefly, and I saw the magnificent windmill of Sloten rise like an apparition on a promontory on the other side of the cloud. It was the biggest, most beautiful windmill I'd ever seen. Beneath it a huge circus calliope was filling the distance with music, and I could see people standing along the narrow canal, dancing to the tunes. Other races had been stopping along the way at little stands selling soup and hot chocolate, but I hadn't dared to slow down, even at the stamping points. I had skated close to 30 miles, and my map indicated the next town was 15 miles away. For quite a while my head had been pounding with a pain I'd diagnosed as jet lag, but I didn't want to stop. Still, how could I just skate past this most glorious of windmills?

I hoisted myself up onto a retaining wall and dangled my legs over the side. As I felt my clothes begin to freeze around me, I stared up at the majestic windmill until I noticed spectators on the other side of the canal pointing at my skates and waving. Soon I was surrounded by people asking me for . . . my autograph.

Eventually somebody talked me into taking off my skates for a while and coming up to a thatch-roofed inn for a bowl of soup. The inn was full of warmth and good cheer, and inside, Dutchmen with long, curving pipes watched the A-class racers fly past one of the forty television cameras spaced along the route.

I sat at a table with a group of policemen and numerous Dutch tourists who recognized me. One man contended with certitude that a visiting Canadian had once unofficially attempted the Elfstedentocht on hockey skates, but he'd been dragged from the course, exhausted, before he had reached the first village. This overwhelmed me with pleasure—especially since I realized I had to immediately put my head down on the table next to my soup and go to sleep.

I remember several bus rides after I called it quits in Sloten and at least one train ride back to Leeuwarden and the finish line, but I don't remember getting on or off any of them.

As darkness fell over the course again, thousands of people were still racing. Bands played late into the night for them, and spectators stood in the cold singing them songs. Sometimes, skaters would stop and stand in front of a crowd with their hands raised in the air, or even pause for a minute to dance with the spectators.

Hours earlier, a young farmer named Evert van Benthem had won the race in just 6 hours, 46 minutes, breaking the old record by 49 minutes. The next three finishers, who'd paced Evert all day, crossed the finish line so close behind him that all four shared the same time.

The sun never appeared to light the day, but the temperature rose enough that by nightfall the skaters were traveling through water above their ankles. At the finish line, I saw exhausted skaters fall to their knees to kiss the ice, then trudge back into the Frieslandhall in Leeuwarden to find much of the skin gone from their feet. Some of them sat in chairs, holding bright bouquets and looking like corpses; others sifted through the thousands of shoes that had been piled on the bank of the canal that morning.

For hours, I watched skaters limp into the hall. Alongside me was Gunther Meyer, a pleasant man in his fifties who was an MP with the Royal Dutch Air Force.

"The ice was really something today, wasn't it?" I said to Gunther Meyer.

"It certainly was," he said. "Best ice I've skated on in years."

Gunther had readied himself for the race by double-timing 40 miles a week with a 25-pound pack on his back because, as he said, "People with easy lives can't do things like this. And only Dutchmen can really race the Elfstedentocht"—a sentiment I'd come to share.

It seemed like everyone in Friesland had come to the great hall by early evening, easily 20,000 people dancing to an oompah band and waiting anxiously for their friends and relatives to appear. By the time the first 12 race finishers had mounted a platform at one end of the Frieslandhal, the huge crowd was singing along with the band. The governor of the province gave a short speech in Fries, and the crowd went crazy with appreciation. Evert van Benthem told the crowd he was thankful for the victory and for the wonderful condition of the ice. He said later that he'd been out of training until just before the race because he had purchased some new cows for his seventeenth-century farm.

J.R. Kruithof had come in 13th, 9 minutes behind the winner, but as he greeted the hysteria his name induced throughout the hall, he seemed so genuinely moved that it didn't seem to matter that he'd lost a race he'd been training for every day for twenty-two years. Then he and a group of skaters—including Crazy Dries, who'd come in tenth—hoisted van Benthem above their heads as the crowd screamed its approval.

A reporter pulled me from the throng and asked how I felt about having to drop out of the race and not receive the cross that more than 13,000 skaters would be awarded. I told the reporter he didn't understand. I said that just a few hours ago I had skated out of a white cloud and found myself in front of the windmill in Sloten, and people had called out my name . . .

Then the crowd rose to an astonishing, keening pitch that drowned us out.

There was more collective passion in that provincial hall than is contained in a decade's worth of Superbowls. The outpouring I witnessed in the Frieslandhall that night was the result of an entire nation waiting a generation so that 16,000 Dutch men and women could show that they were skilled enough and tough enough to skate 124 miles in a single day.

The interminable wait for ice in Friesland had all the elements of an ancient people waiting for a comet, until the endless ribbon of water comprising 14,000 acres of Friesland had frozen and stitched the landscape into a whole, so that Dutchmen could show the world what ice skating really ought to be.

The Deer Hunter

David Mamet

New York was, of course, intolerable.

I found that I was organizing my day around those times when it was possible—just possible—to get a cup of gourmet coffee without standing in line a half hour.

But whose fault was it if not my own, who'd chosen luxury and fashion (at least for the fall) over a healthy life in the outdoors? I wasn't writing a word of any worth, either; and to complete the indictment, I was frittering away yet another deer season. Up in Vermont, archery season was over, as was centerfire rifle, and Morris, my neighbor down the road, had gotten a 175-pound buck in the orchard just across from my house.

And I had just turned fifty.

My friend and hunting companion Bob turned fifty some five or six years ago. An outdoorsman—a hunter, trapper, and forester—he had, his wife reported, spent his forty-ninth year complaining and full of crotchets about encroaching Old Age. But when the clock ticked over onto fifty, he was cured, and went back to an uncomplaining, aggressively active life. I had spent my forty-ninth year emulating his. But now I had turned fifty, and found myself still the slave of habit, sloth, and urban depravity; deer season was waning, and I had to get out of town.

I thought I'd look for an adventure somewhat greater than tripping around the back yard, but not quite as Herculean as going all the way to Maine. So I contacted Uncle Jammers (Jim Ehlers) out of Sugarbush, Vermont, who said he'd put me on some tracks up in the Northeast Kingdom, for the last days of blackpowder muzzle-loading season.

I flew to Burlington, Vermont, and drove to Plainfield for lunch at the River Run Restaurant. Jimmy Kennedy was in the kitchen. He made me bacon and eggs and reminded me to take along a safety pin on the hunting trip. What for? To use as a touchhole pick for the muzzleloader.

Friend of his, he said, had a safety pin, and it saved the day on a blackpowder shoot when the touchhole clogged. Great idea. I remember old Pennsylvania guns, with a hole bored in the forestock, right below that for the ramrod, and in the hole was carried a long quill to clean out the touchhole.

I remembered hunting with blackpowder shooters in east Texas, sitting around in the evening at Bill Bagwell's forge, discussing the contributions blackpowder shooting had made to the language: hang fire; flash in the pan; lock, stock, and barrel; skinflint; keep your powder dry; shot his rod (corrupted into "wad"); chew the rag; spruce up (sprues up, i.e., with the sprue—the nonspherical portion of the cast ball, that portion left when the molten lead overflows the mold—up, that is, pointed toward the muzzle); and (which prompted this reflection) ramrod, used as a verb. So much of the appeal of field sports, at least to me, who practices them infrequently, is the gear and the language pertinent to the thing. I get out there only several days a year, but I, along with the legion of my sedentary coeval enthusiasts, am always up for an outdoorsy book or catalogue (anything's better than playing golf).

Here, blackpowder shooting was reminding me that the simplest gear—in this case, a safety pin—is the best.

Jimmy and I spoke about ice fishing for a while. I paid my check and headed out to my house. My first stop was up at my cabin to get my gear. I took down my .58 caliber Hawken and cleaned it. I blew through the barrel, but I found it clogged. I pulled the nipple and saw the lube had set up in the touchhole, and that, happy day, I could clean it out using a safety pin. I cleaned the nipple, cleaned the bore, polished the thimbles, got the

DAVID MAMET

whole thing shining, and went outside and set up a target at fifty yards. It's a pretty good range, as (a) it's going to be about the limit of any shot in the woods, and (b) it's a range I can actually hit from.

I put a couple of half-inch red Targ-Dots on the cardboard, and put my first shot 2 inches left and on for elevation. With a second shot I obliterated the Targ-Dot, and felt about as good as I'd felt since I first went down to the City.

The rifle exhibited a degree of forgiveness positively feminine. I was standing out there, waxing rhapsodic about the blackpowder rifle, its excellencies, its forgiving nature, its lack of recoil and general friendliness, when the sun went down. I cleaned my gun by the oil lamp, hurried back to the house, threw much too much gear into a pack, and got into the pickup for the drive to Sugarbush.

I remembered a cold and hungry Vermont holiday season, thirty-plus years before. I was out of work, and heard of an opening for an experienced bartender at the Sugarbush Inn. I called and made an appointment for an interview. I went to the Montpelier Library and found the *Old Mister Boston's Official Bartender's Guide*, and studied it night and day until the date of my interview, when that person upon whom I had counted for a lift to Sugarbush disappointed me. I sat out the remainder of the holiday season hungry, cold, and grumbling.

The awful thing about not winning an Academy Award is this: you don't get to give your speech. It just rather sits there and festers. *Yes, you think, it's all right that I lost, that's only fair, and that's the game. But there must be some way that, having lost, I can still mount the podium and give my most excellent and philosophical speech.*

But no. And neither did I ever get to display my (granted, theoretical) excellence as a bartender. And never before had I gotten to Sugarbush, that momentary Oz of my youth.

I arrived at the Snow Ridge Inn. A young woman told me that everyone was out snowmobiling, but that I could fling my stuff into one of the cabins, and work out the details of my stay later on.

I think snowmobiling, at least in Vermont, contains the story of a particularly American triumph. In my youth, up there, in the turbulent sixties, snowmobilers had the reputation of being rowdies—outlaw bikers on ice, bent on inebriation, vandalism, and whatever mischief one could get into whilst wrapped like a puff pastry at 40 below. But their image was changed, and by the most unusual of tactics—by changing their actions. Makes one think.

So I drove the pickup over to my cabin, where there would be no phone. No television. Privacy. I could enter and spread out and check and moon over my gear, I could sleep till dawn the next morning, I could open the windows, accountable to no one, I could live, for the moment, a free man.

I lugged my gear up on the porch and opened the door. I looked down, and at my feet was a note: "Call Norman Lear immediately."

Well, then, I was strong enough to get myself out of New York, but I was not strong enough not to call Norman Lear immediately. He told me he was working on a project and I was the only one to write it, and other irresistible flattery, and I made an appointment to meet him the next week, back in New York.

For, yes, *of course*, I was a fraud. Whom was I attempting to kid? As there was no one there but myself, I sussed that answer out fairly quickly. But was I not, on the other hand, nevertheless entitled to Go Hunting? Yes. I put away my gear and went out to meet Uncle Jammer's guides, Jim and Nathan, for dinner, and we made a plan: we'd meet at the Snow Ridge at 5:30 a.m. and drive up to Wenlock, the preserve by Island Pond. Fine.

I went shopping down in the town: tea, butter, eggs, bread, cheese, and ham. I went back to my cabin and fell asleep. The radio woke me at 5:00 with some symphonic music. I took a quick shower, dashed into the kitchen to make breakfast and a perfect sandwich: eggs, butter, cheese, bread, ham, put it inside several wax paper bags, closed it with a rubber band, and Jim and Nathan arrived.

I had, of course, high hopes for that rubber band. It was to fix my filled-out deer tag to my fallen buck. It, like the safety pin, was to be the talisman signifying foresight, and would therefore ensure an increased chance of success. It was not to be.

I am a bad rifle shot, and an inexperienced, inept (but happy) hunter.

Larry Benoit, the king of hunters (*How to Bag the Biggest Buck of Your Life*), writes, and experience proves, you've got to get out there *every day*—you have to know what the woods look like before you start recognizing the unusual: the magnificently camouflaged animal standing there. It seems to me a lot like writing—one may write only an hour a day, but that hour can't be scheduled in advance—it may come as part of a day devoted to reading or napping or skiving off, but the writer has to spend a lot of time alone and quiet before he's capable of recognizing the difference between an idea and a good idea.

Larry Benoit also wrote that the way to get a monster buck is to follow a merely large buck, and when you get your shot, don't take it—let the buck go. This seems to me to equal Hemingway's advice, to write the best story you can and then throw out all the good lines. Best lesson I ever read about writing.

So there we were, up where the big bucks were. Nathan and James and I were crammed into the front seat of an old pickup, drinking vast travel mugs of coffee, driving two hours up to the Wenlock Preserve and talking about fishing. Jim said the thing about fishing is that you learn something new all the time, how there's always something new to be learned. They composed a paean to ice fishing and I wanted nothing more than to go. We drove past Orleans and they talked about the spawning trout jumping the dam there.

Nathan began talking about his Uncle Dwane, who was meeting us in Island Pond, about how he was *always* learning from the deer, about how Dwane had passed that, or was passing that, down to him, Nathan, and about how much there was to learn. This is the constant, and to me, invigorating, instructive, and grateful aspect of outdoors people—their reverence for knowledge and their understanding that knowledge lies not in the self but in the world around them (and if I get philosophic I had better take myself ice fishing and let it burn off).

We rendezvoused with Dwane in Island Pond. Another coffee. We began talking, for some reason, about traveling. Dwane had been on the road. "With what?" I asked. It turned out he is in antiques. Not only is he in antiques, he and Nathan are relatives of the late Albert May, the great, lamented auctioneer of Molly's Pond, Vermont.

I used to go to Albert's auctions Saturday nights, back in the mid-sixties. He was the quintessential entertainer; he knew his material, he knew his audience, and he loved being up there, and they loved him for it. He would auction off a bag of clothespins and then say he had "just one more," and sell *that*, and be surprised that it seemed there was just one more. And he'd sell clothespins for half an hour.

Dwane said one time there was some hippie from the college down the road who came to the auction; and the hippie, not finding a chair, had perched himself in the tree outside the auction shed. Well, fine, but he was dressed in the tatters of that clan and that day. His clothes were rags, and his genitals hung down through a rent in his jeans. Albert espied him and remarked to the crowd that it beat all of his knowledge of nature, how early the squirrels were putting nuts in the trees.

It was still early, not quite light. We ordered more coffee and talked about the estate auctions, the old farms broken up, the antiques business. I once found a 32 Winchester Low Wall, first year of manufacture (1885), for $25, covered in rust. They cleaned it up for me at Orvis, brought back the exterior metal (the bore was fine) and polished the wood. Lovely little rifle. Into the buttstock some early owner had carved his initials, C.K. It hung for a short time right above my desk, until my good friend and hunting companion Chris Kaldor stopped by one day and took the gun down to examine it. He and I registered the initials at the same time. Chris, gentleman that he is, handed the rifle back and mentioned something about the weather. The next week, after much soul searching on my part, the Low Wall went where it (obviously) was destined.

We'd had enough coffee, and it was up the mountain. We found the logging road Dwane and Jim had scouted, and we cut the track of a buck. I was given the lead, and started packing all of my useless gear onto my belt and back. Dwane suggested that the deer weren't going to wait while I festooned myself, and I acknowledged the logic of his position by watching my rifle fall apart.

"Works all year, but Not Up Here," the old phrase has it.

The wedge, which keeps the barrel in the stock and which had never in a decade budged without my deliberate intervention, dropped straight out of my rifle and into the snow.

Well, we found it, and pounded it back in with the hilt of a knife, and I was ready to set out when the rawhide holding my "possibles" bag onto the cunning period strap shredded, and my bag fell in the snow.

The bag was a loss, so I decanted powder-patch and ball into two plastic speedloaders, stuffed them, a full capper, my third spare compass, and a candy bar into the various pockets of my old red Johnson coat, and nodded to my similarly ready fellow hunters.

"Meet back here in four hours," Jim said. "Road runs north and south, you're going up the mountain west. To come back to the road, all you got to do is walk east."

Excellent. Up the mountain I went, tracking the buck in the snow. He went here, he went there, he eventually cut back east, onto the road, walked the road for a while, and jumped down into the lowland down below. He played me like a violin. He found some old tracks and walked in them, he jumped from one old set onto another, he'd spring down a little hill, and he was *never* walking fast—he had a city boy behind him, and his flight was a necessary but nontaxing academic exercise.

My morning was a bit more strenuous. The buck ran me down and up, across the road, and up the mountain. By noon I'd been tracking him over four hours, and I was drenched to the skin, and cold. My legs were shaking as I came down the mountain.

I met Nathan and we split my sandwich, which he pronounced excellent. We went back for lunch to Island Pond.

I changed into the spare silk underwear I had brought along (about my only display of hunting savvy, along with the safety pin and the rubber band). My shirt and coat were soaked through. I went next door to the gun store and bought a new green-and-black Johnson (short) jacket and one of their shirts, glad to be warm. I love that long red coat. I've hunted and worked and walked and slept under it the statutory twenty years, and it always proves to be too heavy for hunting. It's fine for sitting on a cold stand, but when you start moving it's too warm, too long, and has too many pockets into which I've put too much useless stuff. Well, I suppose I have not quite mastered that lesson yet.

James suggested a change of scene. (I think he took his cue from my physical state). He said he knew a good spot to wait out a buck at sundown. Back in the pickup I slept the deepest sleep of my life on the two-hour ride to Sugarbush.

The sun was just going down, we had that extra half hour of legal hunting. We walked through a field of thigh-high snow. The moon started to rise.

Jim put me in the corner of a field. I sat the last half hour still as a log, and saw nothing. We walked back in the dark to the pickup truck. We had a bourbon at the Sugarbush Inn. I went back to the cabin and slept 14 hours.

We spent the next day hunting around Johnson. It had turned cold and was blowing sleet. We were in fairly flat country and Jim said that they most probably bedded down around a given-up orchard he knew. He and Nathan walked in to start them, and put me on the inside, and back from them; that is, they planned to drive the deer across my path. To hunt deer in thick woods in a snowstorm is one of the most beautiful, the happiest, things that I know. I was enjoying it so much that I missed the deer. They'd passed right before me, 20 yards out.

We got on their trail and kept on it several hours, and then I was played out. There was a half hour left to the season. We went back into the woods, I stopped on the edge of a small clearing, the sun came out. I just sat there, delighted.

What a successful hunt.

I kept up for a couple of days, and told myself it was not a bad performance for a dissipated city fellow with a desk job. I drank some good bourbon in Sugarbush, and remembered that cold winter thirty years ago. I fell asleep three nights in a row at 8:00 p.m. and remembered what it is like to sleep well. I'd had a moment by myself. A very good way to celebrate the transition of my fiftieth birthday.

Back at the inn, James, Nathan and I shot at a stump some 30 yards off to clear the guns. I drove home, cleaned the Hawken, hung it in the cabin, and flew back to New York.

As a hunter, of course, I am a fraud. But it was a hell of a good vacation.

DAVID MAMET

Across the Disappearing Finish Line

Bill McKibben

Barring the odd World War or Depression, being a man was once a fairly simple task. My grandfather, for instance, lived to be a well-adjusted ninety-five—he visited Costa Rica on a banana boat at ninety—by walking a few brisk miles every morning and avoiding between-meal snacks.

But it's not easy anymore. Here are some things you need to know if you're going to be a healthy man, according to a recent issue of *Men's Health*; Chronic, day-to-day stress can lower your sperm count by a third; a diet rich in garlic keeps your aorta flexible; vitamin B2 fights off migraines; shrinking your waist from 40 to 37 inches cuts diabetes risk in half; you can build your triceps by doing dips off the edge of a swimming pool; if you're determined to have sex in an elevator, a spokesman for the American Elevator and Machine Corporation recommends using a freight elevator ("Many lack security cameras, but check the ceiling to make sure"). Not only that—but negative sit-ups can build muscles faster than crunches.

None of this would surprise women. For a long time—say, three or four million years—being a woman was hard work. But sometime around 1985, when men in their underwear began reclining on Times Square billboards, manhood became nearly as time-consuming. A sampling of *Men's Fitness* covers over the past year promises "24 Ways to Customize Your Physique," "6 Dangerous Foods," "12 Instant Nutrition Fixes," "7

Best Bicep Builders," "Better Sex—10 Ways to Drive Them Insane," "7 Super Shakes for Peak Energy," "5 Awesome Back Wideners," "5 Ready-Made Seduction Dates," "20 Hospital Survival Tips, "6 Moves for Bigger Arms," and "50 Ways to Improve Your Life, Guaranteed."

I'd never paid much attention to this kind of thing before the winter of 1998, when at the age of thirty-seven I embarked on, well, a quest. I decided to spend a year training pretty much full-time to be a cross-country ski racer—I knew I wouldn't win any races, but I wanted to understand my mind and my body in new ways, before age closed certain doors. Maybe I was tired of living mainly through my head; maybe I was just freaked to be growing old. In any event, I found a coach, Rob Sleamaker, author of *Serious Training for Endurance Athletes*, who drew up a yearlong program that called for more than 600 hours of training—daily, 2-, 3-, 4-hour runs and skis, long bouts of uphill sprinting, my heart-rate monitor bleating softly all the while. Add to that endless sets of crunches and bicep curls and tricep extensions, and before much time passed, muscles—not underwear ad-size muscles, but still—actually began to appear on my formerly smooth body.

And vanity began to infect my formerly oblivious consciousness. I found myself posing in front of the mirror as I shaved—flexing my pecs so they'd pop up and down, tensing my butt (my glutes, I mean) when I showered, feeling the indentations in my upper arm that marked the birth of my triceps. You couldn't really make out my washboard abs, but I could count the ridges of riblike muscle whenever I tightened my stomach. I read Arnold Schwarzenegger's 1977 autobiography, *Arnold: The Education of a Bodybuilder*, with new understanding.

Unlike Arnold's, however, the veins in my arms bulged like phone cords, not tug lines; my forearms bloomed from celery stalks to broccoli stalks. My wife, Sue, was the only one to notice I was sprouting muscle mass, and even she, in my opinion, paid far too little attention to the details of my emergent triceps. Of course, endurance athletes are not supposed to Popeye up—more muscle takes more blood to feed it, eventually reducing your efficiency. Still, self-image matters, I was finding out. As a boy, resolutely unphysical, I supposed I should exercise in order to get girls. I got girls anyway; eventually I got married and fathered a child and so fulfilled my genetic mandate, and the fact that I couldn't reliably open pickle jars did not prevent my DNA from passing down yea unto generations.

And yet did I measure up to my forebears, those sturdy small-town Westerners, on the manliness scale? My father, growing up, had spent his summers at a log cabin on the edge of Mount Rainier—a place without lights or running water, in the shadow of the great Douglas Firs. We'd visit the cabin every few years on some vacation driving trip, and usually we'd find my cousin Craig there. A mountaineer, Craig was forever heading off to Pakistan or Baffin Island or some other place with high icy cliffs to conquer. Sometimes he'd open his pack to show us his collection of carabiners, pitons, and ropes. Dad loved it—this was his fantasy life, long before Everest mania. But he'd reared us in the cushy suburbs of the East, where SATs counted more than sit-ups, and sometimes it seemed to me as if I was devolving, defying Darwin.

That summer, as I roller-skied and ran and lifted and interval trained in preparation for the winter race season, Mom and Dad celebrated their 40th anniversary. Dad had recently retired after a lifetime as a journalist, and the whole family joined them at a slightly down-at-the-heels resort in the White Mountains that offered a shaggy 9-hole golf course out back. It was a great pleasure that summer to head out onto the green with my dad and my younger brother, Tom. I'd never played before, and I had no swing; they had to show me how to grip the club. But when I connected I had power—the ball would sail away into the middle distance. It didn't bother me that it went left or right or onto the neighboring fairway. I just liked the idea that it went long and strong.

The more I trained, and especially the more I began to race, the more I understood that my mind needed toughening at least as much as my body—that endurance was about going until it hurt, when the natural impulse was to slow down, and then deciding whether to listen to that impulse or not. Not long after my golf date with my Dad, I went off to Australia, which has the planet's bet August snow, eager to test out my hepped-up lungs. I'll never forget the morning of the Paddy Pallin Classic, a 25-kilometer race through the twisted snow gums and eucalyptus trees on the shoulder of 7,310-foot Mount Kosciusko, the continent's highest peak. I remember exactly how good it felt when the gun went off, how I bounded up the hills on my new legs, how I fantasized about catching the wave of skiers who had started 5 minutes before me—and how immediately I lost all that sweet focus at the first real sign of adversity. A racer came blowing by me, chest tightened, and suddenly I was just plodding along, concentration gone. I still had some work to do.

But there'd been enough glimpses of transformation—races where for a few minutes I'd drop into the inescapable now of competition—to keep me going. When I came back from Australia, I began the longest, hardest month of my training schedule, an endless September that peaked one Saturday morning with a 238-minute run. My parents were visiting our Adirondack home, and they offered to watch my six-year-old daughter, Sophie, while I worked out. I ran and ran and ran some more, finally stumble-charging up the last rise, congratulating myself that from now on the whole year would be downhill. I was peeling off my T-shirt and savoring the smug aura of finishing something hard when I noticed Dad. He was about a hundred yards away from Mom, walking back and forth, and he was lurching a bit. "He's testing himself," she said, with a frantic edge in her voice.

Slowly the story started to come out. In August he'd been hiking hard in the Cascades, feeling fine. But when he got home he'd begun stumbling a bit—and once fell right over. Some days, Mom added, he slurred his words. Dad had chalked it up to the late-summer humidity, or perhaps a sinus infection, and had rallied (and reassured) himself by walking faster, working up a sweat. But when I took him aside that afternoon he confessed that his right side felt weak. Could I have had a small stroke? he asked me. As soon as he said it, I felt myself starting to panic—it had never even entered my mind that at sixty-eight he'd start to decline. But I knew it must be true; it would explain the balance, the speech, even a few recent mild displays of uncharacteristic temper.

I bade my parents good-bye with a sour taste in the back of my throat. The next day Dad phoned from home in Boston to say that his doctor

BILL MCKIBBEN

was convinced that indeed he'd had a very mild stroke. He'd scheduled an MRI for later in the week just to make sure, but he told Mom and Dad to go ahead planning a trip to Mexico; I could tell from his voice that Dad was immensely relieved.

And I was too. I spent a little time thinking about the Meaning of It All—how your body would eventually betray you no matter how fit you got—and then I went back to work, because racing season was coming into distant view. The weather began to change; a front came through one of those early autumn nights, dropping temperatures down into the low thirties, threatening the tomatoes. The weatherman talked about "the possibility of sleet or snow on the high ridges." The S word hadn't been heard in these parts since early May, and it made me quiver inside.

I started stacking firewood in earnest that week, and while I was working Friday afternoon I looked up to see our dog, Barley, trotting toward me with something in her mouth. At first I thought it was a shoe, but when she dropped it for me I saw it was a hawk—dead but utterly unmarked, a broad-wing, all strength and sinew. Sophie and I spread its strong, gray feathers, examined its powerful beak and talons, and then wrapped it in plastic and put it in the freezer so that she could take it to school. I went back to the woodpile.

When I looked up a few minutes later, Sue was standing there in the fading light with tears running down her cheeks. My mom had just called. Dad had a brain tumor, "an aggressive non-benign tumor." They were operating on Tuesday. Just like that.

I hugged her for a long time, and headed straight out into the woods, cursing and crying and carrying on. Mom said the doctor had told them that even with the operation, "the long-term average survival" was twelve months, which put a new spin on the whole idea of long term. For me, twelve months was a "training cycle." I was still sobbing when Dad came on the phone. He'd been shaving when I called, and for some reason that made me even sadder. How do you manage to look in the mirror when someone has just told you that in a year you won't be there?

A couple of weeks before, I'd visited some actuarial Web site that let you calculate your life span. Didn't smoke, long-lived relatives, plenty of exercise, low cholesterol—when I tapped the final button it told me I was going to die at ninety-three. I'm certain that Dad would have gotten the same result. He was strong and active; he'd just written his first book. But there was little on the actuarial table for something called glioblastoma, the most virulent form of brain cancer.

When we got to Boston the next day the change was obvious. Six days earlier his speech had been a little slurred. Three days earlier he'd driven to church to attend a meeting. Today, Saturday, his triumph had been walking the 20 yards to the Adirondack chairs in the backyard. His world was shrinking with incomprehensible speed. He told us about finding out the bad news. The surgeon had pronounced his death sentence, and then said he should choose. "I could get a big bottle of scotch and have a wonderful last night before going into a coma, or I could have this surgery that would keep me going a little longer."

The night before Dad went to the hospital, as I was taking off his slippers to put him into bed, I could see the hard, veiny calves that only a month ago were powering him up high mountains in his native Northwest. They were useless now. Was he useless? What did it mean to lose your body in a week? And what would it mean, 24 hours hence, to lose some large chunk of your mind?

That next morning, at the hospital, Dad passed into another, yet smaller world, where his abilities meant nothing. When the surgeon finally came for his pre-op visit, Dad asked only one question: "Will my personality change."

"I hope not," the doctor said.

We watched as they wheeled him out of his room to the operating theater. It was after lunch before the doctor appeared to give us the news. Dad had come through surgery okay, but the pathology was exactly what he suspected: glioblastoma, grade 4. The worst grade. He couldn't get it all; it had already spread to both lobes. Sorry. The next few months, the doctor said, would be "the good time," a phrase that would come to haunt us.

When they finally let us up to see him, Dad looked . . . beautiful. A turban of bandages wrapped his head, but beneath it his face was eerily young, as if he were in his twenties. The sparkle was back in his eyes. When we turned on the TV the Red Sox were leading the Indians in game 1 of their playoff series behind 7 RBIs from Mo Vaughn. Dad was making jokes—he whose head had been sawed open and then the two halves pulled apart by traction. This much was clear: His personality had not changed, not one whit. Doubtless it would darken when the tumor recurred, when the swelling built up again. The hope, though, was that we'd bought ourselves a few months, a window of time to make peace with his passing. Nothing more.

And so we settled into the pattern of small victories and somewhat larger defeats that must mark most terminal illness. They shifted Dad to a "rehabilitation hospital" in the suburbs, where after daily morning trips by ambulance to the radiation ward he would return for afternoons of physical therapy. The therapy rooms reminded me of the world where I'd spent much of the last year—they were filled with weight machines, parallel bars, treadmills. But here, in the place of the ersatz philosophy of the gym, real struggle prevailed. Dad's workouts, as tightly scheduled and as exhausting as mine, involved batting a balloon back and forth with the therapist, folding washcloths, unscrewing a jar top, kicking a ball. He could swing his right foot perhaps an inch, enough to nudge the ball along the floor, but no more. When he tried to steer his wheelchair, it inevitably drifted to the right till he hit a wall, reflecting the now-distorted architecture of his brain. His major triumph: learning to apply and disengage the wheelchair brake.

Through it all I kept running. I suppose I should have stopped, if only because it seemed in such poor taste, calibrating my body's improvement as Dad's withered away. But Dad had been the most interested in my project from the beginning. And there was nothing else to structure my life. No one expected me at the office. I was commuting between the Adirondacks and Boston, between my adult and boyhood homes. (I was sleeping on the bed I'd slept on as a boy, the same bed Dad had slept on in his youth.) There was no way I could write—when I tried to still my mind enough to string two thoughts together, I invariably began to weep. Only motion seemed to relax me.

I'd begun this compulsive exercising on the premise that I was at the tail end of my youth. Now it was all too easy to calculate that if I lived as long as my father was going to, I was already halfway used up. But I could feel the second half of my life starting in more complicated ways too. Identities long fixed shifted back and forth. Sometimes I was his son. But then the next morning would dawn, and we'd need yet again to make some impossible decision: more radiation, say. Dad would doze off while the doctor was explaining the options, and we'd be left trying to figure out what he might want, what we might want. The goal of all the physical therapy diminished. Instead of teaching him to regain real function in his muscles, the single aim became training him to help in the process of transferring himself from bed to wheelchair, and vice versa. If he learned that, he could go home and Mom could take care of him by herself. The technique, as detailed and precise as a good cross-country skiing kick, involved lifting his butt an inch up off the bed and then sliding himself in two stages about a foot and a half into the wheelchair. He would push himself up on his knuckles, slide 10 inches, rest 30 seconds till the panting subsided, then make the next assault. Each time he'd forget the sequence and need to be reminded; each time it left him red-faced and tired.

All of this training, and for what? It wasn't like my training. I knew I was getting steadily stronger and fitter. Not Dad. He worked all afternoon stretching his rubber bands, lifting his tiny dumbbells, and yet his body decayed faster than he could build it up.

I went in to the rehab center one morning and found him in an uncharacteristic rage. Some doctor had wandered through that morning (one of the glories of managed care was that unknown doctors constantly drifted in and out of our lives) and remarked to him, on the basis of a handshake, that he was getting weaker. Dad was outraged, agitated. He didn't want to go to therapy that afternoon, but I talked him into it.

You followed your schedule no matter what; sometimes that seemed about all my year had taught me.

If I needed a metaphor for my autumn, it came early November. Back in the Adirondacks for a week, I noticed some fresh new pavement on a back road on the far side of the Hudson River. Fresh pavement, to a roller-skier, exerts a nearly gravitational pull—smooth and fast, it's the next best thing to snow. What I hadn't noticed was just how steep the hills were. I was, as always, wearing a bike helmet, but I'd forgotten my knee pads, and the light was fading. Predictably, I went for it. For an hour I skied the hills, tucking for fast descents, powering up with short, choppy kicks, feeling pretty damn strong. And then, predictably, a dog ran out at the bottom of a hill just as a car passed on my left—and I was down in a second. Predictably, I jumped up, in the way that guys do when they've fallen, as if to say, Oh, I meant to do that. I waved off the stricken driver—and as soon as he was out of sight I sat right back down to consider. True, my knees were bleeding dramatically, soaking my shredded tights, but on the other hand I had 90 minutes left in my workout. I'd snapped a pole, so I clearly wasn't going to keep skiing, but had my sneakers in the car. And so—predictably?—I ran, knees bleeding and stiff. It was clearly stupid. Perhaps I just wanted to hurt, and to keep going through my hurt.

My road-scraped knees healed just in time for me to return to Lake Placid and the giant treadmill at the Olympic Training Center for the final readout on my year's training. I'd passed through this particular crucible in the spring, establishing my baseline numbers and learning just how much the test could hurt—you ran until you couldn't run anymore, or at least until you thought you couldn't. This time, rubber bit clenched in my mouth to catch my exhalations, I lasted two minutes longer than I had in April, but it didn't cheer me up. Because I knew I'd had another minute in me, if only I'd fought the pain a little harder. But when the treadmill tilted toward the gut-check stage, I couldn't keep going. It hurt, that's why.

My coach, Rob, professed delight. "You've had a 45 percent improvement in body fat, your lactate threshold is 25 percent better—your engine is burning hotter at a lower lactate production. It means you can ski at a faster pace longer." Part of me did feel exhilarated. It had worked the way it was supposed to, all those hours and miles. Mine was not the physique of a champion, but what I had done was maximize my genetic potential, grown about as powerful as my ancestry would allow.

But the day left me feeling unsettled. When things had gotten really tough, I had looked for a way out. My *heart* might have become more efficient, but my heart seemed no stronger.

Maybe it was because I was beginning to question whether endurance was such a grand goal anyhow.

From the moment I'd learned of Dad's first conversation with the surgeon—scotch or scalpel—part of me had been wondering whether we should be keeping him alive. We'd press the specialists with questions about whether his condition would improve, and all we'd get was the PhD equivalent of shrugs. In the meantime, he was home, enduring, and Mom was, too. The HMO professed to believe that a couple of hours of nursing assistance a day was all Mom needed; never mind that Dad outweighed her by 80 or 90 pounds. She hired extra aides to come in the evening and help her get him out of bed; the next-door neighbor's son slept upstairs now just in case he rolled out of bed and she couldn't get him back in. New pills piled up almost daily; dosages changed with every visit to the doctor; Mom was awake by 6:00 to give him his first medicines, and still up at midnight to feed him the final batch. When I thought about the burden she was under, I doubted I could handle anything like that. And yet she kept going forward, forward, forward, like—well, like an elite athlete. In her case, though, it wasn't uphill intervals and mental imagery that had laid the base. It was year upon year upon year of loving, so consistently that the giving had become instinctive.

As for me, if watching someone die could perform the same kind of magic, I wasn't sure I was ready for it. When the treadmill got steep enough, I started to look around for someone to turn it off.

Whenever we were with the doctors, no matter how much of a fog he seemed to be in, Dad would ask that they treat his cancer "aggressively." But one night, when I was talking to him very late, he said, "If it's going to be like this all the time, then there has to be a cutoff somewhere." Amen, I thought. Where's the guy with the switch?

We made it to Thanksgiving, and I spent the week in West Yellowstone—my longest absence from his bedside so far, a guilty vacation—at the annual cross-country training camp that fills the town with gaunt, wax-obsessed

Nordic racers trying to cope with the 6,600-foot altitude. I flew home on Friday, though, for a delayed turkey dinner, where we managed to convince ourselves that we had much to be thankful for and that, with Dad propped up at table's end, all was joy. After the pie settled, I went for a run and instantly understood why athletes are so eager to train at altitude. My body had compensated for the thin Montana air by adding extra red blood cells. I ran through suburban Boston on a high—no matter how hard I pushed, I couldn't make myself hurt. My heart-rate monitor showed I was working reasonably hard, but I could have been out for the lightest of jogs. I felt out ahead of my body, as if I was outrunning my feet.

Sadly, the corpuscles quickly disappeared, and with them the sense that I had become a minor deity. Worse than that, the East was still warm and bare as December began. The temperature hit the seventies on the first of the month. The pond by our house was filled with summery ripples. No need for the woodstove; we slept with the windows open.

It bothered me on many levels. For ten years I'd been a nearly full-time student of global warming—worrying, tracking the rising sea temperatures that were bleaching coral reefs, writing about the increase in the strength and frequency of hurricanes. But I felt it most personally come winter. Always my favorite of seasons, it had become deeply unreliable. As the man from Fischer Skis had told me in West Yellowstone, global warming had already damaged their business, interrupting every winter with long stretches of mud and thaw. Business would doubtless carry on; in fact, I'd just come across a series of economic forecasts proving, in the smug fashion of economists, that increases in the greens fees from golfers would outweigh the losses from declining ski sales. But I didn't want to play golf—I wanted to speed sublimely through the woods, riding on an outstretched ski, pushing with every muscle in my body. I wanted the annual remission from friction.

Rob had been pushing me to pick a final race to aim for, something grand enough to be worthy of this whole experiment—and he'd been urging me to think about the Norwegian Birkebeiner, the mother of all cross-country races, held each March on a course that runs over the mountains from Rena to Lillehammer. Open to all comers, it attracts thousands of Norwegians, and most of the world's best marathon skiers. As they race, they commemorate the pivotal event in Norway's thirteenth-century civil war. The Birkebeiners—Birchleggers—were the underdogs, "often in such dire need that they had nothing but the bark of birch trees as footwear." But they were determined that the rival faction, the Baglers, not capture Haakon Haakonsson, the toddler son of their dying king. So on Christmas Day 1205, two Birkebeiner skiers spirited him away on an epic journey across the mountains. The boy grew up to be King Haakon and to finally rout the Baglers, raising Norway to its medieval glory. And hence, each year in late March, racers pound those same grueling 58 kilometers, about 40 miles, mostly uphill, each carrying an 8-pound pack to match the weight of the young king.

I doubted I could go. With Dad dying, the prospect of a transatlantic trip seemed unlikely. And I wondered if I could even finish the race. But I still logged onto the race Web site and clicked the button for an application. Maybe Dad would get better for a while—maybe the "good time" would arrive. I knew I wanted to go; it sounded crazy, hard enough to justify this crazy year.

This crazy year in which winter seemed never to come. By mid-December we'd set up the Christmas tree at church and gone caroling in shirtsleeves. Finally, December 17 brought a little snow to the Adirondacks, and a few phone calls established that the Olympic trails at Lake Placid were partially open. They were barely covered, but it was skiing, and I kicked around and around the same short loops with the junior biathletes, guns strapped to their backs, and the local masters skiers, all of us desperate for snow. The next day warm, foggy air melted big tawny patches in the snow, and it was back to the damn NordicTrack. December was shot.

We got through Christmas Day in Boston just fine—a lot of the ornaments hung at wheelchair height, testament to Dad's pleasure in the work—but then, tired from the strain of this last big celebration, Dad was all but comatose for a couple of days. "Were it my dad," said the surgeon, "I wouldn't do much more."

At which point Dad emerged from his fog for the first time all day to ask

BILL MCKIBBEN

yet again that he be treated "aggressively." Which annoyed the hell out of me—some part of me wanted him to go away and stop bothering us. Stop making me feel guilty for not being more help to my mother; stop pulling me away from my family; stop stop stop being so damn needy, so unlike my father. Which, of course, left me feeling twice as guilty as before.

A snowstorm might have righted me. It usually does. A couple of hours alone in the woods, gliding along, pushing up hills and carving down them, breaking out into the open on Adirondack lakes and tucking back into stands of hemlock, reminding me of the proper order and scale of things.

By late January the ground was still bare, and Dad was setting off on a major journey. Each day he seemed to grow a bit more abstracted from his shrinking world. He was never short with any of us. If his grandchildren were on hand, he would watch them playing around his bed with deep delight, and he never ceased following Mom with his eyes.

Sometimes the world he was visiting seemed inscrutable. Once I asked him what he was thinking so deeply about, and he replied, in a loud voice, "Insects!" But he did tell Mom several times that he constantly saw a white line in front of his eyes. One morning, when he was more alert than usual and when we had the house to ourselves, I asked him if he could describe the line to me. He asked for a pencil and, gripping it tightly in his shaking hand, drew a wavering line about two-thirds of the way across the page and labeled it R. On the edge of the paper, he drew a wavering circle and with great effort wrote "W. Ocean" across it. (In a lifetime of writing, they were the last words he ever wrote.) The picture represented, he said, a "typical western river" leading to a "western ocean."

"And what does that ocean mean?" I asked.

"Infinity," he said. "Completeness."

He nodded off for a few moments and then woke back up. Why didn't the river connect to the ocean? I asked.

There were, he said, necessary tasks still to be done, but he couldn't find the words to say what they were.

"Is death more scary to think about or more peaceful?" I asked.

"More peaceful," he said emphatically, and then drifted back to sleep.

That night at dinner he seemed happy—we'd been discussing "ultimate truths," he told Mom, with just a little smile to let us know he knew how unlike him it was to discuss ultimate truths. But a new man was clearly taking shape before our eyes.

My own journey seemed all but irrelevant, dull even to me, but by now the training was so ingrained that I kept with it almost automatically. And Rob, the one person besides my wife whom I'd trusted with my resolve to mount a supreme effort in some race, kept trying to help me find the right venue.

The trip to Lillehammer seemed less likely than ever, but I came across a brochure for the annual Keskinada races in Ottawa, in late February. The theme for 1999 was Norway; they were trying to duplicate parts of the Birkebeiner in Canada, including sending off one wave of racers carrying eight-pound backpacks. Ottawa was only a quick trip from Boston; this one I figured I could make. And so the images that filled my mind on training runs were suddenly Canadian: the pine forests of the Gatineau Park, the 50-kilometer trail. There was finally a little snow on the ground, and Rob told me to prepare with a 4-hour time trial two weeks before the race. Four hours is a long time, especially with none of the adrenaline of a race to distract you; I headed to the ski tracks and did the same 5-kilometer loop eleven times, till I knew every soft spot in the snow. Every lap brought me by a pigpen filled with noisy hogs; I'd stop there and choke down some energy gel. When the clock finally stopped, I'd gone 55 kilometers, and proved to myself that at the very least I could manage the distances in the race ahead. And I'd done it with my pack on my back, like a true Birchlegger.

Almost in spite of myself, I could feel my body starting to peak. As the really long workouts of the fall dwindled in number and distance, and the brutal intervals built up my speed, power began to accumulate. I imagined that I knew what a racehorse felt like in the gate, pent-up energy ready to express itself. Long, hard uphill skiing left me feeling spent but not wasted; my body craved fuel and burned it evenly; I was eager for a test, impatient for the Ottawa race to arrive. I was, in fact, in the best physical shape of my life.

In the middle of all this, my friend John Race came to visit. We'd met when he guided me up Mount Rainier five years before. Intellectually curious the way I was physically curious, he'd nonetheless spent almost all his energy on things of the body and the spirit. He'd spent months on Mount McKinley, gotten within 500 feet of the top of Everest, climbed 26,000-foot peaks like Cho Oyu. Now he was hungry for intellectual growth, and he wanted to write about his experiences. He was playing on the path I'd been following since I could first remember, and I was playing on his. It made me think of the first notion Rob had taught me when we'd started working together a year before—each of us born to be balanced physically, intellectually, and spiritually.

It hadn't taken me long to figure out how linked all three could be. If exercise was about being physical, then racing—being willing to hurt, to go harder than you wanted to—had an obvious spiritual quality. But the neat progression of my idea ran into trouble when Dad got sick. He was clearly operating at some higher level now, but it wasn't because he was trying. Instead, it seemed to be because he was letting go. Not giving up, not dropping out, but slowly, methodically, patiently letting go of his life. Every so often, I kept trying to ask serious questions, to find out what was going on inside. Partly it was just my curiosity, but I sensed, too, that he enjoyed talking about it, liked the fact that someone acknowledged he was dying and that it was an interesting process. One day he muttered that he was trying to figure out if there was something beyond this "make-believe" world, if there was something beyond "next week." His metaphors, like the drawing of the river, tended always toward the outdoor, the concrete, toward the joys of the Western boyhood that had filled his imagination ever since. "I feel like I'm climbing," he told me slowly one day. "Like I'm climbing up a cliff."

"Are you near the top?" I asked.

"Getting there," he said, with a grin.

I thought of all the climbs we'd taken when I was young, in the mountains of Maine and New Hampshire; of the pleasure he'd taken in the Adirondacks when I moved there; of the long trip we'd taken with his brother and my brother around Mount Rainier. Every time I'd looked at him in those weeks on the Wonderland Trail, he'd been grinning. Climbing wasn't a struggle for him, didn't represent a battle or even a test. It was a great joy, because it carried you higher, to where the view was clearer. And more than that—though the grand view may have started you slogging in the first place, no one kept hiking for years unless they came to like the slog. Sometimes it's bittersweet to reach the top, because there's nothing to do but linger for a while and go back down. This time, however, he wouldn't need to descend.

I'd started this exercise of exercising in an effort to try on a new identity, the way a high school boy might try on meanness, or a college boy might grow a goatee. But now, watching Dad, I realized what a solid thing an identity is. He was unchanged even by this catastrophe—he remained as decent and egoless a man as I'd ever met. As for me, I'd examined my core from a different side, or placed it under light of a different wavelength, and found it to be much as I'd always known it: curious, eager, tempted by deep commitment but afraid of the effort and pain.

I could live with that—it had served me well so far—but now I wondered if I could die with that. Wondered if I could go as gracefully as my father was going, as bravely and yet as peacefully. What would it be like to reach the end of my life without regrets?

Dad took one last trip into the hospital, for one last MRI. The tumor had fired up again, the doctors said, started once more to grow. Don't even bother calling the ambulance if something happens, they advised—you don't want them sticking a tube down his throat. Mom listened, asked Dad if he had anything to say.

He looked up, and in a clear, conversational tone announced, "I have this fascinating vision of a white line along the edge of a riverbank."

So there was Dad, cheerful in the face of a brain tumor. And here I was, gloomy because I'd caught a cold two days before the big race in Ottawa, and was reduced to obsessively guzzling tea, sucking on zinc tablets, and fretting about compromised respiratory efficiency. But on race morning I was up at 5:45, and I was the first to arrive at Gatineau Park. I splurged $30 at the ski-waxing booth and watched the ski techs patiently iron on purple and red and then a coat of klister because the tracks were icy. I took my skis outside, tried them for a few strides, and instantly felt my mood soaring—I had rock-solid kick and lustrous glide. They felt like perfect extensions of my legs, each twitch converted into forward momentum.

The starting pen for my wave filled with other backpack-carrying skiers, about forty of us among the hundreds of more conventional racers. An official weighed the rucksacks, making sure they topped the infant-king-Haakon line on the scale. We shuffled back and forth in the tracks for a few minutes, trying to stay limber, until the Norwegian ambassador to Canada sounded the ceremonial horn and we took off.

Because of the packs, it was easy enough to keep my competition in sight. We hit the first long uphill, and my legs felt so strong I had to consciously rein myself in a little, remind myself I'd be out on the course for a good three hours. One by one I picked off the guys in my wave—a fellow carrying a blaze-orange knapsack, a fellow in camouflage Lycra, a fast-looking skier who somehow managed to fall on the first small downhill. Twenty minutes into the race, a fellow in a brown rucksack was in front of me, and I was pretty sure he was either second or third in my wave—in other words, if I passed him I'd be in the money. I stayed on his tail for a few minutes, pulling abreast occasionally, even chatting for a while to let him know the pace wasn't hurting me. And I passed him.

After that I was skiing by myself. The hills just kept on coming, and my form began gradually to erode; by the halfway point I was laboring. I stopped for a drink of water and a ClifShot, and the people manning the table seemed concerned. "You're shivering," said one. "Are you hypothermic?" Before they could ask again, I skied off.

At some point along the course, a photographer crouched, taking pictures of everyone coming by so that he could try to sell them at the banquet that night. Through his lens, I was just one more tired-looking guy stuck somewhere in the middle of an unimportant race. And yet for me it was an epic. I crouched down in my tuck and let my muscles recover for a few minutes as the trail tilted downhill. Then came a long flat. Finally, at about 40 kilometers, the trail turned back on itself, and for about 500 yards you could see the skiers right behind you. Oh, God—one had a brown backpack, the same fellow I'd passed nearly 2 hours before, now right on my tail, maybe 40 seconds behind. Worse, my limbs were slowing down—I couldn't muster more than a sluggish kick. I could feel myself about to give up, about to be passed, about to turn normal.

And then I didn't. I made it up one hill and coasted down the other side; after that, though I was shaky and absolutely drained, I managed to go hard. Not fast. But fast enough, because I was still passing people. Fast enough, because every time I looked over my shoulder, the tracks were clear. Eventually there was a sign by the trail and it said: "Finish 1,000 Meters." Did a thousand meters mean a kilometer? Ten kilometers? My hypoxic brain fuzzed the question around until suddenly the trail spit out onto an open field, and the finish was only a few hundred good old English yards away. I sprinted, I fell across the line, someone picked me up and wrapped a wool blanket around me. They said I'd come in second in my wave.

My father's race finished on March 3. Though his sickness had lasted barely 6 months, half the impossibly short "long-term average survival" the doctors had given us at the start, he had endured. He'd kept going.

I had spent a year thinking about endurance. Trying to understand it as a function of physiology, of lactic acid and capillary networks. Trying to understand it as the ability to fight through the drama of pain. But now I understood it, too, as a kind of elegance, a lightness that could come only from such deep comfort with yourself that you began to forget about yourself. Something no heart monitor would ever measure.

Dad died in time to let me go to Norway for the Birkebeiner. Once I'd thought that this would be the epic end of my saga, but now I knew that whatever epiphanies I'd been allotted had come at the edge of his sickbed. Now there was just the pleasure of enduring in a great crowd of others doing the same—old men, some of them eighty and eighty-five, a little stiff in their Lycra, but still elegant. They'd been skiing these hills fifty years ago, tracking down Allied airdrops in the woods, and they did so still, for the sheer joy of it.

The course was brutal as advertised, and I was in no danger of letting loose another epic performance. But never mind. I went deep inside, kept track of my weakening calves and my tightening chest, measured my resources against the distance left to go. And it all came out just fine—a little over four hours of hard skiing, ending with a series of sharp downhills into the Olympic stadium filled with brass bands and cheering crowds. I finished just above the middle of my age group, which I declared a great victory, considering they were all Norwegians. But I took my conquest as quietly as everyone else—there was no whooping or hollering on the bus to the showers, just satisfied and tired smiles. The year was over, and it was time for a smoked salmon pizza and a bottle of Ringnes and some Tiger Balm to rub on my aching thighs.

The next morning dawned clear and cold, and Sue and Sophie and I went for another ski. And for the first time in a long time, it meant nothing at all.

The Backstory

Jack McCallum

A few weeks before the 2005–2006 NBA training camps began, I called Julie Fie, the Phoenix Suns' ace director of public relations, to propose a story idea. I would be with the team throughout training camp as an "assistant coach" and would then write a story about my experiences. (I may have even said "quote marks around assistant coach" during our conversation.)

I was looking to do something different, something from the inside. In my twenty-five years at SI, which included two decades of following the NBA, I had covered everything from BASE jumping to the world championship of squash, but had never engaged in participatory journalism, unless you count having Shaquille O'Neal back his 350-pound ass into me to demonstrate how he doesn't commit offensive fouls.

Julie said she'd check with the authorities—General Manager Bryan Colangelo and Coach Mike D'Antoni—and get back to me.

I homed in on the Suns for a variety of reasons, not the least of which was Fie. I had known her for two decades and considered her one of the best in the business, not to mention someone who might actually think it was an idea that would fly. I automatically crossed out a couple dozen or so other PR directors who would either dismiss it out of hand or had a head coach who would rather push a mule cart down Broadway while wearing a thong than open a window into the inner workings of his team.

I also knew Colangelo and his father, Jerry, still the team's CEO and president. I knew D'Antoni and his assistant coaches, though not all that well, from interviewing them for a story I had written about the Suns during the previous season. I knew assistant coach Todd Quinter well—I even wrote a few stories about him three decades ago when he was a high school basketball star in Nazareth, Pennsylvania—but, as the team's chief scout, he was away from the team much of the time. I knew Steve Nash and Shawn Marion, the team's veteran stars, though neither was what I would call a professional confidante. I thought they were good guys who might not mind a notebook-carrying dilettante; obviously, any such project would need the blessing of the team's superstars, tacit or otherwise.

The other reasons were purely pragmatic. First, the Suns were probably going to be good; unless a team is profoundly bad, like, say, the expansion New York Mets or the 2005–2006 New York Knicks (we didn't know that then), it is almost always better to write about a winner. Winning teams are happy, happy teams talk, talk makes stories. Further, the Suns were coming off of a positively revolutionary season during which they had become one of the most entertaining shows in sports. D'Antoni, having spent most of his playing and coaching career in Italy, did not subscribe to the prevailing NBA wisdom that a fast-break team cannot succeed, and so he built a team around Nash that ran like hell and tossed up 3-point shots like so much wedding confetti. And, though no one suggested that D'Antoni and his staff didn't work hard, they seemed to be serious about the idea of not taking themselves seriously. They seemed like good guys to hang with.

Julie called back 48 hours later and said, "Buy a pair of sneakers. You're on the staff." So to speak.

There are certain stories that just work out, that through some weird alchemy present a combination of factors that trigger positive feelings in the reader. The preseason "assistant coach" story was one of them. Judging from the letters, e-mails, and personal comments I received, people enjoyed the inside perspective, the lively interplay (especially the insults) among the coaches, the details of how players and coaches work together, what the coaches say about other teams, and the participatory–Walter

Mitty aspect of the story, i.e., the outsider-amateur getting the chance to do what the insider-pro does. Along with allowing me total access to practices, meetings, and meals, the coaches let me participate in drills here and there; on the first day, Marion nailed me in the face as I held the ball during a shell drill, and I felt I belonged.

Soon after the story ran in *Sports Illustrated*, I was asked to expand it into a book. I had doubts as to whether it would work. As friendly and open as the coaches had been in early October, when workouts and scrimmages were held far from prying eyes, they were not about to allow me to muck up drills during the regular season. But perhaps they would once again grant me the same unfettered access and that would be the essence of the book. The publisher said, "Give it a try." I called D'Antoni and he said, "Sure." It was almost that simple.

I had written one "season-with" book in 1991 (*Unfinished Business*) after spending a considerable part of the 1990–1991 season with the Boston Celtics. I rode the team bus, collected stories from players such as Larry Bird and Kevin McHale, and just generally spent a lot of time hanging around. It was "inside" but not in any way, shape, or form like this would be. Coach Chris Ford didn't invite me to coaches' meetings. I was not allowed into the locker room when the rest of the media wasn't there. I couldn't attend closed practices. So this would be an entirely different book.

When I showed up a couple of weeks into the regular season to begin my research, D'Antoni took, literally, 10 seconds to brief the team on the colossal significance of my presence. "You remember Jack from the preseason," D'Antoni said at the beginning of an off-day practice. "He's going to be with us a lot of the time working on, I don't know, a book or something." That was it.

Rarely was I asked to keep something off-the-record. As the man in charge, D'Antoni would usually be the one to say, with a smile, "I'll kill you if this is in the book," or, more seriously, "Don't put this in." But considering the hours and hours I spent with the team from November to June, the requests were entirely reasonable. They came to trust me (I think) and further believed that (a) transparency is the best course, and (b) we don't say that many controversial things anyway.

The parameters of my access were simple: I went where the coaches did. I attended their meetings, accompanied them to practice, and sat in the coaches' sections of the plane and the bus on road trips, usually next to Dan D'Antoni, the older brother Mike had brought aboard as an assistant. But for me, a journalist who for four decades has been on the outside looking in, nose pressed to the glass, it wasn't that simple suddenly becoming an insider.

I never walked through the Suns' training room, verboten to anyone except team personnel (more than once I saw a player's agent chased out of there), without feeling that I didn't belong, even though everyone welcomed me. I set all kinds of rules for myself. I wouldn't accept an employee pass, and, instead, spent a considerable amount of time snaking my way by any means possible into U.S. Airways Center (which, before January 6, was known as America West Arena) for early-morning coaches' meetings. Yes, I ate the food on the team plane (but not too much), drank the bottled water in the coaches office, and plucked grapes from the pregame fruit plate. But I tried not to avail myself of the postgame buffet that sat, appetizingly, on a table in the locker room.

I went to great lengths to prevent my fellow journalists from seeing me step off a bus or get into a locker room before the prescribed press time. I literally dove for cover when NBA-TV filmed practices at which journalists were not supposed to be in attendance. I was able to insinuate myself behind the bench for many games but refused to adopt what Phil Weber, an assistant coach, calls "the State of the Union look" (white shirt, red tie) to help sell the idea to security guards and other arena personnel that I was actually a coach.

During the season, I wrote about the Suns for Sports Illustrated only once— a long piece about Steve Nash, in which he came across glowingly but no more so than if I hadn't been with the team. (I hope that's the case anyway.) When it came time to vote for end-of-the-season awards, I thought of recusing myself but finally decided I could vote fairly. I put Nash in third place (behind Detroit's Chauncey Billups and Cleveland's LeBron James) in the voting for MVP and put D'Antoni second behind San Antonio's Gregg Popovich for coach of the year. Nash won anyway. D'Antoni finished second, jokingly making the claim, whenever I was in earshot, that "one vote for Popovich spun the whole process upside down in some weird way," preventing him from winning for the second straight year.

I didn't hang out with the players much when the coaches weren't around. For one thing, it's not like their first thought was, "Man, we really want some fifty-six-year-old interloper dude going clubbing with us." But there is also a precise line of demarcation between players and coaches. You can't sit in on all the coaches meetings, then try to pass yourself off as some sort of special-exempt player. There were many times, however, when I would just sit in the locker room and listen to Eddie House's nonstop rap or chat with Shawn Marion, Kurt Thomas, James Jones, or Pat Burke about nothing at all. They are good people, and I enjoyed our conversations.

I had a good enough relationship with a couple players, Nash and Raja Bell in particular, that I could give them a gentle amount of grief, and they could certainly give it back. On the day the team photo was taken, the coaches insisted that I get into one just for posterity's sake, and, as I stood there, silently urging the photographer to hurry up and snap, Nash said, "Okay, be careful. The spy's in the picture." On the one occasion that I did pilfer a chicken finger from that postgame buffet, Nash caught me. "Jack, I hope you're paying for that," he said with a couple of other reporters around.

In the interest of full disclosure, I did two things that I wouldn't normally do as a journalist: I got Nash to autograph a jersey for a charity auction and Raja Bell to autograph for my sister-in-law. She thinks he's hot.

Going into the project, I was curious about one thing in particular—how do professional coaches deal with losing? I had coached an 8th-grade team for several years, and, though I don't consider myself a particularly competitive person, the losses would gnaw at my insides, keep me up nights, and have me on the phone for hours with my assistant coach trying to deconstruct what went wrong . . . with a bunch of 13- and 14-year-olds. What must it be like when the stakes are high? A basketball coach makes so many decisions during a game—substitutions, out-of-bounds plays, defensive alterations, time-outs—that any single one of them can have an impact on the result.

The answer turns out to be: The losses do indeed take a heavy toll. Coaches don't sleep well. They beat themselves up. They look terrible in the morning. They catch colds. They suck on candy. They drink too much caffeine. They snap at each other. Sometimes they order onion rings and French fries together. Then they come in the next day and do it again.

I flew back to Phoenix with the team after it had lost a 140–133 triple-overtime game to the Knicks in New York on January 2. The referees that night had suffered from a case of Madison Square Garden-itis. The Knicks shot 54 free throws compared to just 16 for the Suns. Had Kurt Thomas not been called for a phantom foul with 8 seconds left, the Suns would've won in regulation. It could hardly have been a more agonizing loss, especially since it came to an inferior team. Security at the private airstrip in Newark took forever. It was raining. The plane didn't take off until 1:15 a.m. Some players had brought along their families (they do that on a few road trips per year) and babies were wailing. I felt like wailing, too, and couldn't imagine how badly I would've felt had I been the one presiding over this godforsaken evening.

"Five hours of freakin' misery awaits," said D'Antoni as he boarded the plane. Then he and his assistants fired up their portable DVDs and watched the game, over and over and over, consigning themselves to their own personal small-screen hell.

Yet, no Suns coach—no coach I've ever known, in fact—wants to give up the life. The highs are too high. Though I never in any way, shape, or form considered myself a member of the team, I understood that feeling for the first time.

Bench Press, or Becoming a Girl Again

Leslie Heywood

I meet Billy at the diner. Bill Townsend, thirty-nine, five-foot-five and 250. Bill with the 465 bench. And bench is what's up this morning, our biannual Elmira Best Bench Championship. Billy's done these meets for at least twelve years, and when he goes out to make his lifts, the announcers always say, "And now our Bill, starting at 440 today . . ." I've trained with him now for two years. Billy chokes down eggs and sausage while I swill coffee, as if my nervous system needs any more kick.

"Gonna open with 440," Billy keeps saying. "You think that's right? Then 460, maybe 465." "You got 460 the other day," I tell him. "Think you need to kick it up a bit. I've got 210 as an opener, then 215. Then you think I should go 220? 225?" We go through this until it's time to drive out there, as if saying the numbers will make them so.

Back in the fray. I've been doing this, competing in one sport or another, since I was thirteen. It used to be track, then track and cross-country, then road racing. In the 1980s it was "all pain no gain," and especially in college, NC fucking double A, Division I, you were only as good as your last win. Sitting here at this old upstate New York diner in the late '90s, staring at the anachronism of cigarette-stained waitresses and plastic booths, so nervous it feels like my stomach's up in my mouth, I keep trying to tell myself that's all changed now. Even the hardest-core sports magazines now advise against "no pain no gain" and preach the necessity of rest.

And I'm not nineteen anymore, every fiber of my muscles, every beat of my heart fixed on winning the race, on keeping my number-one spot on the team. Not a frightened girl struggling to hold fast to the only self she knows, with injuries and a body that is steadily breaking down, struggling to keep the college athletic scholarship that is based on her performances and that is putting her through school. Not anymore. I'm thirty-four, reasonably healthy, good job, four dogs, own house . . . But deep-tissue memories are hard to erase, and the idea of anything athletic in front of a crowd is enough to raise all of it, my heart rate so high I can feel it ramming my chest as I sit there sweating metal-scented fear.

Some coaches used to encourage us to think of it as a struggle for existence. You hold on to your place, your value, what comes to seem like your very soul, if and only if you win. Every practice, every meet. And if you were a girl, you had to compete much harder than if you had that Y chromosome instead, to show that you weren't *just a girl*. You had to choose, because girls don't exist, remember? Girls are *seen not heard, be sweet, just go along with it, give of yourself, don't assert yourself*. Girls are supposed to be nice. Smile a lot, meet everyone else's needs. So if you wanted to be an athlete, you had to *not* be a girl. You can't win a race without asserting yourself. It wasn't a choice for me. I lived to compete. Inside, underneath the smiling blond surface, I murdered the girl.

So twenty-one years later I'm powerlifting, doing the bench press, the one exercise that separates the men from the boys. Billy and I drive to the meet, and walk into the high school gymnasium where it's held. Bleachers fold out over the floor, the bench the very center of the gym. The bin of chalk for your hands and your back, chalk your partners rub over you to keep you from slipping on the bench. The announcer's table. The trophy table against the far wall, its rows of shiny lifters perched on fake wood, smirking. The refs will be on either side, waiting to give you a white light (if you get the lift) or red (if you don't). The audience will cheer in support if you get it. Murmur a disappointed "Awww" if you don't.

Half an hour before we start, people are milling all over the floor, competitors swallowing their last strips of creatine, a powder you mix with grape juice for the fastest absorption, a powder that contains an enzyme that increases your explosive strength. Some down PowerBars, or protein-and-chocolate concoctions with names like White Lightning or Steel Bar, or stimulants with names like Ripped Fuel. The biggest guys, the most intense, tuck their ammonia capsules into their pockets, and will sniff them and hit themselves in the head for concentration right before their heaviest lifts. Some faces are faces you see at all meets, easygoing, appraising the action, dispensing advice. There are parents and girlfriends in the bleachers. The bathroom that always runs short of toilet paper is directly adjacent to the gym, and the bathroom that always has it is at the school entrance much farther away.

The warm-up benches are in the room across the hall. We all crowd in and listen to a recitation of the rules: Keep your butt on the bench. Lock it out at the top, and wait for the judge to say "rack" before you drop it. No one pays attention. Some of us sit, some stand with our backs to the wall, everyone swallows and tries to keep the tension in: *Let's get going already.* The voice drones on. I scan the room for other women. There, in that corner. A woman, maybe forty-five or fifty, middle-weight, though this meet's so small that the women are all lumped in one class, regardless of our weight or age. At the bigger contests, there are three weight divisions: up to 132, 132–148, and 148 and above. Usually there's teen, open, and masters, which is anyone over forty. But today we're just women, all the same. So who am I up against? There! Behind the middle-weight woman, Deb, the bodybuilder, from last year. A woman who looks like she must be seventy-five (I find out later that she is). Where's Cindy? I scan. No Cindy of the 280 bench and the national titles, at least not yet.

Then I stop about halfway along the opposite wall. A little girl, with her father. Man! How old is she? I ask the guy next to me if he knows. He does: at this meet, for the first time, there's a very young girl. Thirteen. Exactly how old I was when I first lifted a weight. Could I have been that small, that pudgy? Could I ever have been that young? She looks at her father and he smiles. Everyone wishes her luck.

The charts that list the competitors' flights, organized according to age and weight, are taped against the far wall of the gym. The women's flight is always first, because the women generally start with the lightest weights. Lately, though, the first flight is a mix, with the strongest women starting after some of the men. In a bench press meet you get 3 lifts. You open with a weight you know you can get, then have two more attempts. Your final score is determined by the heaviest weight you get, calculated in reference to your bodyweight. The charts list each competitor's opening lift, so you can gauge who your biggest challenge will be.

As soon as the meet director stops speaking, people gather by the charts to check out the competition, and calculate how many lifters are ahead of them in the lineup, and therefore how many minutes before they will take their turn. Rule of thumb says you should try to take your Ripped Fuel about half an hour before, and to do your serious warm-ups about 15 minutes ahead, making sure to leave time to have your partners help you on with your shirt. Those of us in the first flight stampede to the warm-up benches. You grab a bench, pump out a few, then ask whoever is next what weight they want there. The young girl—who tells me her name is Tracy— warms up with 50 pounds, then 60. The older woman—whose name is Jean—does about the same. The rest of us rush through sets somewhere in the hundreds, trying to get warm and leave a little more time. Because we've got breasts, it'll take us a little longer to put on our shirts.

Most competitors, those who take the meet at all seriously, wear bench shirts made out of the toughest layers of nylon, or the new denim kind, four layers of fabric thick. To bench without a shirt would be like running the Boston marathon in Keds. A shirt with the right fit can boost your bench by 20 pounds. Your shirt is supposed to fit so tight that you can't pull it on yourself, and many guys—who wear their shirts so tight it often takes three people to get them on—smear themselves with baby powder first to help with the burn.

I've got a red shirt, don't use baby powder, and always get bruised under my arms. Whoever you train with usually helps you with your shirt. After the warm-up Billy helps me, and Owen, this other guy from our gym. First I try to get my arms through the armholes, which are small and placed close together to help with the tightness of the material across the chest. My arms way up over my head, Billy and Owen ease the fabric over my forearms and biceps with quick, efficient tugs. They're pros at this. "Your head!" they yell, and I poke it through a small stitched hole. They work quickly, with short pulls down to the shoulders, and finally my head is out and they're putting the fabric down over my chest. Owen tugs the back so hard I get thrown off balance, and then spill the other way when Billy tugs the front, which presses my breasts completely flat. I bounce side to side, cased tighter than any sausage. I can barely breathe. "There you go," they say, my shoulders drawn into each other so stiff I can't put my arms down.

This is the desired effect, and made for a startling sight when I saw people walking around in these shirts at my first meet: big guys, a few women, in blacks and reds and blues, walking with their arms in front of them like some Halloween ball or Frankenstein parody, so big and stiff and awkward I almost expected them to open their mouths with that monster's inarticulate cries.

Most of us go into the mental preparation phase, trying to concentrate and visualize our first lifts. Here's where your training partner really comes in: to keep your blood circulating through your arms once you're in your shirt, you have to keep them propped up. So competitors rest their arms on the shoulders of their partner before they start, and in between their lifts. A good partner will just stand there, silent, and let you concentrate. Billy waits for the weight of my arms without a word, and I prop them, try to clear my head and see myself getting the two plates up (two 45-pound plates on either side of the 45-pound bar totals 225). I think of faceless competitors who can press 250 when I'm only absolutely certain of 210. I think of Cindy last year with her 280. My hands are shaking a little, but when I reason it out, everyone's at such different levels, such different ages, bodyweights, range of experience, it makes no sense at all to compare us. When I used to run races in college, all of us were about the same age and equally trained. Each woman was a potential threat to every other woman's ranking and place. That's why my stomach is rumbling. But that mentality just has no place here. Powerlifting is a distinctly nonprofessional sport, not likely to get much newspaper ink, and it's occurred to me before that the crowd cheers for everyone just the same, that they don't even notice which lifter wins.

Still, my hands are starting to sweat. I'm really wondering if I can get over 220. I'd been doing 225 easily all summer and early fall, but the last couple of months, I'd only been able to get 220 when we practiced in the gym with the shirts. I thought I should open at 210, go to 215, then 220, but Billy said the nervous tension and yells of the crowd would boost me up that last 5 pounds and I should just go for the 225. I don't know. I can hear from the crowd the first lifters are about to start, and I head in.

Jean is first. She looks like anyone's grandmother, short and thin and really frail, a strange sight in this milling pack of Schwarzenegger brawn. She walks to the bench with her head up and a power to her steps that gives some solidity to the thinness of her arms. She's a pro: sits herself down, gives her chest a final stretch by pulling her elbows back, shakes her arms loose, and concentrates, looking straight ahead. Then she's down, her hands placed on the bar like clasps, and the weight's off the rack, down to her chest, and back up again, white light as the judges say, "Rack!" The crowd is rowdy and really gives her a yell, and she smiles, striding off to the announcers to report what her next attempt will be.

Tracy's right after her, and the crowd's really behind her, too. She's less certain of her movements and does everything a little fast, but she has no problem at all with her opening weight. When she racks it, several groups of people in the stands are on their feet. The crowd's voices echo off the gymnasium walls, and Tracy seems to grow taller as she jumps in excitement and runs to report her next lift.

Seventy-five years old, or thirteen, the girls are in the house today, and the crowd loves them. People are on their feet through each of Jean's and Tracy's lifts: boys in their late teens, their chests thick from lifting and football practice. Guys middle-aged, and graying, in nondescript windbreakers and Carhartt boots. Their wives, hair bleached and pulled back for the morning. Some girls in tight jeans, the girlfriends of the guys who will soon be pressing 425. Other girls in clusters, just watching. Old couples, parents, young kids, the rest of the competitors: "Nice! Nice! Way to go! Here we go now!"—Jean and Tracy are cheered like they're the state championship basketball team.

They both get their personal bests. They both look like they've been made Queen for a Day except prouder. They ruled today. They got their lifts. I smile and add my voice to the din. I drag my arms off Billy's shoulders and Frankenstein it on over to where they're changing, and I don't say anything but they see it in my eyes. They move up under my arms and we stand there with our arms around each other tight.

My arms around them, I feel the hammering in my chest, the edginess in my stomach, shift. I've linked arms with a woman who is seventy-five years old, and who has just bench-pressed the same weight as her age. With a girl the same age I was when I started to compete, who will learn who she is at least partly from this world and how men and women like me treat her here. I stop being scared and think it again: this isn't about first place.

"Deb Costanzas on deck, Leslie Heywood in the hole!" I watch Deb get her lift, 150, clean. My arms are propped again on Billy's shoulders, so it's hard to clap, but I yell really loud instead, so loud he covers his ears. When I first started doing these meets I never cheered for the other women, focusing, preparing myself for my own lifts instead. But cheering for my competitors, women showing their strength in public, I feel like I'm cheering for myself. As if the louder the cheers, the more it matters all of us are out here. So I'm still yelling for Deb even as the announcer is calling my name. "Settle down, champ," Billy says, walking me over to the chalk and smearing it over my back. "Down and up. Right off your chest. Let the shirt carry it." They announce my opening weight of 210 and the crowd starts to roar, but I'm thinking about setting myself under the bar just right. "Straight down, then up. Down, then up." And up it goes, like there was no weight on that bar at all. I get the white lights, run over to tell them my next lift's 215.

My arms are propped up until it's time to go again 10 minutes later. The 215 is easy too. But on 225, my last try, the weight heads up but then hangs in the air three-quarters of the way, stopped dead. It's not going anywhere. The spotters grab it—red light. "Awww!" the crowd murmurs. But the announcer's upbeat. Heywood out with 215—an enormous lift!" The crowd goes from disappointment to a rowdy cheer. I get up off the bench and wave. It's the best I've done in a contest. And winning? Yeah,

I guess. But the crowd's cheered all of us. I'm not feeling like I'm flying because I lifted the most. I'm flying because I'm feeling deeper respect for my competitors, my girls. The girl I murdered a long time ago within me. I feel her kicking in my chest: the girls were in the house today, girls and athletes both.

Flight of Fancy

Dana White

This is the last place I ever expected to find myself: strapped into the cockpit of an F/A-18 Hornet on a drizzly February afternoon, moments away from rocketing into the wild gray yonder. My reasons for coming to this airfield in El Centro, California, are complicated, but the rules of the flight are simple: There are things I can touch (the air vents, the seat adjustment switch, the plastic air-sickness bags) and things I can't (the flight control stick, the rudder pedals, anything painted yellow and black). I shouldn't even think about touching the ejection loop handle. If something goes wrong, my pilot would be responsible for punching me out; I, however, would be responsible for not buying the farm. In the event of an emergency egress, I should tuck my chin to avoid decapitation. After my chute opens, I should steer it into the wind. If it fails to open and I go into free fall, I should manipulate the risers so as to cause the chute to bloom with air. "Avoid power lines, avoid mountains, avoid the highway," the plane's crew chief had told me. "Land next to the highway so we can get to you quicker. We'll drive up and remind you that you signed a waiver."

Like most people, I find that my thrill-seeking impulses occupy the vast middle ground between cowardice and death wish. Backcountry snowboarding and crossing against traffic pretty much satisfy my risk requirements—good, clean, earthbound fun. The thought of flying in a fighter jet filled me with dread. Yet when the Blue Angels, the Navy's flight demonstration squadron, invited me to take a 45-minute VIP flight at their winter training ground as part of their publicity efforts, I had to accept. This could be the ride of my life.

My father was a top-drawer Navy reconnaissance pilot, but I did not inherit the *Top Gun* gene. He was handsome and funny and patriotic in an unabashed way that is entirely out of fashion now. Every female who fell within the net of his affections was called "sweetie." His call sign, or pilot's nickname, was Field Goal. Its origins are a mystery; my mother says he didn't care for football, though he was, apparently, quite comfortable with the notion of scoring. He'd joined the Navy in 1955 to avoid being drafted, sacrificing a promising career as a naturalist, and I recall how he could whistle birdsongs so expertly that the birds sang back. My prized possessions are his college copy of Peterson's *A Field Guide to the Birds* and one of his old flight suits. When I hold the suit to my face, I swear I can smell him: that macho bouquet of tobacco, jet fuel, and Brut.

In my father's letters home from his first tour of duty in Vietnam, he called the jets "birds," and they usually seemed to be malfunctioning in one way or another. "Got our bent bird cranked off the boat yesterday late—busy today trying to get it squared away," he wrote my mother in December 1967. "Got to go make arrangements to get one of our birds off-loaded for repairs. It blew both tires on landing." And later: "Air Group lost the first bird to combat. An F-4 hit west of Haiphong."

I was just a kid, and while I don't know what my older brother thought, I felt a rivalry with my father's jets. I sensed that he loved more than anything to fly them, and that this love had something to do with why he was willing to go to war, whatever war was. And on April Fool's Day 1969, when two officers appeared at our door, with hats in their hands and sorrow in their faces, I knew that his love of flight had a lot to do with that, too.

He hadn't been very high when it happened—about 5,000 feet, coming into position to photograph the Ho Chi Minh Trail. Suddenly, without warning, his plane exploded, broke into pieces and spiraled into the jungle. His chase pilot circled overhead, screaming "Eject! Eject!" until antiaircraft fire chased him off.

My father and his navigator could not possibly have survived, it was decided, yet there were no bodies as proof. Their deaths were official, yet hypothetical. In my mind, my father existed in a state of suspended animation, as if he had ejected out of our lives and simply never come down. I spent several years looking up, waiting for him to land. I imagined him picking himself off the ground, miraculously uninjured, his parachute deflating behind him like a botched meringue. When the POWs were released in 1973, I sat by our front door, expecting him to amble through it, reanimated by faith. But of course he never did, and gradually I accepted that he never would.

For almost thirty years my father remained one of the approximately two thousand U.S. servicemen unaccounted for from the war in Southeast Asia. In late 1994, the military task force devoted to resolving these cases tracked down his crash site in central Laos, and in 1997 they excavated it. From 5 inches of damp clay soil they dug up eighty-three bone fragments, pieces of the ejection system, a locker key, and a quarter. In August 1998, at Arlington National Cemetery, we buried all that could be identified as Danforth E. White, CDR, USN: a sliver of jawbone that matched his dental records.

I had volunteered to give the eulogy, but soon realized I barely knew him. So at thirty-seven I undertook my own search, one that has continued long after I turned away from the gravesite, a spent shell casing from the 21-gun salute trapped in my fist. I searched for my father everywhere: on the Internet, in old photos and documents dredged from my mother's garage, in interviews with family and friends. I could find his name on war memorials and plaques from Honolulu to New York City, but I could not access the passion for flying that defined him. To do that, I would have to fly. The chances of that seemed remote. Then one day, as if fate had adopted my cause, the Blue Angels' invitation eased out of the fax machine of this magazine's [Women's Sports & Fitness] Manhattan offices.

A few weeks later, my sister Marda, who lives in Los Angeles, drives me down to El Centro, a desert agricultural community hard on the Mexican border. Eight years younger than I, she wasn't born when our father disappeared, yet despite—or because of—this, she identifies with him intensely. A few years ago she had a tiny replica of his reconnaissance jet tattooed on her lower abdomen. She tells me it's been her lifelong dream to fly in a fighter jet, and she's beside herself with envy. My anxiety only annoys her. "Have fun," she says, "or I'll kick your ass."

Only about 10 percent of VIP fliers are women, which may explain why, when Marda and I arrive at the airfield, I'm handed a blue cotton flight suit that's four sizes too big and makes me look like a mechanic. The pilots' suits are far more stylish: electric blue with double yellow stripes down one side and an elaborate crest on the chest. They're very tight and vaguely retro, like something Elvis might have worn in *Speedway*.

Next we repair to the ready room for a briefing with crew chief Ed Primeau. He goes over the plane's controls and the egress procedures and the air-sickness bags, or "party bags," which are tucked into slots on each side of the seat. (There are eight; the VIP single-flight record is six.) He explains that a G force of 1 is what we're all used to—the earth's gravitational pull on the body. But the Gs increase as the plane accelerates, banks and rolls, and with each additional G, your body weight seems to double.

"It feels like a fat person is sitting on you," he says, "and the higher up [in Gs] you get, the fatter that person becomes." Next he demonstrates the "hook" maneuver. When the G forces get above 4 or so and gravity threatens to suck all the blood from my brain, I might need to do this to force it back up and avoid passing out. I tense my major muscle groups and grunt violently in a way that's supposed to sound like the first three letters of "hook." It's hard not to feel like an idiot while doing this. Finally, we walk out to the airfield. I want to get on with this and forget about this simultaneously.

The "F/A" in F/A-18 Hornet stands for Fighter/Attack, meaning that when fully armed, the plane can both dogfight in the air and bomb targets on the ground. Surprisingly, I find it beautiful, not lethal. It reminds me of an origami bird, folded and creased and set lightly on the tarmac. I give Marda a hug, climb a narrow ladder, and step into the cockpit. Primeau cinches two straps across my shins and two more across my thighs, then hooks me into a multi-buckle harness that compresses my torso and leaves only my arms and head free to move. He goes over the controls and wedges my helmet on, and when he asks for my call sign, I don't think twice: "Field Goal."

My pilot, Lt. Keith Hoskins—call sign "Judge"—slides into the front seat. He has a big smile, a mild Missouri twang, and a running back's build. He can see me in a rearview mirror, and we can hear each other via two-way mikes. Judge starts the engine and begins his preflight checks. A high-pitched whine arises. The jet's systems rev; I sense a steady gathering of energy, of mechanized muscles tensing.

"I'm getting ready to put the canopy down. You all clear?" The lid descends, sealing me in. I reach up to touch it; it feels like glass. Now I am trapped in a high-tech ovoid, an unhatched chick. Judge asks me to arm the ejection seat by pushing down a small lever to my left. I do. I try breathing to relax. Inhale deeply from the abdomen. In, out. Again. It's not working. The plane begins to taxi; the drizzle intensifies. We're lucky to be flying at all. Nerves make me yawn, blink, swallow. My ears pop. My heart bangs against its cage. Control-tower babble fills my headset.

"How you doing back there?" Judge asks.

"Pretty good." Pause. "So we're going to go straight up?" Primeau had warned me about the HPC, or high-performance climb.

"I'm going to accelerate up to 300 mph and pull back on the stick," Judge explains. "The nose of the aircraft is going to pitch up very rapidly, and we're going to do a 45-degree nose-up climb. We're going to pull about 5 Gs during this maneuver."

I take this in with as much equanimity as possible. A few minutes later the Hornet pivots and stops at the end of the runway.

"You all set back there, Dana? All right, here we go!" Judge fires up the afterburners, and the Hornet lurches forward like a dragster and catapults down the runway. Raindrops streak across the canopy. The digital display reads out our speed: 100 knots, 150, 200, 250—we are hauling serious ass—300, 350. The wheels leave the ground and the plane rears back and shoots into the sky with a thunderous roar. I scream and laugh, but before I have time to be terrified, the plane seems to go weightless. It tips on its side, and I tip with it, then turn my head to look out. At that moment the clouds part, just like they do in the opening credits of *The Simpsons*, revealing colorful patchwork fields that seem to rush toward me. I jerk my head back against the headrest, shaken. Judge levels the plane. "How'd you like that?"

"That was quite exciting." It's hard to force words out of my throat, what with my heart being in the way. Looking down gives me vertigo, so I fix my gaze on the smudged horizon. The cockpit's microclimate is warm and noisy and exceptionally arid. I'm thirstier than I've ever been. I remind myself to breathe, and the next time I look down we're over desert.

For his next trick, Judge says he'll demonstrate different G variances. "Right now," he says, "we're pulling one and a half Gs in a left-hand turn." It feels pretty normal. He banks the plane harder, to 2 Gs, and asks me how I feel. I can't lift my head off the seat, and a weight squeezes my chest. "This is what two and a half Gs feels like on our body," says Judge. He tilts the plane even further until we're practically perpendicular to the ground. "How's that feel?" Like I'm Santa Claus and the world sumo champion is telling me what he wants for Christmas. The plane tilts further: 3 Gs. My body feels as if it's hung with lead weights and my face has gone all cartoonish and exaggerated, the flesh pulled away from my teeth like a Tex Avery hound dog. When Judge levels the plane, my relief is profound.

Next Judge says he's going to roll the plane 360 degrees—first slowly, then quickly. He banks the plane to the left, and it keeps going. I lock my eyes to the horizon as the plane rotates, rotisserie-style, and the ground and sky change places, then assume their rightful orientations. A sense of the overwhelming coolness of this situation penetrates my anxiety, and I can't help but feel triumphant: I went upside down in an F/A-18! Wahoo!

"You ready to try a faster roll rate?" It takes a split second to spin. I am breathless, a flipped pancake. Then Judge goes into a sharp turn, and gravity pins me back in my seat. Uh-oh, now I feel breathless and sick. My capacity for coherent thought and speech has been replaced by a visceral, paralyzing unease. My lips are numb; my thighs tingle. My corporal self feels alien, its fundamental matter fuzzy, manhandled, askew. Judge does what he can to ease my building nausea: levels the plane, cools the air, chats me up. But I'm also chagrined, and there's not much he can do about that. I'm not getting this whole flying thing. Where's the life-altering rush? What did I think I'd find up here? I'm not wired for this. Fine. I've resigned myself to worse. I reach for a party bag.

"I think you've probably been to one of our shows," Judge is saying. "What do you think of the Blue Angels?"

It's only a coincidence that at that very moment I lose my breakfast. When I'm done I seal the bag with a twist tie and tuck it into a zippered pocket on my shin. Afterward I feel better—clearer, more positive, capable of polysyllabic speech. I answer his question.

"I saw the Blue Angels as a kid. We were stationed in Georgia in 1968 and they came and did an air show on the Fourth of July."

My father had been there, lifting kids for a peek into his cockpit and demonstrating the same touch-and-go landings they did on carriers in the South China Sea. The Blue Angels were the final act, and as they streaked across the sky, the collective heads of the crowd swept with them, like fans doing the wave in a football stadium. Judge and I talk about the present: our kids, where I live, what sports my boys like. It's a bit depressing to think that I've come this far and mustered this much courage only to have the type of conversation you have in a supermarket aisle. Cloud cover limits our altitude to 5,000 feet—high enough to reduce the landscape to whorls and eddies and other abstractions, but low enough, let's say, to be plucked out of the sky by an artillery unit. We approach a small mountain topped by a radar station, and Judge does a flyby, swooping so close I swear I make eye contact with a guy getting out of his car.

Soon we are back over cropland; the flight is winding down. Suddenly, below us, I spot a flock of long-necked birds flying in a V, brilliant white against the dark-green fields.

"Those white birds. Are they egrets?" I ask.

"I don't know what type of birds those are, to be honest," Judge answers. "Egrets . . . that's something I need to check on."

I'm willing to bet they're snowy egrets, and it's oddly thrilling to look down on them, to observe from above the slow-motion pulse of their narrow wings. Hey, birds, I think, look at me. We're hanging! Then they're gone.

Back on the ground my legs are shaky and I must be helped from the plane like someone being rescued from a burning building. Marda rushes toward me under a bobbing umbrella, asking, "How was it?" "Wild" is my giddy and grossly inadequate reply. I get a certificate and a Coke. That's that, I think. Still, the flight haunts me, a dream I can't shake.

Two months later I'm watching TV coverage of the war in Kosovo—which consists primarily of warplanes taking off and landing—and flipping aimlessly through A Field Guide to the Birds. Without warning it strikes me: It was the egrets, stupid. I had wanted a 1,000-watt revelation, but the truth was subtler than that. For my father, adrenaline must have been a big part of flying's appeal. But what a thrill, also, for a young man who had only looked up at birds to fly among them, to beat nature at its own game. He must have loved it, especially the first time it happened, and I could see how he wanted it to keep happening. My father had been the baddest bird in the sky—and for a brief moment, so had I.

A Ski Mountaineer and a History of Tragedy

Nick Paumgarten

In the ski-bum brain, the chance to ski with a magus like Andrew McLean is the equivalent of an invitation for a night on the town with Don Juan. The allure is great, but there's always a possibility that the excursion will not end well. McLean is a ski mountaineer; he climbs mountains and then skis down them. He is especially fond of skiing chutes—steep, narrow flumes of snow that plunge like elevator shafts through otherwise impassable terrain. Last fall, before he and I met, he'd sent me a copy of "The Chuting Gallery," his self-published guide to the chutes in his home range, the Wasatch Mountains, which are just east of Salt Lake City. He had inscribed it: "I'm looking forward to skiing with you this winter. If you die skiing one of these, I promise it will be renamed in your honor!" I can't say that the prospect hadn't crossed my mind.

McLean has a bit of a history. One of the runs described in "The Chuting Gallery" is named Roman's, after McLean's friend Roman Latta, who, on an outing with him there in 1993, set off an avalanche in which he was buried and killed. Latta was the first of four men who have died while climbing or skiing with McLean. The most famous was Alex Lowe, who was considered by many to be the best mountaineer in the world; Lowe disappeared in a giant avalanche on Shishapangma, in Tibet, in 1999, when he and McLean and others were attempting to become the first

Americans to ski a peak higher than 8,000 meters. In all, McLean has lost more than a dozen friends to the mountains—"lost to the mountains" being a locution favored by alpinists, as though skiing or climbing were a sacrificial rite, instead of a voluntary act.

My family has a bit of history, too. My father's father, Harald, was a devoted alpinist, as well as a ski racer and jumper who competed for Austria in the 1928 and 1932 Winter Olympics. After the 1932 Games, in Lake Placid, he stayed in America. He briefly held a job at a bank in New York (the story goes that on his lunch breaks he'd head out to Central Park, remove his suit, hang it on a tree, and go running in his underwear) before deciding that the office life was not for him. He moved to New England to teach skiing, which is how he met my grandmother, a Philadelphia society girl who was among the early wave of modish flatlanders to take up the sport under the tutelage of the Austrians. In the summers, my grandfather went on expeditions to the Fairweather Range, in Alaska. He lived in Philadelphia during the war, but afterward he began spending his winters in St. Anton, in Austria, in order to ski. He was killed in an avalanche there in 1952, when my father, the youngest of five children, was six. Twenty years later, one of my father's sisters died in an avalanche while skiing. She had two children, ages seven and three. Since then, there have been a few other incidents. My father was nearly killed in an avalanche while I was skiing with him, and between us we have witnessed a fair number of slides. There was also a disturbing encounter with a crevasse—a snow bridge gave way, and I fell in. I hung by my arms over a void until two guides pulled me out.

Friends and relatives treat this high incidence of snow trouble as evidence of a family curse, or plain idiocy. The weight of these opinions is such that every time I head out on a trip that involves the kind of skiing that can lead to trouble—glaciers, powder fields, steeps—a certain premonitory queasiness sneaks up on me. The anxiety that comes of tempting fate, especially in pursuit of such an indulgence, helps generate dreams of death by suffocation or falling. But in daylight disquiet gives way to delight, and I find myself doing things that may or may not be dangerous, half aware that at any second my situation, as well as that of my wife and children, could dramatically change. It's a fraught kind of bliss.

A year and a half ago, I read a story in the magazine Skiing entitled "11 Excuses for NOT Skiing with Andrew McLean." One was "He'll dust you." Another was "Tragedy dogs him." Perhaps with that in mind, I found myself, within minutes of meeting McLean, telling him about my family, under the guise of trying to persuade him to take it easy on me. (A more direct approach had failed. "Don't know what you think you signed up for here, Nick. You're with the wrong guy.") He seemed to home in on the infatuation, rather than on its consequences. "Sounds like you've got skiing in the blood," he said. But later, when I passed along the additional piece of information that my great-aunt—my grandfather's sister—a world-champion racer and fervent mountain girl, had been crippled in the fifties by a runaway ski, he said, "Maybe I should be a little concerned about skiing with you."

McLean's approach to peril is to see humor in it. Certainly, close calls can be comic, and McLean can laugh, in the way of soldiers and crooks, over many of his near-misses. There was the time he cartwheeled down 500 vertical feet of cliffs, only to land upright on his skis, unaccountably alive and intact, or the time a boulder fell and pulverized itself on a ledge just above his head. Although there isn't really anything funny about avalanches, his manner of survival, in a few of the half dozen or so that he has been caught in—clinging to the trunk of an aspen tree, high above the ground, or buried upside down, with his legs sticking straight out of the snow—can sound cartoonish. The only thing that spoils the Wile E. Coyote effect (he is forty-three years old, yet he has never so much as broken a bone while skiing) is that a number of his narrow escapes have coincided with the deaths of other people. This is something he doesn't much like to discuss.

In "The Chuting Gallery," McLean inventories the hazards of his favorite routes with a cheek that, in the solemn and superstitious realm of mountain chronicles, borders on blasphemy. In some quarters it is considered an irresponsible book, as appropriate as a guide to robbing banks. The northeast couloir of a peak called the Pfeifferhorn, McLean writes, is "more fun than running with scissors, sticking paperclips into electrical sockets or taping firecrackers to a cat's tail." Of Hellgate Couloir, a run that involves rappelling down two cliffs, he writes, "Short, stout, steep and scary. What more could you ask for?"

"The Chuting Gallery" begins with a disclaimer, from McLean's mother: "The fact that this is a 'guidebook' does not mean that you, the reader, should take it seriously. Obviously, no one in their right mind would ski this stuff—and you shouldn't either." By "this stuff" she means terrain that is challenging enough to fit under the standard definition of extreme skiing, first codified by the American steep-skiing pioneer Chris Landry: "If you fall, you die." McLean ascends quickly, sometimes with the aid of ropes, ice axes, and crampons. And he descends carefully. He is not a hot dog. What he's after is an elusive blend of anxiety and exhilaration—a level of difficulty that requires physical and analytical prowess, as well as self-discipline and imagination. He also wants to be first. It's the adventurer's injunction: do it before anyone else does, or at least do it differently. His calling takes him to such remote places as Antarctica and the Himalayas. He goes on two big expeditions a year. This month, McLean and three friends are going to Alaska for four weeks in an effort to become the first people ever to ski the Archangel Ridge of Mt. Foraker, a sister peak of Mt. McKinley. It is a gruesome and isolated route, 11,000 vertical feet—dark, cold, high, scary. It has been climbed only twice before. What's more, to reach Foraker the group will have to climb up and ski down another difficult peak in order to avoid sixteen river crossings, not to mention bears.

There are, of course, many extreme skiers in the world, and many mountain climbers, and quite a few who combine the skills of both. The game has changed since my grandfather's day. The vogue is to refer to them as "adventure athletes." They star in films, have sponsorships, and market themselves aggressively, inspiring an ever-growing array of imitators who fan out into the hills and devour fresh terrain, like so many Scrubbing Bubbles. McLean, however, is a true shell-back. He is as hungry for accomplishment as the rest, yet he has learned to balance the ragtag joys of wandering the mountains with the requirements of making a living at it. He'd be doing what he's doing even if nobody was watching. In some respects, he is not an extreme athlete at all but just a lucid and devoted rambler, with high standards and a low pulse—a descendant as much of Kit Carson as of Harry Houdini.

On my first morning in Utah, I met McLean in a parking lot at the base of Little Cottonwood Canyon, which cuts east into the Wasatch, about a half hour south of Salt Lake City. Little Cottonwood is home to the Snowbird and Alta ski areas and the gateway to a vast array of backcountry terrain. It is known for having the best powder snow in the world.

McLean has the trim and sinewy build of a Sherpa (he is five-feet-ten and weighs 145 pounds) and a rubbery, slightly hunched posture, but his bright-blue eyes, bobblehead proportions, and anachronistic helmet of light-brown hair give him an impish appearance. In warmer months, he likes to ride a unicycle on mountain trails. There is relish in his smile; he likes to say, in jest, "It isn't fun until someone gets hurt," and he enjoys watching lesser men attempt to keep up with him. He once wrote, "There is nothing finer in life than enjoying a chilled tin of congealed octopus while listening to the moans and groans of fellow human beings . . . as they struggle on a slick 45-degree track." The sado-stoicism is not big-headed or bullying; it's how he conveys to his partners his own particular blend of enthusiasm and forbearance. It is a more garrulous version of the ethic you come across in the classic mountaineering tales of Chris Bonnington, in which the climbers, many of them former British military men, invariably respond to serious trouble—storms, avalanches, broken bones—by brewing up a pot of tea.

McLean was accompanied by Polly Samuels, his fiancée; they were to be married in two months. Samuels, thirty-five years old and a lawyer in the Utah attorney general's office, has red hair and an aspect of serious-ness. She has become a formidable skier in her own right; last year, she was the North American women's champion in randonee racing—long slogs up and down mountains in touring gear. (Among the men, McLean usually finishes in the top three or four.) McLean drove. As he navigated the winding road up the canyon, he craned his neck and pointed out some favorite chutes, which coursed through the cliffs on either side like wa-terfalls. They were avalanche paths, basically, but if you have a taste for such things you begin to view all terrain in terms of what is plausible and you imagine leaving tracks everywhere—on distant peaks or a neighbor's snowy lawn—much as fishermen cannot regard a body of water without thinking of casting a line.

That morning, we took it easy: we started at the Alta ski area, where in order to gain altitude we took a chairlift, and to warm up we did two intermediate runs on machine-groomed snow. McLean, an advocate of leg power, doesn't often consent to such indignities. But after a couple of hours we ventured into more McLeanian terrain—Main Baldy Chute, a long, regal cataract that, being avalanche-prone, is rarely open. It happened also to be the site of his conversion to chuting, fourteen years earlier. The run required a half-hour hike and several dozen compact rams on old chalky snow, the joy deriving, in part, from the sensation of simultaneously resisting and submitting to gravity. McLean's skiing style was tight and neat, but deliberately functional and in no obvious way vain. At the bottom, McLean called out, "Main Baldy—check!" as though he were planning to have me ski every chute in his book.

We went to the base of the mountain and retrieved more gear. We were using randonee equipment, which weighs less than standard alpine equipment and is designed for going uphill as well as down. For the ascent, the heel of the binding detaches from the ski, as with a cross-country or telemark ski, and you stick a climbing skin, which is a reusable adhesive strip with mohair or nylon on one side, to the base of each ski (people used to use real seal skins); the grain prevents you from sliding backward. To descend, you peel off the skins and lock down the heel. Each of us wore an avalanche beacon—a transceiver about the size of a Walkman, which sends out a signal in case of burial—and a pack that contained a probe and a shovel, for locating and digging out a buried companion.

We left Alta and hiked up a ridge for a half hour or so to a place called Wolverine Cirque, an amphitheater of chutes guarded by cornices. McLean dropped into one called the Scythe. He jumped up and down on a pillow of snow near the top, to see that it was stable, then hopped back and forth down the slope before skirting under an outcropping, in case the next skier, me, set off a slide. I did not. The snow was deep and a little windblown:

not bad. After another pitch, the chute opened onto a bowl that looked like a place where you didn't want to hang around. It was where Roman Latta, among others over the years, had been buried. We crossed a basin, skinned up for 45 minutes, then skied down to Alta.

Back at my desk five days later, I got an e-mail from McLean: "Utah had its first avalanche fatality the day after you left"—the first, that is, of the season. It had occurred at Wolverine. He sent a photograph of the accident site, with a diagram of our route and the victim's. They weren't far apart. "It turns out there was one other fatality, two other people missing, and one person who was buried and dug out." Also, he said, a place called the Meadow Chutes, where we had spent my last morning, going up and down, rapturously, during a snowstorm, had avalanched—"ripped out wall to wall"—right after we were there.

My aunt, whose name was Meta Burden, was skiing alone when she died. She had had an argument, so she did a rash thing. She skied into Cristy Gully, which in 1972 lay outside the boundary area at Aspen Mountain. Half a foot of new snow had fallen atop 10 inches of two-day-old snow, and apparently there had been a great deal of avalanche activity in the area that morning. But she was a headstrong woman, confident in her abilities. She had lived in Aspen for four years, and was intermittently deranged by anger over the encroachment of more and more people into terrain that she liked to consider her own.

That evening, her husband reported her missing, and at half past six ski patrollers began a search in the dark. They followed her tracks into Cristy Gully. There is an account of the search in "The Snowy Torrents," a volume assembled by government avalanche forecasters, with evaluations of avalanche accidents in the United States. The rescuers, it says,

> probed and scuffed in the runout zone, and within 45 minutes they found one ski and one pole. Coleman lanterns were set up at the points where Burden's tracks ended and where the clues were found. . . . At 2230 hours, Burden was found on the first pass of the probe line 60 feet above her ski and pole. Efforts at resuscitation and heart massage were unsuccessful. Her body was buried in 3 feet of snow.

It appeared that she had died of suffocation. The report noted that she was an experienced skier, and concluded, "Burden knew the dangers involved and ignored them."

The novelist James Salter wrote about my aunt's death, some years ago, in an essay called "The Skiing Life." Like many men, he seems to have been somewhat smitten by her. He called her a "goddess." "There was a woman I knew who used to ski every day, all season long, whatever the weather, whatever the conditions," he wrote. "Later someone told me that she died on the very same day her father had, years before. I never bothered to confirm it, but I think it must be true; I think it was part of the pact." It was not true. The pact, though, I could understand.

Her father had died while skiing alone, too. The night before, he had remarked to his sister that he'd witnessed a lot of avalanches that afternoon and that he'd have to be careful. (His family was back home in Philadelphia; he had wanted Meta and her twin sister to cut school and spend the winter with him in Austria, but my grandmother had said no.) Still, the next afternoon, after a day out with a friend, my grandfather decided to take one last run by himself. An avalanche caught him in a gully between the Osthang and the old Kandahar downhill course; when rescuers found his body, they concluded, from the tranquil look on his face, that he had broken his neck.

This winter, I stumbled on a third account of my aunt's accident, a 1987 poem called "The Death of Meta Burden in an Avalanche," by Frederick Seidel. It is a difficult poem, as impenetrable as "The Snowy Torrents" is precise. "You are reborn flying to outski / The first avalanche each spring, / And buried alive." Seidel, who, it turns out, also met and admired my aunt, seems to imagine what it feels like to be entombed in snow: "I cannot see. / I will not wake though it's a dream. / I move my head from side to side. / I cannot move." Later, he writes, "Everything fits my body perfectly now that I'm about to disappear."

It is, not surprisingly, a grim way to go. If you trigger an avalanche, there are measures you can take to avoid burial, or at least to improve the odds of surviving. The first thing to do is attempt to ski out of it, although as the slab of snow breaks from the layer beneath it and begins to move, accelerating down the mountain face like a book sliding off a tilted table, it becomes impossible for a skier to generate enough speed or change direction. Within seconds, the slab degenerates into a whirlwind. The snow has astonishing power, and as it rips off your gear and throws you into a tumble you should thrash and swim, in order to stay near the surface. Any attempt to get one good last breath will likely result in a mouthful of snow. Snow crams into your ears and under your eyelids. You may be dashed into a tree or a rock, but the force of the snow alone can break your leg or neck. As the slide slows, you are supposed to cup your hands in front of your mouth to create a pocket of air. Your chances improve if you are head up and face up—and if some part of you is visible to others, if there are others—but this choice is not yours. As the snow comes to a stop, it is like cement. The weight of it can press your last breath out of you, like a python. Your little breathing pocket, if you have one, will soon become carbon dioxide or a block of ice. After five minutes, the odds of survival drop swiftly. You pray that someone digs you out.

Every year nearly two hundred people are caught in avalanches in the United States. On average, about thirty of them die. The fatality rate has risen steadily since 1991. An increasing percentage of the victims are snowmobilers, who engage in a practice called high-marking, competing to see who can cut a track highest on a steep slope. Still, with improvements in gear and a trend toward backcountry exploration, more and more skiers and snowboarders are venturing out into terrain where survival depends, to a certain degree, on luck.

"Nobody goes out to die," Jill Fredston, an avalanche specialist in Alaska, told me. "Everyone goes out in pursuit of life. We make a ton of mistakes, but we usually get away with them. Luck is negative reinforcement. And you have probability and complacency working against you."

Last winter, Mike Elggren, a forty-one-year-old friend of McLean's, was caught in a slide while backcountry skiing in British Columbia. He was skinning up a slope with ten friends and three guides. At one point, one of the guides decided that she didn't like where they were. She took two steps, and the whole slope jigsawed above them—a molten acre. Elggren was shoved forward and sucked downhill, headfirst. His skis pulled him deeper. "I looked up to see where I was, and the lights went out," Elggren told me. "I got crushed. The pressure was tremendous. As the snow stopped, it made a real squeaky sound." His hand was in front of his face, but he couldn't see it. His nose and mouth were choked with snow. He was indignant at first, incredulous that this should happen to him. "That gave way to utter panic. I was screaming. I remember not being embarrassed to be screaming like a little girl. I wanted to flail, but I was pinned." After a moment, he regained some composure. "My brain wouldn't allow me to have any hope, the situation was so dire. I was rebreathing my carbon dioxide. My diaphragm and lungs were crushed. And then I started going away. I made my peace with the world. I was sad for the people up top and for my family. I was thinking of my parents and my brother and sisters, and my dog. Then I just went away. It felt like fading into black velvet."

Elggren's friends, some of whom had been partially buried and had dug themselves out, picked up his beacon signal. They were extraordinarily efficient, taking turns digging, but he was buried head down, six feet deep. When they got to him, ten minutes had passed, and he wasn't breathing. It took twenty minutes to resuscitate him by mouth-to-mouth. He remembers coming to and wondering why everyone was making such a fuss. They built a sled out of their backpacks, and towed him a mile or so back to a hut, where a helicopter was waiting. Aside from ligament damage to both knees, he seems to be fine. He has gone backcountry skiing regularly this winter (although not with McLean: "Andrew's on a different plane. He's so damn badass."). After the accident, Elggren's mother pleaded with him to give up backcountry skiing, but, he said, "Luckily, she came around to a more rational point of view." A few weeks ago, he returned to British Columbia to repeat last year's trip—same guide, same friends, same hut.

One spring day, when I was eleven, my father and I were skiing off-piste (off the marked trails) in Verbier, Switzerland. The conditions were exquisite but dodgy—a half meter of fresh snow warming in the sun—and my father, realizing abruptly that we were in a place we shouldn't have been (always this belated moment of recognition), decided that we would traverse, one at a time, to more moderately pitched terrain. I stayed behind on a ridge, as he started across the top of a gully. Then the whole slope seemed to explode, and he disappeared. In those days, I had no experience with avalanches, only a dim sense that they killed Paumgartens, so I failed to keep an eye on him or to take any precautions of my own. Avalanche-safety equipment wasn't widely used back then; anyway, we didn't have any. For several minutes, I assumed that he was gone (it seemed fitting that he would be) and sat crying in the snow until I heard him calling my name. I made it down in time to see a snow-splattered ghoul stumbling out of a vast field of debris. The avalanche had carried him a few hundred yards, and then, as it slowed, poured over a bump in the terrain, which caused him to pop up to the surface. The slide was a big one: he was lucky; we were lucky. He was beaten up but all right. When Meta's twin heard about the accident, she wrote him an angry letter. Except for my father, my mother—whose feelings about all this are rather complicated—and their two sons, the family had quit this kind of skiing. My uncle, for example, tends to ski in blue jeans and stick to marked trails. ("I like the groomed part, the avenues," he says.) But my father did not give it up, although he did resolve always to hire a guide if he was going to ski off-piste. In the years since, I have been more than happy to accompany him.

Skiing, McLean wrote me once, "is like some form of religious practice or martial arts discipline." Years of devotion lead to proficiency, which yields a sense of ease and a chance at transcendence. McLean started on the path at Alta; he was born in Salt Lake City. One of his earliest ski memories is of a man breaking his femur on the rope tow at the Alta Lodge. In his recollection, the bone ripped through the man's pant leg, but he was laughing, because he was drunk. McLean's father was an ophthalmologist and a devoted sailor, and the family spent several years trying to find a town where he could both practice medicine and get out on the water. Salt Lake was not the place. They moved around for a few years—Vermont, Connecticut, Florida, Haiti—and then settled in Seattle. McLean's mother taught skiing nearby, at Alpental, in the Cascades. McLean quickly progressed to a point where she had to make a deal with him: she'd buy him a season pass if he promised to ski one run with her a year. He tended to wait until the last day.

As a kid, McLean was an experimental prankster, a troublemaker of the promising kind. He owned a welding torch and used it both to build go-carts and to fill bread bags with oxyacetylene gas, which he and his younger brother would then place in mailboxes and blow up using fuses made of paper. "We eventually worked our way up to Hefty trash bags, which were deafening," he recalled. "Come to think of it, that might be a good idea for do-it-yourself backcountry avalanche bombs." (Explosives are commonly used at ski areas to set off controlled avalanches.)

He went to the Rhode Island School of Design, where he studied to become an industrial designer. His roommate there happened to be an avid rock climber from Oregon, who began teaching McLean how to climb. Rhode Island is not known for its mountains, but the two of them made the most of the available terrain. On one occasion, they were arrested for trespassing when the police found them dangling from a rope on an abandoned railroad bridge. On another occasion, campus police caught McLean on the roof of the museum ("It had this perfect chimney") and mistook his bag of climbing chalk for cocaine. While at RISD, he fashioned a device that he called the Talon, a three-pronged steel-plated climbing aid, which he eventually sold to Black Diamond, a climbing-equipment company. Six years later, after jobs designing medical equipment and boats, he was hired by Black Diamond, and he moved back to Salt Lake, where the company was based, and began designing technical gear cams, carabiners, crampons, ice axes. Many of his inventions, including the Talon, are still widely used.

McLean left Black Diamond a few years ago in order to focus on skiing—a job does get in the way—but he still designs equipment for a number of companies on a freelance basis. When I visited him, he was working on avalanche safety products and ice-climbing equipment; he was also helping a friend design giant dish antennas for the military. Then there's the money he gets from speeches and from writing for climbing and skiing magazines. Last year, he worked as an avalanche forecaster for the Forest Service but found the job constricting. His superiors disapproved of steep skiing, and he felt called upon to preach a gospel of caution that he did not wholeheartedly subscribe to. Now he pursues what he calls a "low-cost life style." He said, "I haven't heard of any other professional ski mountaineers."

Black Diamond, in the early nineties, was a breeding ground for amateur ski mountaineers, foremost among them Alex Lowe. It was Lowe who introduced McLean to a mode of skiing that employed the tools and techniques of climbing, as European alpinists had been doing for decades. "More than anyone, he opened my eyes to what was possible on skis," McLean said. Their first outing together was to Main Baldy Chute, before Alta opened for the year. They started out at 5:00 a.m. and descended at dawn, in thigh-deep powder. When they were done, they were set upon by ski patrolmen on snowmobiles, who informed them that the patrol was bombing the chute that morning, to make it slide, and that Lowe and McLean were lucky not to have been blown to pieces by a Howitzer shell. McLean was hooked.

In a foreword to "The Chuting Gallery," Lowe describes "a loose group of twisted individuals" who several days a week would convene in his kitchen at three in the morning and, to his wife's dismay ("Is this normal!!?"), head off to climb a chute or a peak, then ski down at sunrise and go to work, glowing with accomplishment and stinking of sweat. This regimen, which McLean still adheres to (minus the going-to-work part) was known as dawn patrol.

"You could always spot another chute or two in the distance that needed to be skied," McLean said. "I kept at it for a few years, thinking that I had almost ticked them all off, before realizing that there was no end to them. Some were bigger, steeper, or more classic than others, but there were hundreds of them in the Wasatch and then a few million more around the world."

"The skiing consumed us," Mark Holbrook, a former Black Diamond engineer, told me. "That maybe led to our divorces." (McLean's first marriage, to a graphic designer from Long Island whom he met at RISD, ended eight years ago.)

McLean would like, on his deathbed, to be able to look at a globe and know that he had been everywhere. "It's getting harder and harder to find big classic lines that haven't been skied," he said. "They're a precious commodity." The conquest game can get competitive. Exotic places—the Kamchatka peninsula or Ellesmere Island—catch on, and the athletes pour in. It is difficult to stay ahead of the Scrubbing Bubbles. Sometimes a team spends years planning an expedition to an obscure peak only to find another team there upon arrival. When I was in Utah, McLean said that he and a nineteen-year-old acolyte named Dylan Freed had recently found a chute in the Wasatch that had never been skied. They had christened it Project Schnozzle. He revealed the location to no one, not even to Polly Samuels. "It takes four hours to get there, and it's only 500 feet of vertical," he said. "You've got to really want it." Last month, McLean went and did it by himself. "The Schnozzle has fallen," he wrote me.

In 2002, McLean and a Black Diamond sales rep named Brad Barlage journeyed to Baffin Island, west of Greenland, on a hunch that there were chutes there. McLean had built giant kites, based on a Dutch modification of NASA technology (he'd come across some kiting Dutchmen in Antarctica). McLean and Barlage used the kites to sail across the frozen fjords—at speeds of up to 40 miles an hour, on skis, towing gear-laden sleds. They discovered soaring chutes everywhere. McLean told me, "We ticked off nineteen first descents, of which ten were the best lines I've ever been in—3,000-to-5,000-foot screamers that came straight out of the frozen sea ice, surrounded by monstrous walls, stable creamy powder, wolf tracks, 24 hours of daylight, and surreal scenery." The skiing magazines took note, and the athletes poured into Baffin.

On a trip like that one, the salient requirements, besides being first and having fun, are imagination and ingenuity, as opposed purely to danger and death-defiance. McLean has learned, he told me, that "fatalities are always a good way to ruin a trip." Holbrook said, "We've toned things down a little. That's a good thing for him, with the problems we've had in the past, with the deaths."

Clearly, the deaths have weighed on McLean. "You go to a funeral," he told me. "You know these people as ski buddies, and you see they have rooms and dads and fiancées. It gives it all a human face." And it can give him pause. Thus the toning down. "I'm more conservative, in terms of risking big falls. No more cliff hucking"—skiing off cliffs. "I give avalanches a lot more leeway than I used to," he said. "On the other hand, each thing you ski tends to be a little bit harder. The ambitions keep getting bigger. Foraker may be as hard as anything I've ever done."

On my second morning in Utah, I met McLean in the Little Cottonwood parking lot. He had his pickup truck, on which he had rearranged the lettering of "Toyota" to read "Otto," in honor of his late Bernese mountain dog. He was accompanied by Dylan Freed. McLean had considered taking Freed on the Alaska trip to climb Mt. Foraker, but Freed's uncle, Mark Twight, one of the world's top mountaineers, told McLean, "If anything happens to him and you survive, I'll hunt you down and kill you." ("This kind of raises the question as to why people would get their kids into skiing and the mountains in the first place if they really wanted them to be safe," McLean told me. "Darts might be a better activity.")

On the way up the canyon, we picked up another friend, Lorne Glick, an accomplished ski mountaineer. Glick lives in a sparsely furnished room (ice axes, topographical maps, banjo) inside a small hydroelectric plant just off the Little Cottonwood Road. The generators outside the room roar day and night. For money, Glick occasionally drives a Sno-Cat at Alta or works as a guide, and recently, at the age of forty-one, he got a license to be a helicopter pilot.

Our plan was to hike up Mt. Superior, a peak rising 3,000 feet above Little Cottonwood Canyon, and ski down the south face, which, viewed from Alta and Snowbird, seemed to be a sheer white wall, studded with cliffs. On earlier trips, I had occasionally seen tracks etched on it and been half glad that they weren't mine. "With slides that cover the road 10 to 20 feet deep, Superior should be treated with the utmost respect," McLean writes in "The Chuting Gallery." "Because of the road below, keep in mind that you are endangering others by attempting to ski it in less than ideal conditions." On this particular day, conditions were close to ideal—4 inches or so of fresh snow atop a firm, older layer. I decided not to worry about endangering others.

The trail began at Alta, behind the Our Lady of the Snows chapel, an avalanche-proof box of reinforced concrete and plate glass that was built in 1993, ten years after the original chapel, made of wood, was destroyed by a slide. McLean handed me a pair of Whippet Self-Arrest poles, which he designed. They are regular ski poles with a steel ice-axe blade fixed to each handle. You appear to be skiing with two stubby handsaws. In the event of a fall on a steep slope, you jab the blades into the snow to stop yourself from sliding. The climb was gradual at first, but it took just three minutes for me to fall well behind. The track was slick. My technique was poor. The air was thin. I huffed my way uphill, doing my best to look around and remind myself that there was no place I'd rather be. The panorama was dazzling in the morning light, like the inside of a diamond; unbroken fields of snow stretched in all directions.

After an hour or so, I rejoined the others at Cardiff Pass, and we started up Superior. Here the skinning got more technical: a winding trail through the trees requiring awkward maneuvers. Again, I lagged; after a while, McLean skied back down to check on me—humbling enough, though he seemed glad for the exercise. After another hour, it was time to remove the skis, strap them to our packs, and start climbing up a narrow ridge leading to the summit. The trail was variable; stretches of thigh-deep, drifted snow gave way to wind-cleared rock. Occasionally, there was climbing to do, on all fours; the Whippet blades helped me gain purchase. On my left, there were cliffs, and, on the right, snow-loaded chutes. In places, it was clear that a fall to either side would be highly problematic. The wind had kicked up, and through breaks in a cloud that seemed to have come out of nowhere I got vertiginous glimpses of the valley floor.

McLean, by this point, was waiting for me at the top of each pitch, to make sure that I was all right and to take some delight in the extent to which I wasn't. "You're still smiling," he'd say, to my grimace. After one stretch, when I crawled up onto a narrow shelf and collapsed at his feet, he said, "Nick, does your wife know you're doing this?"

And then we were on top, the slope below us dropping off into a foggy void. Freed and Glick were long gone. They had decided to ski the north side, which looked bright, powdery, and benign. We bundled up, drank water, ate chocolate, and prepared for the ski down. "There's more snow up here than I thought," McLean said. "I think we'll do the chute on the left. Wait up here until I call up to you." He dropped in, traversing back and forth a few times to test the snow—ski cutting, it's called—and then making a series of blocky turns, his wide stance and cautious pace indicating to me that this was no place to make a mistake. And then he disappeared.

I waited awhile in the wind but couldn't hear a thing. Bits of cloud blew past. Rock, cornice, cloud. Probability, complacency, luck. I decided not to wait any longer. I hopped into the wind-whipped snow on the upper face, then chopped my way into a steep, icy trough, intermittently jump-turning and side-slipping, chunks of snow and ice clattering around me like broken glass. When I found McLean, he was hiding behind a rock, a big grin on his face. "Isn't this great?" he said. It was. The pitch eased, and we were making turn after turn in powder. After a while, McLean stopped and pointed up at a steep east-facing shaft. "That's Suicide," he said. He wondered whether I had enough left for one more. The answer, that morning, was no.

Dawn patrol: I met McLean and Brad Barlage in the parking lot at 5 a.m. the following day. We drove up to the White Pine trailhead, donned head-lamps, and started skinning up through the woods, a damp malevolent wind howling in the aspen trees. McLean had mercifully assented to a compromise: instead of going all the way up to White Pine, we'd climb for an hour to Pink Pine. The name suggested achievability. We reached the top before first light. Snow had started to fall, spinning in the beams of our headlamps. We skied a run in the trees in darkness—a curious experience. Not feeling right, I continued down alone, while they went up for more.

That evening, I had dinner with McLean and Samuels. They live at the top of a rise in a modest development outside Park City, on the east slope of the Wasatch, giving them a view through fir trees of the Uinta Mountains. The house is compact but spacious—three stories. McLean poured two glasses of Scotch and showed me around. The ground floor is dominated by his workshop. It contains twenty-three pairs of skis, as well as climbing skins, boots, bicycles, unicycles, and various heavy mechanical saws and drills. In a closet, neatly arranged, were twenty ice axes and an assortment of helmets and backpacks. Shovels, carabiners, headlamps. Next to the workshop is a sewing room, where he assembles his giant kites. Upstairs, he has an office full of maps and adventure books. He reads a lot; on expeditions, when the weather goes bad, he said, "you end up tearing paperbacks into chapters and passing them around to be read out of order."

When Samuels returned home from work, I remarked upon the neatness of the place. "Did you expect him to be living in some cave?" she asked. She and McLean met in the Little Cottonwood parking lot, when he made a comment about a bumper sticker on her car for a ski-mountaineering mecca in France called La Grave. She loves skiing and understands that he does, too, and so she tolerates the long absences, as well as the risks, though when he talks about them—when, for example, he enumerated some of the obstacles on Mt. Foraker—she laid a hand on his leg, as if to keep him near.

For dinner, McLean made cheese fondue. As he cooked, he talked about some of his avalanche encounters over the years. He told the one about being out on avalanche patrol for the Forest Service, early in the season, and getting caught in a slow slide on a seemingly harmless pitch that buried him head down, so that he couldn't move or breathe. There were incidents in which he was buried up to the waist or thrown up against a tree. "I'm having second thoughts about skiing, suddenly," McLean said, laying the fondue pot on the table.

"I've never heard these stories," Samuels said.

"You haven't?"

"I guess I never asked."

The more you learn about snow, the clearer it becomes that skiing—in the backcountry, on glaciers, in deep snow, on extreme steeps—is more dangerous than most people who regularly do it acknowledge. The capriciousness of the snow is hard to figure. And, whether it's because of hubris or probability, the victims tend to be those who know their way around the mountains, or believe they do.

"Many people think that the way they do it is safe but that the way others do it isn't," McLean told me. "The only truly safe way of doing it is to stop doing it, which I don't want to do." McLean is not superstitious; he doesn't believe that this frank assessment inoculates him against trouble. But it does enable him to evaluate the risks more soberly. For all his seeming recklessness, he is a compulsive planner and a meticulous performer—a mountain scientist. He admits to having "nighttime fears" and "trip anxiety," but in the end such sensations manifest themselves in preparation and a fixation on gear. (Carabiners "are all about semi-intangible subtleties.") And, where acumen comes up short, he resorts, as most mountain men do, to a kind of fatalism. "I often torment myself with a theoretical question," he said. "What if you knew how and when you were going to die? If it was an avalanche or falling to your death, then you'd have to keep skiing, as you've already seen the end. If it was in your sleep at a ripe old age, then you'd have to keep skiing as well, since you'd know you were safe. The end result is the same: keep making turns." He does have his limits: a few years ago, he took up parapenting—jumping off mountains with a parachute—and decided it was too dangerous.

What suits McLean may not suit others. "People get in trouble trying to be their hero," Bruce Tremper, the director of the Forest Service's avalanche center in Utah, told me. "People got hurt or killed trying to be Alex Lowe. Andrew McLean has taken over that mantle. A lot of people are trying to be Andrew McLean now, and they're getting hurt or killed, because they don't have his talent or experience. Life gives us cheap lessons sometimes."

McLean and Samuels's wedding was held in February at Our Lady of the Snows and presided over by Lou Dawson, a pioneer of North American ski mountaineering and a longtime mentor to McLean. He had managed to get an ordination over the Internet for the occasion. (Dawson, it turns out, knew my aunt Meta, and he himself barely survived a big avalanche behind Aspen Highlands, in 1982.) Many congregants were wearing touring boots and ski clothes. One friend had skinned over from Big Cottonwood Canyon with a tuxedo rolled in his pack. The skiers, bright-eyed, shaggy, ruddy, and lean, stood out among the many guests who had come from New York. They made me think of my grandfather and his fellow-*Skilehrers*, surrounded by Ivy League boys and debutantes. Samuels was brought up in Manhattan; she went to Brearley and Penn; her father, a prominent tax attorney, served as an assistant Treasury secretary in the Clinton Administration, and her mother is a residential real-estate broker. Eager to partake of the mountain life, Samuels moved out to Salt Lake City in 2000 and insinuated herself into the area's clique of elite outdoorsmen and women by undertaking feats of courage and endurance. (In a toast at the wedding, one of these women said, "We think you have earned the right to marry the icon of the Wasatch.") Also present was Polly's older brother, Colin, who has himself become an avid backcountry skier and climber. He lives in La Grave. Two years ago, his fiancée was killed when she fell down a slope in Norway into a frozen hole. "Polly's parents don't understand it," McLean said. "Colin has moved to one of the centers of alpinism, and Polly is marrying an alpine geek. They're probably not thrilled by it."

McLean and Samuels left the church under an arch of ski poles held aloft by their guests, then put on boots and skis so that they could ski a celebratory run in wedding attire. They took a chairlift, his morning coat and her wedding dress apparently triggering another exemption to the leg-power rule. Afterward, they joined the reception, at a big hotel at Snowbird. The mountain men were scattered about, stooping to stay clear of the potted palms. Bob Athey, the saltiest of them all, sat by the door in his ski gear. He had a rusty beard and a grand frizz of hair, and he smelled of tobacco and sweat. From the way people lined up to talk to him, it was clear that he had not been observed indoors in some time. ("Bob, I haven't seen you since we scattered Alan's ashes," one woman said.) Athey told me, "I figure I got another twenty years of this, before I die in an avalanche."

McLean sidled up. The morning coat looked big on him, as though he were a boy in a man's suit. He had a fixed smile that thinly disguised a groom's simmering embarrassment. "So, Bob, how was the skiing today?" "It was great."

"Where did you go?"

Athey mentioned some backcountry spots.

"How was the snow?"

"Crusty."

McLean nodded and looked thoughtful for a moment, before his father-in-law came by to suggest that he start herding the guests in to dinner.

After dinner and a short slate of toasts ("And that's how my brother ended up in the position he's in now, with . . . no job!"), it was time for "Hava Nagila." Samuels and McLean were hoisted up and borne onto the dance floor. This being Utah, a good portion of the people holding the bride and groom aloft did not have a great deal of experience with this particular number, and it was hard not to notice, as the tempo sped up and McLean, lurching to and fro, gripped the sides of his chair, that the expression on his face contained an unfamiliar ingredient that you might call worry.

Twenty-four hours after the wedding, I talked to McLean on the phone. I was at Alta, he was at home. (The honeymoon, a trip with friends to a backcountry lodge in British Columbia, would come a few weeks later.) McLean invited me to accompany him and his new brother-in-law on an outing the next morning to the Y Couloir, a three-thousand-foot chute that you walk up in your boots, with crampons and an ice axe. ("The Chuting Gallery": "You will be exposed to avalanche hazards 100 percent of the time and getting caught in even a minor slide here could be fatal.") I recalled that earlier in the winter McLean had told me that the only expeditions he has ever regretted were the ones he pulled out of: "Whenever I get invited on a trip, I remember a fortune cookie that said, 'Practice saying yes.'" To the Y Couloir invitation, however, I said something about not having the gear and having a plane to catch. McLean told me he had gear for me, and that we'd make it down by noon. "Come on, Nick. You'll love it!" I hung up and talked it over with my wife, with whom I was supposed to ski the following day. The consensus was that the answer should be no. I called McLean back. I told him that it was snowing at Alta, and he remarked that, if more than four or five inches accumulated, the Y Couloir would be too dangerous to ski. Later that evening, I stepped outside and noted, with more than the usual elation, that six inches had fallen. And it was still dumping. I called McLean and gave him my report; the Y Couloir would have to wait.

The next day was a powder day. At Alta, the Scrubbing Bubbles were out in force, devouring the new snow in less than an hour. Riding up the chairlift, I looked back hungrily across the canyon, at the vast untracked south face of Superior, and then followed the ridgeline east, until I saw a lone figure ascending a pristine snowfield. The skin track looked steep, the pace brisk. Ten minutes later, I saw the figure, a tiny speck, reach a peak called Flagstaff. My cell phone rang, and it was McLean, calling from the top to gloat. "Are you lonely?" I asked him.

"It is really good, Nick," he said. "And I have it all to myself." After a moment, he dropped off the backside, out of sight.

Hockey

George Plimpton

Cherry read out the lines: Mike Forbes and Al Sims at defense, and the McNab line, with Dave Forbes and Terry O'Reilly at the wings, would start.[*]

He read out my name as the goaltender somewhat perfunctorily, I thought, making nothing of it in any jocular way, as if it were a perfectly natural choice to make, and then he looked over at me and said: "It's time. Lead them out."

I put on my mask and clumped to the locker room door. I had forgotten my stick. Someone handed it to me. I was the first [Boston] Bruin in the tunnel. I could hear the Bruins beginning to yell behind me as we started out.

The tunnel to the rink is dark, with the ice right there at its lip, so that one flies out of it, like a bat emerging from a cast-iron pipe, into the brightest sort of light—the ice a giant opaque glass. The great banks of spectators rose up from it in a bordering mass out of which cascaded a thunderous assault of boos and catcalls. Cherry was right. The Bruins were not at all popular in Philadelphia.

We wheeled around on our half of the ice . . . the [Philadelphia] Flyers in

"Cherry" refers to Bruins coach Don Cherry; "Cheevers" is Bruins goalie Garry Cheevers; and "Seaweed" is Bruins goalie Jim "Seaweed" Pettie.

theirs. There was no communication between the two teams; indeed, the players seemed to put their heads down as they approached the centerline, sailing by within feet of each other without so much as a glance. My roommate, Seaweed, had told me: "In hockey you don't talk to the guys from the other team at all, ever. You don't pick him up when he falls down, like in football." He told me about a pregame warm-up in the Soviet-Canada series in which Wayne Cashman had spotted a Russian player coming across the centerline to chase down a puck that had escaped their zone; Cashman had skated over to intercept him and checked him violently into the boards. "Well, the guy was in the wrong place," Seaweed said when I expressed my astonishment. "He should have known better."

I skated over to the boards, working at the clasp at my chin to adjust my mask. The fans leaned forward and peered in at me through the bars of the mask—as if looking into a menagerie cage at some strange inmate within. "Hey, lemme see." A face came into view, just inches away, the mouth ajar, and then it withdrew to be replaced by another, craning to see. I could hear the voice on the public-address system announcing me as the goaltender for a special 5-minute game. The Bruins were motioning me to get in the goal. We were a minute or so away. I pushed off the boards and reached the goal in a slow glide, stopping and turning myself around slowly and carefully.

The three officials came out onto the ice. The organist was playing a bouncy waltzlike tune that one's feet tapped to almost automatically, but I noticed the officials pointedly tried not to skate to its rhythm as they whirled around the rink to warm up, perhaps because they would seem to demean their standings as keepers of order and decorum if they got into the swing of the music. They, too, came up and inspected me briefly, glancing through the bars of my mask without a word and with the same look of vague wonder that I had noticed from the fans.

The Bruins began skating by, cuffing at my pads with their sticks as they passed. Tapping the goaltender's pads is perhaps the most universal procedure just before the game—in most cases, of course, a simple gesture of encouragement, like a pat on the back.

I wobbled slightly in the crease from the impact of some of the stronger blows from my Bruin teammates as they skated by. I felt a surge of appreciation and warmth toward them for doing it. Two of the Bruins stopped and helped me rough up the ice in front of the cage—this is a procedure so the goalie gets a decent purchase with his skate blades. Invariably it is done by the goalie himself—long, scraping side thrusts with skates to remove the sheen from the new ice. It occurred to me later that to be helped with this ritual was comparable to a pair of baseball players coming out to help a teammate get set in the batter's box, kneeling down and scuffing out toeholds for him, smoothing out the dirt, dusting his bat handle, and generally preparing things for him, as if the batter were as unable to shift for himself as a storefront mannequin. However odd this may have appeared from the stands—the three of us toiling away in front of the net—it added to my sense of common endeavor. "Thank you, thank you," I murmured.

Other Bruins stopped by while this was going on, and peering into my mask, they offered last-minute advice. "Chop 'em down! Chop 'em down!" I looked out at Bobby Schmautz and nodded. His jaw was moving furiously on some substance. "Chop 'em down!" he repeated as he skated off. Slowly the other Bruins withdrew, skating up the ice toward the bench of their positions to stand for the National Anthem.

I spent the anthem (which was a Kate Smith recording rather than a real article) wondering vaguely whether my face mask constituted a hat, and if I should remove it. My worry was that if I tampered with any of the equipment I might not have it in the proper working order at the opening face-off. The puck would be dropped . . . and the Flyers would sail down the ice towards a goaltender who would be standing bare-headed, facedown, fiddling with the chin strap of his mask, his big mitt tucked under his arm to free his fingers for picking at the clasp, his stick lying across the top of the net . . . no, it was not worth contemplating. I sang loudly inside my mask to compensate for any irreverence.

A roar went up at the anthem's conclusion—something grim and anticipatory about that welter of sound, as if, oh my! We're really going to see something good now, and I saw the players at the center of the rink slide their skates apart, legs spread and stiff, their sticks down, the upper parts of their bodies now horizontal to the ice—a frieze of tension—and I knew the referee in his striped shirt, himself poised at the circle and ready for the flight once he had dropped the puck, was about to trigger things off. I remember thinking, Please, Lord, don't let them score more than five—feeling that a goal a minute was a dismaying enough fate to plead against to a Higher Authority—and then I heard the sharp cracking of sticks against the puck.

For the first 2 minutes the Bruins kept the play in the Flyers' end. Perhaps they realized that a torrid offense was the only hope of staving off an awkward-sounding score. They played as if the net behind them were empty . . . as if their goalie had been pulled in the last minute of a game they had hoped to tie with the use of an extra forward. I saw the leg pad of the Flyers' goaltender fly up to deflect a shot.

Well, this isn't bad at all, I thought.

There can be nothing easier in sport than being a hockey goalie when the puck is at the opposite end. Nonchalance is the proper attitude. One can do a little housekeeping, sliding the ice shavings off to one side with the big stick. Humming a short tune is possible. Tretiak, the Russian goaltender, had a number of relaxing exercises he would put himself through when the puck was at the opposite end of the rink. He would hunch his shoulder muscles, relaxing them, and he'd make a conscious effort to get the wrinkles out of brow. "To relax, pay attention to your face. Make it smooth," he would add, the sort of advice a fashion model might tend to.

It is a time for reflection and observation. During a static spell Ken Dryden from the Montreal goal noticed that the great game clock that hung above the Boston Garden was slightly askew.

With the puck at the other end, it was not unlike (it occurred to me) standing at the edge of a mill pond, looking out across a quiet expanse at some vague activity at the opposite end almost too far to be discernible— could they be bass fishing out there?—but then suddenly the distant, aimless, waterbug scurrying becomes an oncoming surge of movement as everything—players, sticks, the puck—starts coming on a direct line, almost as if a tsunami, that awesome tidal wave of the South Pacific, had suddenly materialized at the far end of the mill pond and was beginning to sweep down toward one.

"A tsunami?" a friend of mine had asked.

"Well, it is like that," I said. "A great encroaching wave full of things being borne along toward you full tilt—hockey sticks, helmets, faces with no teeth in them, those black, barrellike hockey pants, the skates, and somewhere in there that awful puck. And then, of course, the noise."

"The noise?"

"Well, the crowd roars as the wings come down the ice, and so the noise seems as if it were being generated by the wave itself. And then there's the racket of the skates against the ice, and the thump of bodies against the boards, and the crack of the puck against the sticks. And then you're inclined to do a little yelling yourself inside your face mask—the kind of sounds cartoon characters make when they're agonized."

"Arrrgh?"

"Exactly. The fact is it's very noisy all of a sudden, and not only that, but it's very crowded. You're joined by an awful lot of people," I said, "and very quickly. There's so much movement and scuffling at the top of the crease that you feel almost smothered."

What one was trained to do in this situation, I told my friend, was to keep one's eye on the puck at all costs. I only had fleeting glimpses of it—it sailed elusively between the skates and sticks, as shifty as a rat in a hedgerow: it seemed impossible to forecast its whereabouts . . . my body jumped and swayed in a series of false starts. Cheevers had explained to me that at such moments he instinctively understood what was going on, acutely aware of the patterns developing, to whose stick the puck had gone, and what the player was likely to do with it. The motion of the puck was as significant to him as the movement of a knight on a chessboard. His mind busied itself with possibilities and solutions. For me, it was enough to remember the simplest of Cheevers's instructions: "Stand up! Keep your stick on the ice!"

The first shot the Flyers took went in. I had only the briefest peek at the puck . . . speeding in from the point off to my right, a zinger, and catching the net at the far post, tipped in on the fly, as it turned out, by a Philadelphia player named Kindrachuk, who was standing just off the crease. The assists were credited to Rick Lapointe and Barry Dean. I heard this melancholy news over the public-address system, just barely distinguishing the names over the uproar of a Philadelphia crowd pleased as punch that a Bruins team had been scored on, however circumspect and porous the goaltender.

Seaweed had given me some additional last-minute tips at training camp on what to do if scored upon. His theory was that the goaltender should never suggest by his actions on the ice that he was in any way responsible for what had happened. The goalie should continue staring out at the rink in a poised crouch (even if he was aware that the puck had smacked into the nets behind) as if he had been thoroughly screened and did not know the shot had been taken. In cases where being screened from the shot was obviously not a contributing cause of the score, Seaweed suggested making a violent, abusive gesture at a defense man, as if that unfortunate had made the responsible error.

When the Flyer goal was scored, I had not the presence or the inclination to do any of the things Seaweed had recommended. I yelled loudly in dismay and beat the side of my face mask with my catching glove. I must have seemed a portrait of guilt and ineptitude. "I didn't see the damn thing!" I called out. As I reached back to remove the puck, the thought pressed in on my mind that the Flyers had scored on their very first attempt—their shooting average was perfect.

What small sense of confidence I might have had was further eroded when soon after the face-off following the Philadelphia goal, one of the Bruins went to the penalty box for tripping; the Flyers were able to employ their power play, and for the remainder of the action the puck stayed in the Bruins' zone.

I have seen a film taken of those minutes—in slow motion so that my delayed reactions to the puck's whereabouts are emphasized. The big catching mitt rises and flaps slowly long after the puck has passed. There seems to be a near-studied attempt to keep my back to the puck. The puck hits my pads and turns me around, so that then my posture is as if I wished to see if anything interesting happened to be going on in the nets behind me. While the players struggle over the puck, enticingly in front of the crease, the camera catches me staring into the depths of the goal, apparently oblivious to the melee immediately behind me.

The film also shows that I spent a great deal of the time flat on the ice; alas, just where Cheevers and Seaweed had warned me not to be. Not much had to happen to put me there—a nudge, the blow of the puck. Once a hard shot missed the far post, and in reaching for it, down I went, as if blown over by the passage of the puck going by. The film shows me for an instant, grasping one of my defense man's legs, his stick and skates locked in my grasp as I try to haul myself back upright, using him like a drunk enveloping a lamppost.

Actually, my most spectacular save was made when I was prostrate on the ice . . . the puck appearing under my nose, quite inexplicably, and I was able to clap my glove over it. I could hear the Bruins breathing and chortling as they clustered over me to protect the puck from being probed out by a Flyer stick.

What was astonishing about those hectic moments was that the Flyers did not score. Five of their shots were actually on goal . . . but by chance my body, in its whirligig fashion, completely independent of what was going on, happened to be in the right place when the puck appeared.

A friend, who was observing from the seats, said the highest moment of comic relief during all this was when one of the Flyers' shots came in over my shoulder and hit the top bar of the cage and ricocheted away.

"What was funny," my friend said, "was that at first there was absolutely no reaction from you at all—there you were in the prescribed position, slightly crouched, facing out toward the action, stick properly down on the ice and all, and then the puck went by you, head high, and went off that crossbar like a golf ball cracking off a branch; it wasn't until 4 or 5 seconds, it seemed, before your head slowly turned and sneaked a look at where the puck had . . . well . . . *clanged*. It was the ultimate in the slow double take."

"I don't remember," I said. "I don't recall any clanging."

"Hilarious," my friend said. "Our whole section was in stitches."

Then, just a few seconds before my five-minute stint was up, Mike

Millbury, one of the Bruins' defense men out in front of me, threw his stick across the path of a Flyers wing coming down the ice with the puck. I never asked him why. Perhaps I had fallen down and slid off somewhere, leaving the mouth of the net ajar, and he felt some sort of desperate measure was called for. More likely he had been put up to it by his teammates and Don Cherry. Actually, I was told a *number* of sticks had been thrown. The Bruins wanted to be sure that my experience would include the most nightmarish challenge a goaltender can suffer . . . alone on the ice and defending against a shooter coming down on him one-on-one. The penalty shot!

At first, I did not know what was happening. I heard the whistles going. I got back into the nets. I assumed a face-off was going to be called. But the Bruins started coming by the goal mouth, tapping me on the pads with their hockey sticks as they had at the start of things, faint smiles, and then they headed for the bench, leaving the rink enormous and stretching out bare from where I stood. I noticed a huddle of players over by the Philadelphia bench.

Up in Fitchburg I had been coached on what the goaltender is supposed to do against the penalty shot . . . which is, in fact, how he maneuvers against the breakaway; as the shooter comes across the blue line with the puck, the goaltender must emerge from the goal mouth and skate out toward him—this in order to cut down the angle on the goal behind him. The shooter at this point has two choices: he can shoot, if he thinks he can whip the puck past the oncoming, hustling bulk of the goaltender, slapping it by on either side, or he can keep the puck on his stick and try to come *around* the goalie; in this case, of course, the goalie must brake sharply and then scuttle backward swiftly, always maneuvering to keep himself between the shooter and the goal mouth. I would always tell Seaweed or Cheevers, whomever I was chatting with about the penalty shot, that I had to hope the shooter, if this situation ever came up, did not know that I was not able to stop. All the shooter had to do was come to a stop himself, stand aside, and I would go sailing by him, headed for the boards at the opposite end of the rink.

Penalty shots do not come up that often. Gump Worsley in his twenty-one-year career had only faced 2, both of which he was unsuccessful against—not surprising perhaps, because the goals came off the stick of Gordie Howe and Boom-Boom Geoffrion. But Seaweed had told me—despite the Gump Worsley statistics—that he thought the chances favored the goaltender . . . that by skating out and controlling the angle the goalie could force the shooter to commit himself. Also, he pointed out that since the shooter was the only other player on the ice, the goaltender always had a bead on the puck, whereas in the flurry of a game he had often lost sight of it in a melee, or had it tipped in by another player, or passed across the ice to a position requiring a quick shift in the goal. Others agreed with him. Emile Francis believed that the goaltender should come up with a save 3 times out of 5. He pointed out while the goaltender is under considerable pressure, so is the other fellow—the humiliation of missing increased because the shooter *seems* to have the advantage . . . the predator, swift and rapacious, swooping in on a comparatively immobile defender. The compiled statistics seem to bear him out. Up until the time I joined the Bruins, only 1 penalty shot out of the 10 taken in Stanley Cup play has resulted in a score—Wayne Connelly's of the Minnesota North Stars in 1968 off Terry Sawchuck.

The confidence that might have been instilled by knowing such statistics was by no means evident in my own case. I stood in the cage, staring out at the empty rink, feeling lonely and put upon, the vast focus of the crowd narrowing on me as it was announced over the public-address system that Reggie Leach would take the penalty shot. Leach? Leach? The name meant little to me. I was told afterward his nickname is the Rifle. I had heard only one thing that I could remember about him from my resume of Flyers players, which was that he had scored 5 goals in a play-off game, a record. I dimly recalled that he was an Indian by birth. Also a slap-shot specialist . . . just enough information to make me prickle with sweat under my mask.

I gave one final instruction to myself—murmuring audibly inside the cage of my face mask that I was not to remain rooted helplessly in the goal mouth, mesmerized, but to launch myself out toward Leach . . . and just then I spotted him, moving out from the boards, just beyond the blue line, picking up speed, and I saw the puck cradled in the curve of his stick blade.

GEORGE PLIMPTON

As he came over the blue line, I pushed off and skated briskly out to meet him, windmilling my arms in my haste, and as we converged, I committed myself utterly to the hope that he would shoot rather than try to come around me. I flung myself sideways to the ice (someone said later that it looked like the collapse of an ancient sofa), and sure enough he did shoot. Somewhat perfunctorily, he lifted the puck and it hit the edge of one of my skates and skidded away, wide of the goal behind me.

A very decent roar of surprise and pleasure exploded from the stands. By this time, I think, the Philadelphia fans thought of me less as a despised Bruin than a surrogate member of their own kind. I represented a manifestation of their own curiosity if they happened to find themselves down there on the ice. As for the Bruins, they came quickly off the bench, scrambling over the boards to skate out in a wave of black and gold. It occurred to me that they were coming out simply to get me back up on my skates—after all, I was flat out on the ice—but they wore big grins: they pulled me up and began cuffing me around in delight, the big gloves smothering my mask so I could barely see as in a thick joyous clump we moved slowly to the bench. Halfway there, my skates went out from under me—tripped up, perhaps, or knocked askew by the congratulatory pummels— and once again I found myself down at ice level; they hauled me up like a sack of potatoes and got me to the bench. I sat down. It was a very heady time. I beamed at them. Someone stuck the tube of a plastic bottle in my mouth. The water squirted in and I choked briefly. A towel was spread around my shoulders.

"How many saves?"

"Oh, 20 or 30. At least."

"What about that penalty shot?"

"Leach is finished. He may not play again. To miss a penalty shot against you? The Flyers may not recover."

I luxuriated in what they were saying.

"Is that right?"

But their attention began to shift back to the ice. The game was starting up again. The sound of the crowd was different: full and violent. I looked up and down the bench for more recognition. I wanted to hear more. I wanted to tell them what it had been like. Their faces were turned away now.

SPRING

My Trip to the Show (Part II)

Tom Verducci

Embarrassment. Injury. Blunt force trauma. Estate planning. The mind quickly accelerates the possibility and the amplitude of catastrophe when you are standing on the infield grass, as I am, 75 feet in front of Boston Red Sox slugger Manny Ramirez while he bats with a runner on first base. No infielder ever would be so foolish to put himself this close to the potential harm of a Ramirez line drive, not even armed with world-class hand-eye coordination, a fielder's glove and a protective cup—all of which, as I am most acutely aware, I do not possess at this moment.

I am a major league umpire—for one day anyway, March 23, working a spring training matinee between the Red Sox and the Baltimore Orioles in Fort Myers, Florida. Leaving the observational safety of sportswriting, I have been granted permission by Major League Baseball to experience the pressure, the difficulty and the thanklessness of risking life, limb and public humiliation in front of thousands of people conditioned to dislike you. I am assigned the same spring rotation as my full-time brethren: 3 innings at third base, followed by 3 at second and 3 at first.

The baseball we hold dear is a benign, leisurely sport, a "noncontact" pursuit in which we cherish its sweetly proportioned empty spaces. The interlude between pitches. The flanks in the alignment of fielders. The 90 feet between bases. The flight of a thrown or batted baseball offers elegant interruption to the spatial symmetry.

Working from the interior of the infield, however, reveals the power and speed of the game. It's the difference between observing a funnel cloud from a safe distance on the ground and flying a research plane into the vortex of a tornado. "I tell all the young umpires that come up from the minors, 'Expect a close play every time,'" says Tim Tschida, forty-six, my crew chief who is working home plate this game. "[The play's] only routine here after it's over. That ball three steps to the right of the shortstop? They don't get to that ball in the minors and here they might throw the guy out. Middle infielders get to more balls up the middle that minor leaguers would never get to—and not only get to them, but turn them into double plays. I tell the young guys, 'Don't give up on anything.'"

My proximity to Ramirez, who is poised in that familiar asplike, coiled stance, is gripping, but the responsibilities of the job rattle around in my head, like marbles tumbling in a dryer. I've got to keep watch on the Orioles' pitcher, Erik Bedard, for a possible balk, the Sasquatch of rules violations for its difficulty to observe. (I've already missed one by Boston starter Curt Schilling, but so, too, did the rest of the crew.) I must make all calls at second base, which is over my right shoulder (including a stolen base attempt or a force play, which is the most commonly missed call by umpires), and possibly at third base if the umpire there, Brian O'Nora, leaves his post to track a ball hit to the outfield.

I must also know the rule book and the grounds rules with absolute certainty, a weakness of mine exposed during a mild argument the previous half inning with Boston right fielder J. D. Drew (who had no clue he was pleading his case to a sportswriter until I told him the next day). And one more thought—the mother of all marbles. Being an umpire is like being a jet pilot, a skydiver, or a sword swallower: You're expected to be perfect every time, and if you do screw up it's obvious to everyone. Nothing less than flawless is acceptable. I must get it right.

"God knows if you don't have the mental aptitude for this, you'd ask, 'What are you doing?'" says Fieldin Culbreth, another crew member. "If you're right, nobody's coming in and patting you on the back. If there are ten close plays and you get ten exactly right, they're booing you anyway. The only people who will say, 'Good job' are the other three guys in the [locker] room with you. The teams aren't going to say, 'Hell of a job.' ESPN's not going to say, 'Watch this umpire!' Here's the difference: The players are trying to make a play to get on *SportsCenter*. We're trying our damnedest to stay off it."

I trained long (okay, two days with Tschida and Culbreth) and hard (kicking back watching games in the Florida sun) for this gig. Ominously, the most important advice given to me by the umpires was to avoid utter disaster. My Umpire 101 syllabus looked like this:

1. *Don't blow out the knee of Baltimore shortstop Miguel Tejada by watching the flight of a pop-up near the third base line.* The fielder, who is also looking up, is likely to plow into the umpire, whose proper course of action is to first look for and avoid the fielders. "You getting hurt is one thing," Culbreth says. "The player getting hurt? Now there's a problem."

2. *Beware of balls that explode.* That's umpire terminology for what happens when you try to track a ball as it passes directly over your head, causing you to lose sight of it.

3. *Don't chase down a batted or thrown ball; that's the players' job.* Don't laugh; it's happened. Former major leaguer Ron LeFlore flunked umpire school in 1988 for his instinctive reaction to play the ball like the outfielder he once was rather than getting into proper position.

4. *Don't get spun around by line drives hit directly at you; you'll fall on your butt or, worse, get pegged there.* Culbreth recalls the time that no sooner had he remarked that he had never seen Jeromy Burnitz hit a line drive than Burnitz nailed first base umpire Terry Craft in the posterior. "It went up one side of his [butt] and down the other," Culbreth says.

5. *Make sure your fly is zipped.*

Basically, the job comes down to this: If I can quit worrying long enough about wiping out Tejada, about baseballs that either explode, tempt me to field them or put me on my can, and about keeping my pants on properly, then all I need to do is nail every single call. Great.

"Umpiring is a gift," says ump Tim Timmons, thirty-nine, who also assisted in my training, "like the hitter who has the skill to hit that 90-mph slider or the pitcher who can do things with a baseball no human being should be able to do. Those are real gifts, and so is umpiring. You can't teach instincts."

Major league umpires are, in fact, closer to perfect than you might imagine. There were 167,341 at bats last season over 2,429 games. According to the 2006 "Umpiring Year in Review," a report put together by MLB officials, the men in blue made only 100 incorrect calls, excluding balls and strikes (and in that discipline they were judged to be 94.9 percent accurate). Not once did a club protest a game. (A protest can be filed only if a team believes umpires misapplied the rules.)

For the privilege of having to be perfect, umpires spend about two hundred days a year on the road, hear the same lousy jokes in every ballpark about their eyesight or familial heritage, and routinely get second-guessed by critics watching repeated superslow, frame-by-frame replays in high definition from multiple camera angles. Yet major league umpiring jobs (of which there are 68) open up these days about as infrequently as those on the Supreme Court. What kind of person would love a job in which you get noticed only for your mistakes?

"I've always said there's no player, no fan, no manager and no umpire who could ever be as hard on me as I'll be," says Culbreth. "The fans can boo and throw stuff, and managers can scream and holler and get ejected, and they'll never get to me like I will. The part that bothers me the most is people think we miss a call, change our clothes, get in a station wagon, go have a cheeseburger and go home. That's just not how it is. If people knew how much we cared . . . they wouldn't be able to comprehend how much it bothers us to find out that we are wrong."

> "You're expected to be perfect the day you start, and then improve."
> —Ed Vargo, NL umpire supervisor, 1985

Schilling and Bedard are throwing so well that my 3 innings at third base pass without incident. The best action I get is a conversation with Boston third baseman Mike Lowell about April weather, and a Manny-being-Manny

TOM VERDUCCI

moment when, as Ramirez runs to leftfield, he looks at me with wild-eyed glee and chortles, "Heeeey! *Que pasa?!*" I get no appeal calls on check swings by left-handed batters, an especially tricky call for umpires because the rule book is not explicit about what exactly constitutes a swing.

Says Culbreth, laughing, "Just remember, if it's David Ortiz, he didn't [swing]. Trust me. After you say he did, he'll tell you. He'll faint. If I could hit with his check swings I might have gotten drafted."

According to Major League Baseball's review, in 2006 umpires missed a call in the field only once every 12.2 games. Force plays (43 mistakes), tag plays (14), and steals (12) were the only categories in which umpires missed ten or more calls the entire season. Video replay, however, is just around baseball's corner, at least in a limited scope. Baseball is studying the possibility of using it to assist in making home run calls—fair or foul, and whether or not the ball cleared the wall or designated home run line. Such calls have been made more difficult by modern ballpark designs, which put fans, architectural elements and billboards closer to the action.

"If we don't address this, there will be a major controversy and that's how replay gets in the door," Tschida says. "Last year our crew in the first month had five home run calls where we had to get together [to discuss them]. I was thinking, Are we snakebit? So I started keeping track. We had 43 home runs where the ball came back on the field. It's not supposed to happen, but it happens when nonbaseball people are designing fields."

I have the pleasure of calling a clean, no-doubt home run by Red Sox catcher Jason Varitek in the fifth, but it's during those middle innings, when I am stationed at second base, that the inner game of umpiring becomes dangerous. The second base umpire is the lead dancer of the four-man ballet. I must run into the outfield on balls hit from gap to gap with nobody on base, with the third base umpire rotating to second and the home plate ump rotating to third. "Once you leave, don't stop," Culbreth instructs.

However, in the fourth, I am positioned in the interior infield because there's a runner at first base—"Once in, always in" is the role with runners on—and I make the mistake of chasing a ball hit into the right centerfield gap by the Orioles' Jay Gibbons. It's a blunder most fans would never notice, but understanding the umpires' pursuit of perfection, it rankles me.

Indeed, I'm later told that umpire supervisor Marty Springstead, watching the game from the press box, exclaimed, "Uh-oh, too many umpires in the outfield."

The next batter, Kevin Millar, also drives a double into the same gap. The ball rolls to a stop at the bottom of the fence and is returned to the infield by centerfielder Wily Mo Peña. That play will prompt Drew, after the inning ends, to stop next to me on his way to the dugout.

Drew lifts his arms out to his sides and says to me, "Hey, what's the rule on the ball that wedges under the fence?"

I can tell he's very serious and mistakes me for an actual umpire. This is not good.

"Uh, did it go under the fence at all?" I ask in an attempt to avoid his question. "Because if it goes under the fence it's a dead ball even if he fishes it out."

"No," Drew says, more impassioned this time. "The ball got stuck between the bottom of the fence and the ground. What's the ruling?"

"The ball's in play unless it goes completely under the fence," I reply, in full filibuster mode as I return to the under-the-fence diversion.

"No, not under the fence," Drew says again, more confused than annoyed about not getting a direct answer from an umpire. "What's the ground rule here on a ball stuck under the fence?"

I've tap-danced long enough for Culbreth to rescue me as he joins us from his station at first base. I haven't been this happy to see an umpire since Leslie Nielsen in *The Naked Gun*. Culbreth explains that the ball's in play as long as Peña chooses to play it; if the ball's wedged, Peña can raise his hand to signal a stuck ball. Then the ruling is an automatic double and two bases to any base runner.

"Yeah," I say to Drew, suddenly summoning an authoritative tone with a straight face. "Tell him next time to just raise his hand and we'll stop the play."

I made sure to find Drew the next morning at a Red Sox workout.

"That was you?" he says in amazement. "I came back into the dugout after that and looked at the list [of umpires]. I knew the other three guys, but they didn't have you on it. So I figured you were some Double A umpire they called up to replace somebody."

There's more trouble in the fifth, the same kind of trouble, like the undertow of the ocean, that mostly goes unseen. Baltimore's Corey Patterson whistles a line drive at Culbreth, the kind of missile that can put an umpire embarrassingly on his butt or whack him there.

Any hitter will tell you that late-breaking pitches are hardest to hit because it is impossible for the eyes to track a thrown ball and see it the last 4 or 5 feet. Culbreth is challenged by the same limitation. He can track the ball—it's heading right for his ankles—but because of its speed and proximity to his body he can't see it just as it hits the ground. He's got to make a call. Quickly.

"Fair ball!" he shouts, and signals so, deftly staying off his butt. Patterson races into second with a double as the runner at first, Paul Bako, advances to third.

Schilling pitches out of the jam, but only after he gets away with his covert balk. Stepping off the mound to get a new signal from Varitek, Schilling, a right-hander, moved his left foot slightly back, which technically begins his delivery. Tschida sees something amiss, but in the moment he processes the information, he grants a request for time from Varitek. ("Oh, I balked," Schilling will say the next day.)

After the inning, Culbreth still is thinking about Patterson's line drive. "That one I don't feel great about," he tells me. (Amazingly, according to the MLB report, umpires missed a total of three fair-foul calls all of last season.) "I think I got it right, but sometimes you feel less than great about it."

"I thought you had it right," I tell him. "Was there chalk?"

"No, it didn't hit chalk," he says, "but here's the thing: If you ever have some doubt in your mind, you're better off calling it fair than foul. That's because, if another umpire had a better look and comes in and says, 'No, I had it foul,' then you can just return the base runner and the batter continues to hit. But once you call it foul, everybody stops; so if another umpire has it fair, what can you do? You can't just make up where everybody goes."

"You had it right," I tell him.

Says Schilling, "It was foul by 3 or 4 feet. Wasn't even close."

"We're looking right down the line from the dugout," reliever Mike Timlin says. "It was foul."

Culbreth gets another adventure straight out of the Umpiring 101 syllabus: a foul pop-up into a swirling wind that confuses Millar, the Orioles' first baseman. Culbreth is trying to stay out of the way of Millar, who is circling wildly, as if dizzy. Culbreth is doing his best to zig whenever Millar zags. It's a comedic and ungraceful pas de deux, the punch line coming when the ball plops on the warning track closer to Culbreth than to Millar. Second baseman Brian Roberts looks at me and we both are laughing. So, too, is Tejada, who yells, "Hey, Kevin, I can't wait to see that on bloopers!" Millar, who otherwise spends his time at first base yelling mock insults to his former Red Sox teammates as they hit, or trying to bait me into making appeal calls from second base on ridiculously meager check swings, has to laugh himself.

> "I occasionally get birthday cards from fans. But it's often the
> same message: They hope it's my last."
> —Al Forman, NL umpire, 1961

Here it comes: a close call I will have to make at first base that will impact the game. Boston, trailing 2–1, has runners at first and second with no outs in the seventh when Lowell hits a grounder to second base. Baltimore will try to turn a double play, so I position myself for the call. The throw from Tejada to Millar bounces into the first baseman's glove. It's a close play, but I have Lowell out, the bang of the ball hitting the glove barely preceding the bang of the foot upon the bag. (The umpires' adage is that a blind man could umpire at first base.) The rally is virtually snuffed by the call. Suddenly there's this swell of noise from the Red Sox crowd, a strange mix of excitement and apoplexy.

Is it directed at Lowell? At me? I thought I had it right, but for one anxious moment, I'm not sure. Did I blow it that badly? No, wait. I flush the doubt. Lowell was out. I'm pretty sure of it. That plaintive groan is the sound of disappointed partisanship. Major league umps are tone deaf to such noise.

"They're biased," Culbreth says of fans. "The only time you might hear

TOM VERDUCCI

something is if it's really original, which almost never happens. I still remember one time when I was in Double A. There was this middle-aged lady. She must have been in her fifties, pushing sixty. She gets up and she yells at me, 'Why don't you pull down your pants, bend over, and try your good eye.' Nothing's original. But that was."

Says Tschida, "There was one time years ago when I bought a patent leather belt and thought it looked just great. Well, I wear it in Yankee Stadium for the first time, and those people know how to wait so that you can hear them. This one guy, a real New Yorker, gets up and yells, 'Hey, Tschida. How can you make a call like dat wearin' a patent leathah belt like dat? And hey, what accessories came with dat?' As soon as the game was over, I go in the locker room, rip off the belt, and throw it in the garbage."

Boston ties the game in the last of the eighth. It is only spring training, but I'm struck by the buzz in the crowd, the effort by both teams to win the game—to preserve the tie, Baltimore intentionally walks Ortiz, who spits epithets all the way to first—and it hits me smack in the gut: I am umpiring first base in a game in which the Red Sox and the Orioles are tied at 2 headed to the ninth. Good Lord, if this is Fort Myers, what must the late innings of a World Series game feel like?

The real umpires want the responsibility of the big call. It's what drove them through one of the two feeder umpire schools to professional baseball (94 percent of the students don't even graduate to the next step, a recommendation to an evaluation course), through the minor leagues (earning between $1,800 and $3,400 a month) and earning that big league job with the $87,859 starting salary, the first-class air travel, the four weeks of in-season vacation, and the $363.48 per diem for food and lodging. Me? I'm praying neither the baseball nor my head explodes.

"This is my twenty-second year," Tschida says. "When I'm fifty-five that will be my thirtieth, and if I feel good I'll keep going. I'll do it as long as I can. Few people in this job just retire when retirement age hits. Mostly, we do it until it becomes physically difficult to do it. Until we can't."

I know, especially deployed at first base, I could very well be involved in the outcome of a big league game. "If it goes extra innings," O'Nora tells me, "we don't rotate. You stay at first."

I remind myself of what O'Nora told me in the middle innings, when I was so eager to make a call I'd give the out signal as quickly as a fly ball thwacked into an outfielder's glove: *Don't hurry. It's nothing until you call it.* Even a big league outfielder might drop a ball, and you wouldn't look too sharp with your fist in the air and the ball on the ground. Slow down the game. It's exactly what the better players do as the tension builds.

It's the bottom of the ninth, and Boston's Alex Ochoa lifts a routine fly ball to centerfield. Just as I sneak a peek to watch the catch before I make sure Ochoa touches first base, Orioles centerfielder Adam Stern, fighting wind and sun, flat drops the ball. O'Nora, cooly patient, gives the no-catch call. Ochoa reaches second base. He advances to third on a groundout to second base—my last call, an easy one—and scores the winning run on a single by Kevin Cash through a drawn-in infield.

The four of us, the umpires, depart the field through the same tunnel as the Orioles at the far end of the visiting dugout. It's been a good day. I did not disable any ballplayers. I stayed off my butt. My fly is up. Our dressing room is on the right, the Orioles' clubhouse directly across the narrow hallway on the left. As I walk into our room I hear a short, loud crash from the Baltimore clubhouse, followed by an even louder shout of "F——!"

Not 2 seconds later, the first words out of Tschida's mouth are these, softly: "I think Schilling balked." His face is riddled with disappointment. "We get paid to see that," he says. "I didn't see that. We will Opening Day."

Tomorrow is another day, another game. Tomorrow they'll be perfect.

Foaming at the Mouth

Robert Twigger

"Tether even a roasted chicken."—From the seventeenth-century Samurai manual, *Hagakure*

For the first time in my life I was about to willfully inflict damage on myself.

The school bully, the one who punched me in the face with a cricket glove, had also liked damaging himself. He had a curiously malformed thumb, a stump of scar tissue that stopped at the first joint. Sometimes, during lessons, he would stab himself in the thumb stump with the sharp point of his compasses.

I can remember other friends deliberately cutting themselves with modeling knives. The most barbarous folly was performed by the naughty boys at the back of the class who gave themselves blue ink tattoos with a fountain pen and the ubiquitous pair of compasses.

My parents, when they got the chance, smothered me with kindly concern. I think that if I'd tried to toughen myself up with self mutilation they would have taken me to a child psychiatrist. In Britain, in the 1970s, only skinheads and the deranged welcomed a beating to build their own resistance to further torture.

The first day of the Riot Police course was, appropriately, April 1. There was an inaugural ceremony held in the *dojo* under a huge Rising Sun flag that hung from the wall.

The police would start a month later. They had been running a month late, ever since the Royal Wedding of the previous spring.

Ito, the head disciple, issuing commands in the same voice as Chida, his mentor, lined the international contingent up for the inauguration and made us kneel for ten minutes while a former foreign minister made a long speech. All the VIPs I noticed were seated in chairs. As well as the huge Japanese flag hanging over the shrine there was a purple Yoshinkan eagle flag hanging from a tripod in the corner. When a *senshusei* name was called out that student had to jump to his feet as fast as possible and shout out his name and nationality. It was good form to shout as loud as possible. Riot Police don't mumble, we were told. Kancho was too sick to attend. It was the first police course ceremony he had missed in thirty years.

After the ceremony we stood around at a bit of a loose end. There were two Canadians, both called Nick. The smaller and younger of the two was an Armenian Canadian and told us his name was not really Nick but we ought to call him Nick because everyone else did. Later he told me his real name, but I forgot it. Little Nick had problems writing, despite having been sent to an expensive private school. He had scars on his arms from knife fights. There was something sharkish and cold about his black eyes.

The older and bigger Nick was jovially keen to shake everyone's hand. He was a few months younger than me, so I was the oldest on the course. He had been an outdoor activities instructor in Canada and had studied Outdoor Leisure at university. "My God," quipped Will, "the guy's got a degree in lighting campfires and putting up tents."

Ben and Craig were both Australian. Ben was well over six foot tall and without embarrassment told everyone he had studied ballet back in Melbourne. Ben looked floppy and relaxed, used to a pain-free existence. I guessed he would last a month. Craig was watchful and quiet. He had a bulky body and pale skin and had trained at karate and *iado*, the art of drawing a sword. He had an Ian Botham style haircut, short at the sides with a mane down the back. Virtually everyone else had either shaven or crew-cut hair, which was the expected *senshusei* hairstyle.

R'em, the Israeli, was to be my training partner for the first three months. There was something Tiggerish about him, a bounciness that was appealing. He had a mop of frizzy hair and round glasses which he never removed, even during fist fights, he said. He sold silver rings for a living and told me he had two girlfriends, one Japanese and one Israeli. "But I am Yemeni-Israeli, and Yemenis are allowed two wives!" he said, winking at me. His English and Japanese were both poor but he rarely stopped grinning. Fat Frank didn't appreciate R'em's jokes: "He tries to make out you're just as dirty-minded as he is—I don't like that." Before coming to Japan (via motorcycle across India) he had served as a captain in the Israeli paratroops. He was thin and wiry. He told me he'd always liked fighting.

It was then I realized that we were a kind of foreign legion within the *senshusei* course. Foreigners who had washed up and were at a loose end, dropouts even, who sought salvation in the punishing discipline of *dojo* life. It was too late to worry that I was running away from life, two late to think of all the freedoms I would have to give up. For the next year we were all the property of Yoshinkan aikido.

The *senshusei* course starts from zero. It presupposes no knowledge of aikido apart from a few basics. For those who are already black belts the idea is to strip out bad habits by going back to fundamentals. The course proceeds very fast. In a year we would do more training than someone practicing an hour a day four times a week for five years. The *dojo* demanded a certain level of competence before starting so that the high speed of learning could be kept up.

There would be four tests throughout the course. The third test would be for black belt, the final test for an instructor's license and a police course completion certificate.

We were all given a manual, translated from the Japanese, which outlined a rough diary for the year. It also told us our duties. In each 7 or 8-hour day at the *dojo* we would spend 2 hours cleaning, attending meetings, writing up our diaries, and hurriedly eating meals. When we weren't at the *dojo* there were training camps to attend, as well as excursions and demonstrations.

Twice a week we started at 7:15 a.m. so that a half-hour Japanese lesson could be fitted in before the first aikido lesson.

All aikido classes were an hour or an hour and a half long, though this would be stretched to two if the teacher was feeling vengeful. There were three such classes each day. Including warm-up time and sitting to attention in *seiza*, the painful kneeling position of all would-be Samurai, we would spend five and half hours a day, five days a week, doing hard physical training in the same hard-matted 30-by-15-meter room.

At either end of this room, the *dojo*, were two clocks. They had to be checked every day, sometimes adjusted several times a day since they were always either slow or fast. These clocks ruled our lives.

The first lesson was widely advertised as the hardest. In previous years people had given up the *senshusei* course after the first lesson, some of them giving up aikido for good as well. I wondered who would be the first to crack up on our course.

The first month was used as a way to weed out those who couldn't adapt to *senshusei*-style training. In one year the number of foreign students had gone down from sixteen at the start to four at the end. The previous year had lost seven people throughout the course. The Japanese rarely gave up, except through injury. Foreigners were not always so tough. But they were not doing it on a salary, like the police.

One twenty-three-year-old Canadian had given up after three days. This was the previous year. He told me he just didn't like being shouted at. But instead of fleeing in shame he stayed and trained twice a day in regular classes. And though a *senshusei* black belt is held in higher esteem than a regular black belt, he passed the test at the same time as those doing the course he had quit. This was the plan that Chris and Fat Frank aimed to follow. With luck, all of us would pass black belt at the same time, though I would still have to complete three more months of instructor training.

We were lined up kneeling and waiting for our first *senshusei* teacher to arrive. It was an early class so we knew it would be a foreigner. A minute before the class started five or six other Western teachers knelt down along the same line as us. These were either witnesses or assistants in the mayhem that would follow.

As the clock struck the half-hour, Roland "the Terminator" strolled in. We went through the bowing procedure and then jumped up to attention to await orders.

The lesson was very simple. Everyone was told a spot they should run to and when the order was given everyone had to get to their spot as fast as possible. And then we had to run back to the line. And then back to the spots. And then back to the line. And then back to the spots. AS FAST AS POSSIBLE.

Quickly, Roland's voice become hectoring and hysterical as people made inevitable errors. Every mistake was punished by a round of *usagi tobi* (the bunny hops, which look like fun things to do, but after 15 or 16 rounds the novelty begins to wear off).

When we had learnt how to get to our spots we practiced going into *kamae*, the basic fighting stance of aikido. First we went into right-side *kamae* and then we went into left-side *kamae*.

The shouting by Roland and his five assistant tormentors was like nothing I had yet experienced. It was pure boot camp. I could hear people being abused all around me. "One more fuck-up and you're out," Roland shouted at Adam, who had even less experience of aikido than I did. Again and again we bunny hopped around the *dojo*. It was ludicrous and yet exhilarating. Roland came over and started bellowing in my ear. "Lower your weight. Lower. LOWER!" I got confused and he sensed the victim in me. He came closer and shouted louder. Somehow I realized I had to get it together or his bullying would never stop. It was back to the school playground. I concentrated fiercely and projected defiance. As if things were now working on an instinctual level he backed away and started picking on someone else.

By now the bunny hopping was becoming a little lackluster. We were assaulted by more shouts and insults to get us moving again. Everybody's lungs were bursting for air. People started falling over as they hopped.

Now the "assistants" moved in. They gathered round those who looked like they might be fading and heaped insults and abuse on them. It felt like there were bombs going off all over the place, that I was back in some nightmarish First-World-War scenario, that I could run but never escape the mortar attack of bellowed "instruction."

Only at one point did I suddenly think, "What the hell are you doing here? Why don't you just walk away? I banished the thought quickly. I knew I couldn't afford the luxury of such thinking if I wanted to stick it out for the whole year.

Compared to the others, I seemed to be doing OK. Adam was having the most problems, but then he seemed to get a second wind and started bunny hopping madly like a suicidal wind-up toy.

And then with a shouted "*ya-me!*" (stop) it was all over. We stood at attention wheezing and dribbling like granddads. Roland gave us barely a look before dismissing the class.

Half an hour to prepare for the next lesson. I drank a little water and collapsed on the floor of the changing room. Stephen Otto, one of Roland's assistants, and a former power-lifting champion of Bavaria, came up and patted me on the back. "You did well out there. I was kind of surprised. But it was good, good."

The next lesson was taught by Chida Sensei. We all expected the worst. Instead, Chida gave us a lecture. He lined us up and laughed at our height. "Too tall for aikido," he said. "All the top people like Ueshiba, Kancho Sensei were small." He told us we were anticipating commands rather than following them. "This is mental inflexibility. A man who anticipates cannot stand still. He cannot wait. His timing is always out. He telegraphs every punch and his opponent knows exactly what he is thinking. You cannot plan a fight!"

We all looked shamefaced. In our last lesson we were told we were too slow. Now we were too fast. What we had to learn was the correct manner.

We were trying too hard. Or trying in the wrong way. The problem was how to try hard in the right way. How to try without "trying." Because, in the end, trying hard is not enough. You have to get results. You have to win the fight, since losing may mean death. How do you win without caring too much about who actually wins?

We made mistakes and Chida said, "This is not the regular class. In the regular class we say something and people forget, so we say it again. In *senshusei* training we only say it once. In *senshusei* training you cannot forget. You are taught once and you learn straightaway."

He said this without a shred of irony in his voice. He paused after he'd said it and the warning hung for a moment in the air like a threat. He continued in a soft voice: "When I joined the *dojo* and became a discipline I made my will. I knew that at any time I could be killed by Kancho Sensei. I made my will because I wanted to be prepared to die." There was another long silence as this final pronouncement was made.

Chida finished with a series of stamina-building exercises. One of the exercises was simply sitting on the floor with the feet raised and outstretched in front. We were all shaking and quivering with fatigue after five minutes. Chida was forty-five years old and completely unperturbed after ten minutes of keeping his feet up. Indeed, he gave the impression, constantly, that he could go on forever.

I later discovered there was a trick to this physical feat—just as there is to most displays of amazing strength or endurance. The trick is that when you tense the stomach muscles you involuntarily tense all the surrounding muscles as well. Some of these pull in the opposite direction to raising the legs so that you are actually working against yourself. This serves to tire out the stomach very quickly, however strong you are. Indeed, the stronger you are the stronger the counter pull of involuntary muscles. Instead, you must relax the stomach and concentrate on the hip tensor muscles that connect the femur to the pelvis. For this the back must be straight. Aikido, since it teaches a high level of body awareness and requires the ability to isolate and relax certain muscles, makes it easier to perform such "miracles."

The early weeks of training were designed to test *konjo*, or guts. It was a traditional Japanese training method. If you were asked to do two hundred press-ups it was for moral rather than physical reasons. The Japanese teachers were not interested in working up to something gently. *Konjo* demanded that they threw us in at the deep end.

The first lesson had been on a Saturday. Training restarted at 7:15 on

Tuesday morning. I had two days to rest before the real onslaught began. Frank observed my attempts to stay immobile in a sleeping bag with amusement. Chris had stronger view. When he suggested a curry rice at the Murakami brothers' establishment around the corner he was annoyed that I rode my bike the hundred or so meters to the restaurant. As the Murakami brothers, cheery identical twins in their sixties, fixed identical bowls of curry with a topping of red pickle, Chris outlined the necessity of not using the course as an excuse for epic laziness whenever I wasn't training. "But that's the only way I'll survive," I protested. "Then you won't learn a thing," he snapped back. Frank was conciliatory: "He's only just started, give him a chance." "Yeah," I joined in, "give me a chance." Chris stabbed at his curry rice with a none-too-clean Murakami spoon and said nothing.

I lay around in the apartment with aching limbs and wrote up my "*senshusei* diary." We had to hand the diaries in each month. They contained detailed explanations of each technique and an assessment of our feeling towards the training. At that point I couldn't summon any feeling so I wrote everything down in dry technical jargon.

By Tuesday morning I was still so stiff I could hardly climb the *dojo* stairs. *Senshusei* were forbidden to use the lift.

Once in the *dojo* we were assigned our cleaning tasks. Adam and I were given the toilets "for at least the next three months." It was definitely the worst job but it had one advantage, providing a chance to properly warm up by vigorously scrubbing the urinals and polishing the pipework. The toilet-roll dispenser lids had to have a mirror finish and so did the electrical socket covers. Adam mopped the floor. Paul had told us that cleaning was an integral part of the course. "It's good training," he said. "I tell you," said Adam, from his position behind one of the toilet bowls, "we're going to be the meanest fuckin' janitors in the world when this is over!"

By the second class Adam was to my left and shaking with exertion. His whole body shook violently as he leaned out over his front knee, arms extended, as if in pathetic homage to the gods. We were doing a basic turning movement which starts in the *kamae* stance and ends with the body leaning forwards with almost all the body weight on the front leg.

ROBERT TWIGGER

The arms reach forward too. The exercise is usually practiced a few times before class. We had been at it for an hour, with long intervals holding the position over the front leg. People screamed with agony. Adam, Craig and Big Nick were the most vociferous—they were also the heaviest, which meant they were putting more strain on the front knee.

The howling and shouting was so bad that some of the *uchideshi* (live-in Japanese disciples) came out of the office to watch. They concluded we were the noisiest *senshusei* course ever.

By this time Adam's defiant shouts had become a low whimpering interspersed with the odd moan. I noticed a quantity of white spittle-like substance around his chin: it was the first time I'd seen anyone literally foaming at the mouth through physical exertion.

Shioda junior seemed unconcerned. From time to time he turned his back on us and looked out the window at the building site below.

Stumpy, the Canadian *sewanin*, former *senshusei*, and now course assistant, ran around trying to "encourage" us. "Use the pain!" he shouted. "Ben, get up, don't cheat yourself!" The one constant chorus was: "Come on, *senshusei*—where's your spirit?"

Adam's spirit was about to desert him. The moans became a yodel of anguish as his whole body rose up in a convulsive wave of shaking. His face had gone bright purple, though his hands were bloodless white. Then he fell to the floor, shook twice, and lay completely still. Dead still. My God, I thought, he's died. He's had a heart attack and died.

Eerily, no one moved from their spots, though a certain lightening up was noticeable, as if Adam's supreme commitment had earned everyone else a holiday.

Stumpy shouted at Adam, who remained unmoving on the floor. Shioda was looking at the clock and had not noticed Adam's seizure. We had been told to never move without being ordered to move. I looked at Will. Will looked at Adam, who was inert and if dead, at least released from the physical pain we were all enduring.

My training partner, R'em, could stand it no longer. He broke ranks and rushed forward to Adam, who gurgled as R'em put him into the recovery position. Stumpy came over, followed by a bemused Shioda. All my frustration was directed at Shioda. Are you happy now? I thought. Now that you've killed someone? At the same time it was intensely interesting.

But Adam wasn't dead. Stumpy ordered R'em back to his spot and then lifted Adam up. 'Don't throw me out!' Adam gurgled deliriously. "Let me stay! Don't kick me off the course!"

Adam was dragged to the side and Shioda ordered Stumpy to take him outside for some fresh air. But Adam wouldn't go. He clung on to the wall bars, whimpering and begging to be allowed to stay. He really believed that if he left the *dojo* they'd never allow him back in again. Shioda shrugged and Adam sat in a heap, his face covered in blotches.

Adam had given everyone a 10-minute rest. The last 20 minutes of the lesson passed in a kind of limbo, the howling reduced to a muted minimum.

Adam even joined us towards the end of the lesson, stumbling along with the proud dignity of a wounded veteran. After the lesson he told us how he had started to hallucinate, imagining that "they" were coming to get him. "They" were the *dojo* staff, whom he held in superstitious awe.

"They won't throw you out for fainting," said Danny.

"That wasn't a faint," retorted Adam. "That was a colossal head rush of fear. That Shioda guy really scares me."

"You went an amazing purple color," I said.

"I thought you'd died of a brain hemorrhage," said Ben.

Adam looked thoroughly pleased at the suggestion. As a lover of attention he had certainly gotten more than his fair share. Even the teachers made comments. In a pep talk before classes, Stephan, the German assistant teacher, remarked on Adam's fortitude. In his Bavarian English he chided us for not trying hard enough: "You know, like in ancient Greece, they had these wrestling matches. Sometimes to the death. Sometimes a guy died because he was trying so hard. And that guy would be the winner, not the other guy. Because you have to give everything. That's what the ancient Greeks believed, and it's true. And right now Adam here is trying the hardest, because he trained so hard he passed out. That is the right spirit. That is *senshusei* spirit."

The next day, in Oyamada's class, Adam threw up. He rushed from the *dojo* with just enough time to make the basins in the toilets.

Dojo protocol was that you didn't need to ask permission to throw up. If you failed to make it off the mats you had to put your head inside your dogi top and throw up there.

In a Chida class Adam's nose exploded in a spontaneous nose bleed.

The first week ran into the second, and then the third, and it seemed that Adam had run out of attention-getting devices. He still moaned softly while we sat kneeling in *seiza* for any length of time. He claimed that a skateboard injury had left his knees skewwhiff and it made kneeling very painful. Probably it did, but by now everyone was beginning to have their own hurts and was becoming less sympathetic.

Suddenly Adam would pop up from a low to a high kneeling posture, spoiling the symmetry of the line. People groused and told him to sit down. The Japanese disciples were snickering and Adam was letting the side down. Reluctantly he would lower his weight back on to his knees, a true martyr to aikido, his unselfconscious whimpering echoing in the large airy *dojo*.

As Chris never tired of pointing out, pain is personal, pain is subjective. You should never judge another man's pain. Not only is the amount of pain subjective for any given injury, so different people are sensitive to different pains. It is difficult to conclude that someone has "a high pain threshold" because he may tolerate a migraine without painkillers but scream blue murder if his finger is nicked by a penknife.

The area is further muddied by imagination—indeed, this is the major contributor to an overreaction to pain. It's not the pain in itself, it's what the pain *means* which is so distressing.

It is one thing to be able to suffer pain. It takes a second level of stoicism to ignore the damage that the pain signifies.

People take hard knocks, break bones, cut themselves badly, tear ligaments, pull muscles in rugby, wrestling, surfing and horse riding, to name but a few sports. And they suffer these injuries with few complaints, usually anxious to be back doing the thing that did for them in the first place.

On the *senshusei* course it was different. The teachers emphasized that we would be in pain a lot of the time, indeed the foreign teachers (who were more masochistic than the Japanese) hinted that learning to live with pain was a large part of *senshusei* training. That created an atmosphere of clenched-teeth heroism, which had little to do with good aikido.

The Japanese teachers were more matter of fact. They gave no outward sign of pain or injury and expected none from us. But they were not judgmental. The Westerners chided us and scolded us, the Japanese simply ignored us and yet gave us no rest. What characterized the Western teachers was impatience. They wanted us to be good immediately. They wanted us to be tough immediately.

Perhaps it is the ability to choose that makes a wounded rugby player take to the field and laugh at his injury. We had no choice in the matter. The rule of the course was to keep training whatever the pain. We had yet to discover how bad an injury had to be before it earned you a holiday.

And we were scared of getting hurt too badly because we knew we'd have to be there the next day, and the next day, and the next day for a whole year. It was either that or give up. There was no halfway house.

As I lay awake at night, unable to sleep because of chronic knee and elbow pain, my mind worked to find ways to heal myself. I should walk less and cycle more, since cycling, with its low-strain, low-level exercise of the legs, had proved to be therapeutic. I should try Stumpy's patent hot towels on the knee joints before going to bed. I should massage the joints with Deep Heat. My mind raced on in the opposite of Zen mind detachment and acceptance. This was not Zen mind, it was survivor's mind.

Others had their own ways of coping. After the first week, Nick the Armenian told Big Nick, his partner, that when the going got tough Big Nick's eyes seemed to pop out with intensity. "You've got a real mad-dog look, all right," agreed Paul, who hung around the tea room, spying on us, I thought.

"Mad Dog," said Big Nick. "I like that. You can call me Mad Dog if you like."

There was a moment of embarrassment. It was a bit much to ask for a nickname, but no one said anything. We were all quite formal and polite at that early stage.

"Mad Dog—more like sad dog," said Ben, as we went into the next class. I didn't say anything. I didn't feel secure enough in my own performance to start insulting other members of the group. Ben was not malicious, he just didn't care that much. He was a natural loner whereas my survival strategy included using the group and not fighting them. That was the plan, anyway.

Will was the other loner. From the start he had taken against Aga. "What a bullshitter that guy is," he complained to me. "What's that shit he's always trying to sell? Nuskin? Forget that, have you seen how expensive their sport drinks are?"

Aga's main problem was that he wanted to be the leader. He wanted it so badly everyone caved in and let him become the unelected spokesman. His first idea was to push for an International *Senshusei* jacket. He brought in color charts and lettering charts and pretty soon everyone had been bamboozled into agreeing to pay for expensive black bomber jackets covered in loud badges.

"I don't like Aga," said R'em. "I know his kind from the army. He is a selfish." I was surprised by this because R'em rarely had a bad word for anyone. But Aga was a curious mix, because he did genuinely want the group to succeed. He was considerate of his partner, and yet you knew he would rat on you if a teacher questioned him. I began to revert to the playground way of judging people—who'd blab, who'd try and get revenge, whom I could trust to be a "best friend."

Two weeks into the course and they decided to toughen up a bit more. We'd suffered the slow anguish of muscular pain, now it was time to suffer the sharp pain of physical blows.

The strikes and blocks in aikido are meant to have force, but their role is to distract and soften up an opponent rather than to finish a bout, boxing style. Strikes in Japanese are known as *atemi*. Shioda senior, who learnt his streetfighting in the vice neighborhoods of pre-war Shinjuku, had pronounced that 70 percent of an actual fight was composed of *atemi*. Obviously it was no good having weedy civilian-style *atemi*, we were *senshusei*, so the *atemi* training would be hard.

Darren, the diffident Australian, was assigned the task of knocking our strikes into shape. Unlike Paul and Stephan Otto, the other assistant teachers, Darren sometimes admitted there were aikido moves he wasn't that good at doing. I knew that strikes wouldn't be one of them. Strikes were, in fact, one of Darren's specialties. Back home in Australia he'd practiced for hours bashing his forearm against tires, trees and even steel.

"Reckon it's pretty strong now," he used to say. "Probably break another man's arm with it." He talked dispassionately about his forearm, as if it were a tool or club, a blunt instrument and not a part of his living, breathing, easily mangled human frame.

Repeatedly striking the forearm against a hard object, like a wooden post, or against another forearm, causes further calcification of the bone and a deadening of the nerves in the arm. Along the way you are supposed to discover the correct way to strike, which is with a relaxed arm. No one told us this because this lesson wasn't about learning to strike properly; it was about willingly inflicting pain on yourself. Not knowing the correct way, we all struck with arms as stiff as iron girders and, after the first few blows, it hurt, with a very uncomfortable dullness, like an extreme ache.

In karate, practitioners deform themselves by repeatedly punching *makiwara*, or punching-boards. In kung fu they drive their hands into hot sand. Scarification and nerve damage follow in both cases.

Turning your hand into a nerveless club of battered flesh and bone seems a low-level approach to martial arts. It is the simplest way to improve the odds if one has little faith in speed and technique. Many tai chi masters eschew it as primitive. Others find the prospect of chronic arthritis at the age of thirty hardly worth the trouble of growing a huge distended knuckle.

Forearm strikes are more sophisticated. A strong strike sets up the correct feeling for an aikido technique. Strike training is also a good way to build up resistance to pain. It is only of secondary importance that you can break down doors and decapitate Doberman Pinschers with one deft swing of the mighty forearm. Or so the theory goes.

Tesshu, as a traditional warrior, believed that any blows received were a good opportunity for self-improvement. He instructed early morning tradesmen visiting his house to give him a punch "anywhere on his body." Eventually the tradesmen complained to Tesshu's brother that they were actually hurting themselves by having to punch Tesshu's hardened body.

We lined up facing each other. R'em's black eyes glinted with mischief and I couldn't help grinning at him. We swung our right arms behind our heads and smashed them together in front of us. This was a *shomen* strike, a front strike. Darren kept the count: "*ichi, ni, san, shi, go,*" and the strange half-strangulated noise he made when saying "*roku*" with his Australian accent.

We did ten on the right, then ten on the left. Then ten on the right and ten on the left. Every now and then R'em's bony wrist would hit mine. Fortunately it seemed to be hurting him just as much as me. I began to search for different parts of the arm which were relatively unbuttered. Darren put a stop to this: "It's not an elbow smash," he said, and demonstrated again by clubbing Aga a few times for good measure.

R'em winced with pain and I struck him more lightly. "No! Harder!" he hissed. "If we go easy now it will be too tough later on." He sounded as if he was talking from experience, maybe the Israeli army did things the same way.

Darren looked on with wry amusement. My arms were bright red from the beating they had received. I noticed an ominous blue bubble about the size of half a tennis ball raising itself on the inside of my left arm. Had I burst a vein? No more looking, I decided, staring instead at R'em's face; too much looking at battered flesh is bad for morale.

We now did 20 strikes against our partner before switching and striking the next man. Another 20 strikes and we moved on again. I became aware of a roaring, bellowing noise from farther up the line. Aga was yelling demonically like a trainee soldier doing bayonet practice. The racket was infectious. It's easier to convince yourself it doesn't hurt when you are shouting. This is the distraction-method of fighting pain, the preferred Western way. The preferred Eastern way is detachment. But this was no time for Buddhist reflection. I started to yell too. What the hell, I thought, I might as well let some steam off.

I faced Will, who looked steadfast, and we gave each other a respectable beating. There was no time to even check my exploding veins before Aga was in front of me. He seemed to have completely lost control. He was not even keeping to the count called by Darren. His face was contorted and his eyes were streaming with tears.

Darren urged us on. Stumpy urged us on. We urged each other on. Stumpy urged us some more with his favorite battle cry: "Come on, *senshusei*, dig deeper!"

I received a methodical hammering from the iron-hard arms of Little Nick, whom I also suspected of being a covert tree thumper. I wondered how much longer I would keep giving "sincerely hard" thumps as opposed to cosmetic swipes. But I was saved from this dilemma. Darren told us to stop.

For some reason everyone started grinning at each other. Huge grins of lamentable stupidity as we stood there rubbing our sore arms. The only people not grinning were Little Nick and Aga, who was still weeping. I later became used to these collective displays of emotion, but at that time it was still strange. I think we were grinning to show each other the aggression was not "really us." In fact we were like schoolboys who become the best of friends after a punch-up.

After the trauma of the forearm-strikes lesson, Danny suggested, in his simple, unaffected, but somehow batty way, it would be more "spiritual" if the group leader (which circulated each week) said "*otagai ni rei*" (all bow) and at the moment of bowing we all shouted "*oos!*" in a loud voice, bowed and slapped the ground in front of us. Surprisingly, everyone agreed. I agreed too, but not for spiritual reasons. It gave the end of a lesson something of a high point, drawing us together. We all slapped the ground in unison like worshippers at a spiritualist gathering in the deep South. It was a Western thing to do, an adaptation of a passive Japanese politeness into a form of rugby-team bonding. And how "in time" the group floor slap was gave an indication of how much the group was "pulling together."

The saying of "oos" at every conceivable occasion is common to most Japanese martial arts. To ignore an "oos" is the height of bad manners. A *senshusei* "oos" was supposed to be loud and full of vim. A frequent criticism of Adam was that his "oos" lacked commitment. He had been taught Japanese by his wife and a certain feminine style of pronunciation infected all his communication in that language. The *dojo* disciples mimicked his way of speaking, finding it a hilarious joke, but the teachers were harsher. They made Adam "oos" endlessly, but it still came out with a startled squeak as if someone had just pinched his behind.

After the collective bow and collective "oos" we all ran—*senshusei* did everything at the double—to get the brooms to sweep the *dojo* floor, which was swept after every class. As we gathered our brooms people showed each other the terrific bruising on their arms. Ben's arms were already black, with sickly yellow edging. I didn't want to look at the blue bubble, but I risked a quick glance and it had subsided a little.

Aga had completely recovered his confidence; he shamelessly reestablished his leadership of the group. It was as if he had never wept at all. "Yeah, I don't know what happened, somehow I just lost control of my eyes out there."

My body was changing. I was changing. The physical shell that surrounded me was growing, hardening, getting more defined by the month. A residual layer of waistlines had melted away, tendons began to stand out for the first time in years, muscles began to bulge. A quick pose in front of the mirror while cleaning the locker room: nice, very nice, the body as it should be, *Homo-activus* rather than his sofa-seated cousin *Homo-sedentarius*. I was careful not to be caught posing, though I knew we were all at it, checking ourselves out with ambiguous ardor, loving our new mirror images, the plates of muscle that connected our creaking joints together.

And I had grown to like pain. A certain sort of pain, a pain that was almost a pleasure. "Not a brandy and cigars kind of pleasure," as Mustard put it, "but a pleasure all the same." This pain was the pain you get from having a shoulder pinned to the ground at the end of an aikido move. Your partner held your arm and twisted it up behind your back, grinding your face further into the mat. The pleasure came from knowing that nothing was being broken, that you could "take it," that the shoulder was being stretched, taken to its own limit and then released just when you tapped out on the mat. Only teachers ignored a tap on the mat, bad-ass teachers like Chino who liked breaking limbs, but partners never did; one rapid tap was enough to get you away from the worst kind of shoulder pain. I was learning. I was becoming a connoisseur of pain.

When one of Tesshu's old commanders heard that Tesshu had the temerity to start his own sword school he flew into a rage. He burst into Tesshu's house and beat him around the head with his fists. Tesshu did not flinch, or even try to move away. Eventually the man tired of hitting Tesshu and left in a huff. When asked the reason for his nonresistance Tesshu explained: "It is essential to harden our bodies and this incident was simply another form of training. It was a contest of will, matching the pain in my head with the pain in his hands. Since he was the one who gave up, I am the winner."

Get Somebody Loose!

Sam Walker

In a summer when three separate hurricanes threatened the mainland of central Florida, Jim Mastropietro knew that precautions had to be taken. He laid down sandbags, boarded up windows, stockpiled nonperishables, and, of course, created a set of emergency provisions for his Rotisserie league in case of a power loss at the transaction deadline. Though Mastropietro had his roof torn off, and other owners had trees fall on their homes, not a single transaction was missed.

"We made it through," he says.

In the introduction to their 1984 book, the founders of Rotisserie baseball issued a warning: "It can be a wrenching experience, this transition from routine rooting to the burdens of ownership, and it has been known to bring on an intense sense of dislocation." When I first read this I had no idea what they meant.

I'm about to find out.

The first official game of the 2004 baseball season is a March 30 showdown between the Yankees and Devil Rays that's being broadcast live from Tokyo at 5 o'clock in the morning. If Halley's Comet, the space shuttle, and the first sunrise of the millennium weren't momentous enough to lure me out of bed before down, I was fairly certain that Rey Sanchez couldn't do the job.

But that morning, lying wide awake in bed at 2 minutes to 5, I decide to revise my original position. And in the third inning, when Sanchez cracks a single and puts my Rotisserie team on the board for the first time, I grab Louise, my semiconscious long-haired dachshund, and hoist her above my head like the Stanley Cup.

I used to think of baseball in April as something like a movie trailer—a montage of short scenes, perhaps significant or perhaps not, that tell you next to nothing about the plot. In any other year, nothing short of chicken pox could have compelled me to watch 6 games before May. But in the first full week of this season, I'm frustrated that I can't watch 6 games simultaneously.

Too fidgety for the sofa, I begin parking myself on a wicker stool four feet from the TV, where I'm able to "interact" with the broadcast. When Matt Lawton steps to the plate and rips Brad Radke's first pitch for a base hit, Whap! the Samsung buys it. When Jacque Jones whiffs on 3 pitches with runners at the corners, I unload a barbaric howl that sends my wife retreating to the bedroom with a book.

"You're so loud all of a sudden," she says.

For as much baseball as I'm watching in these early days, I don't have the slightest idea what the standings are, nor do I care. For the first time in my baseball fanhood, they're irrelevant. The Times and the Journal begin to pile up at the door while I spend most of my "news" time logged on to RotoWire and Rotoworld, the only media outlets one can depend on for saturation coverage of Mark Ellis and his torn labrum.

I have a new set of pet peeves: late games on the West Coast, broadcasters who mispronounce player names, highlights from the National League (who cares!), and most of all, the whole cowardly tradition of bunting. Quite often I can't figure out whether to cheer or boo. If Sidney Ponson strikes out David Ortiz, is that good? Some of my oldest prejudices shift out of whack. Most of the time, I fear and despise the Yankees as much as always, but every time my closer, Mariano Rivera, comes into the game, I might as well be Vinnie from the Bronx: "Go Bombahs!"

The Tout Wars standings are maintained and continuously updated by USA Stats. On the Tout Wars home page, there's a grid where each team's live stats are displayed in all ten statistical categories and their overall point totals ranked in descending order. At this early point in the season, the rankings are so volatile that a single save can cause a mind-boggling fluctuation. In the space of an hour, the Streetwalkers vault from eighth place to fourth and back down to ninth. It's like watching the equalizer display on your stereo while listening to A Chipmunk Christmas.

Bill Meyer, the evil genius who founded USA Stats, tells me his average customer spends 19 minutes on the site, which is a pretty remarkable total for cyberspace. Still, I'm convinced he's being modest. My average is closer to 19 hours.

My social life is in rigor mortis. Phone messages are piling up, dinner dates are being scheduled only for nights when I don't have any pitchers on the hill, and I'm already getting puzzled looks from the uninitiated. Picking up takeout one evening, I bump into Ian, my upstairs neighbor. We talk for a few seconds, then I excuse myself, telling him that I'm anxious to get back to the Orioles game.

"I didn't know you were an Orioles fan," he says.

"I'm not."

If the first full week of my first Rotisserie season was defined by one image, it was the sight of Dmitri Young, my $17 cleanup hitter and the only Tiger on my team, writhing in agony on the Astroturf in Toronto. On the replay I see that Young had tried to avoid a tag at second base while running at full steam. This is a pretty ambitious piece of ballet for any ballplayer, let alone a guy who weights 240 pounds, and Young executed it with all the grace of a Clydesdale on roller skates. He collapsed under his own weight and broke his fibula.

He's out for six weeks.

One of the competitive disadvantages of being a Rotisserie rookie is the inability to maintain perspective. Before the season, I'd been told a thousand times that at some point I would be tested. But watching the replays of Young's grisly flop, I'm not sure if this is the fulfillment of that prophecy or just a minor setback. Six weeks would put him back on the field in May, which doesn't sound so dire.

I sit down calmly at my computer to see what other Young owners are saying in the Rotisserie chatrooms, and the response is nearly uniform. They're about to drink hemlock. "When you lose Dmitri on the second day of baseball, that does make for some troubling times," says one post. "This always happens to me!" moans another.

Checking my messages, the condolences are rolling in. "Sorry about Dmitri," says my friend Hal. "Tough break with Dmitri—pardon the pun," writes Rick Fogel. I get a message from Lawr Michaels, the Zen master. "Breathe. Relax," he says. "If you make a move out of panic, you will create problems for yourself."

The phone rings. "What do you think?" Nando asks.

"I think we're *doomed.*"

The following day, Nando and I are running around the front office under a code orange. I decide to deal with the situation by making eight trade offers, all of them rash, and several of them dangerously stupid. Under the Tout Wars rules, deals can be made at any moment until the trading deadline at the end of August. Once two parties come to an agreement, all they have to do is send an e-mail to the league's volunteer commissioner, Rob Liebowitz, another expert player. If a deal seems woefully unfair and detrimental to the "expert" image of Tout Wars, he's empowered to reject it. But for the most part, I'm operating without a safety net.

Given that it's only the third day of the season, none of my opponents is much in the mood for deal making. Mat Olkin says he'll trade Aaron Rowand but only for two hitters in return. Lawr Michaels says it's too early for him to consider any trade that isn't "totally lopsided," and the cautious Jeff Erickson answers my tentative offer for Gary Sheffield by saying he'll "sleep on it." The only serious bite is from the intellectual Trace Wood, who seems intrigued by a deal that would send Josh Phelps to his team in exchange for Matt Lawton. Hearing this, I dial Sig in California to run the idea by him, and after taking a moment to load Zoladex, he's ready with a typically measured response. "No, No, No! That would be catastrophic!"

Ever since he prodded me to buy Phelps, the Toronto DH has become the flashpoint for our different philosophies. To Sig, Phelps was a stunning bargain at the draft and therefore a shining achievement in game theory. He was so pleased with Phelps, in fact, that he actually broke his scientific code of objectivity and Googled the guy. When he found an old interview in which Phelps said his favorite subject in high school was *Algebra*, Sig was hopelessly besotted. "We can't get rid of Phelps," he says. "He likes math!"

After 10 minutes of hollering at each other, Sig and I hang up in a deadlock. All of my scouting tells me Lawton is more valuable than Phelps, but my statistician has planted a seed of doubt. That night, before I can make up my mind, Lawton settles the matter by collecting two hits and a home run, prompting Trace Wood to pass on the deal. Josh Phelps, the algebra whiz, is officially staying put.

Now that I've exhausted all trade avenues, there's only one place to go to replace Dmitri Young: the market for free agents. In fantasyland, "free agency" doesn't connote the same glamour it does in the big leagues. Here, most of the signable players are minor leaguers who've just been called up or leftover scrubs who weren't claimed at the draft. The only time a bona-fide superstar winds up in this pool is if he's traded over from the National League.

At the beginning of the season, every Tout Wars teams gets a $100 "free-agent acquisition budget" for unaffiliated players. The auction takes place once a week on Fridays, and since the bidding is blind and everyone has the same $100 to play with, logic takes a back seat. Rather than calculating a ballplayer's precise value and pricing him accordingly, the challenge is to guess what the stupidest, most grossly irrational bid is likely to be and then to determine whether you're manly enough to top it. If you're not careful, it's possible to bid $20 on a player only to discover that you could have had him for a buck. The process is known as FAAB, an acronym that can be used as an adjective, a verb, and, more often than anything, an expletive.

When I call up the list of available free agents on USA Stats, I learn another rookie lesson. There are so many pitchers to choose from that they seem sort of like, well, taxicabs. Before the season, I'd been told that one of the reasons pitchers go so cheaply in Tout Wars is because there's always a ton of them available as free agents every week, but until now I'd never seen it with my own eyes.

After scrolling past all the arms for hire, I reach the list of available outfielders, which, in addition to its alarming brevity, reads like a list of cabin assignments at a camp for fat kids.

> Mendy Lopez
>
> Simon Pond
>
> Bubba Crosby

Lopez, of Kansas City, is quickly eliminated. Though he hit a home run on Opening Day, he's all but certainly headed to the minors. The next name, Toronto's Pond, is a mystery to me. All I know is that he put up some decent power numbers in winter ball. The third candidate, Crosby of the Yankees, is the most familiar, only because I'd been reading about him in the New York papers. After six long years in the minors, Bubba caught the attention of Yankees manager Joe Torre by hitting .357 at spring training and covering center field like a water spider. He'd been the last guy to make the team. Trouble was, Bubba hadn't played yet, and when a couple of injured teammates returned he was likely to be dropped.

The next day, forty hours after Dmitri Young broke his leg and one day before the weekly FAAB deadline, I'm standing next to Bubba Crosby in the Yankees locker room. The first thing you notice about Crosby, other than the fact that there's not a grain of dirt on his uniform, is that he looks like somebody's lost kid brother. He might well be five-foot-eleven as the program states, but only in spikes.

Now that he's made the major-league team, Crosby tells me, he's trying to shorten his swing to focus on making contact and getting base hits. He's determined to make things happen by taking walks, stealing bases, and scoring runs, rather than crushing the baseball into powder. If anything, he's given up on the idea of hitting a home run, which is exactly what we need until Young comes back. "I'm not gonna make any money in deep center field," he says.

The next day, with exactly one hour left to submit my free-agent bids,

I still can't decide. Sig has no meaningful data on these subjects. Nando likes Crosby because of his torrid spring, but I'm leaning toward Simon Pond, only because he seems at least physically capable of hitting home runs.

To break the stalemate, I pick up the phone and call Joe Housey, a former pitcher who's now working as a scout for the Chicago Cubs. Built like a lumberjack with a gruff sense of humor, he's the kind of guy who slaps you on the back and nearly knocks you over. I know that he covers Florida, where he'd surely seen both Pond and Crosby at spring training. When I reach him, he's on the golf course.

"Not now," he says, "I'm on the tee."

"Ten seconds?"

"Okay, go ahead."

"What do you think of Simon Pond?"

"He *stinks*."

"What about Bubba Crosby?"

"He's better."

"Thanks, Joe."

Hanging up, I type an e-mail to Commissioner Liebowitz and bid $1 of my $100 budget for Bubba Crosby. Minutes later, Crosby is a member of the Streetwalkers. Mine was the only bid.

About 2 hours later on Friday evening, the White Sox are thumping the Yankees in the Bronx. In the ninth inning, with the outcome all but certain, manager Joe Torre sends our man Bubba Crosby out for his first swing as a Yankee. With teammate Hideki Matsui on second base, Crosby shuffles to the plate, looking as if he'd just finished breathing into a paper bag. With 1 ball and 2 strikes, he uncoils his bat and belts a fly ball to right field that, to the surprise of everybody on earth, clears the fence.

Home run, *Bubba*.

He's not the first Yankee to homer on his first trip to the plate, but he's got to be the most unlikely. Circling the bases, Crosby runs so fast he nearly slams into Matsui's back. "I was just trying to calm myself down," he tells reporters after the game. "Being a rookie and playing in New York, my heart was racing." *SportsCenter* features a highlight of Bubba's blast, followed by a graphic comparing his relatively paltry $301,000 salary to the millions earned by teammates Jeter, Giambi, and Rodriguez.

As a reward for Crosby's Friday miracle, Torre puts him in the lineup on Sunday. It's his first start in pinstripes, and when he jogs out to center field the bleacher bums begin chanting his name. Inspired, Crosby makes a pair of spectacular catches, hurling himself against the outfield wall with abandon.

After grounding out on his first trip to the plate, Crosby comes to bat in the fourth inning with two runners on. He takes two balls from Chicago's Danny Wright and then, with a swing that nearly topples him, drives a ball through the damp April air that bounces off the facade of the *upper deck* in right field. Right before my eyes, the unwanted free-agent outfielder I picked up for one lousy FAAB dollar is taking a curtain call at Yankee Stadium.

The next morning, I buy all the papers. The *Times* puts the story on the front of the sports section. The Bergen County *Record* calls Bubba an "instant sensation," and a New York *Post* headline shouts: "Hubba Bubba!" Gary Sheffield calls Bubba a "throwback." White Sox manager Ozzie Guillen describes him as "the new Babe Ruth in town," and Torre raves like a proud papa. "It seemed like every other inning I was tipping my cap," Crosby said. "This day's pretty much tattooed in my mind."

Crosby is the toast of Tout Wars, too. Hollywood Matt Berry praises my pickup in his nightly blog, and Lawr Michaels gives me props in a column on CREATiVESPORTS. "Keep up the good work!" says Rick Fogel. More important, Crosby's 3-run home run vaults me up two places in the standings to seventh.

I'm quite aware Crosby isn't going to hit a home run in every game, let alone as many as a healthy Dmitri Young. There's still a chance he'll be back in the minors by the end of the month. But he's already given me something more important than a statistical boost: a new infusion of confidence. I'm going to be good at this game, because I know people.

In the pantheon of great sporting events, Red Sox at Blue Jays on April 22, 2004, would rank somewhere between lawn-mower racing and the featherweight championship of the world. At game time, the SkyDome is two-thirds empty.

Here in New York, it's one of the first glorious spring evenings. There are buds on the trees, tables outside the cafes, joggers on the sidewalks, and, for some reason, the faint smell of smoke. (It's an odd night for a fire.)

Nevertheless, I've canceled my dinner plans, turned off the cell phone, shut down the computer, and taken a seat on my wicker stool. In a first for my Tout Wars season, I have seven players starting in this game, including both pitchers, Curt Schilling and Miguel Batista. For me, this is appointment television.

By the fifth inning, Boston has a 3–1 lead, and the game is playing out swimmingly. Curt Schilling is cruising toward a win, and after a rocky start, Batista has gathered himself to retire ten Red Sox in a row. Better yet, every run that's crossed the plate was scored by one of my guys. As I watch Schilling ring up Toronto journeyman Howie Clark, I'm starting to think these pitching duels aren't so excruciating after all.

Just then, I hear a clamor on the sidewalk and, after a few minutes of trying to ignore it, run downstairs reluctantly to see what's the matter. When I return, Batista has been chased from the game, Schilling has just induced a fly ball to end the seventh inning, and the score is . . . tied?

In pitching duels, tie games are the ultimate nightmare scenario. If neither of your pitchers leaves the game with a lead, neither one gets the win, and by virtue of their scarcity wins are second only to saves in the Rotisserie food chain.

With Batista in the showers, Schilling is my only hope for a victory, which means that I should want to see him back on the mound when the game resumes. But now that he's already given up ten hits, I'm worried that he could be on the verge of imploding and dragging down my team's cumulative WHIP and ERA. Before I can come to any conclusion, there's a tight shot on the screen of Schilling, standing on the mound.

Ten minutes later, the bases are loaded, and seven of the last ten Toronto batters have reached safely. Schilling has given up 12 hits, only 2 shy of his career high, and Boston has two relievers getting loose in the bullpen. "That's gotta be it," I mumble to the television.

The camera pans to Boston manager Terry Francona, who's sucking on a wad of sunflower seeds and clearly thinking about skipping up the dugout steps to yank Schilling.

"Dude, get up!"

It's no use.

The only bright spot here is that the next Blue Jay to the plate is Chris Gomez, a guy who hit only 1 home run last season in 58 games. Even in his depleted state, Schilling should be able to get this joker out. As I watch, I'm crouched on my stool, leaning forward, and gripping two clumps of hair. It might as well be Gossage against Gibson in Game Five of the 1984 World Series.

Gomez works the count to one and one, and the sparse crowd in Toronto rises to its feet. Schilling looks whipped. He sets, kicks, and delivers a splitter that hangs up in the strike zone like a necktie.

CRACK.

Lawr Michaels once told me a story about the first time he played Rotisserie baseball, long before his Tout Wars title year. He was riding in the car with his second wife, Ava, listening to a game involving one of his pitchers, Kansas City's Mark Gubicza, who had walked a couple of batters with 2 outs. First there was an error, then somebody hit a single, and the runs started trickling in. "Get somebody loose!" he snapped. On cue, the announcer said the Royals didn't have anybody warming in the bullpen. "Fucking assholes!" he screamed, pounding the dashboard with his fist. "You don't have somebody warming, and it's the sixth fucking inning? You fucking assholes!"

Ava had never seen anything like this. The man she married was a gentle soul, a pot-smoking hippie with flowing locks and a taste for *Middlemarch*. "Lawr," she suggested softly, as he sizzled like a plate of fajitas, "maybe you need an outlet."

"This *is* my fucking outlet!"

I'd like to think my reaction to the Chris Gomez grand slam off Curt Schilling on April 22, 2004, was not quite so Paleolithic. As I try to stand up, preparing to do something violent to the television, my butt skids off the back of the stool and I land on the floor. With the SkyDome crowd screaming like a convention of mental patients, I fumble for the mute button and wrap my arms around the stool, hugging it while moaning. Outside in the street, meanwhile, there are three fire trucks, eighty gawkers, and a torrent of water rushing down the gutters from an open hydrant.

That earlier commotion outside was the response to a kitchen fire in the building next door. The moment the squad leader told me they had it under control, I'd whistled to my dog, headed back upstairs, waved the mist of smoke away from the television with a towel, and turned up the volume.

My wife, having just arrived home to witness the chaos out front, opens the apartment door and sees me crumpled on the floor, clutching my stool.

"Oh, my God, what happened?" she asks.

I raise my head long enough to say four words.

"Francona is an *idiot*."

Three weeks have passed since the "fire" incident, and I now consider myself a recovering Rotisserie maniac. I've had some time to reflect on my behavior the evening of April 22 and to appreciate the misapplication of priorities it demonstrated. I have returned to watching games quietly on the sofa. I have stopped smacking the television and promised my wife to call the fire department the next time our apartment walls are warm to the touch.

At the moment, I'm holding down a café table at Newark Airport eating a breakfast burrito and reading the box scores before catching a flight. In my peripheral vision I have just noticed a thin man in a blue shirt standing 20 feet to my left, taking an inventory of the slim pickings at the food court. After making eye contact with the guy, I have to force myself to turn away. The surest sign that you've had too much Rotisserie baseball is when you start "seeing" your players in the faces of random people in public. And this guy looks a little bit like Mariano Rivera.

Shaking it off, I return to the box scores where I see, to my great relief, that the Yankees are opening a series in Anaheim tonight, clear across the country. I glance back to see the guy who looks like Rivera walking down the terminal hallway, dragging his own black rolling bag. "Man, I need a shrink," I say.

About 2 minutes later, the incident all but forgotten, I hear an announcement over the terminal loudspeaker that makes me drop my tortilla. "In a few minutes we'll begin boarding Flight 287 with service to Orange County."

Abandoning my coffee and burrito at the table, I am suddenly run-walking as fast as my wheelie bag will allow. The Orange County gate is packed with passengers but no thin guy in blue. Then, sitting alone on the other side of the concourse, there he is. I watch him pull out a sleek cell phone and dial a number with movements that are so impossibly elegant, and an expression that's so unflappably cool, there's no longer any doubt.

In seven years of covering sports, I've seen Mo Rivera in person about thirty times. Next week, if I wanted to, I could sit down with him in the Yankees clubhouse and read him my favorite recipes for 15 minutes. Of all the people in this terminal, I should be the least starstruck. But in the last six weeks Rivera has become a significant figure in my life. He was the first member of my first Roto team and the first player selected in the Tout Wars auction. He's been working hard for me, nobly chipping away at his $27 auction price.

I wait politely for Rivera to finish his phone conversation, trying to look nonchalant while standing in the middle of the concourse and blocking traffic for no apparent reason. I'm not sure what to do, although it's hard to ignore the rush of adrenaline.

When he's off the phone, Rivera notices me. He's famous enough that he knows when he's been spotted by a baseball whacko, and he nods at me in a manner that's neither inviting nor rude. I could have introduced myself and reminded him that we've met before. I could have asked him how much movement he's getting on his cut fastball or just told him that he was doing a nice job for my Rotisserie team. But the sentence that comes out of my mouth is something I've never said to an athlete or, for that matter, anybody.

"Hey, Mariano. Can I get your autograph?"

Bad, Brutal Fun

Jeff MacGregor

The first time I drive the car it feels like rage, apocalypse in every cylinder, pistons hammering hot and remorseless as hell's forge, the manifold ravenous, roaring for air and explosives, belts shrieking, crankshaft screaming threats, spinning off metal shavings like a lathe, the oil tortured, a black ruin of subatomic corruption boiling in the spattered bowel, rods, valves, lifters, and springs flying apart, colliding and crashing back, the relentless cycling a hundred times a second, sickle on scythe, shrapnel clattering in the dark, anxious to fail, to escape, blazing, on razor wings, and the exhaust thundering fire and stench and the mourning blast of Armageddon—

"*Don't blow it up.*"

—all of it held together by nothing more than an idea, by the faded ink on an engineer's blueprint—

"*Don't blow it up!*"

—and like everything else in the universe, the inevitability of its own spectacular end was sown in the first moment of its creation—a big racing v-8 is all intricacy and vanity and the outrageous noise of self-love on the way to self-destruction—everything in this engine is beating itself to pieces. Jesus, this isn't a car, it's entropy, a fast unraveling of thermodynamics, it's the cosmic triumph of chaos, it's war!—

"I SAID, DON'T BLOW THE GODDAMN THING UP!"

Oh.

This time I hear him. I ease off the gas. He's leaning into my window while my car idles on the pit road, his face about an inch from mine. I've been revving the engine.

Perhaps more than is strictly necessary.

He's so close to me his nose is out of focus. He's in his late thirties, maybe, very tan and just at the end of handsome, with a slender face, sharp crow's feet framing bloodshot blue eyes, and big pink gumfuls of tiny white teeth. He has the kind of fine platinum blond hair that looks stunning on a ten-year-old girl but makes a grown man seem insubstantial somehow, tricky and about seven-eighths untrustworthy.

"REMEMBER YOUR EXTINGUISHER! 'COURSE, IF THERE'S A FIRE, I SAY SCREW IT! DROP THE NET AND GET OUT FAST! HAVE FUN!"

With that, he pulls his face back from mine, yanks my harnesses even tighter, shoots me a smile that never makes it to his eyes, and eases his shoulders back out the window. I didn't get his name. He's one of the ten or twelve employees here at the morning session of the Richard Petty Driving Experience. He tugs my window net up into place. The net's there to keep my left arm from flying out the window if the car starts tumbling down the track at 165 mph, like Petty himself at Darlington in 1970, when the 43 car got turned sideways and barrel-rolled seven or eight times with Mr. Petty's slender left arm flopping out the driver's window like the free arm of a bull rider, fully extended, circling wildly, while the car bucked and spun, shedding metal and rubber and churning up asphalt until you figured him for dead before the debris even stopped falling. Amazingly, he wasn't much hurt.

That experience, however integral to Petty mythology, isn't pictured in the brochure. We are here, instead, to scare ourselves a little, to show off, to pretend for 8 laps that we're racers, to do a dangerous thing without really doing it. In America this is possible. For $379, Visa or MasterCard. There are twenty of us.

We're in Orlando. Walt Disney World Speedway. Fantasy inside fantasy inside fantasy. The day starts at 8:00 a.m. in an infield classroom. Turn in our liability waivers and medical forms. Just in case. Half an hour of whiteboard instruction on safety, strategy, technique. Gas on/gas off. Half-attentive, we fidget in our seats. We want to get in the cars and *go*. How hard can it be? No camaraderie, just staring at the back of one another's heads. An inventory of male-pattern baldness. We are all of a kind here this morning, white guys on the crumbling brink of middle age—orthodontists, retail managers, salesmen, master plumbers. And one writer poised on a brink of his own.

Out the door, into the blast of that atomic Florida sun. Then a couple of fast laps on the tri-oval track in passenger vans with one of the instructors driving, six or seven of us piled in and hanging on like grim death behind him, as he shouts tips about angles of entry and apexes. There are orange highway cones at the entrance and exit to every turn—we're doing 70, 80 miles an hour, wallowing and squealing around the banking in what amounts to a senior-center ambulette on the worst ride ever to the respiratory therapy center.

"All you need to remember are the cones," he says as we stagger out of the van, weaving like we've been at sea. "The cones remind you when to let off and when to pour on the steam. 'Kay?"

Nauseated, we now gather beneath a trackside tent. We are given helmets and sanitary helmet liners, little white cotton yarmulkes—to absorb the Brylcreem, presumably—and coveralls in Petty's famous medium blue. We look like fat, excited children wearing medieval skullcaps and novelty pajamas. The cars, pure sex, the reason we came, are just on the other side of the low pit wall.

One by one we're going to get in those cars and drive them as fast as we can, following an instructor in another car around the track. "Git tucked in right behind him, now. Stay on him like a tick." First, though, the driver introductions.

Mimicking the canned excitement that precedes every big league stock car race, a voice introduces each of us over the P.A. system. Every balding man-child in his officially licensed fireproof PJs gets his turn at stardom as his name is shouted out over an obligato of arena rock.

Unlike drivers in the Big Show, however, we are not then humbled by the ovation of a quarter-million ardent fans. We blush, rather, at the bland applause of nineteen indifferent strangers and a few of their sunburned wives and children while we walk 12 feet from one side of the tent to the other. The infrequency with which his own children bring their hands together for Dear Old Maximum Dad, to say nothing of the nearly audible rolling of their little Oliver Twist eyes, would indicate that in some degree their applause is to be taken ironically.

Helmets cinched tight, jowls bulging, the first two drivers are led to their cars. They struggle to squeeze themselves in through the driver's window. They fiddle with the safety harnesses. Then they're gone.

Two instructor-student pairs are sent out half a lap apart, so there are always four cars on the track. We have been divided into four teams, on the theory that we will pull together to post the fastest aggregate team time, thereby earning brag-and-swagger rights and a complimentary four-by-six color team photo in a decorative cardboard sleeve. The Petty folks want us to have a rooting interest in our teammates' performances. We do not. We will remain strangers until the day we die. Team member or not, we mock and kibitz about the others as they orbit the track.

"He's too far behind the instructor. He's not getting the draft. Slow-poke."

"Yeah, that's some chickens—— bulls——all right. You gotta tuck right up in there."

"Christ, he even *sounds* slow."

The one thing no one wants to do is drop the clutch and stall the car as he's trying to pull away. Of course, some do.

"Weakling!"

"Candy ass!"

"Oh, you gutless sumbitch!"

Per the dentist, so much for team building. That's for sniveling middle-management lickspittles on corporate outings anyway, not for Rebel heroes and Yankee hot shoes and men who stare down gingivitis every goddamn day.

After 8 laps run at increasing speeds, the cars roll back onto the pit road.

The drivers are helped out of their harnesses and hauled out through the small windows and walked back to the tent while the next pair of students jogs to the car. Flushed with what they've just done, the returning heroes are red-faced and engine-deaf and loud with excitement.

"Man, that was just unbelievable!"

"Incredible! Just incredible!"

"WHAT?"

"I said it was UNBELIEVABLE!"

"OH, YEAH! INCREDIBLE!"

Then, invariably, overwrought with recreational adrenaline and caught up in the moment, Maximum Dad hugs the wife and tries to high-five one of his kids. And while the wives are tolerant enough ("I'm just happy to see him happy," I heard one say, "especially for 379 G.D. dollars"), the kids want very little to do with that big sweaty palm. The younger ones suffer Daddy's new enthusiasm with a flaccid, noncommittal hand, but the adolescents, knowing the rudiments of public cool, blush with shame. One, a girl about thirteen, refuses entirely. Her father comes at her with that high-five raised like he's won the Super Bowl, and she just stares at him like he's exposing himself at the junior sock hop. I have never seen a man look sadder than he did in that instant, high-five hanging there unreturned and the future all at once upon him.

This is the moment when the instructors announce that another 8 laps can be had for only $249 American, and lots of the dads start digging for their wallets, anxious to get back in the car, where there is only speed and freedom, and where time, paradoxically, stands still.

I am beckoned to the pit wall by an instructor. With my helmet on, all I can hear is the rumble and buzz of the cars and the quickening pulse of the blood pumping in my ears. *Lubdub. Lubdub.* He points me to a car.

It is small. On television the cars seem huge, monstrous, in part, I think, because of all those low-slung onboard camera shots, the wide-angle lens in the rear end of one car looking back at 200 miles an hour to another car nosing up behind it so that it fills the entire frame and blocks out the very sky. But everything you've ever seen on television looks bigger and grander than it really is—let's face it, that's what television's for. Any video engineer will tell you that it's a function of the aspect ratio of the screen, that things appear proportionately wider than they really are, and farther apart (Matt and Katie and Al are practically sitting on top of each other every morning!) but that misses the point. Mythology, not technology, is what makes these cars big.

The real thing, though, is small. Lower and sexier than what you'd see in the showroom, wide at the front and rear, slender and sculpted at the waist, it's still based on a midsized Detroit sedan, and when you stand next to it your first reaction might be disappointment—mine was—mingled with a bright excitement and the dark fear that I'd screw the pooch in front of that dentist.

Long ago, when these cars were hot-rodded on the cheap from showroom models, the racers would tie their doors shut with a length of rope or a belt—or, like Elly May Clampett, the rope they used as a belt—so they wouldn't fly open during a race. Eventually they started welding them shut. Now the cars are built without doors, so Maximum Dad's first challenge, and mine, is to climb into the car through the driver's-side window. Watching the men who preceded me, there seem to be two ways to do this.

One: Lift the right leg up as high as you can. Now higher. *Higher*. Now, right foot into cockpit. Right foot onto car seat. Two hands on roof. Lift left leg. Crush testicles on windowsill. Pause. Breathe. Left leg up high. Higher. *Higher*. Bend left leg. Fold into cockpit. Unfold. Crush testicles on steering wheel. Pause. Breathe. Slither down into seat.

Or, Two: Lift right leg. Right foot into cockpit. Two hands on windowsill. Bend forward at the waist. Farther. *Farther*. Now lever torso into cockpit. Reel in left leg. Smack face on steering wheel. Fall across roll-cage crossbar and crush testicles on fire extinguisher. Pause. Breathe. There.

Eventually it dawns on some of us to wait for the instructor to remove the steering wheel before we get in. That's why the steering wheels are removable.

Compounding the entry problem is the horse collar they tell me to put on right before I climb in. It works just like a neck brace to limit the range of motion between your head, neck and shoulders. This will be helpful in a crash, but it also limits the range of your vision when you're trying to hoist your testicles over the windowsill over the car, which explains the strangled screams of my classmates.

The cockpit of a stock car is small, too, of course, nearly claustrophobic.

Tucked tight in the seat, you're surrounded by the thick tubing of the roll cage. The seat is designed to hold you almost immobile, so you don't go sliding all over the place when you're running 150 mph on the track and the Gs are pulling you out toward the wall. The seat also restricts your range of motion in a crash, so you don't go ragdolling all over the inside of the car. The seat seems to grip you from the back of your head all the way down to your calves. It's like falling over backward into a giant pile of modeling clay; when you're idling on pit road, it's a restrictive feeling, but on the track at a buck and a half the seat feels natural and necessary. Cup drivers, like astronauts, all have seats custom-molded to fit them.

The tubular-steel roll cage runs around the entire interior of the car. It's there to prevent the cockpit, and the driver, from being crushed in an accident. It also makes it impossible to see out of the car through anything but the windshield or the rearview mirror, which is fine since you can't move your head in any case.

Like an amusement park fun house, everything in the cockpit of a stock car is comically scaled. The steering wheel is the size of a manhole cover. The gearshift lever comes up out of the transmission hump like a sight gag, as long as your arm. The tachometer, a gauge the size of a pie pan for reading your engine speed, is, in this car, centered above the steering wheel. Strung along the dashboard are seven or eight other gauges so small as to be useless, even if I knew what they were for.

The entire interior is sheet metal painted with a couple of coats of gray semigloss primer. Worn down to bare steel in places, the interior of my car shows a lot of use. Down near the firewall, just a few inches behind the engine, the pedals are tiny and very far away. My right foot knows why it's here, though, and immediately begins tickling the accelerator. The throttle-return springs on racing cars are stout, like the springs on the screen door of a west Texas bunkhouse, and it takes more than tentative pressure from a nervous foot to make any real noise. Flexing your foot forward from the ankle, the way you do it in your Maximum Dad minivan, isn't going to get it. You need to put your leg into it.

Once you do, the results are very satisfying. The whole car resonates as the engine spins faster. You come up out of that mudlumpy vibration you get at idle with a big racing v-8, the exhaust thumping so arrhythmically that you can't focus your eyes, and you begin to get that urgent, perfect frequency of everything spinning and oscillating and pounding in harmony. Your vision clears, and the exhaust rumble tightens into a growl into a whine into a scream.

The sound of a race engine is the biggest part of its appeal, I think, even more than the power it might actually deliver. There's excitement in that noise, of course, and brutality and the promise of bad fun, and for those who love cars and racing and speed, the sound of it is what grabs you first and it grabs you low in the belly and shakes you hard. A big v-8 sounds like America.

The ridiculous steering wheel is angled nearly straight up and down like a ship's wheel and almost brushes the top of my thighs. I am trying to figure out how to overcome this, and relentlessly revving the engine, and musing absently on the nature of chaos and internal combustion when that blond man sticks himself in the window and buckles my five-point harness.

Shoulders, hips and peevish man-tackle all have their own heavy, webbed belts to secure them. All the belts meet at a quick-release locking mechanism just below my navel, and when Blondie cinches them down, he's not kidding. I can barely breathe. He's also not kidding when he yells that reminder not to blow the car sky-high before I even get going. And, last of all,

"*REMEMBER YOUR EXTINGUISHER! 'COURSE, IF THERE'S A FIRE, I SAY SCREW IT! DROP THE NET AND GET OUT FAST! HAVE FUN!*"

And while I'm wondering if anyone's ever died doing this—if any Maximum Sansabelt Dad from Pleasant Valley, USA, has ever come here for a morning's fun and instead gotten loose at speed and lost the rear end and gone hard into the wall fully locked in a hopeless slide, bracing his

JEFF MACGREGOR

feet against the firewall and watching the infield and the wall and the infield and the wall spinning past him, the tires screaming and sending up billows of yellow white smoke, the Gs twisting him in the seat until the movement of absolute deceleration, instantaneous, 50 Gs in the opposite direction, and in the same second hearing the terrible noise of the impact and the utter quiet that follows it and people running and the car rolling slow and broken down the bank of the track—the instructor in front of me pulls away. *Don't think and drive.* I'm already behind.

Left foot hard to the floor, I slam the shifter all the way left and forward—*Whatever you do, don't stall in front of the dentist, don't stall, don't stall!*—right foot hard to the floor, left foot up to drop the clutch, light the tires, up through the gears out of the pits, I'm thrown back in the seat—*lubdublubdublubdub*—lift that right foot a quarter of an inch, left foot hard to the firewall on a clutch sprung like a squat rack, the shifter throw laughably, impossibly long, slam it a yard and a half back into second, right leg locked again, foot back to the floor, power shifting, the acceleration almost yanking my hands off the wheel, the noise fantastic, the carb gaping wide open and gulping fuel and air up front and the exhaust thundering unmuffled out of the headers down by my left hip, wind ripping through the netting now, out of the pits and onto the track apron, steering hard left with both hands because the car wants to go right, up the track into the wall (!), steer hard left with both hands—*lubdublubdub*—hard left foot for the clutch, feather the throttle, right hand off the wheel, yikes! Grab the shifter, throw it right and up to the dash, slam it into third, back hard on the gas—*stay on the gas*—coming out of the second turn now, down off the bank, the car bouncing on the shocks and drifting right, floating out toward the wall, right foot to the floor, halfway up the backstretch and running at redline, grab the shifter and pull all the way back and right and at last I'm in fourth gear, and by the time I'm into the bottom of the third turn I'm running 90 miles an hour.

I've also caught the instructor. This would be a good time to lift my right foot, so I do, barely feathering the pedal so I don't rear-end him. You're supposed to stay close, but ramming your instructor—much less bumping him up the track out of your way and then slipping under him for the win, Rusty Wallace–style—is discouraged.

My instructor's name is Chad. Running down out of the fourth turn, I'm tucked up right behind him. A single car length off his bumper. I'm not scared, but I'm *very* busy. And ricocheting between sensory deprivation and input overload.

I don't have to worry about shifting anymore, but the steering wheel has every bit of my attention now. The principles of driving a stock car on an oval track are as simple as you imagine. Gas on/gas off, and turn left. The physics of it, though, and the sensation of it—the stress and effort of it, the very things that make it so challenging—are the things for which you're utterly unprepared.

Howling down the frontstretch now, for example, I'm trying to inventory what I can actually see. It isn't much. I can see the hood of my car, sort of, the short blur of track between my car and the one in front of me, the rear window of Chad's car, and the back of Chad's car seat. I can just see the top of his helmet. I have a general idea that somewhere in front of him is more race track, and the horizon, but I'm not actually seeing it so much as remembering that it's out there. My eyes have got their hands full. The faster you run, the more your field of vision narrows and the shorter it becomes, until everything in the world telescopes down to the 40 or 50 feet in front of your car in an arc about 10 feet wide. That the shatterproof windshield is etched with scratches and smeared with oil and explodes with glare every time the sun hits it doesn't make the driving any easier.

Seeing things inside the car is even harder. Everything is vibrating like mad and my head's vibrating like mad and banging side to side as centrifugal force is pulling me and all my soft tissue up, up, up to the right at a couple of times the force of gravity, and where the dashboard and the gauges used to be is only a colorful Impressionist painting of a set of instruments. By tightening my jaw muscles and stiffening my neck and concentrating on the immense tachometer, I can just make out the orange needle pointing to about the nine o'clock position. In the time it takes me to see it, though, I've run 100 yards down the track at well over 100 miles per hour with no idea of what was in front of me. I could be picking shards of instructor out of my grill. No more looking at the gauges. I can hear the exhaust noise and that's all. The pitch changes a little when I move my right foot. I can feel the lubdubbing in my ears, but I can't actually hear it. As we come up on the end of my first lap, I'm lubdubbing like Krupa drumming the first eight bars of Sing, Sing, Sing.

The front straight of a tri-oval track isn't strictly straight but in fact has a very gentle dogleg in it. At the apex of that dogleg, at least here at the Disney track, is the start/finish line. You don't turn hard, but you do aim your car for the inside of the track so as to make the shortest route possible from the exit of Turn 4 back to the first turn. By the time Chad and I run across that line nose-to-tail, we're probably running 110 mph or so. There's no speedometer, of course, and I couldn't read one if there were.

Going hard into the first turn now, I catch a glimpse of the orange cones at the base of the wall. Chad's car slows slightly in front of me. I lift my right foot a quarter of an inch. Gas off. Sort of. My hands and arms are cranked full left on the wheel to make the turn. Oops. Still going straight. Lubdub. Heading for the wall. Lubdub. If I don't hit Chad first. Lubdub. I take my foot off the gas altogether and the car dives left, back to the bottom of the turn, but I've lost some momentum so I stomp the pedal back to the floor. By now I'm halfway through the second turn. This is where the rear end of my car starts to ease loose. Lubdublubdublubdub.

"Gas on/gas off" is more complicated than it first appears. Having gone into the turn too hot and stabbing the gas to catch Chad while my arms and hands are still locked over to the left means that I'm now powering the rear end of my car from under myself.

I can feel it in the seat of my pants and in my stomach, and down there it feels just like the first time I spun my dad's vw Squareback in a snowy parking lot or dropped a motorcycle on a rain-slick sidestreet. Sick and exhilarating. The parallel ends there. This time I'm crossing up at 100 mph with 3,400 pounds of car sliding around under me.

I correct by spinning the wheel back to the right, steering into the imminent skid and pulling my idiot foot off the throttle. Now I'm headed for the wall, so I wrestle back left into that impending slide. Where any of this is coming from I have no idea. Kinesthetic instinct roused by panic, perhaps. Latent genius. Dumb luck. But it's just like in the driver's-ed film! Except for the part where I hammer the gas again as hard as I can as soon as the car straightens up. By the time we're down the backstretch, I've reeled Chad in and started breathing again. That Chad is being paid to let me reel him in seems unimportant.

Into Turn 3. Smooth this time. Gas off. Muscle the wheel left.

Halfway through the bottom of the turn, the car starts to straighten up and I pound my right foot down. *That's it.* Chad and I roll down out of the fourth turn a car length apart. Hard down the straightaway.

Into Turn 1. Gas off. Steer. Gas on. Fast. Smooth.

Smooth is a relative term. For a stock car, *smooth* can mean simply that you weren't knocked unconscious by the headrest as you pounded around the track. The car seesaws and wallows and pogos all at once, and violently. A racetrack may look flat, especially on TV, but none of them are, and every surface imperfection is transmitted directly up through that stiff, stiff suspension into your ass and your hands and your brain. A race car doesn't feel right until it's running at speed, and then the ride is purposeful and brutal. Even with power steering, sawing the wheel back and forth to keep the car on the right line is mentally and physically exhausting.

By the time I've made my fourth lap of the one-mile-plus track, I'm pouring sweat. It's in the mid-70s outside, but in here it's closer to 100 degrees, even with the side windows missing. Down by my feet, next to the firewall, it's more like 125 degrees. I've been on the track a little less than four minutes, and I'm spent.

But the sensation of this kind of speed is electrifying, and by the time we circle the track for the fifth time Chad has upped our speed to 130 or so on the straights. If Cup racers ran this track they'd be a third again as fast. I'm running on adrenaline now, and cocky from having kept death at bay for four endless minutes, I start edging my car up so close to Chad's that he waves me off. He raises his hand in front of his rearview and moves it back and forth, lazy and slow—the signal to stop tailgating—and it now occurs to me that while I'm back here struggling to keep up with him, strangling the wheel and yanking it side to side in effortful spasms, kicking at the gas pedal like I'm trying to kill a snake, gasping for breath, heart drumming away, he's up there in front of me going into the turn, the death turn, with one hand on the wheel. He's probably whistling.

In these last few laps, gathering speed and something like confidence, I try to make my entries and exits, conveniently marked by the giant orange cones, gas on/gas off, with something like grace. Once you're over the initial shock—the sensory overload that has you driving that first handful of laps with nothing but your inner ear, your bowels and the reptile core of your brain stem—there's even time to think.

This car is a pig. That's what I'm thinking. This isn't some nimble, responsive little sports car you can flick back and forth with surgical precision on different lines through the turns. It isn't some luxo Japanese ultracar, either, silent and slippery and fast, all silicon-chip efficiency and Tom Swift gadgetry and motherboard performance, polite as an appliance. This thing is a grunting thug, as dim-witted and overmuscled and clumsy as they come. It's a workout to keep the beast running straight, the wheel cycling vaguely in your hands while the nose of the car wanders down the track. There's an arc of about 30 degrees at dead center where the steering wheel can be wrestled back and forth with no discernible effect on your trajectory. The steering assembly has more slop in it than a Tobacco Road hog trough.

Granted, this is a rental unit, the stock car equivalent of a theme park ride, and after a couple of months of hard use in the clammy, clenched hands of overeager money-market managers and cops and bakers and urologists, there's bound to be some play in the linkage, but the fact is, these race cars are brutish and primitive and imprecise from the moment they're built. Maximum Dad's embarrassing Windstar or anonymous late-model Camry (to say nothing of the designs in other popular racing series, like Formula One, or the CART or IRL championship cars) is more technologically sophisticated than a Cup racer by several orders of magnitude. A Cup racer is old-school shop class, simple as brick.

That engine hammering away in front of me is powerful, certainly, but then it has to be to drag the backbreaking weight of all this antique cast iron around the track. And once it gets all that bulk pointed in a particular direction, it's damned stubborn about changing its mind. The brakes, for example, seem largely decorative, and simply turning left starts an argument with the car you can't really win.

This despite the fact that the cars are engineered to ensure that they can't do anything but turn left. They even sit cockeyed on the frame. The right side of the car rides higher on the springs than the left side, and the rear rides higher than the front. Seen from behind, at rest on pit road, the cars all sit tilted from the high right rear to the low left front, rakish as Sinatra's hat brim. At speed, then, with centrifugal force at work on them, they should want to dive smoothly into a left turn and then ride level all the way around its banked radius. No one seems to have explained this to the car, though.

Hard as I try to let the car have its head, it isn't very interested in carving neatly into the turns. Depending on my speed, it either plunges for the infield—Yikes!—or spits the bit and bolts for the wall, lubdub. You really steer the car with the throttle. The car's comic book geometry makes it incredibly sensitive to speed, but horsing that laughable wheel around only seems to make it angry. The constant corrections required to track through the turns are hardest on your arms, your shoulders and your patience. The only thing harder to drive is our motor home.

That I have any unassigned higher brain RAM left to even consider the efficiency with which the car handles comes as something of a surprise to me. On the sixth lap, coming down the backstretch at 140 or so, I notice something else. It doesn't feel like I'm going very fast. This is at least in part because I'm getting used to it. But it also has to do with being 15 feet away from another car going the same speed. If I were out here alone at 140 or 145, I'd be screaming as if I'd been scalded, but tucked in behind Chad, my eyes focused on the back of his car, the speed feels apt, proportional, manageable; no worse than going 60 in moderate traffic on the interstate. Only by stealing a peripheral look at the palm trees stuttering past do I have any real sense of how fast I'm going.

I have no sensation of turning individual laps, either, no sense of a discrete 1-2-3-ness. Rather, it feels as if we're running along a continuous infinite surface, an immense, hypnotic, Möbius strip, along which at intervals recur the same flagman and palm trees and tents and buildings. It's hard to describe, but it feels like one long, seamless process rather than a series of divisible events. And it feels good.

JEFF MACGREGOR

This is the feeling I paid for when I signed up for the class. The Maximum Dads, too. This is the feeling you're trying for when you mash the accelerator at a suburban stoplight or when you're running two dozen clicks past legal on the interstate. This is the feeling they're selling you in those car commercials and in all those video games. It is the feeling of disembodied, concentrated velocity, velocity without consequence, speed freedom—you with your foot to the floor outrunning whatever it is that's after you. You are pure sensation, heart in your throat, internal gyro spinning at the base of your spine, deafened by speed and nearly blinded by it, your vision tunneling down to nothing, your immediate future rushing at you very clearly for a change, as if seen out of the long, hard dark of a shotgun barrel. You are empty—happily, peacefully empty—of everything but the present moment.

Thus, way out past that initial panic, and past the breathless effort of working the car, and way out past the novelty and specificity of driving this car on this lap at this track on this day in this year, lies a few seconds' worth of near-transcendence.

Not that you've shucked self-awareness exactly, or overcome your own piddling and loathsome consciousness. The banal monologue always running in your American head, about your next chicken dinner or the erratic pendulum of your self-esteem or why in the world is Oprah reading *Anna Karenina*, is still whispering, but it's drowned out by the engine noise and the pounding in your ears. Wrestle that snarling mother-effer around the track long enough and you'll drive yourself, if only briefly, to Walden Pond.

It is a version of the experience described ad nauseam on television by adrenaline junkies and extreme-sport thrill-seekers—skydivers, BASE jumpers, free climbers, contestants on *Fear Factor*—in which your squalid little life is briefly reduced to its most primitive psychomotor essentials, and your struggle for personal fulfillment and human dignity is at last made meaningful by endeavoring to soil your fire suit without actually killing yourself. The ennobling effects of recreational terror. An entire industry within our mighty national entertainment complex has been built around it. Extreme sports, extreme theme parks, extreme cruises, extreme fabrics for your extreme technical outerwear, extreme soft drinks. When did they start building climbing walls at the mall?

Only by tugging hard on the trouser cuffs of the infinite can we feel truly alive, the squids and grinders and big-wave surfers tell us; the rest of life is just an unhealthy accretion of errand-running, wage-earning and summers at band camp. The proximity of calamity is what scrubs that callus off your spirit; danger exfoliates your soul.

The quality of your life can only really be measured against the imminence of your death. A philosophy, I'd guess, at which most combat soldiers can only snicker. Before they punch you out.

And while it's certainly true that we might all invigorate ourselves through the rare scrape with death ("I've never felt more alive!" is the line they teach at Hollywood Boulevard Screenwriters Polytechnic to delineate such moments), history more often teaches that prolonged exposure to mortal risk does one of two things. It either desensitizes you to the experience or it drives you insane.

In other words, transcendence out here on the track is possible, perhaps even inevitable, but it is fleeting. And maybe that's enough here in our Sensation Nation.

It is pleasant to get out of my head, though, however briefly, as you might imagine, and drive a hired car much too fast. As proof of same, I spend laps seven and eight with the nose of my car pretty much tucked under the rear roll pan of Chad's car. I'm hoping he'll pick up the pace a little, because, desensitized to the life-threatening nature of what I'm doing as per the above, I believe we should be going a whole lot *faster*. They warned us about this, of course, and insisted that closing in on the instructor would not result in higher speeds. "DO NOT run down the instructor," I believe the emphatic phrase was. "He's going to go as fast as HE thinks you can go, not as fast as YOU think you can go." Still, I'm hoping Chad will make an exception for me, having seen in his rearview mirror my manifest talent for all this.

Sadly, he does not. No matter how far up under him I drive, no matter how elegant a line I follow around the track, no matter how nonchalant

I now seem as I wrench the big wheel to and fro, Chad does not quicken our pace. In fact, he spends our final two laps waving me off with all the indifferent languor of an embarking French sailor leaving his wife and children behind on a Marseilles dock. His wave says, "I see you, *bébé*, but I do not care."

After the eighth lap I follow Chad onto pit road, coasting, as instructed, in neutral, using only the car's brakes to slow down. Overweight as the car and I are, the brakes do nothing. The car doesn't really decelerate, it just loses interest. Brake pedal to the floor, I nearly tap Chad on the turn back into the pits, then come close to mowing down the tricky blond as he waves me into my parking spot. Eventually the car succumbs to its own weight and rolls to a stop.

Blondie shoots me another vampire smile and takes down the window net. "How what is?" he shouts.

"INCREDIBLE!" I hear myself screaming. "UNBELIEVABLE!"

Unhitched from the harnesses I struggle out of the car so the next guy can take my place. I resist the impulse to throw him a high-five as he jogs past.

Back in the tent I give my wife the mandatory post-Experience hug, which, adrenaline assisted, comes off more like a chiropractic adjustment.

Another few students make their laps as the morning winds down. Having stripped off my jumpsuit and my yarmulke, I wander off to make some notes.

When the last Dad unfolds himself from his car, we gather very briefly for the closing ceremonies. They are understated. As the families chatter and mill around the tent, one of the instructors thanks us all for coming and points us to the photo trailer on the way out, in case we want to buy souvenir albums of our day at the races.

A moment later yet another Petty employee approaches me. She presses into my hand a small photograph in a decorative cardboard sleeve. I open it. There in front of a race car I stand with four strangers. We are all smiling and looking straight into the lens. Embossed below the photo in tiny letters: THE WINNING TEAM.

My fastest lap, according to the accompanying printout, was run at an average speed of 124.60 miles per hour. In my ringing head I am convinced that I am the fastest man in that tent. They do not announce anyone else's speed, though, probably to prevent fistfights among the wives and children, so I'll never know for sure. But I know I could have gone faster, so much faster. I will have to satisfy myself instead with being part of the Winning Team. Which sucks compared to individual glory. I brag to my wife, and briefly swagger, but I buy no additional photos.

Our last responsibility before we scatter and return to our separate lives is to fill out a customer response sheet. I grade the whole day very highly and promise to recommend the place to my friends if I ever get home. In the space for suggestions I write two things:

> "Scariest part of the experience was the Porta-Potty."
> and
> "Chad needs to drive faster. So much faster."

But there's something else, too. A small realization. I do not comment on it, because I get the sense suddenly that it's a common enough phenomenon out here. In fact, I suspect that almost every driver who comes here walks away feeling something similar—by their expressions I can tell that a couple of them have caught the same thought and that it excited and then confused them.

Driving a race car? Driving it really fast? Driving it way out past whatever limits the law sets for you on the streets, or way out past whatever limits you've drawn for yourself in your own head? It just didn't seem that hard.

Don't misunderstand—I'm not saying that it's not dangerous, or that doing it week in and week out professionally doesn't require a set of specific, original gifts and long training, or that any Tom, Dick, or dentist can just pick up a helmet and run in the lead pack at Talladega.

I'm only saying that there's a moment after you've gotten out of the car when the voice in your head whispers, I could do this. And for a second or two this is incredibly exhilarating. But in the next instant, the fall back to Earth: Well shee-it, if I can do it, how hard can it be?

For a peek at your dream, you've squandered your innocence.

Our daily familiarity with driving a car breeds not only that initial heroic delusion ("I can drive!") but also leads immediately to the contempt that follows ("Who can't?"). I think it's that very intimacy, our collective love affair with the car, that accounts, at least in part, for NASCAR's popularity. Most Americans can relate more directly to driving than to almost anything else in sports. Driving too fast? You did that last night on your way home from work. And you'll do it again tomorrow.

As we lumber away in our motor home, headed for Daytona and the first race, the biggest race, of the NASCAR Winston Cup season, my wife has two suggestions for me:

"Stop yelling."

and

"Slow down."

Dragon Boat Racing

Unleash the Dragon ... Boats

Dan Washburn

Back. Arm. Shoulder. Side. Backside. Legs. Did I say back? Perhaps it would be easier to list the parts of my body that weren't sore after my first dragon boat paddling practice less than two weeks ago: .

There. You see, all the right parts were sore, but so too were most of the wrong parts. My stroke was bad at the beginning of practice and poor at the end. But that was to be expected, I was told.

"There is a learning curve, and it doesn't come as easy as you might think," admitted Richard Stokes, who captains the AT&T Dragoneers—my team for this Saturday's Hong Kong Dragon Boat Festival of Atlanta on Lake Lanier. "The technique is not what you would choose to do if you just sat down in a boat. It's not intuitive, but it's logical." Logical? I think I was absent the day we learned dragon boating in high school gym class. You too? Well, just in case, here's a little background for those not down with the dragon.

The Internet purports dragon boat racing—which dates back to China circa 400 BC—to be the oldest continuously raced sport in the world. With more than 1 million teams competing worldwide today, dragon boat racing is the second most popular sport on Earth.

Who knew?

All of the furor is focused on a 40-foot wooden canoe with a carved dragon tail and heads affixed to stern and bow. The boat seats twenty uncomfortably: steerer and drummer occupy either end, while eighteen paddlers punch their paddles into the water in unison at more than 80 strokes per minute.

No, I am not my team's drummer. Not yet, at least. But the pressure is on.

Stokes's Dragoneers have won the Atlanta race—a qualifier for August's nationals in New York City—all five years of its existence. No doubt who the paddles will be pointed at if this year's outcome is not the same.

And the drummer's seat at the front of the boat is taken—so there can be no demotion for me. More of a hood ornament than a rhythm keeper anymore, Dragoneers drummer Parisa Johnston likes her vantage point just fine. "When I see the pained expressions on the paddlers' faces," Johnston said, "I'm happy to be sitting right where I am."

Today marks my fourth practice with the team, and I am still trying to get sore in all the right places, still trying to master—or, if nothing else, mimic—the proper stroke.

At least there are others in the same boat, so to speak. Ethan Johnson, a rowing coach at Georgia Tech and another Dragoneer rookie, rubbed his shoulder and winced a bit after practice number 1. "It's definitely different," said Johnson, twenty-four. "In rowing I'm used to a lower stroke rate, a different technique. This is like learning to ride a bike all over again." (By the way, in my twenty months writing this column, I have learned that any new athletic skill is no doubt analogous to learning how to ride a bike.)

Stokes likens the dragon boat stroke to chopping ice, which is an equally foreign science to me. The body leans forward, almost out of its seat, with the outside leg supporting the brunt of the weight. The outside arm remains straight and reaches forward, gripping the paddle right above its blade. The inside arm, clutching the top of the paddle's handle, remains raised at the shoulder, and rotates back and forth, up and down, providing the force behind the blade's entry into the water. Again and again. Hundreds of times in one 250-, 500- or 1,000-meter race. "The shoulder is not used to that for two to four minutes in a row," said Stokes, forty-seven, of Ball Ground. "That causes a lot of pain for most people."

But dragon boating seems to attract those with a penchant for pain. For example, one Dragoneer just finished racing his fiftieth marathon and plans to run a 50-miler in Africa soon. Stokes, a member of the Lake Lanier Rowing Club's racing team, recently competed in the Blue Ridge Mountain Adventure Race and once tried out for the television show *American Gladiators*.

And there's no questioning Stokes's dedication to dragon boat racing, either. Since the actual boats used in the race—authentic models from China—are only made available to the teams two weeks prior to the festival, Stokes took matters into his own hands. He bought a quarter ton of lumber and constructed the Dragoneers' practice boat himself.

"Yeah, that's probably a little out there," Stokes said, grinning sheepishly. But Stokes's extremism is appreciated and, in my case, necessary. Only two more practices to go before race day. And I need every last one of them.

Part II: Exit the Dragoneers

Henry Kannapell and I stood along the shore, studying the sun-soaked waters of Lake Lanier, sizing up our opposition. We were silent for a moment. And then Kannapell—one of my twenty or so teammates for the sixth annual Hong Kong Dragon Boat Festival of Atlanta, held for the first time at Gainesville, Georgia's Clark's Bridge Park Olympic venue on Saturday—spoke. "The competition is really stiff," he said, as the dragon-headed 40-foot canoe glided across the finish line, one drummer, one steerer, and eighteen paddlers on board. "They looked really good, I thought."

I thought so, too. The rest of our team likely did, as well. But never did we think we were actually going to lose to them—or, at least, none of us would admit to it out loud. I mean, we were the AT&T Dragoneers, the event's five-time defending champion, the team that finished fourth in the nation just two years ago. Kannapell and I were two of the team's six rookies this year. We had been training for the regatta for nearly a month. We were confident.

But our primary competition had been training for years. They were the Lanier Canoe & Kayak Club, the reigning sprint paddling national champions. Newcomers to the dragon boat festival, they were eager to defend their course, their lake.

Our early returns were good. We had won our 500- and 250-meter heats by substantial margins. But so did the Lanier Club.

And then we got word of the times. We were 18 seconds behind Lanier in the 500, 8 in the 250. You could hear the confidence start to crumble. We reasoned the 26 seconds away, however. We had more of a headwind during our heats, more of a wake to work through, we would say. We had a leaky boat.

All true. And when we headed into the boathouse to analyze a videotape of our earlier performance, we found few mistakes. Our matching and power were solid. Many of the veterans on the team said our boat moved faster on Saturday than it did in several of AT&T's championship years. We actually felt rather good about our chances heading into the finals.

"I'm interested to get both boats out there together," said my team captain, Richard Stokes, after the heats. "When it's even, we'll see what they really have." Well, we saw what they had in the 500 final. We saw it quite well. We had a nice consistent view of the back of their boat.

It all happened quite quickly. There we were, floating at the start line, listening to the starter: Lane one, back. Lane two, up. Attention, please. He fired the gun. We began our start—a furious 40 strokes designed to get the boat moving quickly and to break us away from the pack early.

Evidently, the Lanier Club had the same intentions. Before the smoke from the starter's pistol had cleared, they already held a boat-length lead. There would be no catching up.

Not in the 500. Not in the 250, either. The same outcome, only sooner. "We've been behind in previous years," said my Dragoneers teammate Phil Webster. "But it was because we had messed up, and then once we got going we would just blow by them. But these guys . . . We just ran into a good team. But it gives us something to work toward.

The two teams couldn't have been more different. Mine was made up primarily of strong, adult males, many of whom were pushing 200 pounds. The Lanier Club, on the other hand, was probably half teenage girls. The team was young, lean and sinewy. They train daily. Lake Lanier runs through their veins.

"Theoretically, it's not that different than sprint racing," said Lanier head coach Tony Hall, after the races. "You've got to feel the resistance. Naturally, a lot of our guys, they instinctively move to the resistance and pull." Instincts or not, there's still something quite humbling about receiving a post-defeat handshake from a fourteen-year-old string bean of a girl who likely weighed several pounds less than my team's 98-pound drummer.

Hall, a former Canadian Olympic paddling coach and perhaps the only Montreal Expos fan this side of, well, Montreal, played it quite coy in the weeks leading up to the race. "If you can't beat us, you're really bad," he would say to me. "Dan, I'm having trouble finding people to fill the boat." Oh, he filled the boat, all right. He filled it good. "We just got outclassed today," said Stokes, who is about as competitive as they come.

I too hate to lose. Don't care for it one bit. But if you must lose, at least let it be to the best paddlers in the nation—fourteen-year-old girls and all.

It Isn't a Snap

Greg Bishop

Jeff Trickey talks with a sense of urgency, like Richard Simmons or Dick Vitale, his arms flailing, his eyes darting, his vocal chords bulging halfway across Qwest Field.

He's standing in front of more than one hundred prospective quarterbacks and wide receivers, all in high school, all gathered for Matt Hasselbeck's annual passing camp, all wide-eyed and soaking in his every word. And one reporter who just looks like he's in high school, all bleary-eyed and sleep-deprived and hoping, above all, to avoid injury and embarrassment.

"We have an opportunity today," says Trickey, a man who spends his days teaching in camps like these. "This is going to be a meaningful day. You have a gift. At the end of the day, you're going to be a better player, and you're going to be a better person."

Trickey splits the campers into groups based on age and position. As I trot out to join the senior quarterbacks in search of understanding the complexity of the position, Trickey grabs my arm.

"At the end of the day, we'll have you throwing better than Matt Hasselbeck," he says.

Or something like that.

Jim Zorn likes to tell Seahawks quarterbacks he coaches that they go through heroics before the ball is even snapped. That's how complicated the position is.

From one tackle to the next snap, Hasselbeck runs through dozens of steps he has spent his life learning, memorizing, and repeating. He's checking the time on the clock, checking the down and distance, and listening to coach Mike Holmgren detail the personnel group coming toward the huddle.

He's sizing up the defense, its formation, its personnel. He gets a play, sets up the formation to match the play, and calls the cadence.

As the Seahawks break the huddle, Hasselbeck checks the play clock, finds the free safety first and the strong safety second, takes his best guess at the defense's coverage, and adjusts. Often, he puts a receiver in motion, hoping the defense will give away whether it's playing man or zone.

All that's left is the only part that everybody pays attention to—the play itself, a play that wouldn't be possible without all those hours in the film room and on the practice field and all the steps that came before the snap.

That's why the quarterback position is like a spider web. There's an intricacy to it.

"When I sat down and counted how many things we do before a snap," Hasselbeck says, "it's complicated. Sometimes, when you get the right protection and the right routes called, then you're sort of proud of yourself that you got the right play called against the perfect defense. You almost forget that you still have to make the play."

The Seahawks recently signed former Indiana quarterback Gibran Hamdan and allocated him to NFL Europe. He came back with a better understanding of the position and a broken collarbone.

Hamdan is one of my group's main instructors. Before we start, he pulls us aside.

"That's the beautiful thing about playing quarterback—all the little things that go into it," Hamdan says. "I wish I had known all the little things about the position when I was your age."

We spend the rest of the morning working on the little things. Starting with the grip—index finger above the line on top of the football, two bottom fingers on the laces, thumb spread wide below the white line, all aligned for maximum friction, which Trickey tells us is the key to the revolutions that make a football spiral.

My passes revolve like an end-over-end punt. There's more grace in throwing fish at Pike's Place Market.

You want to feel like a boxer, Trickey says, vocal chords bulging again for effect. The perfect pass is an economy of motion in that way—compact, quick, and at the expense of as little energy as possible.

He's right in that respect. The more I try for the perfect pass, the more they wobble toward my partner. It's like plugging a garden hose full of holes. Stick your finger in one and water comes bursting out another.

I'm just starting to get the hang of holding both hands on the football, protecting it for the inevitable moment when a defender blasts me from behind, when I start adding an extra hop to my three-step drop. I fix that and my release point is too low, sending balls sideways.

We pass with a partner from one knee, then standing, then running toward our partner. My partner is Ricky Blake, the starting quarterback at Yelm High School. His passes are more like bullets. After the first drill, the thumb on my left hand is numb.

Pass receivers run curl routes and comeback routes and slant routes and fade routes. My arm is the only thing that's fading. My first pass to a wide receiver wobbles toward Mark Anthony of Franklin High School, dropping 5 feet in front of his outstretched arms. The second pass is a spiral, the closest to perfection I'll throw all day.

"Good," Hasselbeck says behind me.

He won't say that again.

The consolation for any Monday Morning Quarterback trying to become a Sunday morning one is that there's not a harder position to learn in football. Trickey calls it "cerebral" in that "the beauty comes before you get to the line of scrimmage. It's a combination of physical gifts and mental preparation on every play."

Lacking both, I seek out Seneca Wallace, the Seahawks' backup quarterback, during lunch. He's athletic enough to warrant consideration as a punt returner next season, athletic enough to play multiple positions on the field, athletic enough to rank positions by degree of difficulty.

"There's so much to the position," Wallace says, "that people don't understand how complicated it is."

He pauses.

"You might want to stick to writing."

Minutes later, I shake the hand of Don Hasselbeck, Matt's father, and notice his Super Bowl ring.

"Be careful," he warns. "You know [ESPN anchor] Stuart Scott once got hit in the eye."

There's so much to learn and so little time. Hasselbeck used to cut pictures out of magazines, paste them into a collage, and study grips in search of the perfect one. My grip? I need to get one.

Hasselbeck learned the nuances of the position during NFL training camps his dad participated in. He learned the tricks of his current trade sitting next to quarterbacks on bus rides home from exhibition games. I'm hoping for a faster osmosis.

Hasselbeck likes playing quarterback because he gets to be an actor. We're given the same opportunity in a drill that teaches you to sell play-action. Really, I'm acting like an athlete.

The uniqueness of the camp strikes me more than anything. For one, Hasselbeck isn't just using his name here. He's actively involved. That includes a film session in the interview room at Qwest Field.

Hasselbeck and wide receiver Bobby Engram break down tape of last season, showing campers how to distinguish between Cover 1 (one safety back) and Cover 2 (two safeties back), showing the difference between teams that disguise coverages well (New England) and teams that don't (St. Louis).

Campers watch Engram nearly score a touchdown, then wonder why he didn't.

"I had a hip flexor," Engram says, while the campers laugh.

The day ends and the Trickey checklist is half complete. Better person? Sure. Better player? Not so much.

I keep thinking back to something Zorn said when he dropped by, when he called football "the greatest sport on earth."

Tell that to my arms and hands. The next day, I can barely sit or walk or move my right shoulder. The thumb on my left hand is swollen and purple. It's what Hamdan calls the "Monday morning rude awakening."

What emerges is a newfound respect for the complications of playing quarterback. I learned more about playing quarterback in the camp than I did in three years covering the Seahawks.

I can grip a football, perform a three-step drop, and read a defense. I just can't pass. And somewhere along the way, Hamdan said I went from being "hopeless"—his first impression—to a passable freshman high-school quarterback. Not bad for a day's work.

"I would say with a little work," Trickey says, "you're on the practice squad. If we work hard, coach Holmgren would have a tough time letting you go."

Reaching Her Peak

Helga Hengge

Finally, after six weeks of waiting, of hiking up and down between 17,000 and 26,000 feet to help our bodies acclimatize to the altitude, the day of our summit bid had arrived. The weather forecasted for May 27, 1999, was clear skies—a long-anticipated window between storms. Although it was nearly midnight here at Camp 4, 27,200 feet above sea level, the full moon made it look like morning. The orange down cocoons next to me had begun to stir, and I could hear the Sherpas slurping soup in the silence. The top of my sleeping bag was crusted with snow crystals. I took off my oxygen mask and got dressed in bed, careful not to overlook anything: two layers of fleece, down pants, down jacket, summit socks, heat liners in my boots and gloves; sunblock and glasses in one pocket, water bottle with hot tea in another; cough drops, crackers, goggles, and tissues in my pack.

To stand on top of the world, to look down over its curve with no higher place to go—it was a vision I'd had in dreams for years. I just never expected I'd climb to the top of Everest and get to see it myself.

I'm not exactly your classic mountain woman. I was born in the U.S. to German parents, and although I grew up in Munich, I work in New York City as a fashion stylist for magazines, including this one, [Women's Sports and Fitness]. The most physical aspect of my job is carrying huge trunks of clothing to and from photo shoots. I like to jog and hike to keep in shape, but I've never been particularly adventurous, either. When I read *Into Thin Air*, Jon Krakauer's 1996 bestseller, I thought everyone in the book was nuts. A huge storm had swept the mountain and killed eight people. The survivors lost noses, fingers, and toes to frostbite. Not bad, considering the odds: one of every ten people who summit fails to make it down alive. Why would anyone do something so obviously self-destructive?

In truth, I did have an inkling. When I was a little girl, my grandparents would spend two months each year climbing in the Himalayas—in places such as Bhutan, Pakistan, Nepal, and the tiny kingdom of Mustang, where they were the first Germans ever to set foot. Once a year, they would invite us to watch a slide show of their travels. My grandmother, who had rugged, tanned skin covered with freckles from her weeks spent outdoors, served my mother, my five siblings, and me tea. My grandfather worked the projector as we sat on pillows and stared at the wall. There, pagodas glowed golden in the sunset, colorful prayer flags fluttered in the wind, and snowcapped mountain peaks towered like waves on a stormy ocean. I was transfixed. One year, however, my grandfather almost died when he tumbled partway down a couloir before his fixed rope could stop him. My mother was so scared by his accident that even when my siblings and I were older and my grandparents had died, she was still reluctant to let us climb anything higher than the mountains surrounding Munich.

And I didn't—until about four years ago. I had never forgotten the beautiful images of the mountains I saw in my grandparents' slides. So in 1996, needing a vacation, I signed up for a trekking trip to Everest Base Camp. The hike was scenic and easy. But as I stood at the foot of the mountain and watched the climbers from other trips preparing to make their ascents, I was gripped with envy. I looked up at a white cloud trailing gracefully from the summit into the sky. I wanted so badly to join them. It was then that I knew that in spite of everything I had read about Everest, I would one day have to try to reach its peak.

I began climbing in earnest. My freelance schedule allowed me the time to train (typically, I run 6 miles each morning and use the StairMaster wearing a backpack) and to take some big trips. Over Christmas of 1996,

I climbed Aconcagua, which at 22,834 feet is the highest peak in South America. I had never even been camping before, but I surprised myself and my trip leader by summiting the mountain with relative ease. Maybe it was my family legacy, but climbing seemed to come naturally to me. In the mornings I'd drag a little, but once I got going I felt as if I had wings on my back and I could literally fly up the mountain. Since then, I'd scaled six 20,000-foot peaks from Peru to Nepal. My only disappointment had come in late 1998, when I made it nearly to the top of the Himalayas' Cho Oyu (at 26,750 feet, the world's sixth-highest mountain) but was forced to turn around in a snowstorm.

That's how, five months later, I ended up on Everest. Russell Brice, who runs the expedition outfit Himalayan Experience and who had led me up Cho Oyu, was planning a trip up Everest's north ridge in May, a steeper and more exposed side of the mountain than the popular south side. I called and begged him to take me along, even though the trip was only six weeks away. After some reluctance, he agreed. Fittingly, I spent my inheritance from my grandfather—all $35,000 of it—for the chance. The only hitch was I couldn't tell my mother I was going.

Our group included Geoff, a banker from Australia; Kozuka, a Japanese spark plug designer; and me, the only woman. I soon gained a reputation as the resident slacker. During our long wait for the weather window, the guys at camp would obsess over every aspect of our route—how we'd negotiate the steep ridges, how much oxygen we would need, and what kind of gear they'd brought. The men saw themselves as warriors, waiting to conquer the great mountain. To me, climbing Everest wasn't a matter of prepping for battle. I considered myself a traveler. Determined to take the trip one day at a time, I was happy to have six weeks to walk over crisp snowdrifts, gaze at Everest's elusive peak, and socialize with fellow climbers, especially the few women from other expeditions.

Sometimes my attitude got to Russell. One afternoon, after our first foray to Camp 2 at 24,606 feet, he admonished me to be more serious and focused. "Summit day will be the hardest day of your life," he said sternly. I smiled at him. "Look, Russell—I'm here on vacation," I said, only half joking. I didn't doubt the climb would be extremely hard. But

HELGA HENGGE

unlike those who were sponsored by big corporations or who had been training for this one crack at the summit for years, I felt I had nothing to lose. I honestly hadn't a clue whether I would make it to the top, but I was determined to enjoy trying to get there.

Now it was midnight, and as we prepared to head to the summit, suddenly the enjoyment was gone. For the first time in my brief climbing career, I thought I might be in over my head. I was tired and dizzy. All I had eaten in the last two days were four or five Ritz crackers—the altitude had made me queasy, and I couldn't keep anything down. Russell, who had gotten ill, was back at Advanced Base Camp (ABC for short) and was monitoring our every step by radio. There were seven of us at Camp 4: the three climbers and four Sherpas—Loppsang, Karsang, Phurba, and Narwang.

Russell had paired me up with Loppsang, our head Sherpa, and had instructed us to leave camp by 12:30 a.m. to be sure we could make the noon turnaround deadline. The majority of the climbers who have died on Everest died on the way down, so it was crucial to stick to our schedule. Our climb would take us from Camp 4 at 27,200 feet, across a steep incline called the Yellow Band, up three vertical rock-and-ice ridges and, finally, across a deep snow triangle to the tiny summit cone at 29,028 feet. As I fumbled with my oxygen mask and crampons, Loppsang stuffed two 15-pound oxygen bottles into my pack and lifted me up. I adjusted my headlamp and began walking slowly, my body stiff from lying in the cramped tent. I stumbled clumsily uphill over patches of snow, my crampons catching on the rock. My 30-pound pack weighed heavily on my shoulders. Breathing hard into my mask, I was unable to gather strength. I leaned over into the snow, exhausted.

In the previous weeks I'd earned the respect of my teammates—some of whom had looked at me (a tall blonde from New York City) a little skeptically at the beginning of the trip—by beating everyone up the mountain. Like that first time on Aconcagua, I'd been accustomed to flying upward on invisible wings, passing my teammates one by one. Where were my wings today?

After a few more labored steps, I called for help. "Loppsang, wait.

Something's wrong with my oxygen," I pleaded. He didn't hear me. I began to panic, worried that I might have to turn back.

Many climbers had died here, three in the previous two weeks alone. Our crew had tried to guide them by radio from ABC when a snowstorm covered the mountain and we lost contact. Was I completely insane to think I was up to this climb? I didn't have half the experience of some of the others. I called out to Loppsang again and this time he heard me. He took off his gloves and dug into my pack. "Is okay now," he said, and told me my oxygen had been on low.

I felt a flood of relief. I'd been about to give up. Every step now seemed light, and the moon danced gloriously on the snow. Ahead, the round circles from the lamps of other climbers bobbed like fireflies over the black-and-white patches of the rocky Yellow Band. Within minutes we overtook Karla, a climber from the Mexican expedition, and her Sherpa. We continued up steep rock, holding on to our jumars (which fasten to the rope) with one hand and pushing up with the other.

Suddenly, Loppsang stopped and whispered, "Helga not afraid now." What did he mean? I smiled, motioning with my head that everything was fine. Then I looked down. In the shadow of a big rock, I made out the shape of a body lying on its side, hands tucked under its head, as if it were sleeping. I grabbed Loppsang's hand, kept my eyes fixed on the body, and let myself be pulled along. As I stepped over the dead man's faded lime-green boots, I lost my nerve and began to cry. The tears were cold on my cheeks. Here was this man, wearing the same jacket and pack as I, only he was dead. This was what distinguished Everest from the other mountains I'd climbed. It was a terrifying reminder of its power.

At 3:00 we reached the bottom of the First Step, at 27,559 feet. The stars brightened and I felt like an angel tiptoeing on top of the world. A steep wall rose 65 feet above us. I clipped onto the rope and used my ice ax to scale it. Halfway up, I traversed a rocky ledge and tried to scramble over a big boulder. In thick down clothes and crampons I could barely feel the rock, but I made it. On top, the ridge continued, and as I began to walk I realized I could no longer feel the toes on my left foot. I checked the battery of my boot heater and saw the light had gone out. In these subzero

HELGA HENGGE

temperatures, serious frostbite can turn your toes black; sometimes they need to be amputated. My mind was foggy from the altitude, but I decided to switch the batteries on my boots. My right foot was toasty and would be fine for a while.

Behind us, the sun had started to come up and the horizon began to separate from the sky. A confetti of green, red, orange, and yellow down-suited creatures, about a dozen in all, appeared over the ridge above us. We arrived at our first oxygen-changing point, littered with orange oxygen bottles. Loppsang changed mine and put a fresh one in my pack. Ahead, a line formed on the ridge where the Second Step began, a 90-foot rock wall. Ten Tibetan climbers were struggling up one by one, and we had to wait our turn. A bottleneck. A similar situation had occurred at the Hillary Step on the south side in that 1996 ascent; the disaster that ensued was in part attributed to the delay. Here I was at the top of the world, and I had to wait on line. Loppsang wasn't worried, though, since we had been moving fast all night.

We sat down in the snow and watched the sun rise. We could see the white-and-blue glaciers flowing from other mountains to meet in the wide valley. Cho Oyu, 26,750 feet high, caught the sunlight, which streamed red and orange down its south face. It was incredible to be higher than any other place on earth and to feel the sun touch you first.

Finally, it was our turn. To get over the rock face of the Second Step required climbing an aluminum ladder rigged by a Chinese expedition some twenty years ago. It dangled precariously from the rock and swayed as I stepped on it. My crampons screeched on the metal. Many of the other climbers had fumbled here for a long time, but I had watched Loppsang and did exactly as he had done. At the top, I wedged the front spikes of my crampons into a small rock crevice and pulled myself up onto the snow.

After exchanging bottles again, we trudged on. It was nearly 7:00 a.m. To our right was a scree field falling away into the Great Couloir, near where only three weeks ago climbers had found the fully preserved body of George Mallory, the legendary British climber who had been lost in what may have been the first successful attempt to reach the summit of Everest. It was also the final resting place for another body, clearly in view now, whose red jacket had faded in the sun. He lay on his back, arms flung over his head, like a heroic sculpture. Even in daylight I had to avert my eyes. If I had let thoughts of disaster creep in, I wouldn't have had the courage to continue.

By now the sun had climbed well into the sky. When we had topped the Third Step, about 750 feet from the top, we started traversing a large triangle of snow. From ABC we had watched other summiteers crossing it like little black ants moving slowly over an ice cream cone. Most of them had crossed it after 12:00 p.m. We were a good 5 hours earlier than that, and I was still full of energy. In many accounts of the final ascent, I'd heard that you have to stop to breathe between each step, but I was able to take five steps before stopping. My wings were buffeting me upward.

The final ridge, at 29,028 feet, rippled with three large snow waves. It took half an hour to trudge across a distance that at sea level would have taken just 5 minutes. Then, suddenly, there was only deep blue sky all around us and no higher place to go but the tiny summit cone. The Tibetans crowded the cone, which was no bigger than 10 square feet, taking pictures for their sponsors. I stepped into the crowd as if I were squeezing into a small kitchen at a party, threw back my oxygen mask, and turned off the regulator. We'd made it!

I beamed at Loppsang and hugged his thick down suit. After weeks of looking up at more snow, rock, and ice walls, now the only direction to look was down. It was incredible. Lhotse, the world's fourth-highest mountain, stood below us, its white flanks falling away in fluted ridges. Everywhere around us, snowfields danced in the light. I wanted to lift my arms up into the air and spin around like Maria in *The Sound of Music*, but I would have fallen off. We radioed Russell and told him we had made it. "How does it feel to stand on top of the world?" he asked. "It's great! It's so beautiful!" was all I could think to say. "I want a Sprite. Save one for me when I come down!" It was an embarrassingly mundane request. But I was so thirsty and sick of drinking tea that I could think of nothing I wanted more right then.

As soon as the rowdy Tibetans left, we had our chance to take pictures. Loppsang unfurled his Nepalese flag, and I snapped photos of him holding

HELGA HENGGE

it high into the wind. At our feet, the Dalai Lama smiled at us from a golden frame that a Sherpa must have placed there years before. Multicolored prayer flags flapped quietly in the breeze and hundreds of white katas (silk scarves) were tied to an ice ax, honoring the mountain gods. To our right was the south ridge and the famed Hillary Step. I knelt down and tied my kata to the ax and uttered a prayer of thanks to the gods.

It was only 8:00 a.m., but already clouds were hovering over the north side. After 45 minutes on the summit, Loppsang put his mask back on and signaled for me to descend. On the ridge down we ran into Kozuka, the Japanese climber from our group, and Phurba, his Sherpa. Kozuka looked exhausted and was taking long rests, but they were close. Walking down was easier than I'd expected. I became so overheated I even took my jacket off. Further down I was surprised to find Karla, the Mexican climber, also proceeding slowly. Karla, who had tried to summit from the south side the year before, had a sponsor and seemed very confident at ABC. "Only 2 more hours," I told her, trying to be cheerful.

I hoped I hadn't discouraged her. I honestly can't say why I felt so energetic throughout what is undoubtedly one of the most difficult climbs there is. It's not as if I were more fit than the others. But I do know this: The only person I was there to prove something to was myself. If the stakes had been higher, I might not have been able to feel so confident. Nerves have undone more than a few of the best climbers.

Rappelling down the Second Step, swinging high over the world, was actually fun. As we continued down the ridge after the First Step, however, thick clouds streamed up around us. Loppsang radioed to Russell that we were below the First Step, only an hour from Camp 4, which we had left 11 hours earlier. Russell said he wanted us out of the "death zone," so called for the lack of oxygen above 25,000 feet, and that we should try to make it down the 1,600 feet to Camp 3. Suddenly, walking became torture. The path was sometimes no more than half a foot wide, over brittle rock. I felt so weak—I still hadn't eaten anything all day—but I walked cautiously, making sure to clip into every rope. Trip over your crampons just once and you can fall thousands of feet into a couloir.

At 11:30 a.m. we reached Camp 4. With my last bit of strength I removed my crampons and stumbled into my tent. I fell immediately into a deep sleep, but soon Loppsang woke me. "We must go down," he said. "I can't," I mumbled. "Come on—we go," he repeated. I don't know how I was able to put my crampons back on, but I couldn't disappoint Loppsang, who had been so helpful. We left camp slowly, following Karsang and Geoff. It was snowing lightly, and every few feet I stumbled and had to sit down. I was thirsty and kept refilling my bottle with snow. Loppsang and Karsang kept waiting for me, but I wanted to take my time. I told them I would be fine by myself and that they should go ahead.

When I reached Camp 3, Loppsang and the others were already far ahead. Unexpectedly, Geoff, who had been going to stay with me at Camp 3 for the night, had also left. Narwang had gone further up to help Phurba and Kozuka down. Were they going to make it back here in time? I didn't want to spend the night by myself. It was already about 3:00 p.m. Suddenly, I was terrified. I searched the tents for a radio to contact Russell but I couldn't find one, only sleeping bags and cooking gear. Soon, night would come. My legs were tired and my back was killing me, but I decided I had to get down another 1,300 feet to Camp 2. I put my mask back on and turned the regulator up. Negotiating the rock scree in the swirling clouds and fading light was awful. I hung on to the ropes but slipped many times. Each time I fell I started crying, feeling sorry for myself, and then got up again and took a few more steps. My crampons got stuck in the leg of my down pants and feathers started flying everywhere. I remembered one night when I had been sick and Geoff had handed me a down feather saying, "Feeling a bit down today?" Right now, I was feeling very down.

Nearly 3 hours later, I made it to Camp 2. In one of the two tents I found Ian, a South African, and his girlfriend. I crawled into the tent on all fours as if I'd just crossed the Sahara and told Ian that if he didn't give me water I would die. He laughed and handed me a cup. "It's not cooked yet," he said. I didn't care and gulped it down. They had a radio, and I called Russell, who had been worried about me. He told me Phurba, Narwang, and Kozuka had all reached Camp 4 at 7:00 p.m.—exhausted after summiting but fine. They were not coming down any further tonight.

At 5:00 a.m. I heard a voice calling my name. Suddenly, Phurba fell into my tent, snow-blind. He had lost his eyes, he said, and was crying. Phurba had dropped his glasses on the Second Step while helping Kozuka down. He then turned back to find Karla, who had returned late from the summit. When he realized that he was snow-blind—a temporary condition caused by the glare of the sun onto the cornea—he started to descend at 10:00 p.m., stumbling downhill all night. I radioed Russell and tried to sound calm, although I wasn't. Russell instructed me to cover a pair of glasses with tape so only a pin-size hole of light could get through. I put these on Phurba and packed him into my sleeping bag, trying to comfort him. Suddenly I felt so exhausted that I blacked out.

Later that morning, after Loppsang had arrived to give us a hand, we set off for ABC. The sun was so strong I had to wrap my neck scarf over Phurba's eyes. Loppsang short-roped him from behind to guide him. It took us 3 hours to get down. The snow was soft and slushy, and descending the 1,000-foot ice fall was treacherous. I stumbled behind Phurba and Loppsang like a complete beginner. I would have tried harder if I had known that Russell was watching us through binoculars, but my body was too tired to care.

Russell and Karsang picked us up an hour above ABC with hot tea—no Sprite, of course. Russell hugged me and told me how proud he was. Lachu, our head cook, had prepared a huge celebratory dinner of pizza and "summit cake," chocolate cake made with Everest snow. Some of the other climbers came and we drank wine and celebrated until we were too dizzy to stand.

The last 36 hours felt like a dream. We had stood on top of the world. No one had died, no one had gotten frostbite, and Phurba's eyes were already getting better. Everest was glowing gold in the sunset, and by the time I dragged myself back to my tent that night the mountain was like a bright candle, reflecting the light of the moon in the dark sky.

It was while gazing at Everest that I realized that Jon Krakauer, in his harrowing account of the 1996 summit attempt, had never adequately described the beauty of the mountain that could so capriciously take life away. And yet climbers have let him have the final word. For six weeks, I had been awash in beauty: the brightness of the stars the night we tiptoed like angels along the ridge; the sun ribboning honey-colored down the mountain's flanks; being so high that we could see the earth's graceful curve. To me, these images were the real reasons to do what some might consider insane—to experience unimaginable, celestial beauty. I couldn't have gotten any closer to heaven. And I knew that from there, my grandmother was watching me standing in Everest's shadow, and that she would have agreed.

Pickles

Mark Jenkins

We were discussing the accident again, trying to figure out how it could have happened. It was early morning and though the highway was striped with sunlight, the bush was as black as ever.

"Maybe one of 'em was injured," said Rick, sitting up front in the passenger seat. "Hit by falling rock."

"There's to be an inquest," said Derek, the driver. "And autopsies."

Three days earlier, on June 14, the accident had made the front page of the *Syndey Morning Herald*: "Two experienced abseilers froze to death in a wilderness waterfall in the Blue Mountains after their ropes became entangled, leaving them trapped and dangling against a steep escarpment as night set in." The article went on to thinly outline a three-day canyoning adventure that had been advertised on the Web site of the Newcastle University Mountaineering Club as a trip with "more abseils than you can poke a piton at." The story was accompanied by a large photograph of helicopters hovering against a cliff face above a green forest, like dragonflies above a garden.

"They died on Corra Beanga Falls," said Derek, turning off onto a narrow dirt road. "You've done that haven't you, Rick?"

"That'n. Yes, I 'ave."

At last count, Rick Jamieson, fifty-nine, had descended some two hundred canyons in the Blue Mountains of Australia. He wrote the book on canyoning Down Under, *Canyons Near Sydney*, now in its third edition. He made his first technical descent in 1961, two decades before canyoneering, or canyoning, as a sport would develop in the deserts of the Western USA. A big rock of a man—thick in the hands and feet, with curly gray hair, a grizzled beard, a heavy Aussie accent, and an uncanny resemblance to the late British explorer-mountaineer H. W. Tilman—Rick tended to think more than he spoke.

Derek Cannon is Rick's canyoning partner. They've done most of the canyons in his guidebook together. Derek, sixty-two, is a retired limnologist who worked for the Sydney Water Authority for thirty-three years while simultaneously rising from private to lieutenant colonel in the Australian army reserve. He's trim, indefatigable, and has led trekking expeditions around the world.

Derek and Rick go canyoning forty-plus weekends a year. We were driving to Bennett Gully, a small, virtually unknown slot canyon that had never been descended. Bouncing in the back seat, I kept brooding about the two dead canyoneers.

"They must not really have been experienced," I said. Derek held the wheel steady and glanced at me in the rearview mirror. Rick didn't look back.

"They must have made stupid mistakes," I said.

"Or," Rick said, shrugging his shoulders, "'ey might 'ave just made a simple error in judgment."

Geography is destiny. Australia's Blue Mountains are ideal for canyoning because they aren't, in fact, mountains at all, but rather a long sandstone plateau riven with gorges—an incised geography of 500-foot cliffs, steep talus, and crayfish creeks all buried beneath what Aussies call "bush" and we would call rain forest. Gorgeous, pale-skinned blue gums, ferns the size of fountains, fens of 8-foot razor grass, shawls of green moss on every stone, and steep wall. Imagine a bony Utah fleshed over by Louisiana foliage so dense all the slot canyons are hidden beneath a python's nest of roots. Most slot canyons here don't even show up on maps; Rick decried topos as "bloody useless."

The Blue Mountains rise like a wave just west of Sydney. Sydney: the beach-blonde antipodal sister of raven-haired San Francisco, with a better port, a bigger gay pride parade, cleaner streets, swimable seas, and a week of sun for every day in the rain.

June in Australia is winter, putatively the wrong season for canyoning. I'd been warned by a vocal American canyoneer that it would be impossible to go canyoning in June. "You'll freeze to death!" he warned hysterically. When I mentioned this to Rick in our first phone conversation, he said something that sounded like, "aaarrruhhgg," then grumbled about "bloody whingey Americans." I bought a ticket.

(Thank God for earth's vestigial incorrigibles, the outdoor atavists, the few who still go outside in all seasons. Hate to say it, but there aren't many left in the U.S.—many good men having devolved into fair-weather adventurers. In Australia, perhaps due to its isolation, the breed is still thriving.)

The morning Rick turned up to drive me out to do our first canyon (Derek was busy that day) it was snowing in the Snowy Mountains, south of the capital, and newscasters were calling the weather "bittah cold." The city people were hiding inside winter coats and wool scarves. Rick was wearing exactly what you'd expect of a man whom one local canyoneer described as a "fokkin legend": ratty sweater, threadbare khaki shorts, flattened sneakers.

Rick is one of those old-school bush veterans who live in shorts. Long pants are anathema to him. So too a coat of any kind. "The best plan is to wear a woolen jumper next to the skin," he writes in *Canyons Near Sydney*. Same goes for the misery of heavy hiking boots: "We recommend Volley sandshoes [cheap canvas sneakers], as they are quite good on slippery rocks."

Brushing aside the beer cans in the back of his station wagon, I saw that his backpack was no better: a potato-shaped lump of such great age and abuse that all the buckles were gone and the nylon fabric, stitched and restitched, worn to fuzz. Crammed in with the rest of his gear and supplies was a dark, unidentifiable object.

"What's that?"

"Whut? Me wet suit?" Although still vaguely blue, it resembled some ragged animal skin, with sleeves cut off at the biceps and legs cut off above the thighs. Most appalling, the crotch was ripped from the belly button to tailbone.

"That keeps you warm?"

"Nah," said Rick sheepishly, "caun't say that it does. But I brought me balaclava."

I took all this as a good sign. The older the gear, the better. People with new gear scare me: the scanty wear-and-tear of their equipage is too often indicative of the scantiness of their experience, which means you don't want to go on a hike with them, let alone descend into the orifices of the earth.

That day we did a canyon called Yileen, an Aborigine word for "dream." It had numerous rappels that dropped straight into icy ebony pools.

"There go me family jewels!" Rick would howl, then rapidly half-wade, half-swim down the penumbral corridor and stumble up onto the next sandbank, chortling. I was wearing an intact wet suit and it was still bone-chilling.

By the time we got to the final rap, a stunning 200-foot drop alongside a vaporous waterfall, our feet were wooden blocks and our fingers rubber bananas. It took an hour of hiking fast and hard uphill with packs to warm up. Rick declared the day "a beauty." One good measure of an adventurer is how he acts when he is uncomfortable. Does he whine, keep quiet, or revel? The former is unforgivable, the second acceptable, the last admirable.

That night we sat close to the woodstove in Rick's home at the edge of the Blue Mountains and drank hot tea. After some prodding Rick told me about a 950-mile canoe trip he made down the Mackenzie River in Canada right after getting his Ph.D. in electrical engineering and marrying Jane (pronounced "yana"), his Danish wife. That somehow led to another adventure that he inexplicably referred to as "the fahs."

"Fahs?" I said.

"Yap. F.A.R.C.E. Fantastical Australian Rock Climbing Expedition. 1972. Six months. Drove a combi from Denmark to Australia, right though bloody Asia." Rick stretched his muscled legs, which, if it weren't for the lumps and scars and half-century tan, could belong to an Olympic runner. "Wanted to climb a mountain in Afghanistan, an' almost did."

Yileen was just a warm-up. A chance for Rick to see if I cut the mustard.

"Got one!" he said one morning, as if snatching a trout from a stream. "Canyon's called Oronga." Which inaptly means "sleep" in the Aborigine language.

No one had successfully completed a descent of Oronga. Even today in our nothing's-left-everything's-been-done world, the Blue Mountains are still not explored out. No matter that they're a mere 2-hour train ride from four million people. Five years earlier, Rick and some mates had attempted Oronga but had been turned back by a drop so deep they couldn't see the bottom. "Was one a 'em misty mornin's," Rick said, "an the stream fell over the cliff and just vanished into the clouds."

So it was, on another freezing, misty morning, that Rick and I attempted Oronga Canyon. The descent started with a short rappel through overhanging vines, followed by another rap from a tree limb into a black abyss. Down inside Oronga we followed one passageway after another, each as dark and dank as a dungeon, before crawling out atop a series of enormous, undercut cliff bands. It took four consecutive rappels—never knowing if we might get stranded halfway down a wall—before we reached the bottom of the canyon. We'd done it . . . almost. In fact, the hike out turned into a grueling bushwhack. Forced to struggle our way through miles of thorn-spiked vines, by the end, Rick's legs were so severely gouged and scratched I could follow the drips of blood through the forest. Still, 8 hours after we'd started, we were back at the car.

"Whuh a bahgain," roared Rick, tossing me a beer from behind the seat.

During the hike out I learned that Rick had been a freelance computer programmer since the dawn of the damn machines. "Don't like to work more'n couple days a week." Which left time for raising two sons and one daughter, voluminous reading, and writing books on subjects other than canyoning, including *A Religion Without a God* (a treatise on the faith of atheists) and *Let's Spel Lojicly: Wi stic tu the hard old way ov spelling?* (an argument for the simplification of English orthography). He had also managed to lead thirteen trekking expeditions to the Himalayas, climb the Matterhorn twice, and drive overland from Munich to Cape Town.

"We got 'rselves into heaps of pickles in Africa. Mighty! Spent a whole month in jail in the Congo. 'Ey thought we were bloody mercenaries. Ten days in a hole in Brazzaville, and then shipped down the big river—pygmies would paddle out and give us bananas—to Pointe Noire, where we spent another three weeks in jail before gettin' out. At any one time we were always in at least two pickles. Tryin' to get 'rselves out of one of 'em while straight away pulling 'rselves into another."

The three of us stepped out of the car above Bennett Gully and looked at the map. Derek was outfitted just like Rick: wool sweater, shorts, Volleys.

Dropping into the head of the canyon, we were instantly engulfed by bush and began creeping through tunnels of vegetation, one after another, sometimes wading through the water, sometimes balancing along a latticework of deadfall suspended like a bridge above the streambed. When the brambles became impassable, we would scrabble up the canyon sidewalls and work our way along slopey, discontinuous ledges.

Slithering, clambering, and clawing through bush—literally bushwhacking—is distinctive to Blue Mountain canyoning. To be a good canyoneer here, you must be a great bushwalker. It was instructive to watch how gracefully Rick and Derek tiptoed along the alligator backs of logs, contorted through cobwebs of vines, and leapt rock to rock. As a team we were as efficient as guerrillas, the man in front rotating as each of us ran into vegetal cul-de-sacs and advised the two behind to find a different path. At any drop, or whenever we got rimrocked, the point man would already have a rope ready by the time the other two arrived.

We were down in the dark, passing from one chamber to the next, when, right in front of us, sky appeared. A brilliant wedge of blue between two black walls. The stream at our feet rushed toward the drop-off, pooled in a cleft as if psyching itself up, then slowly slid over the edge like a suicide jumper who has second thoughts a second too late.

We took turns stepping carefully to the lip, hanging on to a limb and looking down. It was a tremendous drop. The rock was undercut and the stream came apart falling through the emptiness. The yawning space made Derek cock his head like an officer, Rick squint, and my nuts involuntarily contract.

A hundred feet down and to the right there was a long ledge. Unfortunately, below it we could see nothing but blank walls. "She may not go," said Rick. "After the ledge it's a hell of a long ways to the ground an' looks like there's nothin' for abseils."

I volunteered to check it out. Reaching the ledge required traversing a fragile trellis of branches suspended in space—something akin to crawling out onto a lilac bush dropping off the side of a fifty-story building—which I managed, barely. On the ledge I hung out as far as I could in different places, searching the walls below. Unless I found something from which to set up another rappel, the descent was over: I would have to jug back up the rope and we would be forced to somehow back out of Bennett Gully.

I was about to give up when I spotted something beautiful: a dead tree. A slender, limbless, blackened trunk leaning out of a seam. I immediately rappelled down to it and attached myself. I was now two ropes below Rick and Derek.

"It'll go!" I yelled up, exhilarated.

Rick's voice was barely audible. "Will . . . the . . . ropes . . . reach . . . the . . . bottom?"

Looking straight down it's hard to judge distance. I studied the surrounding cliff faces vanishing into the forest. Our ropes were 200 feet long. It couldn't be more than 200 feet more to the bottom.

"Yeesss . . . " I wasn't sure. I thought they would reach. It was a judgment call.

"Abseiling!"

Rick and Derek rapped down to the ledge, pulled the ropes, set up the next rappel, and started down again.

The one foolproof way to get yourself killed in a canyon is to get stranded halfway. If it starts to rain, you'll either be drowned, swept over the cliffs, or die of exposure. Even if it doesn't rain, but you're wet and the temperature drops, or the wind picks up and blows the waterfall over you and you subsequently become wet, you'll be popsicled in a matter of hours.

The one foolproof way to get stuck halfway is to pull your ropes down from above, eliminating all chance of retreat, only to find that they won't reach the bottom. Unlike in mountaineering, where you can usually turn around at almost any point, serious canyoning is a one-way trip. Once you pull your ropes, the only way out, the only way back home, is down.

Derek and Rick completed their descent and pulled the ropes. Then we were all three hanging from a small dead tree in the middle of a remote cliff face in the middle of the Blue Mountains. We knotted the ropes through a sling I'd tied around the tree, and dropped them.

They dove down through space, and stopped. They didn't reach. I couldn't believe it. We could see the ends dangling in midair, snapping lazily like tiger tails, the forest floor still somewhere far below.

"They're really close," I said.

"Fair dinkum," said Rick. "We get down there and we'll be laughin'."

Derek chuckled.

"You have the extra short rope, right, Rick?" I was trying to sound imperturbable. They knew what I was about to suggest: tie the short rope permanently to the dead tree, put a loop in the end, and hang the long ropes through the loop. It would require a mid-wall transfer from the fixed rope to the double, a dangerous maneuver, but it would give us an extra 30 feet or more.

"Tricky," said Rick, obviously pleased.

"If it doesn't reach . . . " Derek shrugged and didn't finish his sentence.

We rerigged the ropes and I went first. Down the single line, making the transfer onto the double; then came a great swing out into midair several hundred feet above the earth, something that always gives one a minor synaptic shock. As I slid down the ropes, 15 feet out from the overhanging wall, I still couldn't tell if they reached the ground. Near the bottom the ends were coiled in the top of a tree. I anxiously descended through the forest canopy to the very end of the rope. I was 10 feet from the ground.

Close enough. I dropped.

"The . . . ropes . . . reach!"

Derek let out a battle cry and swung into space.

When Rick reached the ground he looked up and said, laconic as ever, "That dead tree. She won't be there for long."

By twilight we were walking through the tall grass between the ghostly blue gums. It began to rain and Rick and Derek started singing "April Showers," the Al Jolson tune. Then a cold night set in and it began to pour.

Fishing with the Shad King

T. Edward Nickens

It's 10:00 a.m. on a brilliant spring morning and the Shad King is sweating. It's not from heat. It is two days before the commencement of "National Shad King Week," as the King's wife describes it, a self-indulgent time in which he and a handful of his cronies, the Shad Heads, do little—do nothing—but fish, sleep, and eat. (Some people refer to this eight-day stretch as the Forks of the Delaware Shad Tournament, based in Easton, Pennsylvania. It is the country's largest shad tournament, and there are a pile of them.) But two weeks ago the worst flood to hit the Delaware River in half a century wrecked the valley. When the water crested, trash, silt, and muck floated 4 feet deep in the Shad King's river cabin. Nearby boat ramps were swept away. Riverside roads crumbled into heaps of macadam and mud-caked concrete. The river was a mess and the shad fishing—well, the King didn't want to think about it.

Then, just a week ago, a beluga whale showed up in the river, under the Trenton, New Jersey, bridge, feeding on about a billion shad and herring every day. Right now it's attracting hordes of onlookers and sending shad fishermen into a tizzy over what measures the tree huggers might take in order to keep anglers at a safe distance—say, 6 nautical miles—from the navigationally challenged marine mammal during the peak of the American shad migration up America's greatest shad river.

And there's more, for into this quagmire steps a writer for a national magazine who has come to see just what the Shad King can do, to go where the Shad King says the heart and soul of shad fishing in America is, and to try to figure out why American shad fishing has a heart and soul to begin with.

Quickly, now, because it's already late and the Shad King is getting antsy—one more addition to the King's burdens: Today he and his new writer friend are to meet a man named John McPhee, and the Shad King is a little rattled by the prospect. McPhee is one of the most respected natural history writers of our time. A staff writer for the *New Yorker* magazine and a Ferris Professor of Journalism at Princeton University, McPhee won the 1999 Pulitzer Prize for general nonfiction for his twenty-year-long book project, *Annals of the Former World*. None of that matters as much to the Shad King as the fact that in 2002 McPhee published his twenty-sixth book, *The Founding Fish*, a tome of 358 engrossing pages parsing every possible detail and attribute of the American shad and American shad fishing. During his research for the book, McPhee tried to hook up with the Shad King, but it never happened. Now it's happening.

So the Shad King has a few things on his mind. Months in advance of a migratory period that can shift by weeks on either end, he'd chosen a date for us to fish. Now it's late in the morning, later than he'd like it, and we step into his fishing partner's 19-foot Monark metal skiff, dubbed the *Shad II*. We push off into the Foul Rift pool, a mile-long slack below the largest rapid on the longest undammed river in eastern America, a place where generations of the Shad King's family have cast for the world's largest herring, to see what he can do.

Let me tell you up front that this is going to be a fishing story in which relatively few fish appear, and that you shouldn't hold it against the Shad King. That's not the way he wants it. It's not what he's accustomed to. But these are American shad, and that's the way it is.

The Shad King is Jim Flynn, a fifty-year-old husband, father, fisherman, and field supervisor for a propane gas company from Phillipsburg, New Jersey, hard on the Delaware River. He is red-faced and blue-eyed, boisterous and boyish and blissful that he lives in a small town where being a big kid at fifty years of age does not go unappreciated. There might be more dissimilar figures than the Shad King and the unassuming, self-effacing, professorial John McPhee. It is, for example, unlikely that conditions would ever exist to prompt McPhee to parade up and down the Delaware River in an $8 Park City crown adorned with plastic rubies, as the King has done. But for all their differences, a few things they share. Each is utterly convinced that this untrammeled, largely agrarian swath of northwestern New Jersey is a little piece of heaven on earth. And each is in love with the American shad.

It could be argued that the American shad presents a greater possibility for future gains in recreational fishing opportunity than any other fish. They are native to eastern rivers from Labrador to Florida, and in recent years along the eastern seaboard, dam removals and new ways of passing migratory fish around dams have opened up thousands of miles of spawning habitat closed to shad for decades. On the West Coast, the fish aren't native, but they've been there since 1871, when four milk cans of Hudson River juvenile shad were carted by railroad and stagecoach and poured into the headwaters of California's Sacramento River. In the Columbia River states, American shad populations have quadrupled since 1970 and now support an enormous recreational fishery.

Shad fishing is built on the premise that the fish don't eat anything at all during their migrations from the ocean to the freshwater rivers where they spawn. Instead, American shad are said to slash and strike out of annoyance, or irritation, or instinct, or some reason other than hunger. But here's the trick: For whatever reason they strike, when they do, the result can be spectacular. The same morphological attributes that allows shad to swim for an average of 2,000 miles each year give them plenty of ways to trip up a reel drag. They sport the deeply forked tail of tuna, bonefish, and other speedsters. A flat, compressed profile slices through current like a scimitar, and when a shad turns its deep, wedge-shaped body broadside to the current, the fisherman has to fight the force of the entire river, and the fish knows it. Sounding or leaping, American shad are, as an old saw goes, "pound for pound, the fight'n'st fish around."

Which is a good thing, because the odd pound of shad is all we're going to get.

Foul Rift is a half-mile run of ledge-slashed haystacks, souse holes, and standing waves. At certain levels, jet-drive outboards can pick their way through, but not today. We hug the "Pennsie side," as the King describes it, worming our way along boulders silt-blasted to baby-smooth finish. Tufts of leaves, trash bags, and a pair of gym shorts are tangled 12 feet high in the trees. My stomach knots at the thought of so much water thundering through.

We anchor up at a strong eddy line, what the Shad King calls a "backwash," and he and his buddy Tim Clymer go to work on the downriggers. McPhee draws a finger through a clear plastic lure box and ties on a small dart—pink and white with a tail of pearl Flashabou. He snips off the tag end of line with the scissors from a Leatherman tool.

To catch a shad, according to McPhee, the fisherman must be able to read the river like a whitewater kayaker. Below rapids, where the roiling, swift currents unspool downstream from the rocks, eddy lines form on both sides of the pool. Pods of shad hold beside the seam, and whether the angler is casting or fishing with downriggers, eddy lines are where the action is. When there is action. In good years, McPhee tells me, the fish are everywhere. Most years, however, it's a game of patience, frequently giving way to outright endurance. "It seems like I can spend a month waiting for something to happen," he says, "then you can have your whole season in a day or two."

His right leg is crossed over his left, forming a shelf on which he rests his hands, twitching the rod tip to life every few seconds. "That's all it takes," he explains, "just a little *took . . . took* every now and then."

But it's not working. Not today, not here. We catch the occasional shad, but none are overly large or feisty. None are showy or jumpy like shad are supposed to be. They surge for a few moments, but not in a manner that makes memories. It's a long time between fish, but it's still early in the day. There's time.

To fill it, Clymer explains the genesis of the Shad King's royalty. In 1998, the King won the Forks of Delaware Shad Tournament with a 7.23-pound buck fish. Winning this is the regional equivalent of coming home with the Heisman Trophy; even the lady at the convenience-store checkout knows who wins, and she can likely quote a lot of the last decade's winners. "It's big around here," Clymer says. "I'm telling you—people cover that tournament." The following winter, the King's cronies at deer camp dubbed him the "Shad King" and held a coronation ceremony with a cheap party crown. It was an adolescent prank, fueled by deer-camp liquor and small-town friendships. It got better.

That spring, the Shad Heads solicited friends to pony up $10 apiece to place an ad in the local paper, complete with a photograph of the crowned king with a fishing-rod scepter, wishing the Shad King "Good Luck from your Loyal Subjects" for the next tournament. It was designed to be a "bust"—the Shad Heads' term for good-natured ribbing or practical jokes, such as drilling a hole in a boat angler's pee can—but Flynn seeks the limelight like a shad seeks shade, and he can take as good as he gives. Embracing the name, the crown, and the benefits of local notoriety, he became the darling of tournament boosters and turned into the go-to interviewee for reporters covering shad fishing. He motored up and down the river in his crown. He attracted the attention of McPhee. "If we'd known it was going to be this big," Clymer says with a laugh, "we'd have thrown that crown in the trash can."

But the King is not delivering today, when the spotlight is on him. McPhee tries to relieve the suffocating pressure of no fish. "My being here doesn't bode well," he offers, softly. "I consistently catch the fewest fish. I don't know what it is."

"What it is," says the King, "is that these are not fish. They're damned shad."

"Yes," McPhee says. He's quiet for along moment, as if that's all there is to say about it. *Took . . . took.*

We give the spot 45 minutes of effort, changing depths, spoon colors, spoon sizes, the orientation of the boat in the current. Four men in a shad boat on the Delaware in spring shouldn't have to work this hard for fish. "People take off their week of vacation to fish for shad here," McPhee says, shaking his head. "This is the Yankee Stadium of shad fishing."

The Shad King's shoulders slump.

We motor downstream, to a wide spot in the river beneath the 500-foot-tall smokestacks and cooling towers of Pennsylvania Power & Light's Martins Creek plant. It's a surreal atmosphere, fishing for wild fish in the shadow of such a monolithic industrial presence. Clymer is on the throttle, watching the depth numbers on the fish finder. The Shad King is on his knees in the bow, a white anchor line snaking through his hands. He knows with precision where he wants the boat and keeps one eye on the shore for position, but he's a little handicapped ever since the flood ripped away the refrigerator that long ago had lodged itself against a tree just opposite the underwater shelf. Now it's all about the numbers telegraphing the bottom profile.

"Eleven feet," Clyner drones. "Eleven. Ten. Ten."

"Keep it coming," says the King. "I want it up on the ledge."

"Ten. Ten. Ten. Nine."

"Now. Shut her down."

In my mind, the King says he imagines the river's bottom as the shad see it. They are on the run, moving with urgency that pushes a fish from the deep ocean to river shallows hundreds of miles from the sea. The buck shad are "squirrelly," and they'll venture into shallower water. Not so the roes. "I think they keep their noses buried in the river channel and just go."

He explains the strategy. The Foul Rift pool is deep, 20, 40, 60 feet in places, but at the head of the pool there's a change. The water starts to foam. The fish can hear, or feel, or sense in the way that fish sense the world in a manner fishermen can't understand, the rapids ahead. Below the power plant the river channel snakes away from the Jersey bank to the Pennsie side, and so do the fish. Right there the bottom starts to rise, and so do the fish. "We want metal in their faces right as they bump up on the ledge."

McPhee looks out over the broad, nearly featureless run. He deadpans: "I don't see how we can miss."

Five seconds later the Shad King's rod bends deep. "Right as I was feathering it over the ledge." He nudges me and crooks a finger at me, at the rod, at the place where the line disappears into the Delaware, grinning, a red-faced cherub of a man for whom it's all a little better now.

Clymer is right there for him. "Don't get all puffed up. One isn't the magic number," he says. I can hear the air leave the King. "You'll know when we have them dialed in."

So we wait for the next fish—hoping, wishing, trying to believe that the shad just landed was the first or second or fiftieth in a phalanx of migrating shad that at this very moment stretches from Foul Rift to the sea. We're greeted with nothing. An hour of nothing. Two. It's not a bad way to spend a pretty spring day. But I'm glad I'm not the Shad King.

It's 2:00 now, and before every cast, every time, without fail, the Shad King first checks the action of his flutter spoon. He studies it for flotsam fouled in the split ring or draped over the willow blade. He dips it in the river current beside the boat, quiet for the moment, making sure that it flutters just so. Because when the spoon is fluttering, so too is the bright gold long-shanked hook hand-soldered to it. And it is that agitated, quivering action of the gold hook, the King is convinced, that entices the shad to strike.

"Not the spoon itself?" I ask.

"Nah," says the King.

"What about color?" McPhee queries. Most shad fishermen carry spoons in at least a dozen color combinations, all hand-painted, all requiring multiple coats of pigment and clear coat and glitter. Pink-on-white. Orange. Chartreuse-on-green. Some are speckled, others striped. "Does color seem to make a difference?"

"Nah," says the King. "It's the flutter of that gold hook. The shad just can't take it."

But the shad are tight-lipped despite the flutter spoons fluttering all around our boat. In two hours of fishing, our four rods take three fish. The slow fishing means long periods of silence in the boat. We haven't been fishing together long enough for the quiet to feel altogether comfortable, not like guys such as the King and Clymer, who sometimes fish for fourteen hours a day, day after day, within a rod's length of each other. The occasional shad yanks the line, but these fish leave in their wake silences that beg to be filled by something—other fish, preferably. Instead, they're filled by the whine of the downrigger wires vibrating in the current.

In McPhee's defense, this is not his preferred method of fishing for shad. He is an advocate of the traditional shad dart, offered to shad in the traditional manner, meaning cast across the current, with the river's flow swinging the dart into the eddy lines below.

That's how most anglers caught shad for decades. But over the last fifteen years or so, downriggers have altered the landscape of American shad fishing, at least in the Delaware River. Just the day before, I'd stood in George "Pappy" Magaro's 19-foot skiff, on a current seam at the confluence of the Delaware and Lehigh Rivers. (This is actually the "forks" of the Delaware, the Lehigh was long considered a branch of the main stem.) The boat bristled with downriggers. Magaro is a retired Bethlehem, Pennsylvania, firefighter, festooned with tattoos and turquoise jewelry, subtle as a gaff. He pours untold hours into the Delaware River Shad Fishermen's Association, of which he is the current president, and fishes this very same current seam sixty, seventy, eighty days a season.

For a long time, Magaro told me, it was shad darts and nothing but. Then someone showed up with a downrigger. "My catch rate went up 70 percent," he said. A lot of people don't like downriggers, he admitted. "They think it's cheating. But fishfinders and downriggers put your bait right where the fish are. Since when is that cheating?"

In only one place in McPhee's opus to the American shad does he mention the notion of a downrigger. It is in a passage about one of the Delaware's great icons of shad fishing, Buddy Grucela, a guy who grew up near Foul Rift. In 1982 Grucela wrote *The Original Guide to Better Shad Fishing on the Delaware River*. A man who not only made his own shad darts but had a machinist custom-make his own shad-dart mold, Grucela "spurns downriggers," McPhee wrote. McPhee then observed, not so subtly, "He prefers to do the fishing himself."

Now it's 4:00, and we're all a little antsy. We've been anchored in a new spot for 2 hours and the only action has been a fish lost when the downrigger failed to release. If I'd had x-ray vision to see through his hat brim,

I am sure I would have seen McPhee wince. A man with a fish pole in his hands might have landed that fish.

We pull anchor to try something new. For an hour we've watched a small boat filled with Herberts, another stalwart Foul Rift family, pull in half a dozen shad by trolling flutter spoons up the pool, inching slowly upcurrent. With each Herbert fish I could feel the noose tighten on the Shad King. Then, suddenly, as McPhee reels in his line, his rod tip blows. The King tenses, but unfortunately it's not a fish. McPhee's line has wrapped ingloriously around the downrigger apparatus. I reach over to unbraid the snarl, and the line breaks. I wrap the loose line around my left hand, bringing the dart back to the boat, and that's when a silver-green shape slashes toward the surface. After we've spent hours analyzing bottom contours and dialing in downriggers to put out lures within a foot or two of the channel bottom, a fish porpoises in 14 feet of water to take a shad dart a foot deep? Why would a shad do that? What's it doing this close to the surface?

A mere 6 or 7 feet separate me from the fish, so there's no line stretch to work with, nowhere the shad can go. The King and Clymer hoot at the spectacle, and for maybe 15 seconds I fight the fish by hand, no downrigger to blunt the electric jolt of every surge, no limber rod to take the brunt of each swift change of direction when the fish turns its fat, hatchet-head belly into the current.

Shad have notoriously fragile mouths, and I know the papery membrane that holds the hook won't be able to sustain this kind of abuse. It's a fine line shad fishermen walk every time they hook a fish. "Don't horse it!" angling partners yell, unhelpfully, knowing full well that the guy with the rod in his hand is trying his level best to avoid just that. I desperately try to unwrap a few coils of line to feed the green fish a bit of slack, careful not to jerk or pull too hard, and that's when the line goes slack, the shad disappears, and the dart dangles behind the boat. I groan. But there, for a few seconds, I'd come as close as anyone could to reaching out and touching a live, migrating American shad with as few physical intermediaries as possible. It left me momentarily speechless.

Not so the Shad King. He is beside himself. "Craziest thing I've ever seen!" he hollers. Clymer whoops with glee. When I glance at McPhee, he is behind his hat brim, quietly running a finger through his lure box, ciphering the future.

At 7:00 the trollers pick up another shad. We catch nothing. The sunlight coming through the trees on the Pennsie side is gorgeous, filtering through young leaves. Birds begin to sing their evening songs—a mourning dove, a meadowlark. We catch nothing. Minutes, a half hour, tick by. A peacock crows from someone's backyard. Clymer looks at the King. "That's usually the signal that it's getting ready to bust loose," he says. We catch nothing. My heart's breaking for the Shad King. I know these guys can fish. The King and Clymer have caught fish so fast that they couldn't keep the downriggers locked and loaded. They've caught 40, 50 fish in a day and more. They've won dailies, won the tournament. A sparrow sings. Nothing. The sun drops down to another branch. Nothing. Arms crossed, hands in pockets, McPhee is in the right-hand seat, jiggling his shad dart half-heartedly with a bump of the knee.

The Shad King shrugs. "Sorry there weren't many fish. I wish we could have caught a few more." It's the shoe-shuffling apology every fisherman has heard—and offered.

But nobody's holding anything against anyone. No one is here to dethrone the Shad King. And that's when it occurs to me that this is the heart and soul of shad fishing. Not the good days, when you work double hookups for hours on end and the paint and glitter and depth don't matter. This is when the heart and soul of shad fishing comes to the surface—when the fish are in the river and you are on it and the water temperature is just right and the light is low and shade is creeping and the peacock crows and all day long you have caught next to nothing. And then nothing at all. And still, you fish.

McPhee seems genuinely happy to have spent a half day on the water, in the company of a crew of rabble-rousers quite unlike himself, ribbing each other with inside jokes.

Quiet. Then: "I've been to the Bonneville Dam, on the Columbia River, where 5 million shad pass through every spring." McPhee tells the story softly, as an aside to the falling light and the hush of fishermen with few fish to discuss.

The Shad King's thin eyebrows arch over his glasses. "Five million shad?" In recent years, the Delaware has hosted somewhere between 100,000 and 300,000 migrating fish.

"Oh, yes. People in this part of the country rarely think about shad being in the Pacific Northwest, but the Columbia is home to the largest run of shad in the world."

"Five million shad?" says the Shad King. It's a figure he seems to have trouble grasping. It's not a matter of disbelief, not that he thinks it can't possibly be true, or that McPhee is mistaken or dishonest. But standing in the boat dubbed the *Shad II*, afloat on the Yankee Stadium of shad fishing, this man whose life revolves around shad—he just can't get his mind around a river full of 5 million shad.

"Five million. Did you hear that, Timmy?" He grows quiet. It is a very un-King-like moment. But then he reaches down to study his flutter spoon and to pluck away part of an oak catkin caught on the shank. It's only the size of a mustard seed, but it's just enough to foul the flutter. And whether there are 5 million fish in the river or the fading hope of a single one, the Shad King is taking no chances.

SUMMER

Running Like Hell

Michael Finkel

I kissed Janet Runyan because I fell in love with the way she ran. I fell in love with her stride—the way her legs appeared to arc instead of scissor, the way her feet seemed to brush the pavement rather than pound. The swing of her arms. The slight, steady bob of her chin. These are not the only reasons. I kissed her because she is beautiful. I kissed her because her life had become a jumble of sleep deprivation and physical pain and a training schedule that was the equivalent of running nearly five marathons a week, and I wanted her to know that I, an outsider, did not condemn her for her choices, however unorthodox they were, nor did I pity her or want to change her. I kissed her because there seemed no way to explain all this. It was 5:00 in the morning, and everyone around us was paired off. Kissing seemed to be on the agenda. So that is what we did.

I met Janet early last summer, in Boulder, Colorado, in the midst of a long and extraordinary run. I had come to Boulder for two reasons. First, to conduct research for a book I am writing about the motivations and lifestyles of people who seem addicted to excessive exercise. Second, I wanted to aid my own pursuit of exhaustion. Over the past year I had been methodically preparing to run an "ultra"—that is, a race longer than the standard marathon distance of 26.2 miles. The race I had my sights on was the Western States 100. But in June, less than a month before the event, I found myself daunted by the enormity of running 100 miles and overwhelmed with doubts. My training began to stagnate. I came to Boulder seeking inspiration. I came to find a group of people known as Divine Madness.

Nearly everything I knew about Divine Madness I'd gleaned from a pair of articles published in the *New York Times* and *Newsweek* during the summer of 1997. The articles had a strong effect on me; I cut them out and pinned them to my office wall. According to the stories, Divine Madness was a strange and insular group consisting of a guru and approximately forty followers, men and women whose ages ranged from mid-twenties to late fifties. Their way of life included communal living, all-night meditation sessions, and no shortage of unconventional sexual behavior. There was also a lawsuit, filed by three ex-members (two of them women), accusing the guru of systematically destroying their lives.

What fascinated me most was the running. Spurred on by their guru, about twenty-five of the Divine Madness members had taken to ultra-running. They logged incredible distances—sometimes 50 miles in a day—hours upon hours of running; an entire lifestyle, it seemed, built around running. All this training had resulted in some remarkable performances. A Divine Madness member named Steve Peterson had triumphed in each of the past four years at the Leadville 100, a race that is the equivalent of running nearly four successive marathons combined with an elevation gain in excess of 15,000 feet, more than the rise from the base to the summit of Mount Everest. His winning times were usually between 18 and 19 hours. In 1996 Janet Runyan won the U.S. 100-kilometer national championships, covering the 62 miles in less than 9 hours. This guru is on to something, I thought. His runners had evidently tapped into an energy source I had not discovered, one I hoped they'd be willing to share.

Establishing contact with the group was not difficult. I phoned a Boulder running-shoe store (where, it turned out, Divine Madness members get a discount) and asked how I could get in touch with a member. I was promptly given the phone number for Art Ives, one of Divine Madness's strongest runners. I called and left a message.

Art rang back a few hours later. I told him that where I live the mountain trails were still clogged with snow and that I planned to be in Boulder the following week, in order to train for my ultra. I told him about some of my recent training difficulties. Neither of us mentioned the name Divine Madness.

"We do a pretty good run on Wednesdays," Art said. He paused. "I suppose you could join in."

I told him I'd be honored. "Where should I meet you?"

"Well," said Art slowly and, it seemed, a bit evasively, as if he were weighing his invitation, "I won't know that until Tuesday night."

I gave him my cell phone number. The next Tuesday I flew to Boulder and met friends for dinner. Around 8:00 I began to get antsy. Perhaps Art had discussed his invitation with the other members and felt that the presence of a stranger was not a good idea. Perhaps they felt I wasn't a strong enough runner. (I didn't know if I was strong enough.) Two hours later my phone rang. It was Art. "We're on," he said. He gave me the name of a trailhead on the outskirts of town and told me to be there at 8:00 a.m.

"Be ready for 30 miles," he said. "Maybe more."

Ultra-running is a strange, all-consuming sport. There are very few ultra-runners in North America (a rough estimate is 8,000), and for good reason: It is the point, I believe, at which running crosses the line from sport to obsession. Ultra-running is hard on the body: hard on the joints, the muscles, the hips, the spine. It may be punishing right down to the molecular level; doctors are beginning to question whether excessive running can corrupt healthy cells, resulting in maladies such as chronic fatigue syndrome and even cancer.

Ultra-runners are on a first-name basis with misery. For many of us, the longer we run, the more sleep-deprived we are, the closer we come to absolute exhaustion, the more satisfied we feel. I have been in the throes of such an obsession, and it's not difficult to imagine how soothing it would be to find someone who could guarantee my body endless challenges, who was willing to manage and schedule and plan my pain.

Divine Madness, in fact, is not the only guru-led ultra-running community in the United States. The two thousand or so followers of Sri Chinmoy, based in New York City, include a large contingent of ultra-runners, several of whom have completed the group's annual 51-day, 3,100-mile-long race. A few weeks before meeting with Divine Madness, I spent time in New York, watching and occasionally running with several Sri Chinmoy disciples as they plodded around a 1-mile loop for ten consecutive days, stopping only for catnaps. There was a contingent of ultra-runners in the EST [Erhard Seminar Training] movement who called themselves the World Runners, and a group known as Nichiren Shoshu of America, or NSA, occasionally embarked on long sessions of group marching.

In describing Divine Madness, the *New York Times* bandied about the word *cult*. Divine Madness, of course, hates that label, preferring to call itself an ultra club. But Divine Madness is "definitely cultic," says Carol Giambalvo, director of the recovery program at the American Family Foundation, a group that keeps tabs on cultic groups nationwide. Indeed, the lawsuit supports Giambalvo's belief that Divine Madness meets most of the criteria that indicate a group is operating as a cult. According to the suit (which was settled out of court last year), Divine Madness isolated its members from the outside world; attempted to control members' physical needs and finances; and inculcated fears or phobias.

Divine Madness is centered on one man: Marc Tizer, whom his adherents call Yo. He spends most of his time at the group's retreat in central New Mexico. He is small and gaunt, with wild eyes and an unruly Brillo pad of a beard and mustache. Now fifty-one, Tizer came to Boulder from Philadelphia (via Berkeley, California) in the seventies and began teaching a healing system he called harmonizing. It is a grab bag of religion, mysticism, and self-help programs, including meditation, group therapy, holistic healing, and frequent consultation of the I Ching. The goal of harmonizing is to achieve a state Tizer calls transformation. Yo, his followers believe, has reached the state of transformed being, which gives him superhuman powers: the ability to influence people's thoughts and health, and the Denver Broncos' win-loss record.

Evidently, harmonizing was profoundly appealing to certain people, and within a few years Tizer had enough adherents to establish his group, which called itself the Community. Members rented a series of houses in and around Boulder and began living in groups of five or six, men and

MICHAEL FINKEL

women together. According to the lawsuit, contact with the outside world is limited: "Tizer forbade reading of outside literature; forbade travel outside of Boulder; forbade watching television; and required daily reading and study of the notes of his lectures." Most members are self-employed, working in town as caterers, music teachers, or running coaches, and reportedly donate portions of their incomes to the group. The 160-acre New Mexico retreat is said to have been paid for in cash by a member; another said she turned over a $100,000 inheritance to the group.

Tizer introduced running to his followers about ten years ago, after witnessing an ultra-race at the University of Colorado. Tizer, himself an avid runner, seems to have made the sport a metaphor for the state of one's mental health. Aches and injuries and other troubles encountered on a long run have direct counterparts in deficiencies in one's pursuit of transformation. Extreme distance running seems to fit perfectly into Tizer's ideas of self-fulfillment through deprivation and exhaustion. His rambling, stream-of-consciousness lectures frequently last all night, and group meetings can go until dawn.

The emphasis on ultra-running and sleeplessness, explains Giambalvo, is a variation on a classic cult theme. "A cult leader often seeks to have his followers in a weakened state," she says. "People who are sleep-deprived or physically exhausted are more malleable, more suggestible, and far less likely to disagree with the leader's demands."

According to the lawsuit, one of his demands is sex. Marriage and monogamous couplings are discouraged; Yo believes such relationships sap too much of the spiritual energy needed to accomplish transformation. "I am tired of feeling the sexual pressure," wrote one ex-member in a letter included in the lawsuit. "I am tired of having to field that energy and feeling guilty when I don't want to make love. . . . It reminds me of a battering relationship where the woman is not allowed to communicate with the outside for fear of other influences." The lawsuit states that Tizer has had open sexual relationships with many women in the Community and that he "told female members of the Community that their emotional health required that he control their sexual activity." His regular partners are part of an inner group known as "the Yo ladies."

The guru denied all charges of wrongdoing in the *New York Times* article. "There is such an illusion that I control people," Tizer was quoted as saying. "A cult is where everyone shaves their head and you have to give all your money over. This is something else, where people who are sincerely trying to improve themselves have a teacher who is more or less evolved and is trying to help them lead a more balanced, harmonious life."

Of the forty members of Divine Madness, there are about a dozen men and a dozen women capable of completing ultras. It is no coincidence that Tizer's top students seem to be those who can run the farthest. "The community revolves around the best runners," one former member told me. "Those who don't run work as support crews for those who do; they kiss the runners' butts. When I was in Divine Madness, I was sure it was the coolest running club in the world. It took me years to realize that the price of admission was my mind and my spirit and my independence."

On Wednesday morning I arrived at the trailhead a minute late. Art was already there, looking perturbed. Divine Madness runners are exceedingly punctual; I soon discovered why. Art took off up the trail, which headed across a cow pasture and into the craggy foothills of the Rocky Mountains. It was a gorgeous day: 70 degrees, with puffball clouds meandering across the sky, the peaks still pleated with snow.

Art had a quiet, loping stride and the physique of a spider. He told me he was in his early forties and had run several hundred-mile races, including a twelfth-place finish at Leadville in 1997. It was just the two of us. Two or 3 miles into the run, though, Art began to check his watch. We sped up a bit, came to an intersection with another trail and there, as if by design—it was by design—was another runner.

He was introduced to me as Kevin, and the three of us continued together. A mile later came Rebecca. Kevin and Art soon surged ahead, and Rebecca and I locked into a slower pace. She had long blond hair, a muscular physique, and a perpetual-motion machine of a stride. She wore a pained expression, not uncommon for ultra-runners, that suggested to me she was doing this solely because it would feel so good once she stopped.

Rebecca, it turned out, hadn't run at all until she joined Divine Madness four years ago. Now she was completing runs that lasted upward of 7 hours. In a few months she was scheduled to compete in a 100-kilometer race. She had just turned thirty. I had reached the same milestone a few months earlier, and there was something about this coincidence, I think, that made her open up to me. "The last half of my twenties were the worst years of my life," she said. Had things been better since she'd turned thirty? "Sort of," she said, in a tone that implied not.

I had the impression that she wanted to say more, that the opportunity to speak candidly was a rare one, but it was only a matter of minutes before Kevin and Art slowed down and we were all together. Over the next dozen miles other runners started appearing at various intersections. This was the way Divine Madness operated: an intricate interlinking of workouts, everyone on their own schedule, and yet, as the run reached a crescendo, everyone running together. And then, more than 20 miles into the run, we jumped onto the paved roads and a woman came toward us, running with an extraordinary fluidity, moving as if the road were transporting her.

"This is Janet," said Art.

The woman came upon us, slowed to a stop and pivoted. Then she fired up her stride and continued with us. We'd run nearly a marathon by this point. We ran in a tight, churning group, a sort of runners' peloton. The pace picked up. Seven minutes a mile. We all clicked subconsciously into the same cadence. Our footfalls became synchronous. There was an energy encircling the group, almost a centripetal force, that made me feel as though I'd shed my individual burden and were part of a single multi-legged entity. I was swept along by the rhythm, swept past pain and fatigue and concern. I felt less tired as the miles passed.

I ran behind Janet. A dusty-blond braid fell halfway down her back. I watched her calf muscles flex and relax, pump and deflate, like something on a steam engine. The source of her stride appeared to be not her legs but someplace in her center. Her braid scarcely swung. There was an intensity about her, about the way she ran, that I couldn't quite grasp. Occasionally she would say something aloud, a scrap of imprecise coach-speak to keep the group moving in tune: "Shorten the stride. Round the hips. Lean forward."

We shortened and rounded and leaned. I tried to emulate Janet's pace.

She seemed to be running in slow motion, and yet we were moving faster. Six forty-five. Six forty. We were closing in on 30 miles. I sidestepped to my right, opened my stride, and pulled beside her. We started to talk, in staccato phrasings, to the tempo of our breathing.

She gave me her credentials: winning the 100-kilometer championships and then, the next year, finishing second in the 50-mile championships in just over 7 hours. Later this summer she'd be shooting again for the 100K rifle. She'd come from Texas, she told me, shy and timid and seeking fulfillment. She came to Boulder and found Tizer. She hadn't started running until she was twenty-four, and not seriously until she was thirty-two. She'd just turned forty. We charged up a short, steep hill. Janet burst into the song, "Chattanooga Choo Choo," sung to the cadence of our pace. "I live to train," she said when we had reached the crest. This much was dear: She was radiating the spent joy of exhaustion. She told me she ran 130 miles a week.

What made Janet run? There was her piercing intensity—the single-minded drive endemic to almost all top athletes—but through the slits in that intensity I could sense something else. She had a purity of focus that seemed too pure. "I'll never marry," she said, matter-of-factly. "All I really do is run and eat and sleep." I couldn't help feeling that she was afflicted with an odd sort of low-grade fear, a deep-seated nervousness, as if she thought something terrible might happen to her if she stopped. All I could do was run beside her.

We came to the trailhead where the cars were, and the run was over. Four hours solid, more than 30 miles. One of the best runs of my life, maybe the very best. I mentioned this to everyone, along with my thanks. Rebecca hopped into a car and was off. Janet smiled and glanced at her watch and said she hadn't finished her workout, and she took off down the road.

Art chose that moment to ask me if I knew about the group and its leader. I said I'd read the articles about Divine Madness but had come with an open mind. Art told me he'd been upset by charges against the group. "If Divine Madness is a cult," he said, "Christianity was a cult."

The more I thought about the run, the more I wondered what these runners had subjected themselves to and why. The next day, seeking explanation,

I went to see an ex-member I'll call D. She had joined Divine Madness at twenty-four; she left the group in 1997, when she was forty-two.

D.'s home sits on a bluff overlooking Boulder, where she runs a New Age cooking school that she calls a nourishment center. We sat in her backyard in lawn chairs, catching wonderful tomatoey whiffs of the Tuscany bean soup stewing on her stove.

I began by asking about the guru. At first, D. claimed that much of her time with Tizer was rewarding. "Yo can be an incredible teacher," she said. "At times his ideas seemed magical. He held my essence. He slowed down my aging process. He was the one who told me that my destiny was with food." When I mentioned some of the eccentricities I'd read about—the isolation, the sleep deprivation—her tone shifted abruptly and her eyes narrowed. "You kind of surrender yourself to Yo," D. said. "You live in a cocoon with him. Sometimes we'd listen to Yo talk all night about running. What a waste. Yo said [much sleep] wasn't necessary. He said the organs in the body have their own time to sleep and that as long as you got your liver sleep, between 3:00 and 5:00 a.m., you were okay." D. also said that Tizer did not allow his runners to eat their first meal of the day until after their workout, even if the run was 5 or 6 hours long. "And if you don't finish the run," she said, "you don't eat either.'

Tizer, she went on, had frequent sex with women in the Community, often while drinking. She confirmed the existence of the Yo ladies, though she wasn't one of them. "Oh yeah, I had sexual relations with Yo," she said. "He needed to make love every night. One time, in the morning, I said I didn't feel like it, and he said, 'Oh, you'll get over it.' Just so he could get his rocks off." Toward the end of our visit, I asked D. if she still ran. "No way," she said. "And I don't miss it. I don't miss it at all."

On the drive back to town, my cell phone rang. It was Art, calling to invite me to a party. "You seem like the type of person who wouldn't mind staying up late," he said. There was a gathering that evening, and he gave me an address. "Come around midnight." As I hung up, I was reminded of something D. had told me. I had asked her how she was first enticed to join Divine Madness. "I was invited to a party," she said.

The gathering was held in the loft of a renovated barn behind one of the group's homes. The loft was windowless and steam-room hot and contained at least thirty people, two-thirds of them women. Vinyl records were being played—classic rock, a good amount of Beatles. Many of the men were shirtless and dancing wildly, legs and arms flapping, hips pumping, hair spraying sweat. Women mirrored their moves. A boule of Maker's Mark whiskey was pressed into my hand. I took a long swig and passed it on. Soon another bottle was in my hand. I drank again.

It took me several minutes to realize what was going on. For 30 seconds into each song, there was regular rock'n'roll dancing, but this would soon devolve into dirty dancing and then body smearing and then, quite suddenly, passionate kissing. Some of the couples ended up rolling about on the carpeted floor; others sat and fondled each other. No one, save me, seemed the least bit self-conscious. I took another drink.

Janet and Rebecca were both there, and I stood near the turntable and watched them dance. I saw Janet dance with someone else and, soon enough, kiss him. After a dozen songs I had watched her kiss four men; this stirred in me a surprising jealousy. I'm not quite sure when it happened, but one moment I was watching Janet dance and the next she had flopped down beside me. My pulse jumped; I began to sweat. We got to talking—about running, the mechanics of her exquisite stride, the endless pursuit of faster times—and somewhere during this talk she wound herself about me, so that when she started telling me about her injuries, she'd glide my hand to the site of the wound. I had the feeling I was slipping headlong into trouble, but I did nothing to stop her. She told me about ripping her calf muscle during a 100K race and running through the agony. Down went my hand to her calf. She guided my hand to just above her left knee, where I felt a button-sized scar, and then near her hip, where I could feel a second scar. She told me she'd broken her femur while running and had had a metal rod inserted to hold the bone together. She had even competed with the rod in place.

It got to be late, very late, and suddenly people were pairing off and leaving. I felt that strange dizzy energy on the other side of exhaustion, so I said to Janet, "Let's go look at the stars," and we unhooked ourselves and walked downstairs, holding hands. But there were no stars outside, because the sky was already turning blue. Janet said, "Do you want to go running at nine?" I wanted to go, but I needed more than three hours' sleep, so I said, "I can't, Janet, I really can't," and I leaned forward, and we were very close. The moment seemed to beg for closure, like a first date, so I kissed her—or maybe, in truth, she kissed me—but it was an innocent kiss, dry-lipped and brief. We were too tired for passion, and I think we both knew it, but we tried again, and again it was the same, and so I said, "Good night," and she said, "Good morning," and we laughed again and I walked to my car and drove away.

Two days later Art invited me to join the Sunday run, the most intense workout of the week. I ran for 6 hours, coveting more than 40 miles, and again I found the experience profoundly strength-giving. I spent much of the run with either Janet or Rebecca.

Rebecca and I ran together for some time, just the two of us, and she continued where she'd left off on our previous run. She expressed doubts about her desire to continue running, fears about her spiritual growth. It was impossible for me to remain neutral. As we ran through the foothills, I told Rebecca of the joys of travel, of the pleasures of riding a bike and swimming in the ocean and sleeping late and goofing off and generally being in charge of one's own life. I could tell she was listening, thinking about the path she had chosen, weighing her choices.

For a long time she was silent. Then, suddenly, her foot caught a tree root and she went down hard, skidding on all fours over the rocky path. She jumped up, but already blood was gathering at both knees and tears were pooling in her eyes. She kept going.

"I know why that happened," she said after a few minutes.

"Why?"

Again there was no sound except the slap of footfalls and the rasp of her breathing. "I lost my concentration," she eventually said, "because I was wondering if it would be okay to call you sometime."

Her confession unnerved me. In one intimate moment she had transferred to me all of her pain and chaos and confusion. I told her my e-mail address, and she memorized it, but after one exchange of pleasantries a week later, the messages stopped.

I ran my final miles with Janet. When my 6 hours were up, I gave her a brief hug and watched her push on alone. Janet, I realized, would be miserable if she left Divine Madness, even though I felt she was surely damaging herself by staying. She had become an athletic machine, constantly running, constantly exhausted, never quite finished, never quite transformed.

To unlock the secrets of the group's runners requires a sacrifice I'm unwilling to make. I left Boulder, but not before tucking the memories of my runs into a spot where I could access them when necessary, deep into a difficult workout.

Three weeks later I completed my 100-mile race. I finished in 23 hours and 48 minutes, and I'm convinced my runs with Divine Madness helped me break the magical 24-hour mark. My race strategy was uncomplicated: I simply envisioned Janet's stride every step of the way.

Marine for a Day

Don Kardong

The climax of the Camp Pendleton Mud Run is impossible to miss. It's not at the finish line, as one would expect of a 10K race. It's not at the top of some hot, dusty hill, though there are plenty here. And it's not at any of the walls, tunnels, or belly-crawls in this race. It is, quite clearly, at the final obstacle.

The mud pit.

There, just 100 meters from the finish, the Mud Run reaches its squalid crescendo—fundamentally, horizontally, ineluctably. You approach your mud bath running, maybe even up on your toes. A minute later you exit, a pig-like mess.

Everyone does. That's the point of this event, assuming there is a point. That's also why there are bleachers on the hillside next to the mud pit, where friends and family can sit and shout "encouragement." And that's why, after finishing, I walk back to the pits to have a better look.

There they wallow, mid-pack mud-packers, slithering into the pits on one end, dog-paddling through about 25 meters of ooze, then emerging at the other end.

Wisely, some wear goggles. Others are tentative, less than eager for goop-enhanced hair-dos, but still enjoying the novelty of the day. Still others openly revel, and climb up the slippery embankment at the far end with a whoop.

Everyone remembers that telling hint from the race instructions: "Loose clothing and pockets hold mud." So they clutch and tug at running briefs and sports bras, making sure they're still there, and at least partially drained of gunk.

This scene reminds me of something, but at first I can't place it. We're on a high-powered Marine base 40 miles north of San Diego, but the Mud Run is not the grim, chilled-to-the-bone stuff of military legend. This is more of a wild, sloppy frolic. A-ha. That's it. I know what it reminds me of: Woodstock, 1969. A sea of mud, crawling with youthful energy. Minus the music.

Earlier that warm, June morning, I'm lined up near Lake O'Neill, which is toward the southern end of Camp Pendleton, waiting for the race to begin. This is the eighth-annual Mud Run, organized by the Semper Fit Division of the Marine Corps Community Services at Camp Pendleton, which raises funds to support "quality-of-life programs" for Marines and their families.

There are 3,500 of us, a number capped after the 1999 race to help alleviate parking, course, and other logistical limitations. Without the cap, it's hard to know how big this run might have gotten, but a look at the event's growth shows that organizers were on a fast, muddy track, right from the start. In 1994, the inaugural Mud Run attracted 900 participants. By its sixth year, that number had jumped to 4,700, which organizers deemed too many.

As the start approaches, we hear there will be a 10-minute delay. I chat to a runner next to me, and quickly notice that he's used duct tape to seal up shoe laces, socks, and other openings where muck and gravel might seep in. Others have done the same. I have not, which turns out to be a good thing. I later notice that some orifices that admit mud are not especially amenable to duct-taping. Or at least *removing* it.

While we wait, the announcer gives last-minute advice and a few warnings, including a plea that we not wash off in the lake after we finish. "It's the sole source of drinking water for the facility," he pleads. Then, for the unpersuaded, he adds, "Also, there are seven pairs of breeding anaconda in the lake, and we don't want to annoy them."

I suspect he's kidding, but I'm not sure. Some around me are laughing; others look frightened.

Now we're on our way. It's a mad scramble at first, up a short hill and around a sharp corner. By the first mile mark, we've been doused by a high-pressure fire hose. Next comes the tire obstacle, a high-stepping drill that makes us look like football players at practice. That's followed a half-mile later by a steeple jump—walk through mud, and vault a 5-foot wall—then the sand crawl. None of these really presents too much difficulty.

In this section of the race, Camp Pendleton strikes me as a wonderful throwback to an older Southern California. Marines may have spent the last seventy-five years pummeling this property with artillery shells, but the sun-blanched hills of the beautiful middle miles are oddly peaceful. Despite its serious military function and the 37,000 Marines and their families who reside on base, the 200 square miles of Camp Pendleton also offer the last really big patches of wildlife sanctuary in the region.

In other words, if you're an endangered species around here, don't worry too much about the man with the mortar. Instead, beware the banker with the map of where the next neighborhood will be.

In this back section, I'm able to pass several entrants in the "Boots and Utes" division, a group comprised of anyone willing to run in combat boots and camouflage utility pants. Over half of today's participants are active military—as in tough—but I can't imagine how uniformed soldiers can keep up with lightly clad runners. A surprising number of the Boots and Utes seem undroppable, however.

A long, sharp downhill brings us past 4 miles and another quick river crossing, followed by a sharp right turn. We detour off the main 10K loop to attack a "lesser" mud pit—one you can walk through. Once in the pit, I think of that phenomenon Ross Perot once described as having a "giant sucking sound." No, it wasn't just the sound of jobs going south of the Mexican border, it was also the sound of runners at Camp Pendleton pulling their shoes out of this mud pit.

In any race, no matter the course or the theme, I compete. I just can't help it. No surprise, then, that I suddenly find myself battling two other "mature" runners. I don't know if they're in the fifty to fifty-nine age-group, but they have gray hair, and that's enough of a taunt for my competitive drive to kick in.

Heading back onto the main loop, I try to keep the two in my sights as I vault a 5-foot wall and scurry through a 30-foot-long tunnel. Neither barrier is especially imposing, but I lose sight of both graybeards. Are they still ahead, or did I pass them? Who knows. Keep running.

I reach the final mile, a mostly unimpeded section with one detour up "Slippery Hill." At the top, Marines with hoses make sure the muddy slope doesn't dry out. Thanks, guys.

Soon after that, I prepare myself for the finale: the big, boggy bath. Rounding a turn, I hear Marines standing at the edge of the massive mud pit shouting, "Don't dive! Don't dive!" Despite my fatigue, I almost laugh out loud. But let's face it, there are some incredibly obvious things you still need to remind people *not* to do.

I scuttle in, begin crawling, and wallow. The mud actually feels quite pleasant—cool and buoyant. I can't tell how deep it is, but it's easy to scoot along the surface, ducking under wires now and then. I slither along happily enough, but then feel my shorts start to fill with ooze. Uh-oh. Mayday! Mayday!

When it's time to exit the pit, I check my shorts before standing up. Yep, still there. Heavier than usual, however. Standing carefully, I run the final 100 meters, though with a more self-conscious stride than usual.

I reach the line at 56 minutes, which is about what I expected, around 3-minutes-per-mile slower than my usual 10K pace.

Later, back at the mud pit, I stand mud-covered, baking in the sun. I watch teams of five, which are required to finish together, rallying their comrades. Also, individual runners emerging from the slime, rinsing faces, and marching on to the finish. Eventually I hit one of the showers Camp Pendleton provides to all finishers. Mud everywhere. *In* everywhere.

Washing up takes quite a while, so I almost miss my big moment back at the awards stage. First in my age-group! I must've beaten those two after all. Suddenly elated, I'm tempted to hoist my medal in the air and chant like a good Marine:

> Mud and gunk are everywhere,
>
> But I won this, so I don't care!

But I don't. Instead, I begin pondering something. If, as they say, the Camp Pendleton Mud Run is a civilian's way "to be a Marine for a day," could the rest of Marine life be this much fun?

Ruffians in the Diamond

Corey Levitan

I hover over home plate in my extra-small Las Vegas 51s uniform, focusing all concentration on the bat in my grasp. The crowd at Cashman Center cheers.

But not for me. I'm the batboy. My grammar-school dream of being a pro ballplayer—even just for a single at-bat, in a game where my hometown team is up by 15 runs and can't possibly lose—was flat-out rejected. All the 51s would allow is this.

"Now!" shouts Mikel Yarza, the seventeen-year-old Del Sol High School senior I'm replacing. It's the bottom of the first inning, and first baseman James Loney has singled, moving second baseman Wilson Valdez to third base. (Both players will eventually cross the plate.)

But batboys can't bother with such trivial information as the game's score. We need to focus on more important things, such as where the bats land when the real players get on base, walk, or strike out. Loney's is to the right of the third-base line.

"Go!" Yarza yells. Until the field is de-batted, this game cannot continue.

I sprint out to the diamond, over sunflower-husk hills and tobacco-saliva lakes, to make the crucial scoop. Then I sprint back to the dugout, gently placing Loney's bat in one of three racks. Then I sprint back out to my little batboy seat and wait to repeat the cycle.

"It's warm," says the first-base umpire, making a sour face. Bats aren't all I fetch. When umpires touch their hands to their mouths and tilt upward, I need to make like Gunga Din.

"Hey, where are you going?" the ump asks when I turn around to begin my next sprint. (I didn't realize I needed to collect the empty water cup when he's finished.) "You in some kind of hurry?" he asks as he crushes the cup and hands it to me.

Also high on my to-fetch list are baseballs. I chase after all that are hit up to first base in foul territory. And I must bring 100 new Rawlings out to the home-plate umpire, 3–5 at a time, whenever he holds up fingers corresponding to the number he needs.

Batboys earn minimum wage, which is one reason teenagers usually do it. (Another is that grown men tend not to apply for openings with "boy" in the title.) "I like baseball a lot, so this is a good job for me," says Yarza, who plays on his high school team and hopes to go to college on a baseball or football scholarship.

The most famous batboy ever was Stanley Kirk Burrell, nicknamed "Little Hammer" by members of his team, the Oakland A's, because of his resemblance to Hammerin' Hank Aaron. Burrell went on to music superstardom, and bankruptcy, as MC Hammer.

I have also earned a batboy nickname based on my resemblance to someone famous. "Hey Kazoo, you're cleaning my shoes after the game!" yells 51s relief pitcher Lance Carter. This is not the first time my look has been likened to the 2-foot-tall, floating green alien whose 1965 addition to "The Flintstones" marked the moment that this classic cartoon jumped the shark.

For the record, his name was Gazoo, not Kazoo. But I didn't correct Carter because, as I learned in junior high, those who are ridiculed tend not to be able to effectively correct those who ridicule them. Besides, space aliens are a proud part of 51s culture. The team's name derives from Area 51, and their logo depicts one of the alleged inhabitants of the secret military base, located 80 miles north of Las Vegas.

"Am I saying something funny, Kazoo?" Carter continues, unhappy with my reaction to his comment.

The 51s are the AAA farm team for the L.A. Dodgers. This means players are called directly up to the majors from here. They're also sent directly down, which is what happened to Carter, a 2003 American League All-Star, in May.

Carter's need to unleash his frustration on an innocent bystander is understandable. But when 51s catcher Eric Langill introduces himself by slapping a wad of thoroughly chewed bubblegum atop my batting helmet, I begin to suspect some of my teammates of knowing about my infiltration.

"What acting job?" Carter asks. "I really am a (expletive)!"

I told the front office not to tell the players, so reaction to my performance would be natural. At first, my secret seemed safe. "Did you win a contest or something?" asked assistant clubhouse manager Patrick Bjarage before the game, as I coated baseballs with rubbing mud from a plastic vat. (This ensures that they don't slip out of the pitchers' hands, and that my fingernails remain dirty until they grow out.) But someone has apparently let the cat out of the ballbag.

"Hey batboy!" yells hitting coach Steve Yeagher. "Where's the bag of curveballs?" There is no such thing as a curveball until it's thrown. Even I know that.

"That's not how they normally treat us," Yarza says. My prime blabbing suspect is the team's vice president of operations.

"You'd better know what you're doing!" Nick Fitzenreider scolded me upon entering the dugout. "This ain't no joke!"

I take all my assignments seriously, as I intend to prove in the sixth inning. So far, I've only acted upon Yarza's orders. Now he's retreated to the sidelines. This is the chance to prove the batman I really am.

Like millionaire Bruce Wayne, I spot my signal. It's five fingers. I gather the new balls from my blue Dodgers bag. But the umpire tosses me a curveball (literally). I place the balls down and bend over to field the rolling orb, which he judged too scuffed to use. It encounters no resistance from my catching skills.

After I chase the ball down and deposit it in the bag of scuffed rejects earmarked for batting practice, I re-gather the new balls and sprint out to the field. This is when I discover that the field is currently in use.

"The guy is still pitching!" yells Yeagher as the ump puts up a signal even those in the $7 seats can't miss: Diana Ross and the Supremes' "stop" hand.

During the 2002 World Series, San Francisco Giants batboy Darren Baker ran out to collect the bat flung by Kenny Lofton after he tripled, without realizing that the play would send J. T. Snow barreling into home plate. Baker's excuse was that he was three years old. (As Snow crossed the plate, he grabbed Giants manager Dusty Baker's son by the collar, carrying him back to the dugout.) I have no similar excuse. In fact, I'm fairly sure I'm the only cholesterol-watching batboy in baseball history.

Yeagher rolls his eyes. Postgame payback is already in the planning stages, as I discover in the locker room. "What do you mean you're not showering?" asks one of many naked 51s. "I don't care who you are, it's (expletive) gross if you don't take a shower!" My decision can't have come as a surprise, considering the anticipatory towel-snaps that were audible as he spoke.

"You ever tasted duck sausage?" asks another nude dude who brushes up against me. (I can't tell who anyone is without their shirts.) "It's pretty good, I promise."

It is no stretch to declare these the very guys who would have beaten me up in school. "We can do it now if you want, too!" one informs me.

And in This Corner, the Ghost of Ernest Hemingway

Randy Wayne White

Considering the tragic possibilities, Lorian Hemingway might now be reluctant to admit that it was she who coaxed me into fighting her grandfather Ernest's favorite sparring partner, Kermit "Shine" Forbes, on the docks of Key West, where every sun-giddy Buckeye and wandering Parrot Head could watch and potentially testify against me if the worst happened and the coroner started sniffing around.

"The man is eighty years old," I reminded her.

"Exactly," Lorian said. "Shine's a professional fighter with a lifetime of experience. He was more than a match for Ernest."

"Yeah, but we're talking about a very old guy."

Lorian said, "No, we're talking about Shine Forbes. Have you met him?"

I didn't have to. I live in Florida, where invalid octogenarians are only slightly less common than dead German tourists. I said, "What happens if I miss and actually hit him? We're out there clowning around, he moves the wrong way, and I cold-cock him? My picture would be tacked like a wanted poster on every nursing home wall. Old ladies would thump me with their canes. I'd have to drive to Georgia just to buy groceries."

"Cold-cock Shine?" Lorian said. "If someone moves the wrong way, it'll be you, not Shine Forbes. He's still all muscle, and he's still got the moves. But if you're afraid he'll hurt you . . . "

"Ha! Manipulation won't work."

"Huh?" said Lorian, temporarily puzzled. "All I'm saying is that I told Shine about you, that you used to box a little but that you're big and clumsy and not too proficient. So he said he'd try to take it easy."

"Sure he did."

"And that he'd already heard how slow you are."

"Hey—the old bastard said *that*?"

"Yes. He said he'd 'carry' you if it was necessary. That's a boxing term."

"I know it's a boxing term." I was starting to get angry.

Lorian said, "Three rounds, 10-ounce gloves. You and Shine on the docks just down from Sloppy Joe's Bar. Are you game?"

"Rap on his hearing aid a few times, then tell Mr. Forbes I'm at his service."

She was pleased. "Shine in an exhibition fight—Ernest would've liked that. It'll be a nice addition to the Hemingway Days Festival."

Hemingway Days is not to be confused with Key West's other cash-flow-creating events, such as the Gator Club Dolphin Derby, Key West Womenfest, the Goombay Festival, and especially Fantasy Fest, a masquerade so weird and twisted that afterward the city has to scour the streets with fire hoses.

No, this festival has a cleaner—and more historically resonant—theme. In the late twenties and thirties, Ernest Hemingway lived and worked on the island and, through his name and his descendants, has been paying the Chamber of Commerce exorbitant rent ever since. So every summer, on the second weekend in July, Key West hosts ten nonstop days of Hemingwayesque events, including the Hemingway Flats Fishing Tournament, the Cayo Hueso Arm Wrestling Championship, the Leicester Hemingway Storytelling Contest, the Hemingway Golf Tournament, and the Hemingway Regatta, plus a music festival called the Moveable Musical Feast. Add to this a national short story contest, a national first-novel contest, lots of writing workshops, tours and readings, and the annual Conch Republic Prize for Literature, and there is reason enough to visit an island that has otherwise lost much of its charm as it's descended willy-nilly into tourist whoredom.

Yes, to enjoy Key West these days, one must emulate the island's happy inner sanctum of society: ignore the chemically challenged, avoid Margaritaville and its Buffett pretenders, spend a lot of time on the water, and shun at all cost the geek magnet and drunk hatchery called Duval Street.

But I hadn't come to enjoy Key West. I'd come to fight. And because my first order of business was to meet my opponent—know thy enemy—I went straight down Duval, turned west past a two-story restaurant called Blue Heaven, and pretty soon was knocking on the door of an old conch bungalow, the outside of which looked to be part museum, part curio shop. Out on the lawn there were crab buoys, mannequin heads, paintings, plastic flowers, license plates, stuffed animals—pure Keys Deco. I expected to be greeted by a doddering casualty of the ring. Instead I was welcomed by . . . well, I'll admit it, by an extraordinary being, a man of wit and humor and strength. He still had the look, tendons, and veins that moved independently beneath skin, a fast-twitch muscularity. Not good news.

Shine Forbes said, "Man, get yourself in here! Want an Old Milwaukee?"

I got myself in there and accepted the beer. Inside, the walls were papered with photographs of his family and lots of old friends. "Many of those folks, they dead," he said. The house was also decorated with memorabilia related to Hemingway Days. "Yeah, I look forward to it every summer. Some folks, they complain about all the tourists. Me, I like it."

There isn't much about his life, past or present, that Shine doesn't like. He grew up in Key West, used to dive for coins thrown by people on visiting cruise ships. "I wouldn't dive for pennies, but quarters? Man, we'd dive 40 feet for those." He started boxing in his teens and later got drafted by the army. He served in Guam and Honolulu and later got a civil service job working at the Key West naval base. The whole time, he kept boxing: amateur fights, pro fights, didn't matter. Shine loves the sport. "I fought twenty-some real fights. Only lost two. I'm *sure* of them two losses. All the ones I won, they're harder to remember."

He began to dance around the room, snapping jabs at me. Good jabs, too. "Now I think I'm ready to go a couple rounds!" he said.

This guy was eighty?

Shine said, "Yeah, Mr. Ernest and me, we used to go 'round and 'round." We were at Sloppy Joe's Bar, crowded into the judging area of the Hemingway Look-Alike Contest—lots of gray-bearded Papas peering down from the stage—but everyone allowed Shine his own respectful space. It was a time-warp situation: Sloppy Joe's, all these guys in safari khakis. Looking over at Shine, I had to keep reminding myself that he was real: This man once laid some leather on the beezer of Ernest Hemingway.

Many times, in fact. They used to put on their gloves beside the saltwater pool behind Hemingway's house on Whitehead Street. Once under the spell of that lunatic sport, Shine was probably closer to E. H. than F. Scott Fitzgerald ever thought of being. "Now Ernest, he didn't go 'round looking for trouble like some says," said Shine. "No-o-o-o, he weren't like me." Shine, a troublemaker?

He shook his head. "This one time I was, yeah. You remember the place by my house, the Blue Heaven? It was a sporting house where we used to put on boxing shows on Friday nights to make a little change. This one night, this big ol' man come down to referee. I didn't know who he was. Well, I was in Black Pie's corner. Black Pie was fighting Joe Mills, and Joe was beating Black Pie so bad I threw in the towel. What's this referee do? He picks the towel up and throws it back, hits me right in the face."

Shine, wearing a Sloppy Joe's muscle shirt, his left eye droopy from so many fights, had to smile, remembering it. "So I take the towel and throw it in *again*. Same thing. Referee throws it back, hits me right in the damn face. I had a little of this in me"—Shine indicated the Budweiser in his hand—"which is no excuse for what I did."

What Shine did was vault over the ropes and take a swing at the referee. "That man, he was so big, he could have hurt me. But he just held me off till the other boys could pull me away," Shine said, "I was *mad*. Somebody said, 'Hey, you want us to take this man to jail?' But the referee said, 'Anybody got the nerve to take a swing at me, I don't want him in no jail.'

That's when somebody took me aside and says, 'Hey, man, you know who that referee is? That's Ernest Hemingway.'"

Shine walked over to Hemingway's house later that night to apologize. "That's when Mr. Ernest invited me and a couple others to come over, do a little sparring with him. He was a real gentleman about it."

Shine became a regular at Hemingway's house. "We'd take turns with him, three rounds each. He weren't no real boxer, just did it for sport, see? But he so big, you could hit the man all day and not hurt him. And he'd pull his punches on us. We wore these 16-ounce gloves, and we'd kinda bounce off him. Only this one time, I got under him and was working inside when he let one go and knocked me down. Didn't hurt me, understand, but what I'm saying is, the man could hit when he wanted to."

They continued to spar throughout the mid and late 1930s, when Shine was in his twenties. "Times were tough for us back then," Shine told me. "One Christmas Eve, we didn't even have change for a quarter, so Ernest let us put on a boxing show at his house. It was Black Bob, Black Pie, Iron Baby, and me, with a bunch of Ernest's rich friends there to watch. After we done boxing, Ernest passed the hat, and it had over $200 in it. That was some good Christmas."

"Then one day, Ernest just left. They said he moved to Cuba or something, I don't know. But we missed him."

The Hemingway Look-Alike Contest wasn't over yet—there was a Hemingway on stage right then, carrying a stringer of fresh dorado to impress the judges—but Shine had had enough. He wanted to drive me around in his old Chevy, show me some Key West shortcuts. "I'm not the kind to stand around and drink, drink, drink," he said. "I know when I got enough. I know when I got enough of anything."

The day of the fight, here's what I was worried about: I didn't mind contributing to the Hemingway Days burlesque. Some people wore beards and carried dorado on a stringer. Others put on boxing gloves. What I wouldn't do—nor would Lorian allow it—was play a role in a sideshow in which Shine was diminished. The man had class. Unlike most things in Key West, he was real.

That afternoon, we talked about it as I followed him from boutique to boutique on Duval Street, looking for a new pair of boxing shorts for the fight. "You know that it's just an exhibition, right?" I said. "We're only *pretending*."

Shine was considering a pair of shorts—metallic silver material with blue and red stars. "You believe this?" he said. "Forty-five bucks for these? I can get me a nice *suit* for that."

I pressed the point. "What I'm saying is the whole thing's fake. Nobody expects us to really box. It's more like . . . theater."

Shine gave it a few beats. Finally, he said, "Gawdamn, Randy, you don't think I know that?" Now he was laughing at me. "I was putting on boxin' shows before your daddy was born, so you don't need to say no more about that. Sure, we put the gloves on, dance around, pull our punches—make the people happy."

Later that afternoon, on the Ocean Key House docks, I boxed three 1-minute rounds with Kermit "Shine" Forbes, Ernest Hemingway's old sparring partner. Our audience—mostly fans of literature—grew as the fight continued and came to include a typically Key West cast of sun-giddy Buckeyes, wandering Parrot Heads, and maybe a few living, breathing German tourists, too.

Jeffry P. Lindsay, author of *Tropical Depression* and *Red Tide*, was the referee. The man had flair: "Representing *Outside* magazine, desperately overweight at 220 pounds . . . " Lorian was my cornerman ("You've got a cold, so I'd prefer not to wipe the sweat off you"), and Jeff Baker, an editor of the *Oxford American*, ably worked Shine's corner. "Go for Randy's belly," I heard him tell Shine. "He had barbecue for lunch."

When I threw my first punch, Shine picked it clean and said, "Hey, hey. Pretty stiff jab you got there, boy!"

I said, "I hope you said 'Roy.'"

Shine liked that, and laughed. "Then come on, Roy. Let's mix it up some."

We did, too. Lots of fake lefts and rights, then bear hugs with body shots. But every now and then, Shine would jab and follow with a right that touched my jaw or cheek, using his gloves like a secret communiqué, just to remind me who I was dealing with.

The judges gave the first and second rounds to Shine, 10–8. Then, in the third, I rallied with a flurry of body shots only to be knocked to the deck by Shine's big right hand. When Lindsay helped me to my feet, he studied my eyes and asked, "You OK? Where are you?"

I surveyed the area: turquoise water, purple sunset, freaks juggling torches at Mallory Docks. "Dubuque?" I guessed.

Lindsay waved his arms—the fight was over. "The winner by a knockout, 20 seconds into the third round—Mr. Shine Forbes!"

And Shine stood there grinning, gloves outstretched in victory, enjoying the people enjoying it, part of a long, long show in which he'd always known precisely who he was. Then he glanced at me and winked, this old guy who looked like he ruled the world . . . and deserved to.

It's All in the Game

Melissa King

Eckhart Park, Noble and Chicago

I like my husband, but I love my snowmobile. That's what his T-shirt said. He didn't speak English too well, and I bet he bought the shirt at a thrift store because he liked the color—an appealing purple, actually. Somebody must have told him what "husband" meant, because he had obviously tried to eradicate the word with white shoe polish. You could still see it, but I guess he succeeded in changing the message. *Yo soy heterosexual.*

I don't know his name. I played basketball with him, his brother, and their roommate today. They were new to the game, but they played hard. The most experienced player (also the tallest and the best English speaker) was the one who asked me to play. I had been at the other end of the court shooting baskets, stealing glances at them, knowing they were returning the favor. When you're a thirty-year-old white woman shooting around by yourself in a park populated largely by Latinos, everybody looks at you.

This is the way it works. I shoot around, make a point to have them notice me clandestinely checking them out. I stand tall and swagger a little, as if to say, "I got skills. I play all the time. I know what you're thinking. The question is, are you good enough to play with me?" I can't actually say "I got skills" or "My bad" or "I got next" or any of that stuff. I hate it when white people try to talk street. But that's how I feel.

So I did my little routine and the tall good-English-speaking guy asked me to play two-on-one. My team won both games. And I played some more after that, with another group of guys; the teams just kept melding and interchanging, with new groups of people coming to play. The sun was beating down and a slightly sickening chocolate smell wafted west from the Blommer factory on Kinzie. I played for hours.

Horner Park, Montrose and California

Tori, Melinda, and I got into a discussion tonight about whether or not the person we'd all seen as we walked into the gym was a teenage boy or a woman in her twenties.

Tori was changing into her basketball clothes right there on the side of the court. It was a little brazen, but people hadn't started arriving yet for the Monday night women's open gym.

"It's a guy," Tori said, standing there in her bra.

"She has breasts," Melinda argued.

"He's not wearing a bra."

"So?"

There's a television commercial where Sheryl Swoopes is talking about what she likes to buy with her Discover Card. "I'm very prissy," she says, and then you see her playing playground ball with a bunch of men, screaming like a crazed warrior, *Put up or shut up!* as she drives the lane.

"I love to get my hair done, get manicures, pedicures, but my greatest weakness is shoes," she says in the next cut, walking through a mall in a trendy outfit.

We never did decide.

John, who for some reason plays with us at the women's open gym, was there; it was just the four of us because it was really too hot to play and no one else showed up. John's not quite as good as he looks like he would be, but he looks like he would be good. A guy I used to date has a poster in his house captioned "Shirts and Skins." It's a drawing of a bunch of black men going up for a rebound, stretched out all long-limbed and elegantly gangly toward the sky, everyone moving in what looks from a distance to be a synchronized unit, like a flock of geese falling in instinctively for flight.

John looks like one of those guys. John likes us. He's there almost every Monday, and I always notice him listening to what everybody's saying, even though he never says anything. So I said, "John, do you think that person out front is a man or a woman?" He was shooting around, looking like he was in his own world (he's a little cross-eyed). "Boy," he said.

"This guy walked by me once," Melinda said, taking a shot, "and he goes, 'Hey dude.' I told him, I said, 'Hey, I'm a woman.'"

Then Tori said she was in a car wreck once, and while waiting for the ambulance to arrive she was laid out on the floor of a convenience store. People kept coming up to her and looking over her and saying, "What's up with that dude?" She said she kept fading in and out of consciousness saying, "Hey, I'm a woman."

I've never been mistaken for a man that I know of, but when I'm going for rebounds, screaming like a karate master, wringing the sweat from my shirt, making faces I probably wouldn't want to see, I feel kind of weird. Sometimes it occurs to me that I'm aggressive. Not "assertive"— aggressive.

Tori said to me once, "Girl, you're like a Reebok commercial. This is your world. You go."

It's a good way to feel.

Wicker Park, Damen and Wicker Park

Sometimes I really like white people. Not always, and you might say not even very often, but sometimes I really like them. Today I rode over to Wicker Park on my bike and got stuck in the rain, and waited it out under an awning. Afterward three white guys came over and played with me. We played two-on-two, and they were so without egos.

As they should have been—they sucked. They were fouling the hell out of each other, totally laughing, having a good time. I think they were a little drunk. This guy, Vince, who had been the first one to come over and shoot around with me, was my teammate. After one particularly good play he stuck both hands behind his back, palms up, while he was running backward down the court, for me to slap him ten. It was stupid, but he knew it was stupid. That's kind of fun. In fact, I think it's pretty evolved.

Another time in this same park I was shooting around with a kid called Orlando. His three friends rode up on two bicycles to watch us. The Gap can only dream of capturing the urban slouch of these kids in their baggy jeans, sitting on two-thirds-enough bicycle. They kept saying, "Yeah, she's going to the WNBA next week. She got a right, she got a left, she got a shot, got some D." Orlando was teasing me too, pretending he was shoving me around and laughing, saying stuff like, "All right, it's on now" and "You know I'm mad now." I was kidding him back, saying, "Thanks for the warning, Orlando." I like that kid.

I tried to tell Orlando about how, when you're playing defense, you need to look at someone's belly. How you don't look at his face, because he can fake you out with his face but he can't fake you out with his belly. I wanted Orlando to be good. He liked it that I was telling him something, but I think he already knew about the belly.

A group of older guys started playing on the other end of the court. They were playing twenty-one. I hate that game sometimes, because it's so rebound-oriented. I love to get rebounds, but I can't get any rebounds against those guys. "Orlando," I said, "do you think those guys would let me play with them?" Orlando looked at me funny. "I don't think so. They're kind of rough," he said.

Orlando left with his friends. I did my thing, hoping the older guys would ask me to play. They never did, even though I know they saw me wanting to get in the game. I rode home thinking those sons of bitches made me sick. They didn't know if I could play or not.

Vince had written his phone number on my arm with a felt-tip pen after we finished playing. I wrote it down somewhere else when I got home, but I don't know what I did with it now.

Eckhart Park

Snowmobile wasn't there today, but his two compadres were. They court was so crowded I couldn't get out there. The other Snowmobiles were having the same problem, so I sat down on the ground next to them.

It makes me so mad that I can't speak Spanish. I had three semesters of it in college, for God's sake. And I made A's all three times.

So I chatted in English with Snowmobile #2 and Snowmobile #3. They told me they were both taking English classes four times a week. They kept saying they still couldn't speak English. I told them yes they could.

I couldn't understand why they weren't getting in the game. I mean, for me, being a woman, sometimes you just get the sense that a court is not exactly an equal opportunity situation, but they're guys. It seemed like any guy should be able to play. They said they weren't good enough. I told them yes they were.

When I was in college taking those Spanish classes, I used to have dreams where I could really speak Spanish. In my dreams the words would just be flying out in whole sentences with a perfect accent.

A young black guy was bouncing his ball around on the side of the court, screaming at the players in the game: "I'm gonna kick ya'll's tired asses when I get in there!"

Snowmobile #2 was telling me I could come to play with them next weekend at this park they play at sometimes where there's always plenty of room. "They have sodas," he said.

I have those same kind of dreams about basketball. That I'm making every shot, flying toward the basket, never tired, no one can stop me. When I wake up I feel like those dogs too old to run anymore. You can see them chasing rabbits in their sleep, their legs twitching.

Wicker Park

"What's up kittycat?" That's what this old park dude was saying to me as I sat on my bike scanning the court, seeing if I wanted to play.

"What's up kittycat you gonna shoot some hoops you gonna play me some one-on-one can you dunk it?"

Damn. I almost turned around and rode off, because I knew this guy was gonna stick to me the whole time I was there, but there was an empty hoop and I all of a sudden felt irritated about having to leave a court because of this old park dude.

The guy I told you about earlier that I used to date, the one with the poster, used to say I should stay away from the criminal element. He thought I was reckless. He won't ride the el, and he never gives money to homeless people on the street. But he volunteers at homeless shelters around the holidays and sits on the boards of several charitable organizations.

Park Dude was walking away, so I shot for a while. Then he came back and started shooting around with me. There's a certain etiquette when two people shoot around. One person shoots from the outside and the other stands under the hoop and rebounds. When the shooter misses he goes in for a lay-up, and it's the other guy's turn. Everybody knows that.

Park Dude was not so great to shoot around with. He kept throwing the ball back to me too hard, or over my head, or off to the side so that I had to jump or make a quick move to catch it. Every once in a while it got past me and I would have to run after it, trying to stop it before it went onto the other court or rolled into the middle of the softball game going on 20 feet away. It was really pissing me off. If I were a male or truly urban I would have said, "Man, would you *watch* that shit? What's the matter with you? *Damn.*" But I'm not.

The thing about Park Dude was that he could really shoot a hook shot. Who the hell shoots a hook shot?

A bunch of kids trickled onto the court. At this particular park I sometimes find myself in a game with kids of all shapes and sizes. It's my ball and no one else has one, and I know they want to play, so I play.

A little white girl asked me how old I was. She nearly fell over when I told her I was thirty. "How old are you?" I asked her. "Ten."

Park Dude let fly with one of his hook shots, missing the hoop completely this time. "He's weird," the girl said. "He smells like beer." He was, he did, I thought, but far as I could tell there was nothing wrong with his hearing.

Park Dude said he was getting hot, and he took his shirt off. He had a long, vertical scar running down his rib cage and stomach.

There's a sign in the park that says, WARNING / YOU ARE IN A SAFETY ZONE / PENALTIES FOR SELLING DRUGS OR OTHER CRIMINAL ACTIVITY IN THIS PARK ARE SEVERELY INCREASED. I've seen guys walk past each other making secretive handoffs, or drive up in separate cars, walk off together, then come back a few minutes later and go their separate ways. The park is segregated, with the park dudes sticking to the Damen side and the hipsters playing Frisbee with their dogs in the back corner. All over, savvy little independent kids are running around.

I worry about what happens to a harmless park dude's brain when he's treated like dirt by arrogant white girls. My personal opinion is that inclusion is safer than exclusion, but I'm not positive about that.

All of a sudden I did feel a little reckless, not for being there myself but for being the thing that brought the Park Dude and the little girl together. After the game petered out, I hung around for a while, making sure everyone had scattered before I rode home.

Wicker Park

I wanted to play so bad today. This morning I couldn't get up to save myself. I hit the snooze alarm for an hour.

I muddled through work, came straight home, got on my bicycle, and went looking for a game. I ended up at Wicker Park, shooting around with a little kid, another little kid, and his toddler brother, killing time until a game developed.

I kept grinning at the toddler because he was cute, but his brother didn't grin; he included him. He expected him to play, but he wasn't too rough on him. The toddler just ran around with the ball, happy as could be. He could dribble pretty good for a three-year-old.

All of a sudden a commotion broke out on the other court and we all got still, watching. "Why you testin' me, nigga? Why don't you test summa these other niggas!" one kid was saying to a shorter kid, pushing him in his face. Two middle-aged guys were standing on the side of the court. They were Park District employees; I could tell because they were wearing those plastic ID holders on their shirts. One of the other boys got between the kids, and then one of the Park District guys walked over and said something. It was about damn time.

"Gentlemen, Gentlemen," he said. "Let's just play ball. Gentlemen." But those two kids didn't care about some middle-aged white guy with a pot belly and an ID tag. They just kept on. "Man, if you ever touch my shit again, I'll kill you. Come on, nigga, swing! Do it!"

I don't know why it ended, but it did. The taller kid stalked off, daring the other kid to follow and fight him. The older brother on my court looked over at the toddler and said gently, "Boo, wanna go see a fight?" The toddler just laughed, running around in his stiff-legged toddler way, holding the ball.

After a while the game on the other court disintegrated and an older guy asked me if I'd like to play with him and some other guys. I said sure. I was the only woman and the only white person. I played the best I've ever played, only erring a few times, when I misjudged how fast these young guys were and how high they could jump. I'm not that great a shooter, but that night I was. They kept yelling at each other, looking for someone to blame every time I made a shot. "Who's guarding that girl?" They started calling me "little Larry Bird."

We all have our moments.

The guy who asked me to play was an adult; everyone else was a teen. He was intense, and the kids were kind of laughing at him until we started kicking their butts. The guy who asked me to play kept saying to the scoffing teens, "You know I play hard." The rest of them got into it in spite of themselves, though nobody could ever remember the score.

Riding home, I remembered how I used to sit around the house waiting for something to happen. It was good not to be doing that.

Eckhart Park

My friend Laurie used to tell me how she couldn't go to church without about three guys asking her out. It was the biggest pickup situation you ever saw, evidently, because everyone there wanted to meet somebody at church. She would joke that all the single people at her church were "datin' for Jesus."

Well, the same thing happens in basketball. I met a guy on the court today. Let's call him Peter. I saw Peter looking at me all intense from the other end of the court. He made sure he got in the game I was in, and then he hung around afterward and asked if I wanted to go have a drink later. I said I did; he was very cute, and he was a good player. A guy doesn't have to be that good for me to like him, but it doesn't hurt.

The thing about some guys is, the most important thing about you is where they met you. For instance, I met a guy at a dog party once. It was a dog party because it was a party everyone brought a dog to, and it was supposed to help you mingle and meet other dog owners. The dogs kept fighting with each other and trying to get at each other's butts, which was potentially embarrassing for strangers trying to chat, but people just kept acting like they didn't notice and trying to meet one another.

I went to the party with this girl I worked with, who kind of talked me into it. Neither of us actually had a dog, so we borrowed one, that's how hot she was to go. Single women in their thirties are always latching on to me to do stuff like this. We don't even really like each other necessarily, but they need someone to go do these man-meeting things with. It's incredibly depressing, and usually I run the other way when I smell these situations coming, but this time I went, mostly because I was always telling this woman no.

So at this dog party, this guy, Ed, decided he liked me. And he did everything right. He asked me out for a polite date, and I went, and it wasn't too terrible so I said I'd go out with him again. He introduced me to his friends, always asked me for the next date before he left. He was sweatin' me, as they say.

But there was no connection. The only reason he wanted to go out with me was that he could just imagine telling everybody how we met at a dog party. The story was all the cuter because I didn't even have a dog. It was very *That Girl*.

People don't want to say they met in a bar or through the personal ads. There's always got to be some damn cute story or you don't have a chance.

Peter was all over me because he met me the way he always envisioned meeting *the* woman: on the basketball court. That's what he said, "I always wanted to meet a woman on the basketball court." Me personally, I don't really care how I meet someone, so long as one of us doesn't bore the other half to death.

Horner Park

There's this other guy that keep asking me out, too. He plays with our coed group on Wednesday nights. Lucky me, he prefers my butt to all the other Wednesday night butts. I should write him a thank-you note, I guess. But I already heard him say he has a girlfriend, the dumbass. Oh, and guess what: the girlfriend lives in another city.

The thing about men is, they'll ruin every last thing you like if you let them.

Peter and I went out for a week. We rode our bikes to the lake, played basketball, sat on park benches kissing. All very romantic.

He was funny, although he wasn't the kind of funny where he knew he was funny. The day we went riding I met him at his house, and he came out carrying a bottle of wine, some plastic cups, a corkscrew, and two sheets to sit on, all in a white plastic garbage bag. That kind of stuff can be funny.

When he kissed me he was always pulling the back of my hair. I have short hair, and I kept thinking he was wishing I had longer hair so he could really grab on and pull. I really wanted to say, Hey, what the hellareya doin', but I didn't.

One night he asked me to come to his house and watch a Bears game. I was a little late getting there, and when he answered his door he just looked at me kind of sternly and said, "You're late."

I think he was drunk, and there were two joints sitting on the kitchen counter. He was talking a mile a minute. In fact, I was starting to notice, Peter was the sort of person who didn't let you get a word in edgewise. And, if he didn't think you were listening closely enough, he would move closer and talk louder.

We sat down to watch the game, and he lit up one of the joints. I hate to admit it, but I smoked some. I used to smoke in college, but I don't anymore. I used to get too paranoid. I'm kind of self-conscious already and pot just makes it worse.

All of a sudden I couldn't tell if Peter was really stupid or just pretending to be as a joke. And I hadn't really noticed he was stupid before. I mean, he wasn't by any means the smartest guy I had ever run into, but I just thought he was really physical, that he related to the world in a physical way. If I think a guy is kind of cute, and he entertains me at all, and if he seems to like me, I can kind of make excuses for him and overlook a lot of rude and just plain stupid behavior. A lot of women do that. Decent men without girlfriends must really get sickened by it.

So I was sitting on this chair, really stoned, trying to sit up straight. Peter sat down beside me in the chair and put his arm around me, and he was kind of absentmindedly diggings his fingers into my arm, hard. It seemed compulsive. It was like he couldn't help himself, it felt so good to him. And then, and this is really embarrassing, Peter got up and started gyrating around like a Chippendale dancer, saying, "So, what should I do . . . do you want me to dance for you?" I just kept hoping he meant to be cheesy, to make me laugh. But I didn't laugh, because I was afraid he was serious. All I could think of to say was, "Man, I'm stoned."

All of a sudden, Peter picked me up and carried me over to an open window. I never like it when guys physically pick me up. I know it's supposed to be all romantic, but I just think it's embarrassing. It's too dramatic unless they're going to laugh and maybe act like you're so heavy they're gonna throw their back out or something.

Then I started to worry that he was going to sort of chuck me out the window. I squirmed to get down without saying why, and then Peter said, "I wouldn't throw you out the window." That's when I really got scared. Peter's face looked really brutish to me, and when he moved anywhere near me it felt like he was trying to dominate me, not just get close. After I got out of his King Kong–like grasp, he tried to pick me up on his back, like we were going to play piggyback. And his movements were slow and, I don't know, just slow, like a dumb animal's. I got the distinct impression that he wanted to hurt me. That even if I said I would have sex with him he would still want to hurt me. I kept thinking about the post-racquetball scene in *Cape Fear*, the new version, with Robert De Niro. If you saw the movie, you know what I'm talking about.

Peter kept saying, "Why are you so afraid of me, try to have a little self-confidence, why don't cha . . . I know I can make you feel good," and other creepy stuff like that. I got the hell out of there. I was afraid to drive but I drove home anyway, thinking I was going to go mad the whole time if I had to drive that car one more inch.

But like I said, I quit smoking pot because it makes me paranoid.

These three girls I had seen before came running over, saying, "There's that girl again!"

They looked like a female version of the Fat Albert gang. I asked them if they wanted to shoot around, and the youngest one, who wore about twenty-five colored barrettes in her hair and jeans about three sizes too big, took the ball.

"I can't do it," she said every time she missed a shot.

"Yes you can, you just need to practice some. Nobody makes it every time."

"Why aren't you shootin'?" she asked me.

"I'm all right, go ahead."

These girls, you had to draw them in. I've never seen any boy worry about if he was keeping you from playing.

One girl wouldn't play at all. We tried to play two-on-two, but she just wouldn't play. She kept saying she didn't know how, and she couldn't make it, and all that stuff. The youngest one's younger brother came up and tried to play. He was running all over the court, never dribbling, a big grin on his face, saying "almost" every time he shot the ball.

The girls didn't play long, but they didn't leave, either. They hung around at the edge of the court, watching. You could see them kind of whispering together and looking at different boys.

"Where's you girls' boyfriends?" I asked them, just to see what they'd say.

"Twanisha got her a man," the little one said.

"Where's Twanisha's boyfriend?"

"He over there with his boys."

"That why you won't play basketball, Twanisha? What's his name?" She shrugged her shoulders.

They were doing it already, waiting around for something to happen. Damn, it made me sad. It reminded me of this story I saw on TV, on 20/20 maybe, about whether or not little girls could learn as well when they had boys in their class. They couldn't, some researchers had decided, because the boys just got in there first, talking faster and talking louder. I wanted to shake Twanisha and say, "Listen here, young lady, you're gonna spend your life falling for arrogant men and sitting around a dirty apartment waiting for them to call if you don't start taking an interest in some things."

If I ever have a daughter, she'll have to learn how not to be stupid about men. I don't know how I'll teach her, because I don't entirely know myself. But somehow she's got to know early on it's okay to miss some shots on your own, that you can't let other people always do your shooting for you.

I started playing with some adults, so I told a bunch of adolescents who had walked up that they could play with my ball if they took care of it. They had a big game going before long.

One of the guys on their court was mad because one of his peers has defected to play with us. Leon was on my team. He was two feet shorter than almost everyone else out there, but he could play. He was smart and serious about it. This other kid was screaming at him: "Oh, yeah, I see how it is. You wanna play over there with them. Man, I hate people like you!" He was joined by a glaring fellow malcontent who ran up to us and said, really sarcastic, "Can I play?" Suddenly the tension was racial, because most of the adults were white.

Once our ball flew over onto their court, and the loud kid shot it into their hoop like he thought it was the ball from their game, or I should say my ball. He looked over at us and went, "Oh, is that your ball?"

Leon ignored them. He wouldn't even look at them. We just kept playing. I kept looking over to make sure my ball was still there, and sure enough, the next time I looked up, all the kids and my ball were gone.

So as our game was winding down, I asked Leon, "Hey, do you know those kids that were over there?"

"Which ones?"

"Those ones that were playing with my ball over there?"

There they were, standing about a hundred yards away with my ball. I wondered if Leon had seen them.

"Come on man, you got that girl's ball! Bring it back! Bring it back now!"

Thomas threw it across the playground at us, and we went back to our game.

Oh my God, David. That child is pure love. He comes to the park with his mom on Saturdays. She's a good player; you can tell she was really good in high school. She coached a bunch of girls in the gym at Wicker Park.

I played with her in a pickup game once, and after it was over I shot around and David came over to talk to me.

"Where's your friend?" he asked me.

"What friend?"

"Your friend. She wears black shoes too."

David thought he remembered me from somewhere, I guess, so I told him I didn't know who he meant, was he sure it was me he had seen before, and he said yes, he was sure.

I asked him how old he was. He's five.

"I play with my mama."

"You do? Was she the one who was playing with me a little earlier? She's pretty good." She came over to shoot around with us.

"She made me in her stomach," David informed me. I said, Really, how 'bout that.

He said something quietly to his mom. "Well, she's pretty good, too," his mom said.

A few months later I was playing a two-on-two game and saw David's mom again. She told us to come inside the gym and play if we wanted. After the game, David came running over to me, shouting, "Hi Melissa!"

I couldn't remember his name. What an asshole I am, I thought, as I talked to him, said it looked like his front teeth were growing in and asked what he had been doing. Then he ran around all over the gym with kids his age while his mom and I and a bunch of teens played a game.

In the middle of the game David came over and said, "Maaama . . . maaaama . . . maaaaaaama!" His mom, the point guard, picked up her dribble and said, "What!"

David hesitated, caught off guard by her attention. "Do you want me?" he asked. He looked at his mom expectantly.

"I want you," she said, "but not right this minute."

Satisfied, David resumed running around, and we went on with our game.

The First Fear Fandango

Tim Cahill

Last year, at a dinner party, the subject of high-school nicknames came up. I said that I had never had one, but that, if the truth be known—I must have been shithouse at the time—I'd really like to be known as the Falcon. Everyone around the table burst into hysterical laughter.

"Oh boy," these supposed friends of mind said, "the Falcon." And that set them all off on another choking orgy of whoops and guffaws.

Well, the fact is, I've been doing a little skydiving lately, and when one learns to fly, when one begins to swoop and soar in the wind thousands of feet above the rolling, golden hills of California, then, by God, he's earned the right to Falconhood.

Not that the first jump was all that graceful. That time Falcon dropped in a kind of terror, and he danced the first fear fandango. The plane banked above, the earth lay 3,000 feet below. Instantaneously, all the gears and levers, all the intricate wiring of the Falcon's body reached flash point and burst into a magnesium-bright, adrenaline-fueled flame. There was nothing to fight but the wind, and so the Falcon fled, running hard and without hope in the indifferent, empty sky.

It was a long time ago, before we had taxes or bowling or bubblegum, and the theory runs that we lived an arboreal life, swinging through leafy treetops in the equatorial forest. There followed, it is said, a prolonged dry spell, and the forest dwindled. We climbed down from the trees onto the savanna, adopted an upright posture, and became nomadic food-gatherers and cooperative hunters. Later we became farmers, city build-ers, philosophers, artists, winos, and sex therapists, all of which led, in a straight unbroken line, to the very summit of our culture, the Styrofoam coffee cup.

But sometimes in our dreams we fly. We exist above the ground as we must have in the equatorial forest. In our waking moments, when we fall, we startle and grab. At the top of the stairs, when we catch our foot in the rug and pitch forward, a hand goes out to the banister, the side wall, grandma—anything, seen or unseen. The instinct may be inbred, something we developed in the trees, before we were men.

Indeed, it seems that children are born dreading a fall. Eleanore Gibson constructed a "visual cliff" consisting of a flat board on one side and a steep drop-off on the other. A solid sheet of glass, heavy enough to sup-port a small child, covered the deep side. Infants old enough to crawl, six months and over, were placed on the center of the board and called by their mothers from different sides. Although they crawled freely over the flat board, the children refused, uniformly, to venture out over the deep side. Gibson concluded that the development of depth perception—at least the sort of self-protective mechanism that keeps us from falling off things—does not depend on prior experiences. Falling is something we fear instinctively, and it may be our oldest and our first fear.

All this relates with devious exactitude to skydiving, the sport of jumping out of a perfectly good airplane with a sack of brightly colored nylon on one's back. Veteran jumpers refer to their terrestrial brothers and sisters as "whuffos," which is the first word of the oft-asked question, "Whuffo they jump out of airplanes?"

Well yeah, whuffo?

In the very early stages—the first 10 jumps or so—I think we are dealing with junkies—adrenaline junkies. The phrase comes from the mountain-eer/photographer Galen Rowell, who uses it to explain why he habitually hurls himself into life-or-death situations. And so it is with skydiving. The

TIM CAHILL

sport is a form of staring into the abyss, of confronting our oldest and deepest fear. From the moment you leave the plane until the moment you pull the rip cord—an interminable length of time that usually lasts about 30 seconds—you are effectively dead. It's all the fun of suicide without the messy consequences.

Those consequences—"You mean that big red spot used to be a guy?"— tend to weigh heavily on the mind when one considers taking up skydiving. It is a risky sport, and while I take risks—especially for money—I spend a lot of time computing the inherent necrological density. To this end, I did a bit of research this summer after a couple of smirking desk-bound editors insisted that I write a personal account of skydiving. From a parachuting handbook by Dan Poynter: "In the United States, over the last eight years, an annual average of 35 people have been fatally injured while parachuting . . . it is interesting to compare numbers with other activities: last year over 200 people perished scuba diving, 900 bicycling, over 7,000 drowned, 1,154 succumbed to bee stings, and 800 were even hit by lightning."

I took training for my first jump at the Pope Valley Parachute Center, a drop zone about 2 hours north of San Francisco. The first order of business was to learn the proper touchdown technique. The landing shock, we were told, would include some horizontal movement and would be roughly equivalent to jumping off a Cadillac doing about 3 miles an hour.

Our instructor, Bill, a short, sandy haired man with a dry, almost sour sense of humor, spent a full hour teaching us how to fall from a 4-foot platform. It seemed to be his theory that an action, repeated often enough, is stored in memory in the muscles.

There were twelve people in the class, and they ranged in age from the early twenties to late thirties. One young woman was about 5 feet tall and weighed maybe 150 pounds. She was the sort of blond often described as "perky." She looked like someone who ought to be named Betty.

Every time Betty jumped off the 4-foot practice platform, her face twisted into a pinched, apprehensive grimace, like someone who, for some reason, has elected to jump into a vat of vinegar. This was a constant source of amusement to a young gas station attendant out of a hot, dusty central-California agricultural town. He had driven over 100 miles to Pope Valley in a hot muscle car and pretty much figured he was going to burn up the sky with his natural ability. He combed his thick black hair straight back from the forehead and looked like somebody who ought to be named Duane. Every time Betty got up on the platform, poor Duane had to stifle a laugh that invariably came snorting up out of his nose.

We learned the arch: legs apart, arms outspread about shoulder level, spine bowed until you can feel the strain at the small of your back. The arch is assumed upon exit from the plane. It puts all the weight in the stomach and forces the body into a horizontal position, facing the ground. The classic demonstration of the efficacy of the arch involves a badminton birdie. Dropped with the tip down and the feathers up, it falls straight to the earth and is stable. The skydiver wants that stability in the air; his arms and legs are the feathers, his belly the tip. When the birdie is turned upside down, it flips over in its fall. A skydiver who arches his back the wrong way, like a hissing cat, will also flip over, and the opening chute may come up, say, between his legs and foul.

We examined the jump plane, a red, white, and blue Cessna 182 with room for the pilot, three student jumpers, and the jump master, Bill. We practiced getting into the "go" position, which involved stepping out onto the wheel and hanging from the wing strut. Betty said she wasn't sure she could hang from the strut since she couldn't even do one pull-up. Duane rolled his eyes skyward so that we could all appreciate how hopeless Betty was. Bill said that nobody should worry about hanging on to the strut. The problem, he said, was getting people to let go.

We learned that our standard, round 28- or 35-foot canopies would have a forward speed of about 9 or 5 miles an hour, respectively. (More advanced–class chutes do about 14, and square canopies can do about 20.) We learned how to steer the chute with toggles attached to directional lines, how to tell a bad chute from a good one, what to do in the rare case of water landing, and spent half the afternoon working on emergency procedures. Bill would get a student up in front of the class, strap a harness on him, and yell, "Go."

The student was to make like a badminton birdie, and count "Arch thousand, two thousand" on up to five thousand. The static line, attached to the parachute, deploys the chute in about 3 seconds. If, by the count of five, there is no opening shock, the main chute has malfunctioned, totally. You must immediately pull the rip cord on the reserve chute strapped to your belly.

"Go."

"Arch thousand, two thousand . . . "

"Bam, opening shock. Whatta ya do?"

"Check to see if it's a good chute."

"It's bad. Whatta ya do?"

"I cut away the main chute." The procedure is to unsnap the capewells—two hinged metal plates near each shoulder on the harness—revealing two thick wire rings. Thumbs go in the rings, you pull, and the main chute goes free. Meanwhile, you look down, sight on your reserve-chute rip cord, and pull.

Betty stood up in front of all of us, nervously arching, which is not the most flattering thing you can do when you have a few pounds to lose.

At this point in his session with each student, Bill would begin throwing insults—often hitting close to home. Apparently he thought that real anger and confusion were as near as we were going to get on the ground for the feeling of dropping from that wing strut. "God, are you *fat*," Bill told Betty. "Do you belong to Weight Watchers? Because if you don't, you should."

Duane started off on a series of horsey snorts that lasted for a full 30 seconds.

"Lost 40 pounds this year," Betty said through clenched teeth.

"Who are you talking to?" Bill yelled. "There's no one up there. You got a bad chute. Whatta ya do?"

Duane was curled up in his chair, head buried between his knees, and his back was shaking like a man in the throes of intolerable grief.

Later, during a break, I talked with Betty. Her face was round, even a little puffy, but it was clear that she would be very pretty a couple-dozen more pounds down the line. I imagined that skydiving had something to do with her weight-loss program, that it was simply another method of demonstrating to herself that she could do anything she put her mind to. Betty was the least physical person in our class, and most of the rest of us, with one notable exception, had come to admire her perky determination.

"The only thing I worry about," she said, "is if he tells me I can't jump." Bill had made it clear at the start that he would allow no one to jump until he felt certain they could handle it. "I told everyone at work that I was jumping," she said.

"But what if you chicken out?" I asked.

"Oh, that's fine. People understand that. But to be told you don't even have the choice . . . that's the worst thing."

I was in the second planeload of students to jump that day. With me were Betty and Duane. No one talks in the plane. The mouth is too dry and there are too many things to think about.

I remembered an old newsreel I once saw of a blimp disaster and its horrifying climactic moments. The airship was in dock, but something happened and it began to lift off. Two workmen grabbed at a hanging line, trying to hold the blimp down with their weight. It rose rapidly, and quite soon both men were too high off the ground to let go without risking serious injury. The camera tracked them as they hung there, helpless on that rope. One man's arms gave way and he fell, hurtling out of the frame. The other held on for several more seconds until he too fell, but this time the camera followed him as he plummeted toward earth. There was nothing for the man to do, and he must have known, with sickening certainty, that he was dead; but something called on him to live, to do something, and so he ran. The sequence is terrifying: the man flails his arms, then pumps his legs, like a sprinter in a dream. And he ran until he died.

Bill had told us that we'd have a tendency to run in the air. It was a natural reaction, like that of the man in the newsreel who ran to his death. I promised myself I would hold the arch and not run, not give in to the misinformed bleating of instinct.

It didn't happen that way. I was first out of the plane. Bill opened the door. The wind howled past. He spotted the area where he wanted to cut me loose, told me to sit down and swing my legs out—they blew toward the back of the plane with a frightening jerk—then told the pilot to cut the engine.

I stepped out onto the locked wheel, grabbed the strut, then hung there, arching hard. We were 3,000 feet in the air, and everything below seemed to be carved in microminiature. We were going about 70 miles an hour.

I was supposed to look at Bill, but I didn't think I did a very good job of that. He shouted, "Go!" I let go of the strut and arched. Everything happened very fast and very slow at the same time. I was supposed to shout out my count—arch thousand, two thousand, and so on—but I was silent as a stone. Those movies you see with guys falling off cliffs and screaming all the way down have nothing to do with reality. People who fall from great heights have too much to think about. They don't scream.

Having blown my count, I arched all the harder, arched, in fact, until I could see the plane overhead. A good sign. I had been possessed of this idiot fear that as soon as I let go of the strut I'd be chopped in half by the tail of the plane. It was no use telling me that if the plane was going 70, then someone hanging from the strut was also doing 70, and would drop out of harm's way well before the tail passed overhead.

Now, all this happened in the first second. I had held my arch admirably, which pitched me forward so that I was looking straight down, 3,000 feet. Some autonomous voice shrieked inside my head. I was falling, I was going to land on my head, I was going to end up as a crimson crater in the field below. Another more conscious voice reminded me that I had promised to hold the arch. So I compromised. I arched from the waist up. Everything below took off at a dead run.

No one really knows why this happens, why we feel compelled to spring away from the long fall. We are frightened, certainly; and our instincts tell us, in such situations, to fight or flee. Since there is nothing up there to fight, we run.

Fortunately, on the static line, your chute will open, you will not die, but giving in to a sprint is hilariously funny to those watching you from the plane. It is rather like one of those cartoons where Wile E. Coyote, having eaten a year's supply of mail-order pep pills, pursues the Road Runner at speeds he himself can barely believe. The Road Runner and Wile E. are moving so fast that they are only a blur in our vision. But then the Road Runner stops—"beep beep"—standing stock still on the edge of a cliff, and it seems as if the law of inertia has no dominion over him.

Too late, Wile E. Coyote perceives the cliff and attempts to stop. His heels plow twin trenches in the dirt. Nonetheless, he is carried over the precipice, and he experiences that moment in which everything moves very fast and very slow at the same time. He turns back toward the face of the cliff, his horrified eyes bulging in his head. He hangs there, motionless in the void. Absurdly, he begins to run. He gains an inch, two, three. A gleam of hope enters into his eyes. Then gravity asserts itself and things begin happening very fast. Wile E. falls more rapidly than one might have thought possible. He falls, in fact, so fast that he leaves an inexplicable puff of smoke in his former position, and he makes a whistling sound all the way down to the mute canyon floor.

And so, a second and a half out of the plane, I was running like Wile E. Coyote, dancing the fear fandango. Then, suddenly, there was a jolt on the chest strap and I was brought upright under a bright green canopy, a good one I was relieved to note, all round and shaped like a jellyfish. Over the nearest range of hills—in California's summer they are smooth and golden, looking almost like suede from a distance—there was a great blue lake shimmering in the late afternoon sun. The sky was silent, like the inside of a vast cathedral, and I could hear the beating of my own heart.

The steering toggles were exactly where Bill said they would be and turning the chute was as easy as driving a car. I looked down through my feet to the 5-acre plowed field where I hoped to land. A gentle breeze wafted me toward the small target area and I sailed with it, occasionally checking the altimeter mounted atop my reserve chute. At 2,500 feet I was still above the wrong field, one with bulls in it; 2,000—I was coming in over the plowed area; 1,800—a problem was developing. In all that 5 acres there was one tree, and it was between me and the target. At 1,250 feet I seemed to be hovering, motionless, above that damned tree. The wind was with me—I could see that from the windsock—and my chute had to

TIM CAHILL

be making 5 miles an hour; but still I couldn't seem to clear the tree that was becoming a very large and distressing sight.

At 500 feet we had been instructed to turn our chutes into the wind and prepare to land. Bill had said that if there were obstacles, turn to the nearest open space. Never try to fly *over* an obstacle under 500 feet. And there I was, dropping out of the sky directly into a tree. You land in one of those, you're supposed to cross your legs. Straddling a branch is no fun for man or woman. You're also instructed to cover your face and neck. Jagged, upward thrusting branches can blind you, pierce your throat. I thought about these things and decided, quite definitely, not to land in the tree. I rode the chute to 450, and finally 400. I was sure I was clear of the tree. Then I turned into the wind.

The parachute, which was doing 5 miles an hour, swiveled neatly into a 10-mile-an-hour wind, giving me a ground speed of 5 miles an hour, backward. I was still tracking toward a target I could no longer see. At about 200 feet the ground stopped swaying and became hugely immobile. I picked a spot on the horizon and forced myself to stare at it.

There is controversy about this. Some instructors prefer to have first-time jumpers look at the ground; but Bill insisted that people who stare at the ground tend to do one of two things: they either stretch one foot down to the dirt, like a swimmer testing the water in a pool, or they protect themselves by drawing their knees up to their chests. Both moves break legs. Because Bill had been right about that strange run—the first fear fandango—I tried hard not to watch the ground, which is like trying to walk a mile with your eyes closed. Even though I was staring at the nearby hilltop, I could see the good brown earth looming up under me in the lower periphery of my vision. In a moment, I thought, I'll hit. I was, understandably I think, apprehensive about that, and so I began barking, a perverse reaction that rather surprised me.

The sound was something like that made by a sleeping dog when he is partially awakened by, say, the distant backfire of a car. The dog has no desire to investigate, but he feels that he must note the intrusion, so emits a halfhearted, drowsy bark—mmmmm-woof—and drifts back into his dream.

So there I was, at 50 feet, and I discovered, to my horror, that I was humming in a shaky, scared sort of way. "Mmmm . . " The hum went up a notch in pitch: "Mmmmmm . . ."

I hit, rolling over onto my back in the prescribed manner and barking like a sleeping dog. "Mmm-ooooffff."

All at once, to my utter amazement, I was up on my feet, running around the canopy so the wind wouldn't drag me across the field. I had landed a few hundred yards from the target, on the very bosom of that sweet, brown, plowed field.

After my chute had opened, the plane banked, came back around, and dropped Betty. I saw her come in low over my head, turn into the wind, and land closer to the target than any of the other first-time jumpers. Duane was still up there, last one out. We waited for a time, Betty and I, but we never saw his chute. Bill was up there, stunting under his more maneuverable square canopy; but otherwise the sky above the field was empty. By the time we gathered up our equipment and got back to the hangar, the Cessna was landing, ready for another load. Duane wasn't on the plane.

Bill clapped me on the back. "You did about 50 miles before your parachute opened," he said.

"Yeah," I said, "and I blew my count too."

"Well, you did okay for the first time. Give yourself an eighty-five and remember what you did wrong."

About that time we caught the sight of Duane. He was on foot, pulling his equipment over a fence about a mile away. By the time he got to the hangar, he was sweating profusely and he didn't seem to want to talk to anybody.

"Man," Bill asked him, "what did you do *right*?"

"I did all right," Duane muttered sulkily.

"All right?" Bill was incredulous. "All right? You wouldn't let go of the strut. That's why you landed all to hell and gone. I was yelling at you."

"Yeah, yeah, yeah," Duane said.

Later, I ran into Duane as we were both hanging up our jumpsuits, and I couldn't resist sticking it to him a little. "Had some trouble letting go of the strut, did you?"

"What?"

"Geez, you must have landed 3 miles away."

"Yeah, yeah, yeah."

"You should have seen her," I said, nodding toward Betty, who was smiling serenely and accepting congratulations. "She damn near landed on the target."

"Yeah, yeah, yeah," Duane said. He was staring at the ground. "Look, I gotta go."

In the next couple of weeks I jumped about a dozen more times. By my fourth static-line jump, I was arching well, stable in the air, and pulling a dummy rip cord. On the fifth jump I thought I did everything right, even to the point of not barking on the touchdown. The sixth time out I pulled my own rip cord, a bright metal handle—about the size of a Cracker Jacks box—located just about on my right pectoral muscle. It was a pretty fair jump. I arched for the thousand count, then looked. You always have to look. It's no good pulling, say, the latch that loosens your harness. The handle was right where it should have been. I pulled and it came out smooth as eggs through a hen.

On the seventh jump I was instructed to go a five count before popping the chute. In practice, a 5-second delay plus the pull may take up to 8 seconds. In that time the skydiver reaches speeds of over a 100 miles an hour and will cover some 800 vertical feet.

The sensation becomes that of flying. You can control it. It's like standing on the edge of a high diving board. Lean out and you can feel the point at which you will fall, tumbling over in a front flip. In free fall, from the arch position, a simple downward movement of the head accomplishes the same thing. Bring one arm in, under your body, and you'll do a barrel roll.

Eventually, such acrobatics become second nature. Aside from flips and rolls, experienced divers can go into a hellaciously fast headfirst dive, or modify that position to track horizontally across the sky. Starting from the classic 7,200-foot level, on a 30-second delay, they reach terminal velocity—about 190 miles an hour—in about 12 seconds, provided they are in the "slow" arch position. At subterminal velocity, maneuvers feel a bit mushy; but once at terminal, the greater wind resistance makes a well-executed roll feel crisp and controlled.

Experienced skydivers make a door exit—no more clumsy hanging from the strut—and can track across the sky in a fast dive toward another skydiver who may be in the slower arch position. At some point above his man, the tracking skydiver will flare out into an arch, then "dock" with the first man by grabbing both his wrists. When four skydivers do this, they form a star, and bigger stars and formations may be accomplished with six and eight and even twenty skydivers.

This is called "relative work," and it is the highest expression of a skydiver's art.

On my eighth jump the rip cord stuck—it wouldn't come out with a onehanded pull—and it seemed to me that I handled the situation with a good deal of grace. Observers on the ground insist that they heard a loud and obscene word come booming down out of the sky, but I tend to discount this because I remember what I did and what I thought. With no hesitation, I reached over and gave the handle a vicious two-handed yank. Moving both my hands to the right had put me out of position, so I arched hard and was falling stable when the main chute deployed.

The experience taught me that I will not panic or freeze during an airborne emergency. Consequently, on subsequent jumps, I've been able to forget myself a little and take a tiny sip of the rapture of free fall. Experienced divers court this sensation—it is more sophisticated than those first few adrenaline-charged jumps—and often they must remind themselves to pop the chute. Some veterans have run that rapture all the way to earth wearing two good chutes that they never pulled.

In my case, during that eighth jump with the tight rip cord, fear turned itself inside out and I made the important transition from falling to flying. And if, in fact, I did shout something nasty during that flight, I prefer to think of it not as an obscenity, but rather as the Call of the Falcon.

The Master Grappler

Donald Katz

By the time I saw the huge snake cruising in, its black eyes rising just a quarter-inch above the primordial bog, I was submerged to my earlobes in a Louisiana bayou so completely decorated by plant and insect life and so thickly muddied by alluvial silt that the master catfish grappler beside me looked for all the world as if he'd been buried alive. We were two disembodied faced, pointing up into a ghostly, ancient forest of desiccated cottonwoods heavily festooned with gauzy moss.

The dense curtains of moss sucked the noise of the day from the air, though the huge mosquitoes sitting atop the water beside me sounded like helicopters, and nearby bullfrogs the size of 2-month-old kittens sounded like foghorns on ocean vessels.

And I could hear the big snake swimming my way. It sounded not unlike a rowboat oar being dragged through a still lake.

"Pat," I hissed. "Big snake."

But Pat Mire was concentrating. He kept disappearing under the surface of the cold and viscous Bayou Mallet. He was feeling around in the bed of the bayou, searching for holes big enough to house a 20- or 40- or 50-pound catfish, which he intended to catch with his bare hands.

"Pat, you got water moccasins down here, don't you?" I wondered, casually as I could.

"Yes sir," said Pat. Then he took another breath. When he came back up, several gigantic mosquitoes lighted on his high forehead and began to poke him with prongs that looked like safety pins.

At thirty-nine, Patrick Mire is considered both an accomplished student of Cajun folk culture and the best of all the grapplers—or *pêcheurs-le-main*, a term that translates as "hand fishers"—in the entire tri-parish region of Louisiana's Prairie Cajun country. Mires going back several generations have risen early in the morning, dressed up as if to go duck hunting, and proceeded, with their shoes and hats still on, into the local bayous, there to catch very big, uncommonly strong fish with their hands.

A grappler dives directly into the holes and huge hollow logs and stumps where the biggest catfish live. Once inside, he attempts to entice the heavily barbed animal, which looks and behaves like 10 to 60 pounds of pure muscle packed into a slime-coated wetsuit, to swallow a bare hand. At the first tentative nibble, the grappler kind of pets the great grotesque head of the fish. Slowly at first, and then with whatever violence becomes necessary, he slides his other hand ever deeper into the fish's gullet, hoping to reach out through one pulsing gill slit and grab hold of the other hand.

The fish perceives this violation as you might perceive a strong man threading his hand into your mouth, through your sinuses and auditory canal, and out into the light through your ear. The violent underwater confrontation that ensues often results in a 225-pound tough guy being dragged underwater and down toward the Gulf of Mexico by an animal with a pedigree dating back to the dinosaurs. On a good day—depending on the hand fisher involved—the man wins.

"You got to grab 'em there," Pat said when I asked if there wasn't a less disputed spot by which to lay hold of the fish. "They just too damned slick 'n' slimy and strong to grab anywhere else."

Most Cajun hand fishers will readily note that a catfish can "make you a bad sore," a reference to the fact that through a combination of particularly powerful jaw muscles and a mouth lined with high-grit sandpaper, a catfish can flay back the skin of a human arm and hand like so much peel off a ripe banana.

DONALD KATZ

A typical catfish lying on the ground next to a river wears one of the meanest faces observable in all of nature. Given a few drops of water and a little mud, a catfish can kind of crawl off a bank and go home. (One exotic Asian breed is said to manage long portages through sheer willpower.) Catfish can bleat like wounded mammals at times, and if you stare hard enough, you can easily become convinced that an angry cat is just a half an evolutionary step from rising up, kicking your ass, and eating you whole.

The Catfish Book, a wonderful volume by Linda Crawford, reports Russian catfish measuring 15 feet in length and weighing in at 750 pounds. Mark Twain once reported the sighting of a 250-pound specimen on the Mississippi, and the fish can still get up around 200 pounds. Catfish apocrypha are of an appropriate scale: Waterfowl, various pets, and one small child—the poor youngster placed in stories all over history and locale—have all been snapped up by hungry cats. Innumerable *pêcheurs-le-main* have been dragged to their deaths, locked up shoulder-deep in some big cat's jaws, though you won't find any names or dates.

"An Obsoloosa cat will just destroy a hand," Pat had said when we stopped in at Mowata Store, his friend Bubba Frey's country eating place, for supplies (ice and lots of beer) before wading into Bayou Mallet. Mowata Store lies 8 miles outside Eunice, Louisiana, right in the middle of Cajun country.

"A flathead is easier to handle," Pat continued. "Grab his lip just right and get his jaw outa position, and you're okay."

"You really goin' in?" Bubba asked me, just enough disbelief in his voice to make me nervous.

I'd agreed to be the guy who blocks the fish's escape route. I had no intention of feeling the inside of a catfish's mouth. There are few things better to eat than a well-cooked catfish, but the truth is I've always found the live version of the meal too repugnant of aspect even to touch.

Bubba pulled out from a great steel pot a couple of his hand-packed boudin sausages, delicious Cajun creations just hot enough to singe your nose hair. Bubba is known far and wide for his boudin and for his capacity to play an extremely clean Cajun fiddle, but his loyalty to the proud traditions of his culture stops just short of grapplin' with the cats in the bayou. "They'll roll you on over and take you down," he said, tugging at his T-shirt.

Bubba showed me a significant scar on his thumb where one of the local loggerhead snapping turtles once removed a bit of flesh. Loggerheads, Pat had explained, favor the same kind of holes catfish do.

"Loggerhead's got a head on him big as a 12-inch softball," Bubba said. "Things can take half your foot away."

He grinned at me. "So you really goin' in?" he asked again. I just smiled and shot a trusting look at Pat.

Out at the bayou, Pat and I donned suitable protective hand-fishing gear—jeans, sneakers, and long-sleeved flannel shirts. Pat loitered quite a while alongside his pickup, heartily diminishing a case of beer and talking of catfish battles past. He sorted out piles of red and purple mesh crawfish sacks that would be used both to stop up escape holes and bring the fish to shore. He wound a rope around his waist to hold the sacks, just as his father had taught him to do when Pat was only six.

Felix Mire, a farmer and retired butane delivery man, still joins Pat in the mud at seventy. He likes to string a rope through the fish's mouth and out the gill slit when he grapples it, which makes it easier to drag the catch up onto the bank.

"You really comin' in?" Pat said, his tone causing me to think upon the pre-immersion beer as part sacramental Cajun tradition and part application of a liquid foolhardiness sufficient to the craziness at hand.

Then we got wet.

Walking in a slow-moving bayou is a special sensation. You'd move slowly even if you hadn't heard it was safer that way, because each step deposits you thigh-deep in fine delta silt. This water was icy, and the air didn't move at all.

Up along the tributarial edges of the Kankakee River in Illinois, where I first heard about men catching the least sightly of all freshwater fish with their bare hands, the little-known pastime is called "hogg'n'." In Arkansas, where it's against the law, they call it "noodlin'." In East Texas, it's called "grabblin'," while in certain parts of Louisiana it's called "grapplin'" or grabbin'." In Mississippi, where the emphasis falls more to the tactile mesmerization of the fish than to the actual wrestling of the animal onto the land, they call it "charming." "Graveling" and "hand grabbing" are other variations on the same sport—if sport is what this tribal bit of manly endeavor can accurately be called.

Technique and style vary according to region and relative claim to historical tradition—the most outlandish variation I've come across being the application of a protective layer of duct tape to the hand and forearm. All practitioners share a reverent tone when they claim to understand certain transcendent secrets tethered to the dying art. I often heard that a grandfather or a great-grandfather had learned how to do it, usually from somebody who lived downriver, farther to the south. I kept asking who invented hand fishing—who was the first to even imagine such a thing—and I asked all the way down to the bayous of south-central Louisiana until I found a window to a deeper past. In Pat Mire's isolated piece of the republic, Cajun men say they learned to put their hands into a big fish's mouth from the local Indians, and the local Indians claim they've just known how to do it all along.

A few years ago, Pat Mire made a film about hand fishing in the bayous called *Anything I Catch: The Handfishing Story*. In it, he reported that an old-timer was once asked what he did when a snake occupied the hole he was exploring instead of a fish.

"Why, you jus' find yo' another hole," the old-timer said.

I kept thinking about the line as the big snake swam closer. I was sure I saw it smiling. I kept looking over at Pat, just to make sure he saw it too. I sensed that an intricate etiquette was involved in joining the animals in the swamp. I tried to stay cool like Pat.

"Whoa, Pat," I said. "Before you go back down, just tell me if this big snake here is poisonous."

I watched four huge mosquito bites enlarge on Pat's head like small balloons. He seemed oblivious now, as if he'd moved into some altered, meditative state. He was actually "fishing," feeling things with his feet, occasionally touching submerged logs with his hands and then diving down to feel the edges of holes in the banks. He'd said the catfish—*goujon*, as the Cajuns call them—tend to smooth out the entrances to their holes.

"Don't worry," he said. "I can smell water moccasins. You know, my dad, he won't ever back away from a snake. He feels one in a hole, and he grabs it by the tail and tosses it up on the bank. I've seen him throw water moccasins out many a time.

"Now, come on under and feel this log," he said. I jumped when he grabbed my hand under the clouded water. He directed me to a huge log, the hole in its side marked by rough and deep ax cuts.

"Very old," Pat said. "Even in the late nineteenth century they would have used a rough-cut saw. Not many people have ever felt this log. They put the hole there to block off one side of the log. Okay, now. Let's just see if we got a fish inside."

I bunched up some crawfish sacks as Pat instructed and plunged my hands into the hole. I could barely keep my mouth above the surface, and I was sure that much of one hand was still exposed to whatever lurked inside the log.

"If you feel a bump, don't move," Pat said as he felt his way to the far side of the log, moving in huge, elliptical steps, like an astronaut across a stretch of moon. "The hardest thing to learn is not to move when he touches you. Just try. If you jerk back from a loggerhead, that's when he clamps off whatever he's got in his mouth."

"Can they see us, Pat?"

"Who?"

"The fish."

"Who knows?" he said, drawing in a big breath.

And with that, Pat went under, and in the next second I felt a powerful, wriggling force slam like a hard-swung baseball bat against my bare hand.

The Cajuns are descended from the French Acadians, whom the British deported from Nova Scotia in 1755. They began fishing with their hands because the nets and weirs their fishermen brought south didn't work in the tideless swamps and bayous of Louisiana. Over the years, as the refugees and their descendants and additions settled in the boggiest realms of the Deep South, they were known first as Cadiens and finally as Cajuns, the term applied by locals with whom they blended through the years. "'Cajun'—as 'Indian' became 'Injun,'" Pat explained.

Most of Pat's films are based on his research into Cajun folkways. He left Eunice after college and grew out his hair. He hit the gringo trail in South America and lived on the Kenai Peninsula in Alaska.

"I came back starving for this," Pat said as we floated and shivered in the morass. "I came back for the music, the food, the talk, and to do things like this—things that set us apart from other people."

The previous evening, out at Bubba's uncle's camp, some men had gathered for Cajun music and Cajun food and, apparently, to compare their scars. A local rice farmer was contending that it was a "big ol' blue cat" that had years ago pulled the skin off his left thumb.

"That's not what you said last time," somebody replied.

Camps are a Cajun institution. The one owned by Bubba's uncle is a ramshackle two-room dwelling with a big table and a bunch of plastic kitchen chairs. The 13,000 inhabitants of Eunice have seen better times than now, with the oil business dried up. The camps become more important when it gets like this.

Though the camp is not far from town, the area nearby is heavily wooded. Hooks and chains for skinning fish and game protruded from several trees. An extremely heavy iron pot, very black, was sitting on a fire. Pat whipped up a fragrant catfish étouffée; a tray full of fat catfish steaks and another full of bullfrog legs the size of jackrabbit hinds sat nearby. Cayenne pepper was poured into the pot, and strangely sad and medieval music filled the night.

Pat was stirring in time with the music when somebody said, "We shoulda invited some women."

"What, and fuck the whole thing up?" Bubba replied.

I told Pat that a senior parks-and-wildlife official in Texas had told me that Texas, like Arkansas, outlawed grapplin' because it was thought unsporting, tantamount to dynamiting or electrifying a body of water. The official had added that catfish that will let you get a hand in their mouths are usually spawning. "One of those boys gets real good at it," the man had said, "and he can clean out a river."

"First," Pat said, "it's the male that guards the hole. The male shoves the female in there, but then she leaves. He stands guard until the eggs are hatched, upon which he begins to eat as many of his children as he can. I pull out a big old male, and the babies live. As to it not being sporting—compared to the sporting way of tricking a fish into thinking there's not steel hook inside his food—I jus' don't know what to say."

Several of the men at the camp offered me ironic compliments about my plan to follow Pat into a swamp full of snakes, turtles, and a particularly trashy sort of fish that's changed little since the Eocene epoch. One or two put their one arm not holding a beer around me and said that I must be fully accoutered in the anatomical sense.

By the time his transcendent étouffée was ladled over plates of steaming rice, Pat was sitting on one of the frayed plastic chairs, waving away mosquitoes and trying to explain what you have to know to risk the primal vagaries of deep, dark holes. He tried to talk of what you had to feel inside to be able to convince a great big fish to fall into your grasp.

"You have to become part of the environment; you have to feel part of the same exact thing as that fish. You have to become larger than your own impulses. And you have to really use those hands."

As he spoke, I thought about watching my six-year-old daughter playing in a pond a few weeks earlier. Several of her friends had been trying time and again to capture one of the hundreds of darting newts that teemed below the pond's surface. As the others gave up in frustration, my daughter—who likes to stand back and take in a scene before plunging in—slowly put one hand into the pond and waited. She drew it out and handed a wriggling newt to one of her friends. Then she reached back in and came out with another, handing a newt to each of her playmates, steady and calm. I waded in and tried to catch one for 10 minutes, obviously out of sync, utterly in awe.

"I do it because it won't be done much longer," Pat was saying by the time the fiddles were being packed away. "I fish with my hands, well, jus' 'cause I can."

DONALD KATZ

"Be mentally prepared," Pat said before he went down after the fish again. "Concentrate on not drawing back."

By now my feet had floated to the surface, but I was determined to block up the hole. A hogger from up north had told me that in the 8-foot waters he fished, one man will stand on a submerged hogger's back and others will pile on until sufficient weight is brought to bear to keep the bottom guy down; other times, two men will dive down and physically insert another into a deep hole.

Pat was underwater for a very long time. He had told me that in the old days a hand fisher who could spend a few minutes underwater was revered as a true *plonger*. Pat said it often takes some time to stroke and pet the fish.

"Otherwise they get wild," he said. (All the talkers on the subject pronounce it "while.") "And a wild cat you really don't need. You have to slowly feel what you've got. Then you've got to move in."

I felt another hard bump. Whatever hit me was very hard and even colder than the frigid water. Seconds later Pat shot out of the bayou, rising up like a Polaris missile, gasping for air. His left hand was spurting blood from having been deeply spined, but he was hugging a hideous-looking bit of prehistory to his chest, clutching as the fish slapped him hard in the gut.

When the fish was finally glowering in the dust beside the bayou, two bare-chested teenagers in feed-store caps strolled onto the bank. "You the boy made the fee-ulm," one of them said to Pat.

"You teach us to fish?" said the other. "My great-grandfather could do it, but I don't know anybody who still knows how."

"Yeah, sure," Pat said, panting, bleeding, his wound swelling up like an extra digit, insect bites rising from his pate, mud coating his soaked clothes. "I'll teach you."

The two boys smiled broadly as the incensed catfish below them just stared off into the eerie woods.

The Running of the Bulls

He Who Hesitates Is Lunch

Billy Anderson

"Why am I here?" This is the thought going through my mind as I prepare for the *encierro*, the famous Running of the Bulls in Pamplona, Spain. *Los Sanfermines*, as the festival is known by the local Pamplonicos, has been famous ever since Ernest Hemingway described it in *The Sun Also Rises*. If you don't run fast, I am told, your sun will never rise again.

For four weeks I had been backpacking around Europe, hearing stories of the infamous Running of the Bulls: a week-long extravaganza of drinking, dancing, and partying, highlighted by the bull run itself—a mass of lunatics chased by six extremely large and unhappy bulls. Thus far, my European adventure had gone smoothly. I hadn't been mugged, maimed, or laid waste, and I was feeling the need for a little excitement. That cute town in the Austrian Alps suddenly seemed stale. At that moment came something I don't normally have a surplus of: courage. I thought to myself: "I'm a pretty fast runner. I could outrun a bull or two. What the hell, let's give it a go."

So now, three days later on a sunny July morning, I'm standing on Santo Domingo Road in Pamplona for what could very well be the last day of my life. I wait impatiently with a few hundred adrenaline seekers, listening anxiously for the rockets signaling that the gates have opened and the bulls have been turned loose. The night before, I'd been cruising

Pamplona's bars, full of sangria-induced bravado, boasting of my upcoming adventure. Now my knees are shaking and my mouth is parched. The guy beside me in the crowd leans over to me with a look of panic and says, "I don't think my travel insurance covers this."

Boom! The rockets sound and I have one sudden wish: "Beam me up Scotty!" But Scotty is obviously asleep at the Transporter switch, because I'm still standing in the cobblestone street as the crowd begins running like men possessed. I have a sudden flash of complete sobriety. Every ounce of machismo drains from my body. People are yelling and hollering; it seems I'm one of them. As I start into a full-out sprint, I have a horrifying realization: I can run only as fast as the people in front of me. At this moment, self-preservation takes over, and I switch from a running-in-sheer-terror tactic to a run-push, run-push strategy.

The buildings lining the street overflow at every orifice with spectators who are smart enough to just watch. Side streets are barricaded with fences—and the remainder of the Spanish spectators, who kindly push you back into the running throng should you attempt a quick exit. The end of the run empties into the *Plaza de Toros*, or bullring. It is at this bottleneck where most of the accidents usually take place. A fatal goring is not uncommon. I dash into the ring, the bulls' hooves pounding toward me. I'm convinced that, out of all these people, the only target they see is my plump rear end. The red shorts might have been a bad idea.

Some of the spectators in the stands boo us as we enter the ring. We're near the front of the running crowd, which is apparently for the wimps. It seems it's more "honorable" if you're at the back of the crowd, with a better chance of getting trampled. In my opinion, the wimps are the people sitting in the stands. Shouldn't I be booing them?

The bulls charge in behind us as we position ourselves around the perimeter of the ring, simultaneously catching our breath and thanking the Lord for sparing our lives. I'd been told that once the bulls were ushered out of the ring, mid-size bulls would be let in and we would spend the next half-hour horsing around with them, trying to keep a healthy distance. It is at this point that I get a little confused about which bulls are which. Maybe it's the adrenaline of the run or perhaps the sleepless night and crate of sangria coursing through my veins, but I peel myself from the crowd and run up to the lead bull. Suddenly I'm not so confused anymore. I am downright petrified. I am in something like a Bugs Bunny cartoon as I stare level-eyed at this behemoth with steam pumping out his nostrils. From out of nowhere come two locals with bamboo sticks. Their job is smacking the bulls on the behind to keep them in line. But instead of hitting the bulls, they wind up like Babe Ruth and whack me in the head.

As they walk away, their sticks broken, I reach up to discover blood streaming down my face. A young Spanish boy takes me by the arm and ushers me to the infirmary under the bullring, where I am cleaned up. I either don't need stitches or they're too busy to give me any, but I don't care—I just want to get back to the ring and the excitement I had traveled three days to experience. And if my head wound turns into a scar that I can show off for the rest of my life, all the better.

Back in the ring, the crowd tries to stay away from the bulls. With so many people blocking the view, you have to watch the movement of the crowd to determine where the bulls are. If you get too focused on one bull, another can charge up from behind and flatten you like a tortilla. Suddenly the crowd parts, and there, much to my chagrin, is a bull bearing down on me. My brain is yelling, "RUN!"—but from head to toe I am frozen with fear. The bull's head crashes into my paella-stuffed stomach, sending me through the air to land in a heap of 100 percent terrified tourists. Luckily it doesn't come after me to attempt a disemboweling. I don't feel any pain. I may have lost a few brain cells, but I'm so scared and my heart pounding is so fast that all I can think is, "I've been trampled! I can't wait to tell my friends!"

Back home, long after the event, I fondly remember my brush with death. *Los Sanfermines* is still as popular as ever with Spaniards and tourists alike, and when I see it on TV or in the newspaper I proudly say to those around me, "I was there, man! I did that." I often contemplate a return to Pamplona, but . . . in the end, the desire to live until my midlife crisis prevails.

Fortune's Smile

James McManus

I flew in on American Airlines, the nickname for two pocket aces, and I take that as a very good sign. I've got my poker books, sunglasses, and lucky hats, including the White Sox cap I got married in. My room at Binion's Horseshoe overlooks downtown Las Vegas's dolorous, last-gasp attempt to keep up with the billion-dollar resorts 5 miles south on the Strip, which in the last few years have siphoned off most of the city's 34 million annual tourists with pixilated facsimiles of Paris and Bellagio, Imperial Rome and Renaissance Venice—all the more reason to be happily ensconced way up here at the Horseshoe. Even better this evening is that the 2000 World Series of Poker is in full swing downstairs. Tomorrow, with a $4,000 stake, I'm going to try to win a seat in the million-dollar championship event, due to begin in five days.

I ain't superstitious, as Willie Dixon once sang, but my second daughter, Beatrice, was conceived in Bellagio, Italy, so my lucky hats include a sun visor sporting the logo of the local version. I've also been playing poker for thirty-nine years now, everything from penny-ante family games in the Bronx to $80-$160 hold'em at the Bellagio, but never at anything close to this level. The championship event costs $10,000 to enter, and always draws the top two or three hundred pros in the world. I'm good, but not that good. I was taught by my uncle and grandfather, both named Tom

Madden, then got schooled in caddy shacks by guys with names like Doc and Tennessee. My current home game in Chicago involves day-traders, attorneys, a transit-systems planner, and a pizza delivery man. It's a game that I fare pretty well in, but I still have no reason to doubt T.J. Cloutier, the former Canadian Football League tight end who is now one of poker's best players, when he says: "The World Series is a conglomeration of local champions. There's Joe Blow from Iowa who's the champion in his game at home; hundreds of local champions like him come to Vegas to play the World Series. But it's like the difference in going from playing high school football to college football: It's a big step up."

To reduce the long odds that I'll only embarrass myself, I've spent the last year practicing on a computer while studying the four poker bibles: Cloutier's *Championship No-Limit & Pot-Limit Hold'em*, cowritten with Tom McEvoy, the 1983 world champion; David Sklansky's seminal *Theory of Poker* and *Hold'em Poker for Advanced Players*, the latter cowritten with Mason Malmuth; and *Doyle Brunson's Super/System: A Course in Power Poker*, cowritten with (among others) Sklansky, Chip Reese, and Bobby Baldwin, the 1978 champion and current president of the Bellagio—which is good luck right there, I figure, as I switch on the light in the bathroom. These little yellow horseshoes on the shampoo and soap might help, too.

The crowded main tournament area has forty-five oval poker tables, each surrounded by ten or eleven chairs. The size of a grammar school gym, the room has an 18-foot ceiling fitted with cameras and monitors but not quite enough ventilation for the number of players who smoke. Posters along the walls give results from previous events, including a color photograph of each winner. There's precious little else in the way of adornment, no music besides the droning announcements of poker activity and locust-like clacking of chips. Shangri-la!

The $3,000 no-limit hold'em event starts tomorrow at noon, so that's when I'll play my first satellite—while the best two or three hundred players are otherwise engaged. Before I go to bed, though, I need to take a few notes on the action. In satellites for the Big One, ten people pay $1,000 apiece and play a winner-take-all freeze-out. Which will make me a 9–1 underdog tomorrow, assuming I'm evenly matched with my adversaries, and of course I will not be. But a night's sleep and diluted competition will give me the best, or least bad, chance of winning.

Most of the satellites have $300 buy-ins and generate a seat in tomorrow's event, but one table along the near rail is reserved for $1,000 action. A harried blond floorperson with a microphone—her nametag says CAROL—is trying to fill the next one. "Just one more seat, players! Chance to win a seat in the Big One . . . " Nine hopefuls already have chips stacked in front of them, along with their Walkmans and water bottles, ashtrays and fans. As Fyodor Mikhailovich confessed to his second bride, Anna Grigoryevna, who'd conquered his heart while taking down *The Gambler* in shorthand: "Once I hear the clatter of the chips, I almost go into convulsions. Hear hear! Down I sit, forking over $1,015, the $15 being the juice. Tired schmired. Once I receive my own $1,000 stack of green ($25) and brown ($100) chips and the dealer starts shuffling, I've never felt any more ready.

Hold'em involves nine or ten players receiving two facedown cards each (called "the pocket"), followed by three faceup shared, or "community" cards ("the flop"), a fourth community card ("the turn," or "fourth street"), and a fifth community card ("the river," or "fifth street"). Two rotating antes called "blinds," small and large, initiate a round of betting before the flop, with a round of betting after the flop, after fourth street, and after fifth street. Starting at $25 and $50, the blinds double every 20 minutes. Since the game is no-limit, a player may bet anything from $50 up to all his chips at any point in the sequence. No-limit action seldom reaches a showdown on fifth street, where, if it did, the best five-card poker hand wins. Most often, an intimidating wager before or just after the flop gets no callers, and the bettor receives the whole pot.

Things get much trickier when factoring in your position. Acting last from the dealer's button (which rotates hand by hand) is the strongest position, since you see everyone else's action before deciding whether to fold, call, or raise, and can therefore get away with playing slightly weaker hands; whereas only big pairs, Ace-King, or suited connecting face cards (Queen of Diamonds, Jack of Diamonds, for example) are likely to make money played from an early position. As early shades clockwise into middle, then late position, the valences of wagering assert themselves and less savvy players get soundly outmaneuvered.

My satellite rivals are mostly middle-aged guys of all stripes: the anxious, the collected, the pocky, the sleek; ex-beatniks, ex-jocks, and ex-hippies. So I feel right at home on all counts. Although one of us will stroll off with everyone else's money, the table has a friendly, if not quite munificent, vibe. When someone gets edged at the showdown, the usual response is, "Good hand." We also tip the cocktail waitress for one another. None of this fools me, however.

A gray-haired Vietnamese woman in round mirrored shades has taken the lead, winning three of the first eleven pots. Doing less well is the toothless varmint in seat one, just to the left of the dealer. His scraggly beard starts high on his cheekbones and covers his Adam's apple, with scalp hair of similar aspect, the entire gnarled package tentatively winched together by a powder-blue UNLV cap. Yours truly sports poker face, titanium shades, and Bellagio visor but still hasn't entered one pot. Him too scared.

Most of my no-limit experience is on Masque's *World Series of Poker* program and Bob Wilson's *Tournament Texas Hold'em*. By playing hundreds of thousands of hands (and winning three virtual tournaments), I've sharpened my card sense and money-management skills, and developed a not-bad sense of no-limit wagering rhythms. Yet computer play affords no opportunity to read faces and body language for "tells," and may actually diminish the mental, fiscal, and physical stamina required for live-action poker. The $1,015 I'm risking is real, with 9–1 odds that I'll lose every cent. I can't sit here with T.J. and Brunson and Sklansky open in my lap, thumbing an index or two for advice about playing an unsuited Ace-Jack.*

The main thing I need here is feel, and for this, books and computers can't help much. Right now the pot has been raised by the muscular Arab in the salt-stained tortoiseshell Wayfarers, not Masque's "Player #4." What is Stains thinking that I'm thinking that he's thinking? Is his

---

Author's Note: In a poker tournament one plays hundreds of hands a day; the hands discussed in this article have been reconstructed as accurately as I and others can recall.

visceral aplomb all an act? The only things I'm sure of is that he wants my money more than Player #4 ever could and that he's already knocked out Madame Ho. But if I can't look into his eyes, at least I can observe how hard his lungs are working. If I've tuned him in right, I can feel it.

Right now from middle position I'm playing Ace of Diamonds, Jack of Hearts, having called Stains's $200 preflop raise. The flop has come Ace, Five, King—all of Spades. With flushes abroad, there's a bet and three calls ahead of me. That no one has raised makes my pot odds about 12–1, with my shot at a full house a lot worse than 1 in 13. But I call, God knows why, and fourth street comes up Jack of Spades, giving me Aces and Jacks. After Stains bets another $200, two hands get folded, but the guy on the button reraises. Two other calls on my right, then a fold, then . . . the next thing I know the dealer is staring at me. So is Stains. So is the Pakistani guy to his left. With only four outs (the two remaining Aces and Jacks), folding Aces-up makes me groan with irrational pride, but when the dealer turns over Jack of Clubs, I no longer have a good feeling.

I need to take a piss about now, but I hold it, and the poker gods deem fit to reward me. Fifteen hands go by in which I can do no wrong. I win six good-sized pots, three in a row toward the end, using check-raises, semi-bluffs, traps—the whole works. By midnight I have $4,900, almost half the chips on the table. The slender Pakistani guy, who's named Hasan Habib, has roughly $2,700; a big, bearded guy named Tom Jacobs about $2,400.

With the blinds at $400 and $800, Jacobs moves all-in on the third hand we play. Habib calls, turning over two Sevens. (In heads-up action, when one player goes all-in usually both expose their hole cards since no more betting is possible.) When Jacobs flips over A-10, Habib becomes an 11–9 favorite, and I get to watch the do- or-die "race" from the sideline: J-J-3, followed by a Trey, then a Deuce. I'm down to one adversary. The only problem is that it's Hasan Habib, who finished second last month at the World Poker Open no-limit event down in Tunica, Mississippi. And he now has me slightly outchipped.

We fence for a half dozen hands, neither of us willing to call preflop bets, before I discover a pair of Queens peering back up between my thumbs.

Betting first, I can try to trap Hasan by (1) merely calling his big blind, (2) putting in a modest raise, or (3) moving all-in, hoping that he (a) calls, and (b) doesn't have Aces or Kings. I decide to try door number three. And he calls, then puts the frighteners on me by turning over King of Diamonds and . . . 10 of Diamonds. When the board fails to improver either of our hands, the dealer yells, "Winner on table 64!" Yawning yet flabbergasted, I sit back and try to relax. Carol takes my name and address, then issues a printed receipt for $10,001, the last buck being the token entry fee. Event 25, it says, World Championship, 5/15/2000, and assigns me to Table 53, Seat 6. I'm in.

Besides drawing record numbers of entries, the 2000 WSOP, I've discovered, has already produced a few of what might be called cultural achievements. The $1,500 seven-stud bracelet, along with the $135,975 first prize, went to Jerri Thomas, a forty-one-year-old from Cincinnati who had given birth only three months earlier. She and her husband, Harry, are now only the second married couple with a WSOP bracelet apiece. The following event, limit Omaha, was won by Ivo Donev, a former chess pro from Austria who'd spent the past two years reading Sklansky and McEvoy and practicing on Wilson software.

A week ago, on May 4, Jennifer Harman won the no-limit Deuce-to-Seven event. Because of its steep degree of difficulty, the event drew only thirty entrants, but the Deuce (in which the lowest hand wins) is the title poker professionals covet almost as much as the Big One. No satellites get played for it, so only by putting up $5,000 can the cockiest, best-bankrolled players compete. Harman is a blond, thirty-two-ish, dog-crazy gamine who plays high-stakes lowball games every night with the likes of Brunson, Chip Reese, and Annie Duke, but she'd never played no-limit deuce. Neither had Duke, for that matter, but that didn't faze either of them. They took a 10-minute lesson from Howard Lederer, Duke's brother, and 10 hours later Harman had the bracelet and $146,250. And then, on May 5, Phillip Ivey took home the Omaha bracelet, defeating Thomas "Amarillo Slim" Preston with a series of fifth-street miracles at the final table, coming back from a 5–1 chip deficit. In thirty years of World Series play, during which he's won four bracelets, Slim had never lost at a final table. Playing out of Atlantic City, the twenty-three-year-old Ivey has been on the tournament circuit for less than six months but is now the only African American with a wsop bracelet.

The World Series of Poker (and tournament poker in general) was invented by Benny Binion in the spring of 1970. He simply invited a few of his high-rolling cronies to compete among themselves and then vote for the best all-around player; the winner, Johnny Moss, received a small trophy and whatever money he'd earned at the table. The current freeze-out structure, which continues until one player has all the chips, was instated in 1971, and Moss won again, this time taking home $30,000. The next year's winner, Amarillo Slim, won $80,000, wrote a book, and went on the talk-show circuit, boosting the public's interest in tournament poker. By the time Brunson became the second repeat champion in 1977, first prize had quadrupled to $340,000. It was up to $700,000 by 1988, the second year Johnny Chan won. From 1991 until last year, first prize was an even $1 million, with the number of entries and total prize money steadily climbing. Last year's championship event drew 393 entries, with second place paying a record $768,625. Almost from the wsop's inception, the total prize money awarded has dwarfed the purses of Wimbledon, the Masters, and the Kentucky Derby. There are now twenty-four preliminary events. The buy-in to the Big One remains $10,000, but these days the majority of players gain entry by winning satellites or super-satellites, mini- tournaments designed to democratize the competition; they are also thought to be the most legitimate route in, since they reward poker skill instead of deep pockets, though the two often work hand in hand.

T minus 70 minutes, and counting. After half an hour of lazy backstroke in the rooftop pool, I open my Cloutier and start cramming for my first big exam since I was an undergrad twenty-seven years ago. I'm reviewing all twelve of T.J.'s practice hands, poring over underlined phrases to see if I've absorbed the logic of his analyses. "Cardinal rule number one in no-limit hold'em is: If you limp with Aces, you will never get broke with Aces." And this, on the luck factor: "You can set up all the plays in the world, you can play perfectly on a hand, and you can still lose. And there's nothing that you can do about it." The rest of his advice I've tried to reduce to four memorizable aphorisms.

1. Don't call big bets; fold or raise.

2. Avoid trouble hands like King of Diamonds, Queen of Clubs, King of Hearts, Jack of Clubs, or any Ace with a kicker smaller than a King in the first four positions.

3. Don't always steal-raise in obvious bluffing positions (the small blind, the button), and play big hands (even Ace of Diamonds, Ace of Clubs) slowly from them.

4. Drawing hands are death.

This last one means: Don't risk your tournament life chasing big pairs with small ones or medium-suited connectors, as is often correct in a limit game. You'd win a big pot if you filled your straight or flush, but aggressive no-limit players make you pay too high a price to draw against them. Mistakes in no-limit tend to be costlier by an order of magnitude, and the chips that you lose in a tournament can't be replenished by digging into your pocket. Amen.

Furious satellite action is still underway as I arrive in the tournament area just before noon, with the overflow crowd getting denser by the second. Judging from their faces, a few of these hombres have been playing all night. Dealers raise the betting levels every 3 minutes instead of every 20, eliminating players tout de suite but reducing the caliber of poker to little better than all-in crapshoots. Railbirds are six or eight deep, clapping and whistling when their hombre survives, as four camera crews roam the aisles. One guy they're focusing on is tournament director Bob Thompson, a silver-haired cowboy with a dulcet basso drawl. With his big jaw and narrow-eyed gaze, he effortlessly personifies the American West, Texas hold'em in particular. And that's what we came here to play: cowboy poker. Thompson runs the floor with his son, Robert, and Tom Elias; his daughter, Cathi Wood, coordinates the administration. Her fact sheet says that if five hundred entrants sign up, nine players more than the usual thirty-six will be paid; first place will pay $1.5 million, second will pay almost $900,000, and all other payouts will escalate. Her father just announced that last year's record of 393 has been shattered, then pointed to the line of new entrants with $10,000 in their pocket still snaking three-players thick out the door. Clearly no cards will be in the air for a spell.

In the meantime, Puggy Pearson, the 1973 champion, holds court in a gold- and-lemon silk Genghis Khan outfit, including a crown with tasseled earflaps to go with his broad smile, eponymous pug nose, and Abe Lincoln mustacheless beard. Elsewhere I see little black dresses, tuxedos, and a short, wild-eyed black guy in a cloth airman's helmet hung with a dozen pink or yellow rabbit's feet. The leading sartorial choice, though, is Poker Practical: baseball cap, sunglasses, sateen casino jacket. Among so many corn-fed middle-aged guys in goatees and Levi's, Slim still looks clear-eyed and rangy at seventy-seven, bedecked in pressed khaki trousers, platinum belt buckle, mother-of-pearl buttons on his crisp cowboy shirt.

However unlikely this sounds, the World Series of Poker has evolved from its good-old-boy roots into a stronghold of, yes, functional multi-culturalism, proving, if nothing else, that there is such a thing. The field is an ecumenical crazy quilt of players from twenty-three countries on all six inhabited continents, among them Scotty Nguyen (the gold-bedecked 1998 champion) from Saigon, Hasan Habib from Karachi, and, from Pam-plona, a Carlos Fuentes. Any all-name team would also have to include Tab Thiptinnakon, Jesus Ferguson, Exxon Feyznia, David Plastik, Chip Jett, Spring Cheong, Sam Grizzle, Lin Poon Wang, and Huckleberry Seed, the 1996 champion. Among toned jocks like Seed and Layne Flack and Daniel Negreanu we have equal numbers of the obese and the skeletal, plus plenty of folks who are youthful or ancient, wheelchair-bound or in dance shoes. Evangelical Christians are competing with Larry Flynt, CEOs, and dot-com millionaires against call girls and poker dealers, gay men and lesbians, cowgirls and golfers and artists, black poker professionals and Jewish physicians, Jewish pros and black docs, at least one Aramaic scholar, and several Vietnamese boat people. All told our number is 512, breaking last year's record by 119 and bringing the purse to a staggering $5.12 million.

I fail to recognize any stars at my table, cause enough for slightly less pessimism. After showing our receipts, we each receive a stack of $10,000 in chips: one orange five-thousand, three white- and-royal-blue "dimes," two black- and-yellow five-hundreds, and seven slate-colored "ones" topped by a dozen green "quarters." The cards finally go in the air at 1:35, with the blinds at $25 and $50, no antes. Our dealer flicks out a card apiece to determine who starts on the button—and, with the sad-eyed King of Spades, that would be *moi*. On the first hand, I look down and find Ace of Clubs, Six of Clubs. No less than five limp in front of me, i.e., they call the big blind by tossing $50 each into the pot, trying to get a cheap look at the flop. Not on my watch! I make it $250 to go, get no callers, and, with $10,325, take the lead.

Not for long, of course. I start playing far too impulsively, overriding my own blueprint by entering pots with small pairs, King of Hearts, Jack of Diamonds or Five of Hearts, Four of Hearts, getting smoked. Is someone else pushing my chips in or making my mouth say, "Let's raise it"? The main person making me pay is an unfearsome cowpoke five seats to my right. Wearing the same puzzled grin, he rakes in pot after pot. The worst hammering comes when I turn an overset of Queens—make three Queens on fourth street, that is, with no higher card on the board—and bet $2,000. Henrik calls. Even when I fail to improve on fifth street, I feel that six titties, or three Queens, are worth another $2,000, a foolish amount at this stage. My logic is that if I could only get Henrik to call—I'd put him on two little pairs—I'd be back up to even: lesson learned, tabula rasa, ready to start playing solid. But not only does the little shit call me, he shows me a Seven-high straight.

By the first 15-minute break at 3:35 I'm down to $2,200 and change. I skulk up to my room and call my wife, Jennifer, in St. Louis. I give her the ball-crushing news, and she sighs. What I need is a kiss and a head rub, she says, but all she can provide is a suggestion to page through my brag book, the 4x6 photo album with pictures of our girls and my two other children. "Just keep it in your pocket and think about us." It's truly a sorry idea, but since I don't have a better one I take the book with me downstairs. My goal all along has been to go to bed tonight still alive, and it looks like I'm not gonna make it. Yet I have absolutely zero reason to be surprised by this turn of events. Competing against inspired professionals, I'm not even heeding my pedigreed battle plan. Entering this event was an act of mind-bending hubris, so the only surprise is that I still have some chips to my name.

As we're sitting back down to the tables, word comes that Harman, Ivey, Seed, and Flack have already bitten the dust. So that's something. But have I "beaten" these people? Not really, since we only have to take on eight players at a time. What I've done is outlast them. I should therefore be thrilled to be stroking my orange-free stack while Geraldo yucks it up for the cameras.

The players I'm sitting with couldn't care less. All they want is to eliminate me and one another. But not me! Because as soon as I put the brag book next to my chips and open it to the page on which Jennifer reads *The Little Mouse, the Red Ripe Strawberry, and the Big Hungry Bear* to our daughter Beatrice, my pocket cards start to get better. I manage to steal a few blinds, then take down a decent-sized pot when two pairs hold up over Kings. More important, I've persuaded myself at long last to fold all my trouble hands. With my new leather ass and my talismans, I manage to hang around until the nine o'clock dinner break, when I've scratched my way up to $16,450. I dash to my room, call Jennifer again in St. Louis, and brag. And she lets me.

Back at the poker table, I grab myself by the collar and demand that I wait for big hands in all but the last three positions; and I listen. But escalating blinds and a stretch of cold cards grind my stack down to $13,825 by midnight. We're still at Level 4, anteing $25 a hand with $100 and $200 blinds. Down to $11,700, I can't wait forever for a hand. With the blinds at $200 to $400 and $50 antes, it's costing me $1,050 a round just to sit here and fold all my rags. But finally, one off the button, I peek between my knuckles and discover Jack of Hearts, Jack of Diamonds. Ooh la la. Raising to $1,000, I get three callers, and the flop comes K-J-8 rainbow. Even with the overcard (King) and all these damn callers, I bet $1,500. Seat seven folds, but the Japanese yuppie in seat eight makes it $3,000. Then the shaved head in one cold-calls both bets. Jesus Christ! It's gonna cost me every last chip to keep playing this hand, and without the mortal nuts (at this point, a "set" of three Kings) I'm petrified of set over set; even worse are the obvious straight draws. Yet if I don't get my chips in with this hand, when am I going to? Never, I decide, as I call, then watch fourth street come a darling, a beautissimous, a sideways-infinity 8, providing my first full house of the day—in two days, actually. I nudge the rest of my chips 10 inches forward. "All-in." Japan meditates on his options for a minute, then folds, flashing two queens in disgust. Sayonara! Shaved Head, however, smooth-calls me. Since I'm all-in, no further betting is possible, so we both turn over our hole cards. His are Ten of Clubs, Nine of Clubs, not the cowboys or the other two eights, so it's over: any straight he might make will still lose to Jacks full of Eights—a full house. The pot comes to $36,900. Stacking it next to my brag book, I'd love nothing better than to trudge off to bed, but we still have 52 minutes left at Level 5. I order hot chocolate and sit tight, once folding pocket Sevens from middle position even though no one had raised yet. Me solid!

Bob Thompson calls a halt to our march at 2:09. Sheets are passed around with places to record our chip count. Mine comes to $35,325. Tom Elias recounts them, signs my sheet, stuffs chips and sheet into a Ziploc™ bag, staples it shut. Done. Still alive. It's too late to call my wife, but my rush while it lasted—one hand!—has gladdened my heart as much as any sonnet or fuck or narcotic or shot glass of silver Patron, as much as any three of those things, though it still takes 150mg of Trazodone washed down by room-service cabernet to finally fall off, I'm so wired . . .

Tuesday morning, after 36 laps in the pool, a fast shower, room-service oatmeal and OJ, all in the service of tuning my nerves, muscles, and glucose, I arrive back downstairs to the sunlit fact of my name on page one of the five-page, single-spaced leader board. Two hundred fourteen still have chips, and my $35,325 is good for thirty-eighth place. With par at $23,933, this puts me in pretty good shape, though Mehul Chaudhari, the leader, has me almost tripled with $92,500. My satellite rivals, Hasan and Tom, are in fifth and sixteenth, respectively. Rising star Kathy Liebert is seventh, T.J. nineteenth, Noel Furlong right above me in thirty-sixth. Bunched near the middle are Hayden, Duke, Enright, and Erik Seidel, runner-up to Chan in 1988. All of these folks are my heroes.

By the end of today we'll have to lose 169 more of us, but every survivor will be guaranteed at least $15,000. Am I ready for this? Maybe not. My first big mistake is walking pocket Kings, failing to protect them by raising in hopes of building a pot, then getting caught by a straight on the river. Exactly when, I have to wonder, did I become a person on whom everything is lost? This game is designed to blast draws from the battlefield, imbecile! Down to $28,000, I resolve, for the umpteenth time, to play solid poker— to stay out of pots until I find what Sklansky calls the Group 1 or 2 hands (Aces or Kings down through suited K-Q), then attack. For the next 90 minutes, it works. I also manage, from later positions, to slip into a few unraised pots with suited connectors, two of which turn into flushes. Bottom line? $98,000. If I hadn't wasted a call with Ace of Diamonds, Three of Clubs, on the previous hand, I'd now have the magic one large.

After dinner I get moved to seat two of a table with Hasan in seat one, J. J. Bortner in three, Kathy Liebert in four, Mickey Appleman in six, and Daniel Negreanu in eight. Scary, but also more fun. Bortner keeps a plastic baby rattler coiled atop her stacks that she's quite fond of shoving toward the pot, snake and all. Appleman is one of the game's veteran pros and melancholy philosophers. He used to work with alcoholics in Harlem, but he's been on the pro poker circuit for twenty-five years now. He's wearing a white Massada baseball cap over his ash-blond Groucho Marx moptop, and losing. The goateed Negreanu is whippet thin under his Sharks jersey and ultimatebet.com hat. Fresh off a win at the U.S. Poker Championship, he's brimming with humor and confidence. "Let's be honest here," he tells Hasan, after a flop comes off Ace of Clubs, Seven of Spades, Seven of Hearts. "You've got the Seven. Why walk it?" As Hasan tries to keep a straight face, Daniel grabs a dozen orange chips, winds up like he's getting ready to throw a left hook, and wings the chips into the pot, which he goes on to win with Ace of Diamonds, Ten of Clubs.

With sixty players left, I'm back down to $82,000, so I play extra-tight for a stretch, waiting for a monster I can sic on these big shots. The leaders are Duke, Liebert, Habib, and a guy called Captain Tom Franklin, all with around $250,000 in chips. With the blinds at $1,500 to $3,000 and $500 antes, it's costing me $9,000 per round. So the last thing I'm in the mood for is a photo op, but here, as the cameras shark in, we have Slim standing up behind Liebert, holding a butcher knife to his throat. Turns out that back in 1972 Slim reportedly threatened to cut his throat if a woman ever won the tournament. (What he said was that he'd do it if a particular woman won, but the misquote makes much better copy.) I'm sure Kathy wants to concentrate on poker, but she's being a pretty good sport, though I'd be smiling, too, if I had big straight white teeth and $270,000 in front of me.

With a dozen eliminations to go till we reach forty-five, I basically hang around for 2 hours, actively avoiding confrontations. Doesn't work. By the time we're down to forty-seven, I have only $36,000 left, almost exactly where I started the day. But if I can only survive two more ousters, I'll not only be good for $15,000 but will be on a freeroll for the $1.5 million.

At this stage we're forced to play hand for hand, holding up the next shuffle until all six tables complete the previous hand, this to keep short stacks from stalling. My table is already a terrifying convocation, but when the player in the eight seat goes out, he's replaced by—oh, shit—T.J. Cloutier. It gets worse. More than content to just sit here and wait, I somehow get forced into a series of make- or-break jousts. The first comes when, one off the button, I find Ace of Clubs, Jack of Hearts. T.J. has already raised it to $5,000, and both the tanned, blond cowboy in nine and Hasan have folded. *Don't call big bets*, I remind myself. *Fold or raise.* Yet I'm also aware that strong players target weak players, especially when the pressure is on, and my guess is that this is what T.J. is up to. I call. Jerry, the mustachioed Latin dealer, raps the felt, turns the flop: Ace of Diamonds, Nine of Clubs, Six of Hearts. T.J. stares at me, checking. If he's got a bigger ace I am cooked, ditto for A-9 or A-6, but with top pair and a decent kicker I still have to bet $20,000, having put him on an Ace with a medium kicker. I meet his warm glare for a second or two, then study the smoke-marbled distance. I must appear terribly frightened, however, because T.J. moves in with alacrity. His stack is smaller than mine, but only by three or four thousand. I call.

Now it's old T.J. who don't look so happy. "I think you've got me out-kicked," he growls hoarsely, then exhales a yard-long plume of smoke as I show him Ace of Clubs, Jack of Hearts. He makes me wait while snuffing his Salem, then turns over . . . Ace of Hearts, Ten of Spades! My heart hurdles four of my ribs.

The turn is Nine of Diamonds, giving both T.J. and me Aces up, with my Jack of Hearts still outkicking his 10 of Spades. Only a 10 will beat me, I figure; any other card comes on fifth street, I win. Instead of going out two off the money, I'm a 44–3 favorite not only to win a big pot but to punch out the number-one badass. Jerry raps the felt, turns over . . . an Ace. Whew! The crowd around us gasps, and I hear Liebert say, "Oh my God!" With so much hot blood in my head, I'm able to parse neither the buzz of commentary nor the looks on the other seven players. All I know is that T.J. is grinning. Even after Jerry announces, "Split pot," and is echoed by dozens of railbirds, it takes me a moment to fathom that we both just made Aces full of Nines. Jerry shoves me my measly half-share of the chips. I try to restack them by color, but my fingers don't work very well.

For the next 30 minutes, Liebert keeps the table pretty much under control, maneuvering her $300,000 stack like Rommel in a short desert war, blitzkrieging our antes and blinds, setting us all-in when we draw. Down to forty-six we are still hand for hand, and sometimes the suspensions last 8 or 10 minutes. When I try to stand up, the tendons in my legs yank me forward. As I hobble into the men's room, Jesus Ferguson is manning a urinal in his trademark unreadable getup: full beard and yard-long auburn locks under black cowboy hat slung low over wraparound shades. "Still have chips?" he asks cordially. Sort of, I tell him. What about you? "I guess I'm still doing all right. Hey, good luck." Heading out after washing our hands, I notice that his feet are adorned with elegant little black dancer's shoes. Strange! Before I sit back down, I try to survey the other five tables. Jacobs and Duke have big stacks, though Liebert still rules the whole tournament. The tiniest stacks are at my table, where Appleman is down to $4,500. Another round of blinds and he's through.

Three hands later I flop two pair in a heads-up pot with Hasan and get elated all over again—until Hasan sets me all-in. The two Diamonds on board are what scares me. If he makes his flush while I fail to improve, it'll be I going out instead of Appleman, and in the worst of all possible places. I've put Hasan on flush draw and inferred that he's semi-bluffing before his own hand gets made— or does not. Only a fool wouldn't do so with those scary looking Diamonds out there, and Hasan is no fool. So I call. And my Sevens and Sixes hold up, doubling me through to $78,000.

During the next break I notice that Andy Glazer, the *Detroit Free Press* gaming columnist, is talking to Jesus. When I introduce myself and ask for a cigarette, it turns out that neither of them smokes. I tell Ferguson that I'm shocked: in spite of the dance shoes, he looks like a Marlboro Man all the way. In fact, he's a gentle-voiced, day-trading wonk with a new PhD in computer science from UCLA who happens to love ballroom dancing; the outfit is "just for disguise." Does he prefer to be called Jesus or Chris? "Both." Both? "Either one. I like them both the same." Helpful! Andy now suggests that I might want to slow down at this point. I tell him that the last thing I want is to keep mixing it up, but the table's not giving me much choice. "Plus my hand keeps grabbing the chips and tossing them into—"

"Almost as though you've been hypnotized."

"Ri-i-ight . . ."

"We understand perfectly," says Jesus.

With me on the button and Liebert in the big blind, Appleman folds one more hand, leaving him with barely enough to post the next blind. The next player, Roman Abinsay, pushes his entire $10,500 into the pot. Appleman, of course, desperately wants someone to knock out Abinsay, in forty-sixth place, but no one ahead of me can call; neither can I, with Seven of Spades and Four of Diamonds. Which leaves it up to Liebert to play sheriff, especially since she already has $3,500 invested in the pot. And that's what she does, calling and turning over King of Clubs, Queen of Diamonds. Appleman's long face never once changes expression, even when Abinsay turns over . . . Aces. Liebert sighs. The flop comes Queen of Spades, Seven of Hearts, Three of Hearts, leaving her dead to either of the two remaining Queens. The turn comes a seven, apparently helping neither of them. When a king comes on fifth street, some overexcited railbirds start chirping that we're done for the night, and I'd love to believe them. But another quick look at the board makes it clear what Liebert already knows: that Kings and Queens loses to aces and *whatever* pair.

On we play. I'm more determined than ever to stay on the sidelines. Even when under the gun I find Aces, I think about mucking them, but it's too easy to imagine kicking myself 15 minutes from now, let alone fifteen years. Deciding to walk them, I bet "only" $10,000 and get called by the cowboy. When the flop comes Jack of Spades, Four of Hearts, Two of Spades, I bet $12,000 more, expecting to win a nice pot then and there, though with part of me hoping he'll raise. When he smooth-calls again, it finally dawns on me that I may well be trapped by three Jacks. Fourth street is Five of Hearts, giving me an inside straight draw to go with my Aces. I can't put the cowboy on anything higher than Jacks, since he wouldn't have called $24,000 with A-3. I almost prefer he has Jacks as my right hand picks up fifteen blue chips, breaking them down into three piles . . . and Cowboy smooth-calls me *again*! Thank God the river card is Three of Spades, backdooring me into a wheel (giving me, in other words, an unexpected Five-high straight on the final two cards). No way is Cowboy holding 6–3, and since the board hasn't paired, he couldn't have filled his three Jacks. I check, hoping he'll at least represent the 6–3 and I can raise him all-in. He had me trapped back there on the flop and the turn, but now I believe I have him. When he shows me two pocket Jacks, I turn over one Ace for the wheel, and then, for good measure, the other one, which Cowboy doesn't seem to appreciate.

All of a sudden I have almost $200,000, second at this table only to Liebert's four large. I'm reminding myself to avoid her, in fact, when, back on the button again, I find Ace of Diamonds, Queen of Spades. When it gets checked around to me, I raise it to $12,000. After Bortner folds, who else but Liebert reraises to $24,000. She does this, of course, with an absolute minimum of anima. Zero. She could care less, she couldn't care less: take your pick. Assuming again that the big-time pros want to push me around, but failing for the dozenth time to heed T.J.'s advice about raising or folding, I call. The flop of Two of Spades, Seven of Clubs, Queen of Clubs bails me out, in a way. Because when Kathy, the reraiser, taps a slender pink finger to check, I catch a faint whiff of check-raise. As the odor becomes more insistent, my overmatched brain seizes up—*chcheckcheckch*—but my thumb and middle finger somehow mange to bet

$20,000 without even pausing to consult with their boss. Kathy stares me down through my polarized lenses like some chick laser surgeon zinging my capillaries. Do they smoke? Do they twitch? I don't know. The hand I'd put her on was a medium pair, but now I ain't so sure—not that I was sure in the first place, though I doubt she reraised me preflop with Q-2 or Q-7. Whatever Queen she's playing I've got her tied or outkicked, but what if she's slow-playing two of them? After weighing and squeezing her miniature blue- and-white soccer ball for over a minute, she cuts out a stack of fifteen orange chips, fondling them as though ready to move them forward, all the while watching me closely. Zzzt . . . zzzzzzt . . . I stare away from the table for 10 or 12 seconds, then pointedly look back at her. I like her a lot, and she knows that.

When she finally mucks, I flash her my Queen of Spades in what I hope will be taken as a comradely gesture. "Show one, show all," Abinsay demands. I pick up both my cards from the edge of the muck and flip them over. Kathy nods twice but doesn't look happy. She also makes a point of sliding her own cards facedown toward the dealer.

Two hands later, after T.J. has raised to $10,000, I find an eminently foldable Ace of Spades, Five of Hearts, but I can't shake the feeling that my new favorite author wants to pilfer our antes and blinds. The longer I think about it the more convinced I become, so I call. My heart thumps out signals visible all over my body—finger, neck, pupils, complexion—of how nervous I am, so I try to persuade myself that they can also be read as elation, as in, "Yes! I'm finally gonna get T.J.'s chips!" I camouflage my relief when the flop comes Ace of Diamonds, Three of Diamonds, Two of Clubs, giving me an inside straight draw to go with top pair and pitiful kicker. When T.J. raps his fist on the table I'm convinced I'll be check-raised, but even if he comes back over the top of me I've got enough chips to survive. I pluck two pink $10,000 chips from the top of one stack and toss them forward. Take that!

Now it's T.J. who's staring me down, an altogether more visceral experience than my face-off with Kathy. While there's nothing overt about it, the man comfortably embodies a lethal threat, even from the seated position. If it happens to suit him, he can reach across the table and rupture key vertebrae with his bare hand, and everyone sitting here understands this down in our helical enzymes—my helical enzymes, at least, not to mention my looping and straight ones. Doing my best to meet his jagged scrutiny, I decide not to taunt him about his run-on sentences or the stench from his Salems. The best way to take care of that is to break him and make him go home.

And he mucks it, God love him! Showing me Queen of Clubs, Queen of Spades, he seems both proud of his laydown and irked at the gall of me, slick little East Coast book-learned weasel that I am, even if it's his goddamn book I've been learning from. It's impossible not to think of Jack Palance staring down Billy Crystal: *I crap bigger'n you* . . . Amid the ensuing buzz, I overhear Andy Glazer speaking about "how spooky things are getting. A few minutes ago he was a writer trying to hang on, and suddenly he's messing with T.J. and Kathy?!" With T.J. perhaps. I certainly didn't think of myself as messing with Kathy. I read them both as messing with me, each time with less than a premium hand. All I did was refuse to lay down my strong hands just because they were who they were and I didn't have the absolute nuts. So even after I get pocket Kings cracked by Appleman's King of Clubs, Ten of Hearts, when the board makes him a straight, everything's still copacetic. A few hands later an unfortunate gentleman at another table gets busted in forty-sixth place and it's time to call it a morning. And this time I do wake up Jennifer.

Eight and a half hours later I have unwelcome company in the pool on the roof. The strong swimmer splashing away my tranquility is a big, dark-haired guy with a mustache. When he finally climbs the hell out, I recognize him as Umberto Brenes, a Costa Rican player I met, along with his younger brother, Alex, back on Monday. He'd shown me his World Series bracelet, for the 1993 seven-card stud event, and invited me down to his poker club in the Hotel Corobici in San José. I saw him at Ferguson's table last night, so I knew he was still in the running. It turns out we're both in our forties and have kids. I have four, Umberto has two; he has a World Series bracelet, I don't. But my $276,000 is good for third place, just behind Liebert's $283,500 and Englishman Barney Boatman's $282,000.

Downstairs we learn that Umberto, with $101,000, is at Table 48, the most hazardous of the five—plenty of chips to win if you catch cards and play well, but with Boatman and Liebert wielding big stacks, you risk being set all-in each time you enter a pot. Tom Jacobs's $229,000 makes him the bully of Table 47, which has four stacks under $39,000. Duke, Habib, and Mike Sexton are all at Table 54, the second most chip-laden group and perhaps the most talented. Duke and Habib are both hot, and Sexton is fresh off a victory at the European No-Limit Championship. In seat six of Table 55 sits its putative bully, yours truly. I've fantasized for decades about having a World Series stack big enough to make brutal sport of my opponents, but I have zero actual experience in the role. I spent the first two days gasping and thrashing to keep my nose above water, and it isn't so obvious how to skim along the top with the current. Another problem is that my four most chip-laden opponents sit immediately to my left. Larry Beilfuss in seat seven, with $121,500, is a bespectacled, all-business guy around my age. Then comes Dae Kim in eight with $127,500, Meng La in nine with $197,000, and Anastassios Lazarou in one with $125,000. Since chips tend to flow clockwise around the table, I'm in lousy position to kick any serious butt. On my right, I have a curly haired Parisian by the name of Angelo Besnainou, who has what sounds like Cuban salsa leaking from his earphones. He's about the sunniest person I've met in Las Vegas so far. Even sunnier is the fact that he has only $64,000, which I plan to relieve him of stat.

At Level 11 the antes alone are $1,000 (five times the buy-in for my home game) with blinds of $2,000 and $4,000. My stacks now consist of sixteen blue- and-white dimes, twenty-four orange five-thousands, and fourteen hot-pink ten-thousands. We've been told to keep our pinks at the fore so that opponents can gauge whom they do or do not want to tangle with.

As expected, the first player eliminated, over at Table 62, is Eric Schulz, who started with a single $500 chip. An old poker adage says that all you need to win is a chip and a chair, but starting from so far behind at a table with Mel Judah, T.J. Cloutier, and Jesus Ferguson, that's what it remained for Mr. Schulz—an old adage. Yet that yellow-and-black chip of his just earned him $15,000, the same prize the next eight eliminatees will receive.

Meanwhile, at our table, Appleman has just raised all-in. Angelo folds, and I'm not playing trooper with Broderick Crawford. After mucking, I have to brush away what looks like cocaine or powdered rock salt from the baize between my stack and Angelo's. Beilfuss calls Appleman, but Kim, La, and Lazarou all fold. (Was someone snorting lines or noshing saltines here last night?) Pair of Fives for Appleman, Ace of Diamonds, Nine of Spades for Beilfuss. The flop comes Ace of Hearts, Ace of Spades, Five of Hearts ruining Beilfuss's day while doubling Appleman through to $180,000. It seems like he was down to felt only a few minutes ago.

The white mess turns out to be sugar, and the culprit turns out to be Angelo. I discover this by watching him sprinkle out more of it. I stare at him, shaking my head. "For sweet life," he tells me. "You know?" He goes on to explain that Tunisian Jews, of which he is one, have a tradition of adding sweetness to life by sprinkling sugar on portentous objects: a new house, a tractor, a child . . . I have to admit it's a wonderful concept, but as its substance combines with the moisture on our fingers we're sugar-coating the cards as we play them. Isn't it bad enough that I've got either the suddenly ill-tempered Beilfuss or the ever inscrutable Kim snapping me off with reraises each time I try stealing blinds? Have they no damn respect for the Bully? A few hands later Meng La comes over the top of me, all-in, this after I've made the heaviest wager of my life by raising his big blind eight pink—eight pink $10,000 chips. I'm forced to lay down the same red Jacks that came to my rescue on Monday.

After licking my fingers and wounds for a round, I'm only too happy to call, with King of Clubs, King of Diamonds, the last $28,000 of Ron Stanley, the player in seat two. Stanley turns over King of Hearts, Ten of Spades. Oh yeah, I gloat, mentally pumping my fist. Time to get back in the lead! But the Queen of Hearts, Nine of Diamonds, Three of Diamonds flop gives Stanley a belly straight draw, and when, sure enough, the beardless Jack of Clubs arrives on the turn, my stack and my confidence plunge to $97,000, a piddling sum at this stage. Just in time, too, for Level 12, when the blinds jump to $3,000 and $6,000. Worst of all, I get high-carded to a table with Habib, Sexton, Jeff Shulman (the chip leader, with almost $500,000), Jacobs, and Cloutier. In my humble opinion, it's over. Not that

I've given up, but I have to be realistic before I get blinded to death. My only chance is to wait, not too long, for a monster to materialize between my knuckles, hope I get called by a worse hand and don't get sucked out on, and so double through. And then I have to do it *again*. And then I have to do it again. At least we have a ravishing dealer named Red, presumably because of her fox-colored shoulder-length locks, to go with wide hazel eyes and a sly grin.

T.J.'s $400,000 threatens to make him boss hoss, a role he was surely born to play. And with Shulman's vast stacks on my right, I'm developing a severe case of big-stack envy. A half hour later we lose Kathy Liebert. She entered a big pot with Queens but lost to King of Hearts, Ten of Diamonds, then got bounced five hands later when someone called her King of Diamonds, Ten of Clubs raise with a pair of Queens, and that time the Queens did hold up. Very brutal. But now I can barely keep from whooping when, sitting in the small blind, I find King of Spades, King of Diamonds. Even better is that Annie Duke, who's playing without shoes or socks, has already raised it four pink. I reraise eight more and flash her what I hope is a friendly but confident smile. Her response is to say, "I'm all-in." Terrified of Aces, I call, timidly flipping my Kings as Duke snaps down . . . Queen of Clubs, Queen of Hearts. This is good. What's bad is that our table has suddenly become the matrix of Annie Duke fandom, all of them training a miasma of estrogen onto my innocent cowboys, willing them to be bushwhacked by ladies. Bob Thompson's reminder that Annie's the last woman left only whips them up further. *Annieee!* . . . *You go, girl!* . . . *C'mon, Queeeen!* Yet in spite of all this, my brag book decrees that the cowboys stand up.

We come back from dinner to antes of $2,000, blinds of $5,000 and $10,000, with the final fourteen reconfigured as such:

Table 1
1. Mark Rose, $223,000
2. Annie Duke, $130,000
3. Hasan Habib, $330,000

4. Chris Ferguson, $305,000

5. Jim McManus, $450,000

6. Steve Kaufman, $400,000

7. T.J. Cloutier, $540,000

Table 2

1. Mickey Appleman, $540,000

2. Roman Abinsay, $330,000

3. Angelo Besnainou, $70,000

4. Tom Franklin, $450,000

5. Jeff Shulman, $440,000

6. Anastassios Lazarou, $105,000

7. Mike Sexton, $385,000

What a player Appleman must be, having started the day with $6,000! I'm glad that he's not at my table as, once again, we play hand for hand, aiming to get down to six. Between shuffles I get up and watch Angelo get bounced when his Ace of Clubs, Six of Spades goes down to Shulman's Ace of Diamonds, Ten of Clubs.

I remind myself how much seven-handed action changes the value of pocket cards. Trouble hands like King of Spades, Queen of Diamonds or small pairs become cautiously playable, even from an early position. It's crucial that I not only adjust but account for the fact that my opponents will, too. The amazing thing to me is how calm I now feel, as though vying for the lead late on Day 3 of the Big One is all in a night's work. I can't see the stacks on the other table, but I figure I'm in fourth, third, or second, and I understand that I can win.

I watch as Chris Ferguson makes what has become our standard preflop raise, $60,000, and with Jack of Hearts, Jack of Spades I am happy to call, especially since I've read Chris's raise as positional. Kaufman and T.J. and Rose and then Annie all fold, but Hasan, in the big blind, calls too. This triggers the blend of *oh, shit* and *oh, well* that's been percolating down through my brain each time I play a big pot. I've risked only $60,000 so far, but we're likely to take it much higher. When the flop comes Ace of Diamonds, Queen of Diamonds, Two of Clubs, it's more like *oh, shit* and *oh, shit*. The fecal sensation becomes more pronounced as Chris moves both hands behind his stacks, clasps them together with pale, bony fingers, and pushes them slowly toward the pot, making sure not to topple any of his precious pink towers. I ask him to count it. "Two-fifty," he says, without counting. I believe him, and the dealer confirms it. Do I call an all-in bet with two overcards already on board? I don't think so. At the same time, I don't want no Fred Astaire wanna-be shoving me off my two Jacks. T.J. and Annie and Slim all have their share of the photographers' attention, but Jesus of late has become the new darling. Both the still guys and film people regularly zoom in on his badass Black Stallion hat with silver buckles adorning the brim, his wraparound shades whose convexity must make for some swank photographic effects—Fred Astaire meets Richard Petty, along with the Youngbloods hair and beard, the bona fide Jesusesque features. I'm sure they're all pulling for him to win the whole thing, as opposed to some puffily unphotogenic dad-type like me. But darn it all, I'm bad as well! Haven't they noticed my space-age titanium shades, or the stain on my top right incisor from smoking Cambodian opium? And what about the four-color tatts of Sade and Genet on my scrotum? . . . I flip my Jacks into the muck. Too many overcards, plus no read whatever on Chris.

But I only have to wait three more hands till I get my first chance at redemption, looking down to find what certainly looks like Big Slick. I peer in again to make sure. Yessiree, it's Ace of Diamonds, King of Clubs. Swallowing as discreetly as possible, I wait my turn before pushing ten orange toward the unraised pot. The instant that Steve Kaufman mucks, T.J. shoves forward a tall stack of pink, snarling, "Raise." He may not have actually snarled, but that's how it registers in my soul. And whatever the participle or verb, it's another $100,000 to me.

In the final chapter of *Super/System*, Brunson claims that A-K are his favorite pocket cards because you win more with them when you make a hand and lose less when you don't; whereas A-Q, just one pip below it, is a hand he famously refuses to play under any circumstance. T.J.'s book stresses that you have to win both with and against A-K. "It's the biggest decision-hand in a tournament." He considers it so decisive that in four of his twelve practice hands, the reader is given A-K. And be still my computerized, book-learnin' heart and suck in my un-Christlike cheeks, but I just have a feeling that T.J. is making a play. And I want him to go on making it. Yet with four hundred large in the pot, what the hay is a feeling? The short answer runs something as follows: T.J. writes that when he gets raised holding A-K, his response depends on *who made the raise*. I've studied the passage so obsessively, I believe I can quote it verbatim. "There are times when I will just flat call the raise. There are times when I will try to win the money right then by reraising. And there are times when I will simply throw the hand away. It all depends on what I know about my opponent." Not to get overly granular here, but I think T.J. thinks he can push me around, so I feel I should give him a call. Playing against him these last two nights has made it clear he's a guy on whom nothing is lost—just his chips in this case, if I'm right. If I'm wrong, I'll be out of the tournament.

"Call."

The flop of my life comes a baby rainbow: Two of Clubs, Five of Hearts, Four of Diamonds. I still have boss overcards, plus a nice belly draw to a wheel; but I also have nada. Same draw for T.J., I'm guessing, since I've put him on a medium Ace. He's not the kind of guy to reraise with A-3—unless he has Kryptonite testes or assumes he can bluff me with garbage, both of which are probably operative. I recall that in Practice Hand 4, the flop comes three babies. If Player A bets, T.J. quizzes the reader, what do you do? "You throw your hand away. Why? Because you have nothing. In no-limit hold'em, you never chase"—about the dozenth time he's restated the never-chase maxim. Assuming he knows that I know this, I chase. The instant I tap the felt checking, T.J. mutters, "Two hunnerd thousand" and his entire stack of pink chips disappears into his hand, to be deftly redeposited between him and the pot in four stacks of five. His fingers don't seem to be trembling.

"Call," I croak finally, making a virtue of necessity by trying to sound like I've lured poor T.J. into my trap, an impression I hope isn't risibly belied as my vibrating digits fumble to count twenty pink. I can't bear even to glance in T.J.'s direction, so I cannot say how he reacts to the turn card, the Seven of Diamonds, which as far as I'm concerned changes exactly nothing. I check.

"I'm all-in," T.J. says. No surprise here, since he's been trying to buy the pot all along. A third enormous bet doesn't scare me any less, or any more, than the first two did. Except now he has put me all-in.

"I call."

Thompson notes for the gallery that T.J. has me covered by a hundred thousand or so. What he doesn't say is that if his fellow Texan has even a pair of deuces, I'm finished. T.J. turns over an Ace and a Nine, muttering something I can't quite make out because of the buzz off the rail. When I turn over macho Big Slick, there are oohs, aahs, applause, and T.J. appears mildly shocked. Amid the gathering uproar, Thompson announces our hands. A Trey will give us both wheels, a Nine and I'm kevorked. Anything else, the pot's mine. My sense, as the dealer's right fist thumps the table, is that T.J. is going to catch . . .

"Jack of Clubs on the river," drawls Thompson. "Jim McManus wins $866,000 and becomes the new chip leader." Benny Behnen and Amarillo Slim have been standing behind the table for the last several hands, and Benny now drawls, "Jesus Chrahst!"

"Ah'd bet on that boy," Slim drawls back. "He's got the heart of a cliff divah."

"T.J. taught me everything I know about this game," I announce. "Read his book and you'll see." If I had my copy on me, I would brandish it aloft for the cameras. T.J. stubs out a Salem, not pleased. "It didn't teach you that, boy," he growls, with what I hear as a trace of contempt. Now, the last man on earth I would taunt is T.J. Cloutier. I also remember how showing my Queen to Kathy Liebert didn't seem to assuage her. Not that it's my job to assuage either one of them . . .

This *former* cliff diver, though, is gonna sit good and tight with his chip lead. After 13 hours at the table and staring down T.J.'s three barrels, he's got cobwebby spermatozoa floating through his vitreous humor. So he's not even tempted to play a Three of Diamonds, Eight of Hearts, Jack of Hearts, Five of Clubs, or even Ace of Hearts, Seven of Hearts. No, sir. He also decides not to raise but to limp. And Duke, one off the button, cooperates beautifully, raising to $60,000. Hasan and Chris fold. Hasan stands up, yawning and stretching, to watch. And then I'm yawning, too, just as I happen to start moving $150,000 toward the pot; judging by the size of Duke's stack, it's enough to have set her all-in. The next thing I know, both Kaufman and the dealer are citing me for a string raise, claiming I went back into my stack for more chips without saying, "Raise." I realize they're right and apologize. The dealer determines that the amount in my hand as it started forward was $60,000, which happens to be the minimum allowable raise of Annie's original bet. And boy, she's not happy. My raise doesn't set her all-in, but since she only has $140,000 left, she's been priced in. She turns to her entourage. "This is the worst thing that's ever happened to me in a tournament!" she shrieks— and *shrieks*, I'm afraid, is the word. "Let me call that myself," she chides Kaufman, and for a moment I'm cheering her on, till she adds, "I would've been glad to let him go to his stack for more!" She runs a hand up through brown bangs, jangling her wrist load of beads, braided leather, plastic bangles. That she would have been "glad" to let me put her all-in suggests she has a premium hand, and that she was so overwrought when she said it makes it impossible to believe she was acting. I have to put her on something better than a lousy pair of Jacks, do I not? But so why, after my raise was scaled down to $60,000, didn't she simply re-raise me?

The flop comes Ace of Clubs, Queen of Clubs, Eight of Clubs, about as bad it can be for my Jacks, so I check to the shrieker. "All-in," she says, sliding her stacks in. She has a live human being inside her—her third— but that's not the reason I fold. No way can I call even a $100,000 more, though the pot odds declare that I should. Not with them overcards squatting pregnantly on the baize. It isn't the toughest laydown I've made, but it still smarts to have to muck johnnies again. This is, after all, two-card chicken we're playing, and things can change fast on fourth street and fifth street . . .

"I changed my mind," Duke announces, then graciously shows me an Ace before mucking. "That's the best thing that ever happened to me in a tournament." Big applause from the rail. *Hang in there, Annie! . . . Chicks ruuule!* Yet who can I blame but myself and Steve Kaufman? If I'd been competent to set her all-in before the flop, when all she probably had was a medium Ace, she almost certainly would have folded; but for only $60,000, she was still sufficiently tied to the hand to make a crying call correct. Then she caught that huge piece of the flop. So my little snafu while trying to put her all-in cost me $120,000 and handed Jeff Shulman the lead. If I'd simply said, "Raise," I'd be sitting on over a million.

To stem this new ebb tide, I resolve to enter no pots for the next fourteen hands unless I find Aces or Kings. I watch two rounds go by without a flop, a single raise being enough to capture the blinds. Meanwhile, at the other table, Sexton and Lazarou get bounced on consecutive hands.

Level 15 brings with it $3,000 antes and $15,000 and $30,000 blinds, but my chips are still copious enough to let me relax, await monsters. Anyone in his right mind would follow this plan, yet when I find Ace of Clubs, Nine of Diamonds, I flash back to what Annie just did to me and call Chris's raise to $60,000. Hasan calls as well. When the flop comes A-Q-5 rainbow, Chris says, "All-in."

"Jim has about $700,000 in chips," declares Thompson, "Chris and Hasan, oh, I'd say about half that."

If I call and lose I'm out of the tournament; if I win I'll not only guarantee playing tomorrow but I'll have a huge lead in the sprint for the $1.5 million. Yet every last piece of advice I've received says no way do you call in these situations unless holding the absolute nuts. I do have a top pair, but I lose to any kicker above Nine. I wish I had some kind of read on this Jesus character. He's certainly capable of bluffing, but he's also extracted quite a few fishes and loaves from his butt in the last 20 minutes. My mouth for some reason says, "Call," and Chris turns over . . . Ace of Hearts, Nine of Spades. I pause long enough to give him decent psychological scourging before I let him off the hook and show mine. Shaking our heads as the crowd goes bananas, we triple-check the board for a flush draw; finding none, we both burst out laughing. His slender blonde wife stands behind him, wrist to her forehead, recounting the split on her cell phone. In the meantime, on the very next hand, Annie goes all-in again, only to have Chris call and show pocket Aces. Revealing the fateful Ace of Spades, Nine of Spades, Annie never catches up, so she's out. As she slowly gets up, Thompson announces that Annie's tenth-place finish is the highest by a woman since Barbara Enright came in fifth in 1995, and the $52,160 makes Annie the leading female money winner in World Series history. After watching her play for a week, I doubt this will cheer her up much. She's a cowgirl.

Down to nine men, we are ranged around one table: Ferguson in seat one with $800,000, then Habib with $400,000, me with $950,000, Cloutier with $550,000, Abinsay with $420,000, Appleman with $240,000, Jeff Shulman with $1,000,000, Captain Tom Franklin with $600,000, and Steve Kaufman with $220,000. Sitting just to my left, T.J.'s in perfect position to hammer his student, like he's been trying to do for two days. Plus he now has revenge as a motive.

For the next hour or so, the standard preflop raise is $90,000 or $100,000, usually enough to take down the blinds. From time to time one of us reraises all-in, but in each case the original raiser gives the reraiser credit by folding. Then, in very short order, this happens: Abinsay, from under the gun, brings it in for $60,000, and Appleman calls with his last $58,000. With the Jack of Spades, Ten of Spades, I'm tempted to make it a three-way, but I follow the no-chasing dictum. Thank God and Cloutier too, because none of my straight or flush cards appear on the board as Roman's Ace of Spades, King of Spades easily holds up over Mickey's Ace of Diamonds, Ten of Clubs. Two hands later Captain Tom wagers his last $118,000 before the flop, and Ferguson calls him with tens. When the Captain shows Fours and the board gives no help, we are seven.

One more unfortunate bet and it's bedtime, but nobody wants to finish in seventh. As in every WSOP event, the last nine players receive commemorative final-table jackets; there's also a hefty difference in prize money ($146,700 for seventh versus $195,600 for sixth); but the main reason for our lull in aggression is that tomorrow's final table will seat only six, owing to the Discovery Channel's need for compressed action in their documentary. Since we all want to be in the movie, not one all-in bet gets a call for the next 40 minutes. The guy forcing most of the action is Jeff, and he steadily builds up his stack. I'd love to know whether he's doing it with legitimate hands, but I'm not catching cards to find out with. One mistake against Jeff and you're gone, whereas he can guess wrong and still play.

Finally, *finally*, one off the button, I find Aces, the first time I've seen them all day. But my ecstasy ratchets down notch by notch as Kaufman, then Chris, then Hasan, muck their hands. At this point I'm tempted to limp, though I know it would be read as a trap. The $66,000 in antes and blinds I'll win by raising is hardly chump change, but when you find pocket rockets you want to *eviscerate* people. Masking my chagrin, I make the minimum raise to $60,000, hoping someone will come blasting back over the top of my show of timidity. Not this time. T.J. even shoots me a rare little smile as he folds, and Roman and Jeff are also untempted to call.

Three hands later, Jeff raises $200,000 from the button. Kaufman ponders defending his $15,000 small blind for a moment, then passes, leaving Chris, in the big blind, to reflect on his options for another 30 seconds. "What would Jesus do?" a shrill railbird wonders aloud, getting laughs. The answer is: move all seven of his tidy stacks toward the pot, re-raising $650,000. Hasan and the rest of us scram. Jeff stares at Jesus for maybe 10 seconds, then shrugs almost meekly and calls. When he turns over Seven of Hearts, Seven of Clubs—not really much of a hand to be calling a big stack all-in with—there are whispers and cries of astonishment. Then Chris shows us . . . Six of Clubs, Six of Spades! In absolute crunch time, the twenty-three-year-old Shulman has somehow made a veteran read of his opponent, leaving Chris with two outs. As auto-advance cameras fire away and the railbirds go silent, the flop comes Ten of Hearts, Three of Hearts . . . Six of Hearts! Having flopped a miraculous set, Jesus vaults from his chair. And yet Jeff, for all his hellacious bad luck, has a flush draw—Nine outs right there, to go with the two other Sevens. Jesus's lean, foxy wife, Cathy Burns, has her palms on her ears, a Munch screamer, as voices call out for Sixes or Sevens or Hearts. When Five of Clubs hits on the turn, Jeff has a straight draw as well, though Chris is still the 2–1 favorite. The dealer turns fifth street: a Ten. No Heart flush, no Seven. As Jeff slumps back in his chair, Chris dances out of his, the sooner to be locked in a tango embrace from Ms. Burns. No celebratory peck for these two, but a lingering soul smooch while they twirl one another around.

"Jesus Makes 6–6–6," I proclaim. "Takes Over Chip Lead, Molests Wife in Public."

"Molests Girlfriend in Public," a railbird amends me.

"Even better," I say. But the truth is, I'm dying inside. Not only is Jennifer not here to cheer me but it's starting to sink in that to win this damn thing I'll not only have to catch a few monsters; I'll need to catch them when someone else holds one a single pip lower. I'll have to play well for four days just to be in a position to get lucky when the big money goes in the pot. If only, if only, I snivel. If only I'd caught Aces on this hand . . . till it dawns on me that if I had, I would've lost every one of my chips. But of one thing I'm certain: Smooching Jesus is due for an epic correction. Having bounced Duke with Aces and Franklin with Tens, he now spikes a two-outer and doubles through Jeff to the lead. What he needs is a quick crucifixion, if only to give his strawberry-blonde Mary Magdalene something to hug him about. Everyone at the table would love to just nail him right now, yet we're terrified of taking him on. Not only does he have the big stack but he's got my old horseshoe lodged miles and miles up his ass.

T.J., of course, isn't terrified. He'd seen hundreds of rushes like this before Chris was even born. I fold Raquel Welch (3–8) in a hurry. "Raise," T.J. mutters as soon as the action gets to him, pushing in $290,000. Abinsay folds, but Shulman reraises all-in. Then Jesus not only calls Jeff and T.J.; he, too, reraises all-in! The big guy can't seem to believe what has happened, but he manfully lays down his hand, claiming it was Jacks. We believe him. What are Jacks, after all, once Jesus H. Christ gets involved? Turns out to be a pretty shrewd laydown when Jeff shows two Kings, and Chris has . . . the Aces again! Get the fuck outta here! The board renders no poetic justice either, because this time the best hand holds up. Just like that, Jeff is out. A couple of minutes ago he was running the table. He congratulates Chris and the rest of us, and then, with his dad's arm around him, walks away like a man with a future.

Ten hours later, the Horseshoe's vast tournament room has been converted to an intimate poker studio, if there is such a thing. In place of last night's four tables there are twenty rows of seats facing a 13-foot monitor.

Bleachers were erected along one side of the final table, flanked by more rows of seats at both ends. The table is lit with four banks of lights, surrounded by cameras and monitors. Everyone else wants to interview the finalists, but the Discovery director has first dibs because of the shoot. One of his tech guys wires me for sound, winding the line up through the fly of my pants and clipping the mike to my collar.

Back behind the bleachers, I peruse the new sheet with Hasan. Chris is in seat one with $2.853 million, Hasan is in two with $464,000, I'm in three with $554,000, T.J.'s in four with $216,000, Roman's in five with $521,000, Kaufman is in six with $511,000. Between us we have $5.19 million in chips, with which we'll be vying for $3.74 million in prize money. The other $1.38 million has already been awarded to places forty-five through seven.

"Good luck to you, buddy," says Hasan in his buttery lilt.

"And good luck to you." We embrace. I'm startled to realize that I meant what I said. For eight days now, we've been throwing haymakers at each other over critical pots, but that makes me love him a little. Plus we'll both need some luck from now on.

Finally, a little after noon, Thompson introduces us one by one. Chris, at thirty-seven, has already won the $2,500 seven-card-stud event, to go with the 1999 Best All-Around Player at the California State Poker Championship and his new PhD, but lists his occupation as "student." I hear Andy note that his nickname stems not from delusions of grandeur but from his hair and the kindness of his features. I also hear that Hasan used to own a video store but has now, at thirty-eight, been a pro for four years; just last month, at the World Poker Open, he finished second in the $1,000 no-limit event.

Now me. On their live Internet broadcast, Glazer and Phil Hellmuth, the 1989 champion, are calling me the "family man's family man," mainly because of my brag book and frequent calls home. Thompson says I'm playing in my first poker tournament and that most of my no-limit strategy comes from T.J.'s book. Down I sit. T.J. needs no introduction but gets a rather lengthy one anyway, followed by a standing ovation. This is his fourth final-table appearance at the Big One; he's won four other WSOP titles, fifty-one major championships altogether. At sixty, he's the sixth-leading money winner in series history, but by placing first or second today, he'd move past Johnny Chan into first. Abinsay, a fifty-two-year-old Filipino now living in Stockton, California, has already placed second in the $2,000 limit hold'em event, so he's hot. Kaufman, fifty-four, is a rabbi as well as a professor of languages (Hebrew, Aramaic, and other Semitic languages) at Hebrew Union College in Cincinnati, sufficiently high-powered as a scholar to be a consultant on the Dead Sea Scrolls. After playing big tournaments since 1997, he made the final table at Tunica. He's also a bit of a noodge.

I may have the second most chips, but we're all basically tied for second behind Ferguson. And with a stack less than half the size of mine, T.J. is at least twice as dangerous. He sits bolt upright and smokes, his gray Binion's polo shirt tucked into beltless beige slacks. I let him know one more time how terrific his book is, but he doesn't want to hear about it. He seems to think it's some kind of gamesmanship, and maybe he's right. Yet it's obvious to him and everyone else who the novice is here, the book-learned tournament virgin. No question, these five other guys see my $554,000 as the most plunderable stack.

The blinds are still $15,000 and $30,000, with $3,000 antes, and will be for the next 81 minutes. T.J. can't wait long to make a move, but it's Hasan who puts in the first raise, to $70,000. I'm tempted to call with Two of Diamonds, Two of Hearts, but come to my senses—duh!—in time to pass. When T.J. and Roman pass, too, it looks like Hasan may have executed the last day's first steal. But then here comes Professor Kaufman blasting over the top of him in a language we all understand: twenty pink. Once Jesus folds, Hasan has the day's first gulp-worthy decision. After gazing at Kaufman for maybe 10 seconds, he lays down his hand with a sigh.

Hand 2: From the button, Roman makes it $100,000 to go, a likely positional raise. Chris says, politely but firmly, "All-in." Roman calls, pushing his entire half million, then turns over Ace of Clubs, Queen of Spades. Chris shows Eight of Diamonds, Eight of Hearts. I want to observe Roman's face, but T.J. is blocking him out as Thompson narrates the Seven of Hearts, Two of Diamonds, Seven of Clubs flop, followed by a Jack and a Trey. Roman stands up from the table to abundant applause. His ouster has just guaranteed me fifth-place money, though it's the last thing I care about now. What I want is to cast Jesus and the rest of these money-changers from the temple and rake in the *serious* shekels. What I don't want is to glance at a monitor and be forced to wonder who's the little homunculus hunched in the seat next to T.J.—this as, on Hand 4, T.J. is moving all-in. No one calls him, certainly not the homunculus with his measly Jack of Diamonds, Five of Clubs. T.J. shows us Ace of Spades, Ten of Spades. And now, on Hand 5, here comes Hasan moving in. I can't call with Seven of Spades, Six of Hearts, and neither can anyone else. Am I playing too passively? I've already bled away 10 percent of my stack while the others are letting it rip.

On my next hand Chris raises $50,000, Hasan folds, and with Eight of Clubs, Six of Clubs so do I; so do T.J. and Roman and Steve. We've thus let Chris extend his lead by $63,000. His chips are arranged in two massive triangles, one on top of the other: ten pink twenty-chip columns in a 1–2–3–4 configuration, topped by six of less regular color scheme arranged 1–2–3. Very scary.

My next few hands are unplayable, but on Hand 9 I find Ace of Clubs, Queen of Clubs. Hasan, in the small blind, has raised it all-in once again. Suited A-Q is a better hand to raise than to call with, but still. Five-handed, it can fairly be called, pace Brunson, a monster. Granted that Roman's Ace of Clubs, Queen of Spades just got him beheaded, but my read of Hasan is that he's caught up in a spasm of all-in steal-raises. In the end I am happy to call him. Pushing my seven stacks forward, I believe that this puts me all-in. Hasan shows Ace of Hearts, Four of Hearts. I was right. When I flip up my Ace of Clubs, Queen of Clubs, everyone sees why I'm thrilled. What a call!

But now comes the flop of Hasan's and my life: Nine of Spades, Six of Spades, King of Spades. So far, so fantastic. Dead to the three remaining Fours, Hasan groans, shakes his head. The other forty-two cards in the deck give me a $900,000 pot and a real shot at taking down Chris. The crowd's yelling hundreds of things, but all I can hear is the Habib Society pleading for Fours. "Ha-san Ha-beeeeeeeb!" someone croons. They outnumber my own fans, such as they are, plus they have a specific card to pray for, but I've come to understand that I'm gonna win not just this hand but the tournament. One and a half million dollars. The heavyweight championship of poker. My faith is confirmed when fourth street arrives as the sacred, the numinous, the preternaturally chic Five o' Diamonds. *Close* to a four, I gloat to myself, but no sucking-out-on-me cigar. Hasan has stood up, getting ready to shake hands. My heart pounds spasmodically, but I'm still feeling thoroughly confident. So that when the fifth street card—*what?*—is—*what!*—Four of Hearts, I "reel," according to Glazer's column that night, "in stunned silence," even though a chorus of f-words and blasphemies and Fours is howling like a squadron of Pakistani banshees on tilt through my skull. Glazer will also write that, "Jim hadn't suffered too many indignities at the hands of fate in the last couple of days. Most of his leading hands had held up. But now, at the worst possible moment, he'd taken a punishing blow." Punished and reeling, then, away from the table, I have to be told by Hasan that I had him covered. "You'rrre still in therrre, buddy. I'm sorrrry. Keep playing. I'm sorrrry . . ." Although it feels like I died, I have life, if only $105,000 worth. Hasan and I are still clasping hands, shaking our heads in amazement. We realize that this is what happens in poker sometimes, that it could have just as—*more*—easily gone the other way, the towers of pink and orange chips being raked a foot to the left instead of a foot to the right.

A round or so later I find Ace of Spades, Two of Spades. I have barely enough chips for the blinds, so I probably won't see another Ace, let alone a big pair. I move in. Kaufman—who else?—not only calls but moves in himself, trying to knock me out on the cheap while making sure it stays heads-up between us. Once Chris and Hasan muck their hands, Kaufman turns over . . . Ace of Diamonds, Queen of Spades. It's perfect. That I'm now in the same spot Hasan was just in somehow inspires an ever more bottomless gloom. Yeah, sure, when Dante was spiraling down into the frozen bowels of Hell he may have also been ascending, without realizing it, toward Paradise, but here in Las Vegas, another frigid desert peopled by faithless demons, three-outers don't spike twice in a row. Forget about the long odds against it—I *know* it's not going to happen. And indeed the

Nine-Six-King flop gives me neither a straight draw nor a flush draw, let alone a sweet Deuce. In the end, with an Ace on the turn, a Ten on the river, it's not even close. I am out.

Now that the Satanic Prince of Noodges has forked me down into the pitch, there's applause. Many zooms. Many clicks. I shake Kaufman's hand, then Hasan's, then T.J.'s. "You played well," T.J. says. And that's something. And now here is Jesus coming around for a hug. "You played great!" he says, bonily squeezing me. Walking away from the table, however, it dawns on me how alive I felt while playing four days in the Big One, and now I feel dead. I mean *dead*. As Thompson and Glazer and Hellmuth and all the other commentators are making clear to the assembled and far-flung poker universe, I've won $247,760 by finishing fifth out of 512. What it feels like is fifth out of six.

Up on the podium, Becky Behnen shakes my hand, pets my arm. "You were wonderful, Jim. And last night! Congratulations!" Shaking my hand in his turn, her son Benny snaps me back to reality. "That Four was brutal, man. *Brutal*. You were playing so awesome last night!" Yeah, last night . . . Tom Elias ushers me a few steps to the left, where the payout booth stands. From his unbashful spiel, I gather that "big winners" have to tip the dealers "between 2 and 8 percent." I have to decide that right now? "We have to take care of our people, Jim. So, I mean, yeah, you do." I decide to tip $7,800, 3.3 percent of my profit and vastly more money than I'd ever played poker for, or made in one week doing anything. After thanking me, Tom details a Horseshoe security guard to escort me downstairs to the cage. Passing a monitor, I see that Hasan has just been bounced, and I desperately want to keep playing! But I know it's all over when the technician starts removing the sound pack. "If you'd just undo your belt . . ."

At the cashier downstairs, I play hurry up and wait with bucket-toting slot players, then start signing form after form. I slide the tax forms, the tip receipt, and a trayful of five-thousand-dollar brown chips into my lockbox, keeping one of them back to rub against the coins in my pocket.

By the time I get back upstairs, it's down to T.J. and Chris. T.J. has 1.5 million, and Chris has about 4. It's hard to get close to the action because of all the film and press people. Then I see what the commotion's about: a phalanx of Horseshoe security has just delivered the traditional cardboard box to the table. Benny's pulling out wads of cash and handing them to his mother, who stacks them at T.J.'s end of the baize. Each wad she takes from her son consists of five hundred Ben Franklins subdivided by five yellow and white paper bands marked "$10,000," these in turn held together with rubber bands doubled near the ends of the bills. When Becky has finished there are thirty such five-inch-thick wads stacked in a ramshackle cube three wads high, five across. She lays the gold championship bracelet across the second gray tier, facing T.J., and T.J. can't help staring back. It's the thing he wants most in the world.

I finally find Hasan and ask him what happened. "I had King-Queen," he purrs wistfully, shrugging. "Chris had Ace-King." Enough said. As we edge two steps closer, Chris makes it $175,000 to go from the button. T.J. calls. When the flop comes King of Diamonds, King of Clubs, Six of Hearts, T.J. checks. (In heads-up action, the player on the button bets first before the flop, second on subsequent rounds.) After thinking for over a minute, Chris bets $200,000. When T.J. says, "Call," there is $800,000 in the pot. Fourth street arrives a red Trey. Check, check. Street five: Jack of Diamonds. No straight draw, no flush draw, but do either of them have a King? T.J. at least represents having one by betting $600,000. Chris takes a while to decide, then calls and turns over a Jack and a Six, only to watch T.J. turn over King of Hearts, Ten of Hearts. His check on the turn, letting Chris catch his Jack for "free," earned him an extra Six large and put himself into the lead, with $2.6 million to Chris's $2.5.

"Only in no-limit," says Andy.

A couple hands later, Chris raises $175,000, prompting T.J. to come over the top for another half million. Chris shows how frightened he is by responding, "All-in." Without a blip of reluctance, T.J. calls. Whoever takes this pot wins the championship.

At Thompson's official request, they show us and the cameras their hole cards: Ace of Hearts, Seven of Hearts for T.J., Ace of Spades, Two of Spades for Chris. An uproar, then relative silence. From 6 feet away in his booth, I hear the Discovery director whisper, "Camera Two, give me Jesus."

Because Jesus is dead to a Deuce or a flurry of Spades and we all want to see his reaction. From my vantage point he looks nervous, unhappy, and pale. The flop comes Three of Spades, Ten of Spades, Queen of Hearts. Although still a 3–2 underdog, Chris's Four-flush gives him nine extra outs to go with the two other Deuces. Both guys have proven they have solid brass balls, but right now all four must feel clammy. When the turn comes King of Hearts, T.J. picks up his own flush draw. But when Ten of Diamonds shows up on fifth street, yielding Ten-Ten-Ace-Queen-King for another chopped pot, the vibe suggests that maybe they'll play on *forever*. Chris looks tapped out. How many deaths and resurrections can the Son of Man suffer per hour? Even the Texas centurion pretends to wipe sweat from his brow.

The next two small pots go to T.J. when Chris is unable to call even modest $100,000 raises, but on the following hand Chris wins $400,000 with a raise on the turn. The hand after that brings no preflop raises, and when the flop comes King of Hearts, Three of Hearts, Eight of Clubs, Chris checks again. T.J. bets a mere $100,000, Chris calls, and we all sense a trap being set. The question is, who's trapping whom? Because when Seven of Spades hits on the turn, this time it's Chris betting a puny $150,000 and T.J. who's warily calling. Four of Clubs on the river, and both of them check. While they stare at each other, Chris flashes what must be a King. T.J. mucks. They've been at it now for four and a half hours—a long time with this much at stake and dozens of lenses and mikes jabbing into your poker space.

Ten minutes later, on Hand 93, T.J. raises to $175,000. When Chris reraises $600,000, T.J. moves in like a shot. The pulse in his cheek makes me think that he feels like he's finally got Chris where he wants him. Certainly, if Chris manages to call him, this will be it—unless we get another chopped pot. Chris scratches his beard, shakes his head, exhales. Two minutes pass. I can't speak for T.J., but no one else seems to begrudge all the time he is taking. "Call him, Jesus!" shouts a rowdy fan twenty rows back. T.J.'s eyes narrow as he drags on his umpteenth Salem. He puts his left fist to his mouth, clears his throat. Won't anyone give him a lozenge?

"T.J. likes his hand," Andy whispers to me, "and I think Chris has Ace-Nine." I remember the matching A-9's Chris and I turned out to be holding last night, how the untranquil mood had been scalpeled by laughter. I watch now as Chris takes off his hat, then his sunglasses—*whoa*—in an instant defanging his aura. The thinning hair above his temples accentuated by the length of the strands, brown eyes a tad bloodshot and sunken, he also looks much more like Jesus.

He calls. As the low-dB buzz from the previous five or six minutes rises to a crescendo, he turns over Ace of Spades, Nine of Clubs. T.J. immediately shows him Ace of Diamonds and . . . Queen of Clubs. The crowd gasps and whistles.

"Pretty astonishing call," I tell Andy.

"Chris's?"

"No, yours."

He nods modestly, as though he hasn't been making reads like this the whole tournament, then elbows my arm. "Ace-Queen look familiar?"

"Oh, boy . . ."

The flop—Four of Hearts, Two of Hearts, King of Clubs—keeps T.J. in the lead. When King of Hearts falls on the turn, Andy groans, "Not again!" Because now any Deuce, Four, King, or Ace will give us another chopped pot. Exuberant Ferguson boosters entreat the poker deities for a Nine. Cloutier fans are more numerous, but it isn't clear what they should beg for. Hollering "Let's go, T.J.!" is pretty much all they can do.

Jesus leaps from his seat with his fists in the air and T.J. thrusts his big paw across the table before I see the last card. What else could it be but " . . . a Nine!" Bob Thompson ejaculates. No one, especially Bob, seems able to believe it. Chris reaches across the table and clasps T.J.'s hand. "You outplayed me," he says. T.J. shakes his head, disagreeing. That he just got harpooned through the ventricles doesn't register on his vast, craggy features. He's smiling!

Cathy Burns and the Fergusons are all over Chris now. Hugs, kisses, pogo hops, shimmying. Chris still makes his way around the table to where T.J. is standing with his wife, Joy, inside a crush of reporters. While Chris is almost as tall, when the two men embrace their difference in mass is straight out of vaudeville: the burly tight end hugs the sinewy swing dancer, steel-wool ringlets meshing with yard-long chestnut locks. "Are we still friends?" Chris asks.

"Of course. Don't feel bad. You played great." But once they let go of each other, T.J. asks, "You didn't think it would be that tough to beat me, did you?"

"Yes, I did."

I congratulate Chris, then try to tell T.J. how brilliantly he played. "There's a lotta luck in poker," he rumbles, "and if you're gonna play this game you better get used to that."

Needing oxygen and sunlight, I go for a walk down on Fremont, then head south along First Street. Strip joints and flophouses, pawnshops and t-shirt emporia, a few dozen down-market tourists. In Las Vegas, Fifth Street is Las Vegas Boulevard South, which also is known as the Strip. Family Vegas. We are far, far away from that world. Already the scorching southwest wind has driven some grit through my lips and made my pale forehead feel crisp. I think of my children, my wife. By this time tomorrow, I'll see them.

At the far eastern tip of the Pacific time zone, Las Vegas sunsets come early. Even at five-thirty or so on a May afternoon, even through polarized lenses, there are horizontal shafts making you squint and ricocheting dazzlements that make you shade your eyes, and then there are glares that make you *duck*. And then there are thermal traps where it must reach 130 degrees. And when these are interrupted by gelid blasts from gaping casino doorways, it's a little like wandering along the perimeter of the eighth and ninth circles of Hell—all of this, mind you, while heading a block north toward Paradise.

But the thing is, I maybe could've won the damn thing.

Q: Why Do You Want to Race?

A: Because My Name Comes Apart

Grace Butcher

Loading up the motorcycle. Tugging on the tie-downs to secure it on the trailer. Heading through the countryside, through a little town: Main Street with the teenagers hanging around the pizza place staring at my bike, the racy little white Yamaha RD250. I am proud to be the driver of this car with the bike on the trailer behind it. People don't expect to see a girl driving the car.

A girl. Am I not supposed to say that about myself now that I am forty-four? My body is a girl's. My long hair is a girl's. From a distance people think I am a girl. From inside I think I am a girl. In bed with my lover I am a woman, but here, now, driving this car to the racetrack, I am a girl.

When I was indeed a girl, I pretended to be an auto racer. My balloon-tired Schwinn was my race car, my Indy car, my blue No. 5 Offenhauser. I lied intensely to my little friends about being a real auto racer at night when they were in bed. For some reason my mother aided and abetted me in this lie; she *almost* verified it, never scolded me, allowed my friends to believe me by not telling them anything different. Now I think maybe my mother *wanted* me to be a race car driver. Or wished she were one herself. People used to gasp when she drove our family car 50 mph! She loved it. You see? My mother was skinny and loved to drive fast. She was always a girl.

My motorcycle is not a race car, but it is what has come into my life now. It is almost the same thing except that I ride it like a horse. It can go so incredibly fast with a flick of my wrist that it could leap out from under me. I lean over it, wrap my legs around it. I am perhaps in love.

I pull in through the gates at Nelson Ledges, the road-race track. "Hi, Grace!" Ah, they know me here, seem glad to see me. I park the car, make myself stroll casually into the big barn for registration. I want to run, to leap around saying, "I'm here! I'm here!" I happily sign all the papers that deal with death and damage and destruction and disaster and doom. (Whose? Not mine, surely.)

And being with my bike-race friends in the shadowy tents and vans of the darkening infield, sitting by the bike-race campfire in my bike-race chair, toasting my bike-race hot dog . . . yes, I am here among these people to do this amazing thing, to ride the 100 mph. I am afraid to ride on the street where cars and dogs and loose gravel and chuckholes all leap out to bring me down. Here there is a clear clean track for me to go fast on, and corner workers who speak to me with silent sudden flags of many colors that tell of oil spills and accidents ahead and one lap to go—corner workers who will run to me if I should fall. Here there is an ambulance, sleek and quiet, quickly coming just for me should my body explode onto the pavement in that terrible surprise of knowing I have crashed.

And tech—the late-night laughter in the brightly lit building where we've pushed the bikes through ruts and dark and dust of the infield. The bikes go through tech inspection. They are declared safe, for look here—here is proof. This is safety wire so nothing falls off the bike except the rider. My leathers, my skintight road-race suit, is looked at. It is declared safe, for here is all the padding that rounds the angles of my skinny body and here are all the zippers that zip me into this additional layer of brown leather skin that has my name on the chest in white letters. And my helmet that may bounce on the pavement so my head does not. Ah yes, I am safe as long as I do not fly over the crash wall and drown in the swamp or cross paths with the woodchuck who ambles across Turn One at least once on every race day. Push the bike back through the dark voices of my friends, through the dark summer night with its red jewels of campfires, through the dark butterflies that rise from somewhere with wings so gentle they seem almost not to be made of fear but of summer wind, through the dark rows of trucks and vans and families and babies and dogs and children. This would be like a picnic tomorrow if it were not for what some of us are going to do.

I pretend to sleep and morning pretends it is never going to come. But finally we stop pretending and I do and it does. Riders' meeting. I am a rider. I am amazed by this, every time. I am again going to do this unreal thing that only incredibly brave young men seem to do. Am I therefore brave by association? I am the only girl in this boisterous gathering. I listen intently as the race director explains the upcoming practice session to us. I look serious or keep my face carefully neutral but laugh at the jokes.

Instructed in the protocol of practice, we leave the hot, crowded little room in the stands. The track shimmers and curls off into the distance like a thick gray snake in the sun. At my campsite in the infield I struggle and wiggle into my leathers on this sticky, hot Ohio morning—like a snake myself now, writhing around to get back into my skin. Now my loins are girded, my feet are booted, my hands gloved, my head helmeted, my pigtails tucked in. *Now.*

Kicking my bike into action I ride slowly through the pits to line up for practice. Where are my friends who also ride this class, the 250 Production class? I keep looking for the big x taped on the backs of the leather jackets of the beginners, the first-year racers. My own x in silvery duct tape from shoulders to waist seems to burn into my back: a reminder. Veteran riders will watch out for me, be aware that I might do something squirrelly out there, something they wouldn't do. While I am waiting, I pray. I also pray while I'm riding: "Please, dear God . . ." (hurling the bike around the 80 mph first turn), "Keep me safe . . ." (scraping my toe in the fast left-hander), "Let the light be around me . . ." (speedometer needle touching 100 mph on the back straightaway).

Practice session. Another one. And the first race. As I line up on the track with twenty other bikes, all of us revving it up—that shrill, sharp, racketing two-stroke howl drowning the pounding of my pulse, drowning all my thoughts—I am turning my throttle, turning it . . . turning it . . . till the green flag swoops suddenly down and I am doing this wild and crazy incredible thing. Going as fast as I dare, feeling good, true lines through the turns, hauling my bike down nearly on its side to keep my line, to stay on track. Getting passed, being whooshed by better riders as they go by. Amazed that I'm going as fast as I can and they are passing me. No, I'm not going as fast as I can, only as fast as I dare.

Spot a friend ahead of me, concentrate on moving up lap by lap, maneuvering, passing him at last when he goes a little wide on one turn. At last! Ah! A small ecstasy finds room to flower, pushing through the dense layers of concentration. Must stay ahead now. No one to tell me how; I'm on my own. He stays right behind me. Oh lord. I lean more tightly over my tank; my neck aches from fatigue, my engine and the wind scream inside my helmet.

Rider ahead goes wildly down, went too high, caught the edge of the track. He is rolling across the track and away out of sight as I pass him, an object suddenly gone like scenery streaming past the window of a train I'm on. I feel neutral about his fall. I don't know who he was. I felt neutral about my own fall once, and I certainly knew who I was.

Oh beautiful for checkered flag! I sit up, slow down, ride an easy lap back to the pits. I think this is one of the most real things I've ever done. I've raced well, smoothly, not been last, not crashed. I ride into the pits, kill the engine, lean the beloved little white bike on a box, dismount, unzip my brown-and-white road-race leathers, let the jacket part flop down around my hips. My T-shirt is soaked with sweat. The wind and sun start to dry me off. I try not to swagger as I walk a little aimlessly, unwinding, feeling as if there is a glow all around me.

Then I grab my stopwatch and head for trackside to time laps for a friend in the next race. "Okay, Grace! Looked good out there!" a white-uniformed track official hollers at me as he hurries by. There's that feeling again, that sort of blossoming, as if I'm leaving flower petals behind me as I go, or a little trail of golden sparkles in the air.

Yes, thank you, and please, I *want* to look good out there. Like a real motorcycle racer. So far, so good. Motocross for three years on a Suzuki 125—the ruts, the jumps, the mud, the foot-down turns; the jolting, slamming speed; the dust so dense I'm riding blind; the aching biceps and forearms and thighs; the wrenching around of my whole body. And now road racing, sinuous, graceful, the track a steady gray blur of speed, the little Yamaha 250 two-stroke shrieking beneath me as the tach climbs to the red line—

Motorcycle racing in my forties. I've always liked going fast: running, horseback riding; driving on long, empty highways. On the street, on a motorcycle, going fast is not cool; it's too dangerous. But on the track the distance opens up into an endless horizon that I can speed toward as fast as I dare. I would call this *ecstasy*. I seek it out again and again.

After the checkered flag says I am through, I feel drained and exuberant, grateful to whatever turns of fate have led me to this track in this lifetime, grateful even for my name, which may be why I do these things. Funny, the way my name comes apart like that: Grace—race—ace. An echo. It tells me what to do, what to be. My parents named me Grace. I must have heard just "race."

"Okay," I said.

Turning It Up

Betsy Crowfoot

Twelve pounds of rubberized clothing and gear lay bunched around my ankles. I squat on the toilet, which swashes with icy seawater as the boat lurches and surges ahead. In the opaque darkness every groan, squeak, thump, and shudder is amplified.

We are pounding in choppy green seas, in the first few days of the Transpacific Yacht Race, a 2,225-mile voyage from Los Angeles to Honolulu. Nine women on one 50-foot sailboat versus 166-million square kilometers of Pacific Ocean.

Offshore racing is not a glamorous sport. This thought inevitably comes to me at 2:00 a.m. when I'm roused to go on watch.

My stomach convulses and a flush of fever radiates over me. I hurry through my business. It is difficult to wipe, stand, pull up the layers of thermal underwear and foul-weather gear while the boat thrashes from side to side. Flicking the lever, I pump the head, and teeny bioluminescent sea creatures sucked up from the ocean sparkle down the insides of the toilet bowl. As I stumble up the steps of the companionway the nausea is in my throat.

Buckling on the last of my gear, I paw into the open cockpit and—*whomp!*—a wave nails me, just moments before I pull on my hood, and chilly brine trickles down my back. I'm wide awake as the others scamper down to bunks still warm.

I've actually worked my tail off to earn a place here, on the sloppy wet deck of this sailboat. Women, more often than not, are passed by when race crews are chosen. So we create our own opportunities to answer the call of the open ocean.

I began sailing only nine years ago and at once felt surprisingly at ease and invigorated. Never graceful or swift enough to compete in tennis, volleyball, or the like, I found my niche in strength and tenacity. When my daughter came along, Saturdays at sea became my "girl's night out." As my career changed, from mobile sales exec to very rooted mom, I looked to my racing adventures to satisfy my compulsion for excitement and accomplishment: a sharp contrast to a drab office job girdled by diapers and baby food.

Begun in 1906, the Transpac was designed to lure tourists to the tropical paradise of the Sandwich Islands. Organizers promised a warm aloha upon landing, hospitality, and parties with exotic "hula hula" dancers. Since World War II the race has been held on the odd years, providing a challenge for thirty-five to eighty boats, 30 to 150 feet in length.

Ninety years after the first Transpac, we are still enticed by the promise of welcome in Shangri-la. Our reward for a fast passage will come in the form of endless parties: the first when we tie up at the docks. Relieved family and envious friends will greet us with buckets of mai tais, fresh fruit, and other delicacies we have missed at sea, and the velvety soft petals of fragrant leis stacked around our sweaty necks.

It is this picture of paradise that helps us press on.

The night is black. We have set sail with 38 other boats during a moonless phase. The billions of stars that normally light the sky are shrouded in dense clouds. Driving blind, using only the compass and wind instruments, I struggle to hold a favorable course: not knowing when a peculiar wave might lick up the side of the boat, or the sea might fall out from beneath the bow, at least just for a moment. The yacht volleys, yaws from side to side; sails flutter, and the trimmers—one each on the main and the jib—inch the sails in and out. We constantly tinker with the sheets (lines attached to the loose corners of the sails) and halyards (that hold the sails up) while we tweak the outhaul and leads (which control the "belly") . . .

all to define the shape of the sails, to get the most speed out of the velocity and angle of the wind at that particular instant. The first few hundred miles our sails will be set tight to help us race into the breeze; days later we'll set a spinnaker for the sought-after downwind rush to Honolulu.

There is nothing between here and Hawaii. We are self-sufficient: our own commissary, hospital, power plant, social structure. Aside from one mandatory radio check-in each day, we are on our own.

We sail day and night, night and day. Our assignments: four women on deck, four off watch below, and one housekeeping. We call her the Bitch of the Day. Each of us will rotate off for a turn as B.O.D. to prepare meals, hang up wet gear, keep the head clean, and sort the garbage (biodegradables get minced into little bits and thrown overboard; other trash gets smashed and stowed). The B.O.D. keeps our water bottles full, sunscreen handy, and dispenses painkillers as frequently as the directions on the Aleve bottle will allow.

We are nine women between the ages of twenty and forty-seven. Although four of us have done this passage before, it is the first time for us as a team. And the first day out we are still stunned at the last-minute withdrawal of our skipper, Linda. Just five days before the race start, after a year of preparation, Linda had a relapse of ovarian cancer. From her hospital bed she commanded us to go on.

An offshore skipper is unique: In what other sport does the captain assume responsibility for the lives of her team? And Linda is the one most familiar with *Baywolf*, the yacht she's chartered (taking out a second mortgage on her home to do so). We feel her absence, we miss her skill as a sailor and driver: her warmth, humor, and management style. Weepy at the onset, soon we are forced to push aside the thought of her lying in a hospital bed, being fed intravenous fluids along with daily race results. She is fighting for her life and we, now out on the ocean, must fight to sustain ours.

Two all-women crews have campaigned this year: a first in Transpac history. In its inaugural year there we no representatives of the "weaker sex" on the three boats that sailed. By 1908 women started cropping up on crew lists: usually the wife of the owner or the occasional cook. In

BETSY CROWFOOT

1933 a Los Angelina was invited to sail with her husband and a crew of six men, but hardly got to see more than the galley and cabin. During the torturous journey the sails were torn and tattered so many times, Mrs. Radcliffe sewed her way across the ocean, cutting up her aprons when she ran out of spare canvas.

After World War II women became more active in the competition. Lady skippers have run the gamut from the brassy Peggy Slater, to Beverly Hills socialite Sally Blair Ames, to Martha Baker, a 1950s single mom who brought her twelve-year-old kid along because, hey, who can afford a babysitter for three weeks? It wasn't until 1979 that the regatta saw its first all-women crew; and here we were in 1997, finally with two expert women's teams on highly competitive boats.

Each of the crew is limited to what we can carry in a yellow 16-by-24-inch Gore-Tex duffel. In addition to standard offshore sailing gear—foulies, rubber boots, fingertip-less gloves, a self-inflating harness and tether—I have thermal underwear, a wool hat and socks, nylon shorts, Lycra leggings, a tank top, two T-shirts, a swimsuit and sneakers. This ensemble, although hardly fashionable, will suffice during the extreme weather conditions we'll see, whether the trip lasts ten days or twenty.

Two years earlier when I did this race I sailed on a seaworthy but older boat. It proved to be one of the slowest Transpacs on record. For one solid week we drifted over glassy seas, clocking a total finish time of just over seventeen days. Had we not gotten along so well we would have killed each other: eight women on a 40-foot yacht in the scorching sun with diminishing water and food stores. But we survived the frustration—nearly more threatening than an angry sea—reading, writing, spying on sea life, and watching one spectacular sunset after another . . . and another . . . and another. I even caught a jellyfish with a spaghetti strainer, I was so crazed.

But this year has been different. The weather reports are rosy, showing a strong and steady breeze all the way, and a tropical depression brewing near Cabo San Lucas. And for once, the weather we find offshore is as surly as the forecast.

As a result, when dawn slinks through the woolen clouds the second morning out, we are met with another setback: in the night our mainsail has developed a tear near the top. We douse it at once, but repairs can't be made until the sail, wet with dew, dries. There will be no race to Hawaii without this powerhouse of canvas. Our new skipper, bumped up from navigator to captain by default, agonizes—and is finally convinced to let us carry on another 24 hours. If we can patch the sail, if it holds, if the wind clocks behind us a bit, if . . .

In near silence—abetted by an epidemic of mal de mer in all but two of us—we push ahead, knowing that each fraction of distance we struggle for, we may have to retrace tomorrow.

In each of the past thirty-eight Honolulu Races there have been boats that turn back, and others that limp into Ala Wai Yacht Harbor with broken spars, missing rudders, shredded sails. Some arrive short a crew member or two—evacuated because of medical emergency—but no one has ever died during the race.

Three days out and the wind has circled behind us. It's a blessing. With the sail cracked off a bit there's less pressure on the main. Hoisting the repaired sail, we are ecstatic when the decision is announced to go on. Despite an insurmountable loss in mileage, we are going to Oahu, not Catalina—the booby prize offered, had we been forced to drop out.

As we advance south, the weather warms up a touch. Seasickness phases out. Our bodies adjust to the schedule of four hours on, four hours off. I am part of a machine. My life, typically intellectual, is now purely physical. I sweat, groan, struggle, and coax my body to its limits. I eat—we all eat—like a pig. Off watch we sleep the sleep of the dead. We share one purpose: to push this vessel to Hawaii.

The wind this year is ceaseless! Tricks on the helm, trimming, or grinding, are kept to 30 minutes, then we rotate through the cockpit. Driving requires stamina, practice, intense focus. The helmswoman holds everybody's fate in the grip of her two hands; skirting the seas, following that just-perfect angle to the wind. As you catch a wave—the boat we sail was designed to do this, skim along the huge Pacific rollers like a 50-foot surfboard—the wind moves forward. It's an art. If you pinch too much you collapse the chute—a 2,000-square-foot nylon spinnaker pulling the boat along at 15 to 20 or more knots (18 to 24-plus m.p.h.) of speed. Drive too low and the wind crosses the back of the boat. This, sailing by the lee, is lethal: sweeping the boom and mainsail 180 degrees across the stern with such force it can take out the rigging and lop off the head of anyone in the way.

Like Sisyphus of ancient mythology, condemned to heave a boulder up a mountain in Hades for all eternity, the trimmer's job is never done. I continually ease out and trim in the sheets with hands gnarled from clutching the slippery, synthetic rope. My job is made possible by a grinder whose sole purpose is to muscle in the line on hefty winches. After half an hour, we trade.

Sunshine is scant. There are few of the stunning sunsets or sunrises I've seen in previous Transpacs, and the omnipresent dolphins, pilot whales, and sea turtles are obscured by rambunctious waves. Now and then an albatross glides unerringly over the ever-moving profile of the sea, and as we approach the islands, tropic birds appear.

Nighttime is sheer hell.

As the sun sets, the wind rises. Lines of squalls, dastardly storm-laden cumulonimbus, are hard to detect in the dense night. The lack of moonlight, and a dense cloud cover that shrouds the starlight, creates the blackest pall. Mesmerized by the LED instruments on the mast, the wind whipping past my ears, the sensation of speeding, swirling—I am overwhelmed. Vertigo is not unusual in these conditions: neither is just plain fear. I beg off the wheel.

Four of our drivers turn out to be better suited for this "simulator sailing." But stints are short.

Lying in bed—not really my berth as we are hot-bunking, snagging whatever sack is free—I hear terror in the voices of the women on deck. A squall has hit and the wind has increased. If possible, it is even darker. The traveling storm system sends the breeze from a new angle and kicks up the seas in its path. We career into the wind: a roundup. Eyes closed, I still can see and anticipate the sequence of events. We're flying enough sail area to carpet a barn, as the gust blasts us with tremendous force. The driver knows she's losing the fight to keep the boat headed down and shrills, "*Ease! Ease!*" Already the trimmer is letting the sheet run to deflate the spinnaker, but the boat has chosen her own course. She crashes up into the wind and on her side; water pours into the cockpit.

I slam shut the little windows above my head so the sea doesn't cascade in. I know that in 2 hours it'll be me on deck, hip-high in water, grinding like a son-of-a-bitch, trying, at times in vain, to keep the boat upright and on track. Eventually the boat will tip enough so the breeze spills out of the sails, and she'll right herself. In the meantime, I turn up my Walkman, roll over, and try to rest.

I dream odd dreams, people out of place and out of context. I think sweet thoughts of my daughter, almost six years old. On my first offshore race, I remember lying shivering and crying in a bunk, weary from a long watch in stormy seas, uncertain of our fate, terrified I would never see her again. We tore the main in an accidental jibe and struggled with a contorted and ineffective sail. Our navigator, I suspected, was way off. The promised glide down the California coast had transformed into a hellish ordeal through 35 knots of breeze on a confused sea the size of a roller coaster. As a final insult, our batteries ran low and we had no power for running lights or radio communications. We couldn't even call for help.

I kissed the dock when we finally straggled into port, and refused to sail for nearly three months. But eventually I realized that offshore yacht racing is at once arduous and exhilarating. It's a matter of who can show up most prepared, with the best-conditioned equipment, then stick with it the longest, with the most focus.

Halfway to Hawaii, and life onboard is rough. A number of problems befall us. Our water-maker refuses to work and we drink lemon-flavored tank water with unidentified floating objects. A hairline crack appears on the mast. Our instruments, so crucial to our night driving, are about to croak: one repeatedly flashes "no data."

Tensions are evident, as the two watches snipe at each other. The B.O.D, now adoringly and rightfully called the Goddess of the Day, referees. We make too much noise while the other watch tries to sleep; they make too much noise while we are trying to sleep.

In truth, no one gets much sleep at all. Jibes (positioning the sails from one side of the boat to the other to get a better angle to our destination in the ever-changing wind) call for all hands on deck. The sails are kept flying while the boat and spinnaker pole are swung to opposite sides of the boat in a perfectly orchestrated maneuver . . . at 18 or 20 knots of speed. Think: *changing the tire while driving down the freeway*—we are racing full-bore and there is no stopping allowed. Sail changes (we use heavier or lighter sails for a heavier or lighter breeze), the replacement of chafed and worn gear, and the mandatory hoisting of Pam to the top of the mast to check the rig, mean no shut-eye as well. Even when we are "down" it's impossible to sleep with the screeching of the on-watch crew, the moaning of sheets as they slip on the drum of the winch, the shuddering of the rig when the boat comes off a wave, and the incessant rush—like a flash flood—of water along the hull.

I have never felt more alive.

A friend who has sailed more than a quarter of a million miles pointed out, "It's like turning up the volume on life." My senses heighten. There is wind in my hair and the taste of salt spray on my face. My body feels toned and fluid. The sound of the rooster tail off the stern is deafening; the laughter of strong, happy women is music. The tropical heat warms my skin; I smell sweat, a delicious dinner cooking, and—at last—a puff from a sugarcane fire which has journeyed for out to sea.

Mostly I feel in place . . . because the ocean equalizes my sensibilities, too. I realize how small and insignificant I am; and with this comes relief. In this greater arena, I remember that life is to be enjoyed.

A spectacular lightning display hovers above the Hawaiian Islands as we approach the final leg—and challenge—of the Transpac. Thousands of miles of ocean and wind converge at the Molokai Channel, shimmying between the towering peaks of Oahu and Molokai. This is the scene of many dismastings and blown-up spinnakers: where the race has been won—and lost.

At nightfall our instruments are declared DOA. The captain appears on deck, her eyes rimmed red with agitation and lack of sleep. This is not the program she's signed on for. She growls, but we disregard it. My personal experience has established that all skippers turn into werewolves at the entrance to the Molokai channel but transform back into humanoids upon docking, plied with a mai tai or two.

Our practiced crew pulls off the final jibe in 30-plus knots, and the quartet of hotshot drivers takes turns helming the boat through the passage. As the lumpy shapes of the islands rise up from the sea, the crew clusters on the back of the boat to keep the bow from burrowing into the waves. Everyone is hooting and hollering like banshees. Joining the driver and a trimmer in the cockpit, I straddle the winch on the low side and grind—mostly submerged—as we scream through the channel on our ear. It's strenuous and eventually Jeanie spells me; I take her place high and aft.

We pick off navigation lights as the glow of Honolulu City outlines the profile of Koko Head. As is required, we radio in our arrival so a squadron of boats can greet us. Around the corner the unmistakable silhouette of Diamond Head appears. Its light dances around and we look for the adjacent bell buoy that marks the finish line, and also the dangerous reef to its north. In the night, with so many lights on shore, it's easy to miss— as one competing yacht did eight years ago, running aground just a few hundred yards before the finish.

Lights spill down the surrounding canyon roads like necklaces of lava; wind cranks down these ravines too, and buffets us with tremendous gusts that knock us repeatedly on our side. Our skipper decides to douse the chute early. Four of us move gingerly forward, harnessed and tethered to jack lines which run the length of the boat. We carry knives, in case we get tangled up in the sail or sheets and need to cut ourselves free. In a matter of seconds we are all soaked to the armpits as the captain brings the boat up into the wind, luffs the spinnaker, and the halyard is let loose.

There is too much wind in the chute—it refuses to come down. Over and over we grab onto it, only to have the brilliant nylon sail fill and rip out of our hands again and again; even though four of us—all pretty hefty—are hauling on it with all our might.

My fingers are raw; I am barely on the boat, suspended over the lifelines by my tether. I am fully aware that if either the stanchion or my harness fails, I am lost. History. This is terrifying.

I am also delighted that it is nighttime and the ESPN camera crew is not out to document our clumsy finish.

Finally we muscle the sail down and stuff it, along with gallons of water and possibly a few unsuspecting fish, down the hatch. We finish quietly, lining up the buoy with the lighthouse; popping a chilled bottle of champagne (our only booze on board), after nine days and 19 hours. It has been a record-breaking race, a twenty-year Transpac standard broken, and we are the fastest-ever all-women crew.

Then it is finished. The crowded skyline of Waikiki unfolds in front of us, as first light creeps up. Despite the hour we are surrounded by boats packed with indecipherable forms but familiar voices. We tuck away the sails and tidy the boat, change our shirts, and enter the Ala Wai Harbor.

"A-loooooooo-ha!" a voice booms across the PA system, even though we have arrived in the wee hours. Each member of the crew is welcomed by name, and a throng of people, alerted by a relentless, sleep-deprived team of volunteers, begins to take form along the docks lining the canal. Figures rise ghostlike from the seats of Hawaii Yacht Club. One is bobbing up and down like a jack-in-the-box. It's Linda! Her doctor has determined she'll recover much more quickly from surgery in Hawaii, as opposed to lying agitated in bed at Long Beach Memorial Hospital.

The tears that have been waiting for ten days finally fall. We have arrived, ranking fifth in class (comparable boats) and seventh in the entire fleet. Six boats have turned back because of difficulties, including three dismastings, a broken rudder, and illness.

I feel strong and alert as pink clouds cluster to the east and we turn into our slip. The plumeria leis laced around our necks are the most fragrant you can imagine. The drinks are icy cold, sweet and strong, and the fruit is so fresh, it must have been just picked yesterday. Linda looks ravishing and the men are more handsome than even I remember. The Hawaiian music that plays has the sweetest melody; as my friend promised, the volume of life turns up—to "high."

Epilogue: Linda Elias made a courageous recovery from this bout with cancer and realized her dream of returning to Hawaii the following year, when *Baywolf* owners Kirk and Jocelyn Wilson invited her to crew in a race from San Francisco to Kaneohe. She did one final Transpac a year later, on a 70-foot sled, *Cheval*. While under treatment Linda continued to buoy race—although at times she had to be lifted onto the boat—saying she savored the chance to maintain the mindset of being in control, and being a winner, in some aspect of her life. Despite her adversity Linda remained a viable competitor, but more so, a generous, enthusiastic, and positive woman with a sense of humor, strength, and grace. It was an honor and a pure joy to race with her.

Linda passed away January 3, 2003, at the age of fifty-two.

Reading the River

John Hildebrand

Whitehorse

My own life had narrowed in all the predictable ways. But the essential problem remained: how to live decently and keep one's head above the crapola. It was never easy. What came easy was everything else—career, house, a comfortable boredom. When a little credibility was called for, I trotted out my cabin-building as an after-dinner anecdote until even I no longer believed it. It was somebody else's story, not my own. When the divorce swept everything clean and I found myself thrown out on my ear, homeless and alone, I whimpered at the unfairness of it, all the while nursing a secret exhilaration. The world had opened wide again and seemed filled with possibilities.

One possibility was to go back to Alaska. I was still haunted by my original vision of the North—the nightless summers and long winters of solitude. But I had no desire to spend a lonely summer in my cabin. I was more curious about the sort of people who had stayed behind, leading a life I frankly couldn't manage. We need our dreams even if we don't live up to them. Flying back now, I meant to find the North that had eluded me before. I needed to verify that the life I had imagined had a counterpart in actuality, that, after all these years, it had not simply been the wrong dream.

First I needed to relearn the country. The choice of routes was important. I lacked the necessary innocence to rumble up the Alcan Highway again in a beat-up van, seeing the landscape in a haze of desire. Whatever mystique the Alcan once held for me had long since disappeared behind cracked windshields and caravans of Airstream trailers. Besides, the road would dead-end in nostalgia, and it was other people's pasts I was after, not my own. Then I remembered the river trip I had once daydreamed to the sea. The Yukon River was the original highway into the country, the main artery, the broad sum of all the northern streams and creeks, including my own. Floating downriver, I would sample a little of each tributary. The Yukon also appealed to me not only because it traversed one of the last great wildernesses of North America but, more important, because it was a working river, where people followed, or tried to follow, a very old cycle. A voyage down the Yukon would be a journey through time as well as geography, back to the world as it used to be. Along the way, I could rub elbows with the survivors of many winters, the pioneers and the veterans of my own generation. Hitching a ride on the river, I could drift into other lives, people I might have become.

In the late afternoon, I left the hotel and went looking for the river. The street beside the railway station was being torn up and the wind blew dust against the shop windows. An Indian girl cradling a boom box brushed past me on the sidewalk, lost in music.

In a riverside park, I fell in step with a group of school children touring a dry-docked steamboat. Proportioned like a shoebox, the paddle-wheeler had three balustraded decks and a single smokestack rising behind the glassed-in pilothouse. On the saloon deck, rattan chairs ringed a circular observation room, just the place to sit with a drink in your hand and watch the treetops slide past. The boat had been beached in the early fifties when the completion of an all-weather road linked Whitehorse to Dawson. In a single stroke, the road had eliminated steamboat traffic on the Yukon, relegating the surviving boats to museum pieces and the river itself to no more than a painted backdrop. But the kids were too fidgety to listen to the tour guide. Swarming over the decks, they turned the open staircases into monkey bars while their teacher shouted after them: "Stay in line! Keep your hands off that! Get down from there!"

After he herded the kids back on the bus, I climbed down the grassy bank for a closer look at the Yukon. I found it sliding beneath a highway bridge, a swift-flowing river the pale, oxidized green of weathered statuary. A truck rumbled overhead and swallows poured from the bridge shadows. I sat down on the bank and skipped a stone across the water. Not so wide as I had imagined, the river looked faster, barreling like a freight train between white clay bluffs, heading north.

In the morning I rented a car and drove south on a gravel road along the river. No one agrees on the Yukon's exact beginning or its length. One source is a glacier above Lake Lindeman in the Coastal Mountains of British Columbia, a scant few miles from tidewater. But if measured from its farthest tributary, the Yukon rises in the headwaters of the Nisutlin River in the Pelly Mountains of the Yukon Territory, two thousand miles from the Bering Sea. (For that matter, one could say that the river begins in the clouds.) But for my purposes the river started at the head of navigation below the tailrace of a hydroelectric plant, a strange beginning for a wild river.

At the power plant beneath the dam, the chief engineer, a short, bearded man with a pocketful of pens, showed me around. He was in charge of the river, at least the first 100 miles before tributaries swelled it. From a control panel of computer terminals and breaker switches, he could fine tune the Yukon into kilowatts and megawatts.

"Most of the river's water comes from glaciers. If it rains up in the hills or we get hot weather, the glaciers melt and raise the level of the river."

The temperature that day was in the high seventies. Someone flicking on a light switch in the Whitehorse would tap into voltage the far end of which was blue glacial ice. In the heat of summer, the glacier's melt water flowed from a string of mountain lakes through Miles Canyon and into the reservoir of Lake Schwatka to drop into lightless penstocks that led beneath the power plant.

We put on hard hats and left the quiet of the chief engineer's office for the humming center of the plant. The floor gratings vibrated from the turbines spinning beneath them.

"We're standing," the engineer shouted, "over the tail end of White-horse Rapids."

The rapids took their name from the foam-tipped waves that resembled the flying white manes of horses. In the first summer of the gold rush, seven thousand rafts and ripsawed scows and bateaux drifted down from the mountain lakes until the river narrowed abruptly in Miles Canyon a few miles above the rapids. Those who didn't portage around the canyon risked drowning in its sucking whirlpool and still faced the roaring cascades of Whitehorse Rapids.

Now the canyon was itself drowned, and the rapids had been transformed into the very heart of the dynamo. Standing over the turbines was a disquieting sensation, all that compressed violence, as if someone had stoppered up a fearsome storm in a bottle and invited you to peek down the neck.

We strolled outside past bulldozers and dump trucks moving earth for a new turbine that would double the Whitehorse dam's generating capacity. This was the only existing dam on the Yukon, but there were proposed dam sites already on the books, waiting for the right circumstances to turn the river into a chain of flaccid lakes.

At the edge of the tailrace we watched the river plunge over the spillway. You could lob a message in a bottle here and conceivably expect it to be picked up by a Bering Sea Eskimo. Across the river, the long flume of a fish ladder ran along the shore for half a mile so migrating salmon could reach their spawning grounds on the other side of the dam.

"They start off from the Bering Sea the first week in June," the engineer said. "When they arrive here in the middle of August, they've only got another fifty miles to their spawning beds."

By that time, I thought, I would be at the river's mouth.

To Build a Fire

The day after the party, I slipped quietly out of Selkirk and drifted down the long corridor of river. The valley rose up green and steeply canted, with castellated cliffs like those on the upper Hudson. Stacks of driftwood were heaped at the heads of islands in great bonfire piles, whole trees stranded high and dry, tap roots radiating like spokes. I watched a dust devil swirling along the long white spit of a sandbar. Every so often a creek came in, thick with alder and willow, a riverboat tied to the bank and a path winding back to a cabin. But I kept on without stopping.

I felt talked out. River travel made for an edgy blend of isolation and company. Days passed when I spoke to no one. Then, falling in with a party, I'd talk myself silly.

The hard part was the transitions, as abruptly felt as barometric changes, these sudden swings from being too much alone to being caught in a crowd. I kept moving between silence and noise. The ghetto blasters that you see everywhere in villages along the Yukon aren't used to create space, as they are in cities, but to fill it in. Here the country is so immense, so full of space, that it soaks up sound. After a long, solitary drift, I wanted company and hearty campfire chatter; a few hours later I'd be ready for some trackless sandbar and life as Robinson Crusoe.

Homesteaders must view the summer with mixed feelings. After a winter of counting whole valleys their own, they have to share them with canoeists who drift by, jabbering in English and German, poking around, asking questions. When I talked to some soft-spoken pioneer in the quiet of his cabin, my voice was so amplified, by comparison, that it seemed to issue from a bullhorn. Behind the questions about trap lines and steamboats, what I really wondered was: Are you happy? Is this enough? Trying to read their faces was like reading the river. Nothing showed on the surface except a wry grin like a two-way mirror that said: Of course we're happy or we'd have left long ago. But also: Why are you here?

Below the mouth of the Selwyn River, I passed a cow moose and calf swimming along the shore. The cow moose had an ungainly, Lincolnesque head with soulful eyes and a pendant beard. Stilt-legged, she scrambled up the willow bank, but her calf couldn't get purchase and drifted down the river with me. The cow didn't care much for this arrangement. She crashed along shore until the calf found a low bank and climbed from the water. I waved good-bye. The cow only shot me an incendiary look and turned, big-hipped, into the willow.

The Yukon was changing day to day, shifting gears, picking up momentum. The White River, entering from a gap in the hills to the west, doubled the size of the Yukon and ruined its clarity. I climbed a hill to see the T-shaped confluence; the mouth of the White was a maze of braided channels with driftwood logs stranded on the sandbars. Robert Campbell named the White for the milky sediment it carries down from glaciers high in the Wrangell Mountains and Saint Elias Range. The Tlingits called it the River of Sand: the water was exactly that buff color. You couldn't tell it from the sandbars except for its pulsing movement. For maybe a mile, the two rivers flow side by side until the White dissolves its glacial load into the Yukon, turning it into a yellow cement wash. From here on, the Yukon is opaque with silt except in winter, when the glaciers stop melting and the river runs clear under the ice. Now at the height of summer flow, the silty water makes a slightly abrasive sound, like sandpaper, against the canoe's hull.

In late afternoon, I watched three big cumulus clouds towing rain and blue shadows across the valley until they jammed up downriver. A flash of lightening, thunder rolling over the hills, and I bumped onto the nearest sandbar. There was the rush to put up the tent and rainfly, then the long wait inside as the heat gathered. The storm when it came broke like a fever, bringing a cool breeze and an end to the quiet. Raindrops fell heavily at first and then settled into a steady drumming on the tent.

A sudden bout of loneliness, nameless and unexpected, overtook me like the rain. It was accompanied by a tightness in the chest and the conviction that I was, literally, shrinking. I lay on my sleeping bag hugging my knees to my chest until the ache passed. Isolation had a scouring quality. While it had left people like Danny Roberts with lilting smiles, having worn down the rough edges, it must wear others down until there's nothing left. I often wondered how I'd do here if left to my own devices. Badly, I think.

Lately, I'd missed my ex-wife, which surprised me since there were more recent women to dwell on. Now, instead of the fights and recriminations, what I remembered were pleasant moments: reading to each other in bed, picking berries, long talks. I would rather have remembered the fights. After a divorce there's an inclination to shift geography and start fresh, but at every bend this place reminded me of her and how it had felt to be

JOHN HILDEBRAND

young in a new country. The irony was that she grew to hate the North and would never have dreamed of coming back. But in my memory she was forever stuck here. I'd hear the four-note song of a fox sparrow or pick up the jackknife she'd given me, and it would all come back—the good years together and all the things done badly.

For lonely nights, I devised a form of tent therapy. First I poured a drink and mixed it with boiled river water, which gave the bourbon an ashy taste. Then I unscrolled a topographical map, the country in miniature, on the tent floor. Canadian charts are very beautiful, rivers a brilliant azure flowing through chartreuse valleys and ranges of sienna mountains. With my fingertip, I traced the Yukon and arrived by dead reckoning at a likely spot below the White River. It was comforting to fix my position, to locate myself at certain quadrants, to say I occupy this precise point in time and space. Here.

The sun reached its zenith by mid-morning and turned my nylon tent into a hothouse. Feeling drugged and thick-headed, I crawled out on my hands and knees to fix breakfast. Coffee was the only antidote. Beneath the sun's glare, the sand and gravel island held a terrible radiance.

In a torpor, I gathered twigs and dry grass stranded from highwater. Scooping a depression in the sand, I laid down a gridwork of tinder and driftwood and struck a match, playing out the pivotal scene in Jack London's "To Build a Fire." As a boy, it was my favorite story, the first one I read without coaxing, and the particular details remained fixed in my head: the amber streak of tobacco juice on the prospector's beard; the brindled, pragmatic sled dog. In the throbbing heat of summer, it was hard to imagine a man freezing to death. But from where I sat, gazing downriver toward the confluence of the Yukon and the Stewart rivers, I looked out over the very country that had inspired the tragedy.

Jack London spent his only season in the North on a spruce-covered island at the mouth of the Stewart River. A square-shouldered youth of twenty-one, with curly brown hair and deep-set blue eyes, he watched from his cabin doorway as the winter sun rose late in the morning over one range of hills and disappeared a few hours later behind another. In London's stories, it was always winter, the temperature falling, the country a sprung trap. Darkness, silence, the unearthly cold—these were the perimeters of London's North.

The year before, Jack had toiled as a work beast in an Oakland laundry, having dropped out of the University of California for lack of funds. His deliverance came when the northern steamship *Excelsior* docked in San Francisco, laden with gold and the first news of the Klondike strike. His brother-in-law, a man of sixty with a heart condition, offered to grubstake the two of them in exchange for Jack's strong back. Eleven days later, they boarded the *Umatilla* bound for the Yukon.

London's brother-in-law, complaining of rheumatism, turned back soon after the boat reached Skagway, but Jack had already joined company with four other stampeders, all his senior. Instead of paying 50¢ a pound to Tlingit packers, Jack lugged his own outfit over the Chilkoot Pass, later bragging of "outpacking many an Indian." At Lake Lindeman, the party hammered together two whipsawed skiffs, rigged them with square sails, and sailed down the mountain lakes into the Yukon River with Jack at the tiller of the lead boat. They drifted past Indians at Little Salmon wearing rings through their noses and, farther on, boatloads of mounted policemen headed for Dawson.

It was early October. With slush ice from the tributaries running in the Yukon, the two boats landed on an island at the mouth of the Stewart River. Stampeders called it Split-up Island since so many partnerships were dissolved there, and London's was no exception. London and his partner decided to stay, while the other boat continued on to Dawson, eighty miles downriver. The decision to stay was logical. Stewart River had been the site of an earlier gold strike and there were abandoned cabins on the island; at Dawson they would have had to settle for a tent on the beach.

The inhabitants of Split-up Island were a far-ranging crew: a German, a Swede, a French-Canadian, a Stanford football star, and an alcoholic physician. The only woman the men saw that winter was a redhead who lived across the river with a ferret-eyed man twenty-five years her senior. Her paramour was a crack shot. Once he took a Winchester from the wall when Jack was visiting and treated him to an impromptu display of marksmanship by putting ten bullets in a piece of tin nailed to a tree.

One of the men had found "colors" across the Yukon on Henderson Creek, and, with the others, London staked 500 feet of streambed on the left fork of the creek. (This was the destination of the ill-fated *cheechako* in "To Build a Fire.") But the hard work of thawing and digging at the frozen muck didn't appeal to Jack, and the claim went unworked. He was content to spend the winter in the smoky confines of the cabin, playing whist, arguing socialism, and reading. He had carried Milton's *Paradise Lost* and Darwin's *Origin of Species* over the Chilkoot Trail and borrowed a copy of Kipling's *Seven Seas*. Earlier, Jack had devoured the writings of Herbert Spencer, whose biological determinism offered a rationale for his own racial theories. In Jack's eyes, the Yukon was a northern Galapagos, an isolated and harsh proving ground where only the fittest survived. Hadn't the white man taken the Indian's country as his own, besting him at his own game as Jack had "outpacked" the Tlingit packers? In London's most popular book, *The Call of the Wild*, Buck the "outside" dog comes to the North, like Jack, from California and by brute strength and cunning soon dominates the native huskies. The novel, at one level, is an allegory of colonialism, and Buck a stand-in for London's Anglo-Saxon supermen.

But by the end of his first winter, London was barely surviving. A steady diet of bacon, bread, and beans had left him bent double with scurvy. His joints swelled and ached, his skin grew pale and puffy, his teeth rattled loose in his mouth. He resolved to leave the Klondike as soon as the river was open.

Spring came late that year. Balmy May winds blew into the valley from the coast, and the river began to rise. Then with a cataclysmic roar the ice broke, great blocks of it crashing along the shore, scouring the banks. With the river open, Jack and his partners tore apart their cabin, built a raft from the logs, and floated down to Dawson, where they sold the wood for $600. The muddy streets of Dawson were filled with dogs, mosquitoes, and new arrivals. Jack met up with two other men ready to quit the country, and together they purchased a "homemade, weak-kneed, and leaky" skiff for the voyage down the Yukon.

They set off from Dawson late in the afternoon, camping the first night in a light train. The open boat was outfitted with a portable cook stove and a sleeping bunk amidships made of pine boughs and blankets, so the men could travel without stopping to cook or find a place to sleep. Days were tropically hot; in the evenings a smudge fire kept the mosquitoes away. Drifting with the stream, the trio played cards, shot at passing ducks, and took turns at the helm.

Jack preferred the night watches, sailing along beneath the northern twilight while his companions snoozed under mosquito netting. He kept a log of the voyage, the only notes he made of his Klondike experience. He recorded the stern-wheelers passing in the night, bound for Dawson, and how the miners in the camps along the river besieged him for news of the Spanish-American War and the outcome of the Sharkey-Jeffries fight.

In the villages and fish camps on the Yukon, London was both fascinated and repelled by the miscegenation of whites and Indians, the mixture of primitive and civilized blood. In his diary he wrote: "Squaw three quarter breed with a white baby" and "Traces of white blood among the papooses everywhere apparent." From these fleeting glimpses, he would fashion the improbable Natives of his fictions, doomed and brutal characters like Nam-Bok the Unveracious, or Makamuk, the shaman of "Lost Face."

London's scurvy worsened as the trip wore on. At Anvik on the lower Yukon, he obtained fresh potatoes and a can of tomatoes, noting in his diary how the Episcopal missionary had implored them to stay "at least one Christian Sunday." Jack proved to his own satisfaction the shallowness of the Natives' conversion by trading them a pack of playing cards for a crucifix. The party sailed through the Apoon Channel of the delta and up the Bering Sea coast to the port of St. Michael. Jack signed on as a stoker on a steamship bound for home, where he would shortly sit down at a writing table and reinvent the North. He wrote his final diary entry on June 30, three weeks after having departed Dawson: "Leave St. Michael's—unregrettable moment."

Stewart Island, at the mouth of the Stewart River, was probably London's Split-up Island. I landed there below a steep cutbank. A manicured lawn led back from the riverbank to a tin-roofed house painted cerulean blue, like a chunk of sky that had tumbled onto the grass. Behind the house, a middle-aged woman pegged white sheets to a clothesline. The scene was unexpectedly suburban for an island in the midst of a wild river valley. The woman came out to meet me and we talked beside the cutbank. Yvonne Burian wore tinted glasses and had a habit of glancing upriver.

"I didn't see you land," she said. "Usually I can spot a boat well before it gets here."

She couldn't say for certain whether this was the island where Jack London had wintered, but even if it had been, the cabins had long been lost to the river's slow attrition.

"There was a big meadow there," she said, and pointed into the swirling water. "But it's gone now. The river took it. Some years the river takes 10 to 12 feet. One year we lost 60 feet."

Whenever the Yukon gobbled up their front yard, the Burians put the buildings on skids, hitched them to a tractor, and hauled them farther back into the cottonwoods.

"We've had to move the house back. The store's been moved twice. The warehouse three times."

Yvonne's father had been an agent for the White Pass Railway when Stewart Island was a transfer point for barge traffic on the river and the small settlement here was optimistically called Stewart City. There were two roadhouses, a store, a telegraph post, a full-time bootlegger, and a summertime Mountie. Yvonne and her sister were the only children, except when a relief telegraph operator brought his family along. While there were few playmates, the roadhouses filled, in summer, with steamboat passengers and trappers in from their creeks, and being the only fair-haired child on an island of homesick men made her a kind of star. In 1940 she married Rudy Burian, who had come up from British Columbia with his brother to cut wood for the steamboats.

When the big boats stopped running, the Burians bought the Hudson's Bay store for their home and stayed to raise five children. In the winter, they trap and chat on the shortwave with neighbors on creeks up and down the river. Summers they run a small clapboard store and rent cabins to canoeists and rafters, letting visitors drift to their doorstep.

Over my shoulder, Yvonne spotted a canoe and hurried to finish hanging the laundry. The canoeists turned out to be the big German in the wooden clogs and his toady wife. The river was a small world: you were always running into the same people. The Germans set up their tent on the front yard, and I headed for the store.

Where his wife was plump and kinetic, Rudy Burian was lean and creased as a walnut, possessed of a woodsman's economy of movement. He wore oily coveralls, like a mechanic, which is what a woodsman has to be these days. Inside, the store shelves were stocked with the Burians' own groceries, as well as the candy bars and soda pop they sold at cost to visitors, since the store was less a business than an excuse for company. Like Danny Roberts, the Burians kept a guest register, which I signed.

In winter, Rudy covered his trap line, up to two hundred miles, by snowmobile. He leased the trap line or "trapping concession" from the territorial government for $20 a year, and he could pass it on, like an inheritance, to his children. He shipped the furs he trapped to auction sales in Ontario but kept a few for the store, "for people to look at," although canoeists these days didn't want to see a pelt without the animal in it. One countertop was lined with pelts of animals Rudy had trapped last winter: mink, marten, red fox, cross fox, lynx, wolverine, wolf, and beaver. The beaver pelt felt the softest, the brindled wolf the deepest. Price tags danged from desiccated muzzles, and the vacant, slanted eyeholes gave the skins the stern expression of ceremonial masks.

"Wolf is about the hardest thing to trap," Rudy said. "They'll see the toggle line and walk around. Best time to catch them is when there's a fresh snowfall. The most I've ever got was a dozen when they were real thick. This winter I only got one. He went up and down my trail, pulling the bait, so I set an extra trap beside the one he'd hit. A blind set. Finally got him on the last trip."

The door swung open, and I heard the clump, clump of wooden clogs on the floorboards. The big German wanted to buy beer, but the Burians had none, and this launched him on a long tirade about liquor laws. His wife glanced around and fixed upon the furs on the counter with a look of horrific disgust.

Outside, Yvonne Burian led me through the cottonwoods behind the store to a frame building, which they had turned into a museum. It had a wonderful collection of old bones and tools, more like someone's attic than a museum. Finding an old, fallen-in cabin, Yvonne would figure out where the fellow had thrown his garbage and start digging. There were old china plates, porcelain conductors from the telegraph line, a woolly mammoth's tusk, rusty guns, a blacksmith's bellows, a hay saw, old bottles tinted lavender from the magnesium in the glass. There was the leg bone of a Pleistocene horse pulled from the tailings of Henderson Creek where Jack London's unworked claim had been. There were skulls of lynx, wolf, and marten and the massive, bony dome of a grizzly bear.

"I'd like to get more of a collection of skulls," she said wistfully, "but no one wants to clean them."

We walked back to the store, past a ripe-smelling shed that held dried fish and haunches of bear meat. I wanted to rent one of the small cabins for the night, but the commissioner's party had arrived and made a clean sweep.

I climbed back into the canoe and waved to Yvonne on the bank.

"Maybe next time."

"We'll be here as long as our health holds out," she said. "Or until we get washed away."

Climb Every Molehill

Rob Story

Dawn was but a rumor on the eastern horizon when our climbing team set off from base camp, heading north toward a mountain so elusive it wasn't even named until 1998. By 11:30 a.m., after a morning of steady advancement, our party of seven had gained the summit ridge. No one was showing signs of edema; we pushed for the top . . .

Suddenly, a large creature stormed our right flank. Crowned by a woolly gray mane, it walked erect and emitted humanoid noises. "Egad!" I exclaimed, flinching. Was this the fabled yeti, terrorizing another doomed high-altitude expedition?

No. It was retired farmwife Donna Sterler, who emerged from her white clapboard house with a hearty midwestern hello.

"Welcome to our home," she chirped. "And the highest point in Iowa!" She passed out plastic key chains that read HAWKEYE POINT, ELEV. 1,670 FT., and then pointed toward some farm buildings and a million ears of corn. "The summit is over there," she said. "To the right of the cattle trough."

We climbed 6, maybe 8 feet and conquered the first of the Seven Summits.

Big-time climbers will object, saying the Seven Summits consist of the highest mountain on each continent, and Hawkeye Point definitely isn't one of them. But that's a modern alpinist for you: an unthinking yes-man, toeing the company line. Do these so-called mountaineers even bother to explore anymore? It seems to me they just mindlessly follow lemming tracks up places like Rainier and Everest, blathering about European knots and turnaround times, rarely attempting anything new.

What would George Mallory think? Would he feel kinship with monkeys who climb "because it's been done—often"? Hardly. I think he'd be more impressed with seven slow-footed high school buddies who decided, for no good reason, to stage a reunion in which they claimed truly unknown peaks far off the beaten path. Namely, the roofs of Iowa, North Dakota, South Dakota, Nebraska, Kansas, Oklahoma, and Arkansas.

It was all my twin brother's idea, actually. A California-based documentary filmmaker who helmed the riveting A&E special on the history of cleavage (called, helpfully, *Cleavage*), Dave figured he could squeeze a film out of our still-close gang—two decades after graduation—as we schlepped around in a van, notching heartland "peaks." Though we wouldn't be the first to take on seven relatively lame summits—way back in 1987, a group of Kansans blitzed through Arkansas, Missouri, Iowa, South Dakota, Nebraska, Kansas, and Oklahoma—we liked to think we would do it with a style and lack of grace all our own.

So it was that, at the start of a long holiday weekend, Dave convinced six of us—Casper, Drew, Spade, Dorrell, Steve, and me—to assemble with him at base camp (that is, our parents' homes in the suburbs of Kansas City, Kansas, where we'd grown up). There, we loaded sleeping bags, mats, climbing gear (sport sandals and Hawaiian shirts), and an ammo box stuffed with ninety-eight Nicaraguan cigars into a rented 15-passenger Ford Econoline Club Wagon. At exactly 5:17 a.m. on a Friday, we set off for peaks that Reinhold Messner has never mustered the courage to challenge, on a journey that would demand more than 3,100 miles of motoring—and fully 17.8 miles of strolling . . . er, I mean hiking and climbing.

And now, just 6 hours and one greasy breakfast later, we'd bagged our first peak and were ready to aim the Econoline northwest, toward the Dakotas. Triumphantly, we descended the summit ridge.

Or, as Donna Sterler called it, "the driveway."

"Traveling to State High Points involves healthy outdoor recreation with concomitant learning of state and regional geography and history . . . . It can expand the senses and bring joy to the heart." This according to a 1997 journal article called "Highpointing"—Summiting United States Highpoints for Fun, Fitness, Friends, Focus, and Folly," written by Thomas P. Martin, a health professor at Wittenberg University, in Springfield, Ohio.

Martin rated America's 50 state highpoints using a 10-point scale of difficulty, with Florida's 345-foot Britton Hill earning a mere 1 and Alaska's Mount McKinley, at 20,320 feet the tallest of them all, getting a 10. He informs us that highpointing was first mentioned in a 1909 edition of *National Geographic* and that a 1986 *Outside* item about the pastime spurred the establishment, in Mountain Home, Arkansas, of a national Highpointers Club, some of whose twenty-seven hundred members amuse themselves by seeking the second-highest point in each state. One of the leading guidebooks, *Highpoint Adventures*, published in 2002 by Colorado highpointers Charlie and Diane Winger, points out that more than eight hundred people have successfully climbed Mount Everest but only one hundred or so have claimed all 50 U.S. highpoints.

Interesting. But we felt disconnected from Thomas P. Martin's world of wonder even before Iowa's flapping cornfields gave way to the arid vastness of the Great Plains. See, traditional highpointers are like birdwatchers: They have time on their hands, and they're willing to spend decades adding to their life lists. We had just one long weekend to get the job done, and as the Econoline chugged westward, our task seemed as immense as the sky.

The basic plan was to bag peak two in North Dakota, then work our way in a southerly and easterly meander through South Dakota, Nebraska, Kansas, Oklahoma, and Arkansas before zipping back north to Kansas City to catch our flights. Friday night found us at the Butte View Campground, in southwestern North Dakota, sleeping under stars that never have been—and probably never will be—sullied by urban light pollution. Butte View also boasted excellent bathrooms, and the next morning its showers wooed six of us. Only Casper—who insisted we were moving too slow, since by this time we'd climbed only one peak in 26 hours of travel—begged off. Little did we realize that his refusal to groom when he had the chance would later imperil our entire quest.

We packed up and drove roughly 25 miles to White Butte, at 3,506 feet the highest point in NoDak. Like Hawkeye Point, White Butte towers above private property. Unlike Hawkeye Point, its owners don't give anything away. We had to pay a woman $20 to climb it—and she didn't even hand out key chains! Fortunately, the cost was offset by the stark beauty of the sandstone formation, which gave off fine white dust that coated everything. Even the bugs, which were big and plentiful. As a note on the summit register put it, "the crickets scared the crap out of me!"

We ate breakfast in Bowman, North Dakota, at a place called the Gateway Cafe, a fine establishment that furnished sticky buns and a local newspaper, *The Dickinson Press*. Its lead story: A seventy-year-old woman touring nearby Theodore Roosevelt National Park had been seriously injured after getting gored by a bison, thrown 20 feet into the air, and impaled on a tree.

This troubling news gave us much-needed perspective. Though a 3-hour drive and our highest summit—South Dakota's 7,242-foot Harney Peak— awaited, we were ready, willing, and punctured by neither horn nor branch: the Chosen Ones of the Great Plains!

I don't know of many high school posses that have stayed as close as ours. This happened, in part, because my buddies and I liked high school so much that we've mythologized it. (Hey, it happens. Call it the Diner syndrome.) Steve served as student-council president; Dave was veep. Dorrell edited the yearbook. I worked for the student newspaper and was lineman of the year on the football team. Spade was a star golfer. Casper was the class clown. Drew, who gets along with everybody he meets, was one of the most popular guys in school. Our friendships have never faded; we would march to the grave for one another. And though we'd all made it to our twentieth high school reunion the summer before, we relished a chance to meet up again.

Which is how we found ourselves roaring past Mount Rushmore with barely a glance—who needs it?!—heading merrily toward South Dakota's apex. On the Martin difficulty scale, Harney Peak is a 4, thanks to its height, its 1,500 feet of vert from trailhead to tippy-top, and its round-trip hike of 5.8 miles. A sign on the summit reminds visitors, incorrectly, that Harney is the highest point between the Rockies and the towering Pyrenees of Spain and France. It's capped with an elegant stone lookout built by the Civilian Conservation Corps in 1939.

Of course, there's a built-in problem with a soaring, 7,000-plus peak: It's a real mountain, so it attracts real mountaineers. At the summit, while taking celebratory sips of whiskey from my Kansas City Chiefs flask, we were approached by an athletic couple from Colorado. Mistaking us for like-minded "serious" climbers, they gushed, "You gotta go sit in the Chair!"

The what?

"An armchair-size divot in the cliff just downhill from here," one of them explained. "You can sit in it and dangle your legs over 300 feet of nothingness."

This intrigued Steve, who just can't resist a challenge—despite his utter lack of coordination and kinetic awareness. One time in high school, Steve tried to hurl a pack of lit firecrackers out a half-open car window and hit the glass instead. The fizzing explosives tumbled to the floor of Drew's mom's Thunderbird, blowing a hole in the carpet.

While Steve managed to sit in the Chair without tragedy, the sight of him wiggling on the precipice made the rest of us hit the flask repeatedly. We drank more that night at dinner, which meant the only sober driver available was . . . Steve. He gave up drinking a while ago, but he remains, quite simply and without peer, the worst driver of all time, constantly alternating between sudden acceleration and braking. His hands shake constantly; throw in his current addictions to coffee and cigars and you get transport that is, at best, fumbling and herky-jerky, at worst, upside down in a ditch, surrounded by flashing lights.

As Steve pointed us toward Nebraska, Spade, Dorrell, Dave, and I nodded off. Drew and Casper claimed they "couldn't sleep in cars" and watched Steve drive—with the color drained from their faces and their fingernails dug deep into Econoline vinyl. Whatever they did as backseat drivers must have worked, because Steve successfully, if shakily, kept us on the road.

It was 2:00 a.m. on Sunday by the time we reached the highest spot in Nebraska: Panorama Point, a 5,424-foot bulge in the extreme western part of the state, near the forlorn three-way junction with Wyoming and Colorado. Though Panorama is more than a mile high, you can't exactly rappel off it. It's a big mound with a crude metal-and-stone marker on top, put there to remind you that it's something special. We pulled the Econoline within 6 feet of the marker, unfurled our bags, and slept on the summit itself.

We woke shortly after dawn to the lowing of bison from a ranch located half a mile south, in Colorado. Dave got on top of the Econoline to get a bird's-eye digicam view of the utterly horizontal summit, and then we were off. Thirsting for a strong cup of joe, we kept our sand-encrusted eyes peeled for any sign of gourmet coffee. But the Great Plains is the only region in the lower 48 where you can drive for four days and never see a Starbucks. We settled on a venerable diner, the Longhorn Cafe, in Kimball, Nebraska, and sat among ranchers sporting their Sunday-best Stetsons. Near a pot of bitter brown water masquerading as coffee, on a platter perched atop red-checked oilcloth, sat the finest apricot turnovers this side of anywhere.

"Mmm. Succulent orange goo encased in flaky, sugarcoated crust," ventured Spade, a telecom executive who now lives in Colorado Springs.

"This transcends mere breakfast pastry," said Dave, his mouth stuffed.

"This is a reason for even jaded coastal dwellers to come to 'flyover country,'" added Steve, a public defender who lives among jaded coastal dwellers in Silver Spring, Maryland.

I didn't say much. I snarfed three turnovers and later wished I'd pocketed a fourth.

People love to laugh at Mount Sunflower, Kansas's highest point, but here's a fun fact: At 4,039 feet, it towers above most of the Green Mountains in Vermont.

From Kimball, we zigzagged east on Interstate 80, south on U.S. 385, east on I-70, and south on narrow gravel roads toward Mount Sunflower, Kansas. Since all seven of us hail from the Sunflower State, we badly wanted this 4,039-foot trophy.

If you're not from Kansas, you don't understand. You tease us with lame *Wizard of Oz* jokes. (Note: "We're not in Kansas anymore" is a line from 19-bleeping-39. Let it go.) You find the very concept of Mount Sunflower—a noble hillock that sits one-tenth of a mile from the Colorado state line—to be automatically laughable. But when we were in elementary school, the fact that Mount Sunflower towers above most of Vermont's Green Mountains was balm to our Kansas souls, like learning to sing the sweet state song, "Home on the Range."

Mount Sunflower earns a meager 1 on Martin's scale, involving fewer than ten feet of vertical gain after you park. Non-Kansan eyes might survey the featureless landscape surrounding it and conclude that the nearest town, Weskan, should have stuck with its original name: Monotony. Yet when the Econoline's doors opened peakside, we saw a dreamscape. Atop a treeless, imperceptible uplift stood a majestic, 10-foot-tall iron sunflower. An American flag waved from its stalk. A small corral surrounded the exhibit, echoing Kansas's rich cattle-drive heritage.

Highpoint Adventures raves, "Kansas gets our vote for the most creative and whimsical highpoint monument!" We couldn't have agreed more. State pride engulfed us, despite the moronic entries scrawled in the summit register: "No hiking stick required!" and "It'd be better if you had naked chix!"

We'd all agreed to fly home from Kansas City on Tuesday. That way, we could highpoint deep into Monday night if necessary. But during the drive from Mount Sunflower to Black Mesa, Oklahoma—a 4,973-footer at the western fringe of the panhandle—absentminded Dorrell dropped a bomb. In the parking lot of a convenience store in Lamar, Colorado, he looked at his airline ticket and mumbled, "Uh, guys . . . my flight's at 6:20 Monday night."

Murmur ensued. Followed by hubbub. Succeeded by malice.

Six-twenty on Monday? That was 25 hours away! And we were looking at 2 or 3 hours to Black Mesa, at 8.6 miles the longest hike of all. After that there would be 700 miles across the Texas panhandle and Oklahoma before we got to Arkansas and the last summit—not to mention the final 4-hour slog back to K.C.

Our spirits were crushed like the Cool Ranch Doritos fragments littering the Econoline's floor. We'd have to forget Arkansas or drive all night or both. We'd been slugging it out against the vexing factor of distance, but now that other awful variable—time—had jumped us from behind and was punching our kidneys.

We rolled up to the Black Mesa trailhead just before sunset. We were tired, grumpy, and about to hike for several hours in the dark. We grabbed three flashlights, two of which worked, and set out across a grassy field studded with scrub pines. We made good time until the trail angled up Black Mesa itself, which is notorious for rattlesnakes. We had to squint at the trail and proceed with caution to make sure nothing was slithering.

Once atop the mesa, we regrouped for the summit push. The marker—an eight-foot-tall dark-granite obelisk—looked eerily like the ape-maddening slab in 2001: A Space Odyssey. We fired up our cigars and read on the marker that Texas was 31 miles away, Colorado was 4.7, and New Mexico was but 1,300 feet to the west. Thank goodness the marker didn't mention the mileage to Arkansas, which would have been depressingly huge.

Hiking down a dark mesa with a lit cigar was a kooky joy, but it had evaporated by the time we reached the van. It was a little after midnight, and mutiny wafted through the air. Casper, the father of an infant son, was especially ready to quit—having skipped his shower in North Dakota, he was desperate for creature comforts.

"Let's call it 6 and a memorable weekend," he moaned. "Let's get a motel. Showers, clean sheets, sleep, glorious sleep. C'mon . . ."

Steve, also a father, and Spade, who wanted to watch ESPN to see how his college football bets had turned out, recognized Casper's patriarchal wisdom and began to cave. Which, frankly, made Drew and me sick. After all this, we were supposed to give up? To tell people that we'd conquered six runts rather than seven, because we couldn't handle the driving?"

"No way," I said, though in much coarser language. "Get in the van now! We're burning daylight standing here! Well, darkness . . . "

Even though I refused to be stopped, I could see Casper's point. All of us could. There would be ramifications if we returned to our families and jobs looking like hollow-eyed carcasses. We were thirty-nine-year-old men attempting a trip that would exhaust guys half our age. We should be proud enough for bagging six summits—two of which required actual effort. Not to mention the logistical wizardry it took just to get us together in one place.

At the moment, though, that one place happened to be an extremely sad parking lot in the Oklahoma outback. We got in the van and hit the road.

Our Econoline featured two captain's seats up front and four bench seats. We had removed the rear bench to make room for luggage, which meant only one guy at a time could catch quality winks by going horizontal.

It wasn't enough. We needed another sleep bay. After arriving punch-drunk at a truck stop in Amarillo, Texas, I positioned a Therm-a-Rest atop the luggage in the very back. I stretched out on it, not caring how many toothpaste tubes I squished. It was absurdly comfortable. Fresh, rested drivers were suddenly a possibility.

We rocketed east, intercepting dawn near Henryetta, Oklahoma. Then came serendipity: In Fort Smith, Arkansas, we stumbled across a restaurant called Sweet Bay Coffee. We caffeinated until we could caffeinate no more.

From Fort Smith, a series of twisty roads took us up into the Ozark National Forest. After spending so much time navigating open range, the Ozarks' leafy glades seemed foreign and wrong. Had we really been in North Dakota just two days ago? Our instincts said it couldn't be possible, though the odometer and our collective stench insisted that it was.

At 2,753 feet, Magazine Mountain was the second-shortest of the Seven Dwarfs but the fourth most difficult, requiring a 20-minute uphill walk. A simple wooden sign marked the top. I touched it. Dave filmed. We sipped bourbon from my flask. And history was made.

Seven up, seven down. As we headed back toward Kansas City, we felt like the heroes we truly were. For about 2 hours. Then, on U.S. 71 outside Butler, Missouri, we came to a screeching halt behind a long train of barely moving cars.

"Good God," Dave groaned. "Do these people know who we are and what we've done? We've been elite road warriors all weekend! But now look at us. We're just more schlubs stuck in holiday traffic."

There was no way we'd get Dorrell to the airport in time if we stayed on 71. Our only option was to cross into Kansas and hope that U.S. 69 would take us to K.C. through less traffic.

It worked. Dorrell made his flight; he even had time to take an ineffective sponge bath in the airport loo. The van was returned and Payless Car Rental called me only once to complain about its condition. Dave went back to Santa Monica, where he has yet to begin editing the alleged documentary that brought us to the Great Plains in the first place.

He has, however, found time to compile our statistics. We were out on the road for 86.5 hours. We drove 3,168 miles. We were cited for zero moving violations, though one or two might have occurred. We returned home feeling like mountaineering legends, but as the numbers made clear, the real champ was the Econoline.

"If you do the math," Dave later wrote us, "you see that, even at the moment we were gorging on apricot turnovers at the Longhorn Cafe, it was still averaging 36.6 miles per hour."

Fall

Football

George Plimpton

Jack Benny used to say that when he stood on the stage in white tie and tails for his violin concerts and raised his bow to begin his routine—scraping through "Love in Bloom"—that he *felt* like a great violinist. He reasoned that if he wasn't a great violinist, what was he doing dressed in tails, and about to play before a large audience?

At Pontiac I *felt* myself a football quarterback, not an interloper. My game plan was organized, and I knew what I was supposed to do. My nerves seemed steady, much steadier than they had been as I waited on the bench. I trotted along easily. I was keenly aware of what was going on around me.

I could hear a voice over the loudspeaker system, a dim murmur telling the crowd what was going on, telling them that number zero, coming out across the sidelines was not actually a rookie, but an amateur, a writer who had been training with the team for three weeks and had learned five plays, which he was now going to run against the first-string Detroit defense. It was like a nightmare come true, he told them, as if one of *them*, rocking a beer around in a paper cup, with a pretty girl leaning past him to ask the hot-dog vendor in the aisle for mustard, were suddenly carried down underneath the stands by a sinister clutch of ushers. He would protest, but he would be encased in the accoutrements, the silver helmet, with the two protruding bars of the cage, jammed down over his ears, and sent out to take over the team—that was the substance of the words, drifting across the field, swayed and shredded by the steady breeze coming up across the open end of Wisner Stadium from the vanished sunset. The crowd was interested, and I was conscious, just vaguely, of a steady roar of encouragement.

The team was waiting for me, grouped in the huddle, watching me come. I went in among them. Their heads came down for the signal. I called out, "Twenty-six!" forcefully, to inspire them, and a voice from one of the helmets said, "Down, down, the whole stadium can hear you."

"Twenty-six," I hissed at them. "Twenty-six near oh pinch; on three. *Break!*" Their hands cracked as one, and I wheeled and started for the line behind them.

My confidence was extreme. I ambled slowly behind Whitlow, the center, poised down over the ball, and I had sufficient presence to pause, resting a hand at the base of his spine, as if on a windowsill—a nonchalant gesture I had admired in certain quarterbacks—and I looked out over the length of his back to fix in my mind what I saw.*

Everything fine about being a quarterback—the embodiment of his power—was encompassed in those dozen seconds or so: giving the instructions to ten attentive men, breaking out of the huddle, walking for the line, and then pausing behind the center, dawdling amid men poised and waiting under the trigger of his voice, cataleptic, until the deliverance of himself and them to the future. The pleasure of sport was so often the chance to indulge the cessation of time itself—the pitcher dawdling on the mound, the skier poised at the top of a mountain trail, the basketball player with the rough skin of the ball against his palm preparing for a foul shot, the tennis player at set point over his opponent—all of them savoring a moment before committing themselves to action.

I had the sense of a portcullis down. On the other side of the imaginary bars the linemen were poised, the lights glistening off their helmets, and close in behind them were the linebackers, with Joe Schmidt just opposite

Two players in this excerpt are identified only by last name: Bob Whitlow and Nick Pietrosante, the latter of whom played fullback for the Detroit Lions.

GEORGE PLIMPTON

me, the big number 56 shining on his white jersey, jumpjacking back and forth with quick choppy steps, his hands poised in front of him, and he was calling out defensive code words in a stream. I could sense the rage in his voice, and the tension in those rows of bodies waiting, as if coils had been would overtight, which my voice, calling a signal, like a lever, would trip to spring them all loose. "Blue! Blue! Blue!" I heard Schmidt shout.

Within my helmet, the schoolmaster's voice murmured at me: "Son, nothing to it, nothing at all . . . "

I bent over the center. Quickly I went over what was supposed to happen—I would receive the snap and take two steps straight back and hand the ball to the number two back coming laterally across from right to left, who would then cut into the number-six hole. That was what was designated by twenty-six—the two back into the six hole. The mysterious code words "near oh pinch" referred to blocking assignments in the line, and I was never sure exactly what was meant by them. The important thing was to hang on to the ball, turn, and get the ball into the grasp of the back coming across laterally.

I cleared my throat. "Set!" I called out, my voice loud and astonishing to hear, as if it belonged to someone shouting into the earholes of my helmet. "Sixteen, sixty-five, forty-four, hut one, hut two, hut three," and at three the ball slapped back into my palm, and Whitlow's rump bucked up hard as he went for the defense men opposite.

The lines cracked together with a yawp and smack of pads and gear. I had the sense of quick, heavy movement, and as I turned for the backfield, not a second having passed, I was hit hard from the side, and as I gasped, the ball was jarred loose. It sailed away and bounced once, and I stumbled after it, hauling it under me 5 yards back, hearing the rush of feet, and the heavy jarring and wheezing of the blockers fending off the defense, a great roar up from the crowd, and above it, a relief to hear, the shrilling of the referee's whistle. My first thought was that at the snap of the ball the right side of the line had collapsed just at the second of the handoff, and one of the tacklers, Roger Brown or Floyd Peters, had cracked through to make me fumble. Someone, I assumed, had messed up on the assignments designated by the mysterious code words "near oh pinch."

In fact, as I discovered later, my *own man* bowled me over—John Gordy, whose assignment as offensive guard was to pull from his position and join the interference on the far side of the center. He was required to pull back and travel at a great clip parallel to the line of scrimmage to get out in front of the runner, his route theoretically passing between me and the center. But the extra second it took me to control the ball, and the creaking execution of my turn, put me in his path, a rare sight for Gordy to see, his own quarterback blocking the way, like coming around a corner in a high-speed car to find a moose ambling across the centerline, and he caromed off me, jarring the ball loose.

My confidence had not gone. I stood up. The referee took the retrieved ball from me. He had to tug to get it away, a faint look of surprise on his face. My inner voice was assuring me that the fault in the fumble had not been mine. "They let you down," it was saying. "The blocking failed." But the main reason for my confidence was the next play on my list—the ninety-three pass, a play which I had worked successfully in the Cranbrook scrimmages. I walked into the huddle and I said with considerable enthusiasm, "All right! All *right*! Here we *go*!"

"Keep the voice down," said a voice. "You'll be tipping them the play."

I leaned in on them and said: "Green right" (*Green* designated a pass play, *right* put the flanker to the right side), "three right" (which put the three back to the right), "ninety-three" (indicating the two primary receivers; nine, the right end, and three, the three back) "on *three* . . . *Break!*"—the clap of the hands again in unison, the team streamed past me up to the line, and I walked briskly up behind Whitlow.

Again, I knew exactly how the play was going to develop—back those 7 yards into the defensive pocket for the 3 to 4 seconds it was supposed to hold, and Pietrosante, the three back, would go down in his pattern, 10 yards straight, then cut over the middle, and I would hit him.

"Set! . . . sixteen! . . . eighty-eight . . . fifty-five . . . *hut* one . . . *hut* two . . . *hut* three . . . "

The ball slapped into my palm at three. I turned and started back. I could feel my balance going, and 2 yards behind the line of scrimmage, I *fell down*—absolutely flat, as if my feet had been pinned under a tripwire stretched across the field, not a hand laid on me. I heard a roar go up from the crowd. Suffused as I had been with confidence, I could scarcely believe what had happened. Mud cleats catching in the grass? Slipped in the dew? I felt my jaw go ajar in my helmet. "Wha'? Wha'?"—the mortification beginning to come fast. I rose hurriedly to my knees at the referee's whistle, and I could see my teammates' big silver helmets with the blue Lion decals turn toward me, some of the players rising from blocks they'd thrown to protect me, their faces masked, automaton, prognathous with the helmet bars protruding toward me, characterless, yet the dismay was in the set of their bodies as they loped back for the huddle. The schoolmaster's voice flailed at me inside my helmet. "Ox!" it cried. "Clumsy oaf."

I joined the huddle. "Sorry, sorry," I said.

"Call the play, man," came a voice from one of the helmets.

"I don't know what happened," I said.

"Call it, man."

The third play on my list was the forty-two, another running play, one of the simplest in football, in which the quarterback receives the snap, makes a full spin, and shoves the ball into the four back's stomach—the fullback's. He has come straight forward from his position as if off starting blocks, his knees high, and he disappears with the ball into the number-two hole just to the left of the center—a straight power play, and one which seen from the stands seems to offer no difficulty.

I got into an awful jam with it. Once again, the jackrabbitspeed of the professional backfield was too much for me. The fullback—Danny Lewis—was past me and into the line before I could complete my spin and set the ball in his belly. And so I did what was required: I tucked the ball into my own belly and followed Lewis into the line, hoping that he might have budged open a small hole.

I tried, grimacing, my eyes squinted almost shut, and waiting for the impact, which came before I'd taken two steps—I was grabbed up by Roger Brown.

He tackled me high, and straightened me with his power, so that I churned against his 300-pound girth like a comic bicyclist. He began to shake me. I remained upright to my surprise, flailed back and forth, and I realized that he was struggling for the ball. His arms were around it, trying to tug it free. The bars of our helmets were nearly locked, and I could look through and see him inside—the first helmeted face I recognized that evening—the small, brown eyes surprisingly peaceful, but he was grunting hard, the sweat shining, and I had time to think, "It's Brown, it's *Brown!*" before I lost the ball to him, and flung to one knee on the ground I watched him lumber ten yards into the end zone behind us for a touchdown.

The referee wouldn't allow it. He said he'd blown the ball dead while we were struggling for it. Brown was furious. "You taking that away from *me*," he said, his voice high and squeaky. "Man, I took that ball in there good."

The referee turned and put the ball on the 10-yard line. I had lost 20 yards in three attempts, and I had yet, in fact, to run off a complete play.

The veterans walked back very slowly to the next huddle.

I stood off to one side, listening to Brown rail at the referee. "I never scored like that befo'. You takin' that way from me?" His voice was peeved. He looked off toward the stands, into the heavy tumult of sound, spreading the big palms of his hands in grief.

I watched him, detached, not even moved by his insistence that I suffer the humiliation of having the ball stolen for a touchdown. If the referee had allowed him his score, I would not have protested. The shock of having the three plays go as badly as they had left me dispirited and numb, the purpose of the exercise forgotten. Even the schoolmaster's voice seemed to have gone—a bleak despair having set in so that as I stood shifting uneasily watching Brown jawing at the referee, I was perfectly willing to trot in to the bench at that point and be done with it.

Then, by chance, I happened to see Carl Brettschneider standing at his corner linebacker position, watching me, and beyond the bars of his cage I could see a grin working. That set my energies ticking over once again—the notion that some small measure of recompense would be mind if I could complete a pass in the Badger's territory and embarrass him. I had such a play in my series—a slant pass to the strong-side end, Jim Gibbons.

I walked back to the huddle. It was slow in forming. I said, "The Badger's asleep. He's fat and he's asleep."

No one said anything. Everyone stared down. In the silence I became suddenly aware of the feet. There are twenty-two of them in the huddle, after all, most of them very large, in a small area, and while the quarterback ruminates and the others await his instruction, there's nothing else to catch the attention. The sight pricked at my mind, the oval of twenty-two football shoes, and it may have been responsible for my error in announcing the play. I forgot to give the signal on which the ball was to be snapped back by the center. I said, "Green right nine slant *break!*" One or two of the players clapped their hands, and as the huddle broke, some of them automatically heading for the line of scrimmage, someone hissed: "Well, the *signal*, what's the signal, for chrissake."

I had forgotten to say "On two."

I should have kept my head and formed the huddle again. Instead I called out "Two!" in a loud stage whisper, directing my call first to one side, then the other. "*Two! Two!*" as we walked up to the line. For those that might have been beyond earshot, who might have missed the signal, I held out two fingers spread like a v, which I showed around furtively, trying to hid it from the defense and hoping that my people would see.

The pass was incomplete. I took two steps back (the play was a quick pass, thrown without a protective pocket) and I saw Gibbons break from his position, then stop, buttonhooking; his hand, which I used as a target, came up, but I threw the ball over him. A yell came up from the crowd seeing the ball in the air (it was the first play of the evening which hadn't been "blown"—to use the player's expression for a missed play), but then a groan went up when the ball was overshot and bounced across the sidelines.

"Last play," George Wilson was calling. He had walked over with a clipboard in his hand was standing by the referee. "The ball's on the tent. Let's see you take it all the way," he called out cheerfully.

One of the players asked: "Which end zone is he talking about?"

The last play of the series was a pitchout—called a flip on some teams—a long lateral to the number-four back running parallel to the line and cutting for the eight hole at left end. The lateral, though long, was easy for me to do. What I had to remember was to keep on running out after the flight of the ball. The hole behind me as I lateraled was left unguarded by an offensive lineman pulling out from his position and the defensive tackle could bull through and take me from behind in his rush, not knowing I'd got rid of the ball, if I didn't clear out of the area.

I was able to get the lateral off and avoid the tackler behind me, but unfortunately the defense was keyed for the play. They knew my repertoire, which was only five plays or so, and they doubted I'd call the same play twice. One of my linemen told me later that the defensive man opposite him in the line, Floyd Peters, had said, "Well, here comes the forty-eight pitchout," and it had come, and they were able to throw the number four back, Pietrosante, who had received that lateral, back on the 1-yard line—just a yard away from the mortification of having moved a team backward from the 30-yard line into one's own end zone for a safety.

As soon as I saw Pietrosante go down, I left for the bench on the side-lines at midfield, a long run from where I'd brought my team, and I felt utterly weary, shuffling along through the grass.

Applause began to sound from the stands, and I looked up, startled, and saw people standing, and the hands going. It made no sense at the time. It was not derisive; it seemed solid and respectful. Wha'? Wha'? I thought, and I wondered if the applause wasn't meant for someone else—if the mayor had come into the stadium behind me and was waving from an open-topped car. But as I came up to the bench I could see the people in the stands looking at me, and the hands going.

I thought about the applause afterward. Some of it was, perhaps, in appreciation of the lunacy of my participation and for the fortitude it took to do it; but most of it, even if subconscious, I decided was in *relief* that I had done as badly as I had: it verified the assumption that the average fan would have about an amateur blundering into the brutal world of professional football. He would get slaughtered. If by some chance I had uncorked a touchdown pass, there would have been wild acknowledgment—because I heard the groans go up at each successive disaster—but afterward the spectators would have felt uncomfortable. Their concept of things would have been upset. The outsider did not belong, and there was comfort in that being proved.

Some of the applause, as it turned out, came from people who had enjoyed the comic aspects of my stint. More than a few thought that they were being entertained by a professional comic in the tradition of baseball's Al Schacht, or the Charlie Chaplins, the clown, of the bullfights. Bud Erickson, the public relations director, told me that a friend of his had come up to him later. "Bud, that's one of the funniest goddamn . . . I mean, that guy's *got* it," the man said, barely able to control himself.

I did not take my helmet off when I reached the bench. It was tiring to do and there was security in having it on. I was conscious of the big zero on my back facing the crowd when I sat down. Some players came by and tapped me on the top of the helmet. Brettschneider leaned down and said, "Well, you stuck it . . . that's the big thing."

The scrimmage began. I watched it for a while, but my mind returned to my own performance. The pawky inner voice was at hand again. "You didn't stick it," it said testily. "You funked it."

At half time Wilson took the players down to the bandshell at one end of the stadium. I stayed on the bench. He had his clipboards with him, and I could see him pointing and explaining, a big semicircle of players around him, sitting on the band chairs. Fireworks soared up into the sky from the other end of the field, the shells puffing out clusters of light that lit the upturned faces on the crowd in silver, then red, and then reports would go off, reverberating sharply, and in the stands across the field I could see the children's hands flap up over their ears. Through the noise I heard someone yelling my name. I turned and saw a girl leaning over the rail of the grandstand behind me. I recognized her from the Gay Haven in Dearborn. She was wearing a mohair Indian sweater, the color of spun pink sugar, and tight pants, and she was holding a thick folding wallet in one hand along with a pair of dark glasses, and in the other a Lions banner, which she waved, her face alive with excitement, very pretty in a perishable, childlike way, and she was calling, "Beautiful; it was beautiful."

The fireworks lit her, and she looked up, her face chalk white in the swift aluminum glare.

I looked at her out of my helmet. Then I lifted a hand, just tentatively.

Le Tour d'Amour

Steve Friedman

The marketing person for the singles bicycle trip wants to talk about the gently rolling hills that will greet me each morning, the velvety, succulent salmon I'll be eating for dinner any night I choose, the cozy inns with individual hot tubs that will await me at the end of every day.

I'm interested in something else. "What's the male/female breakdown? What's the age range?"

"Oh, it's a wide range," she says. "A fun group."

"A fun group. Glad to hear it. Can you be more specific?"

"You're going to fit right in," she says. "Lots of different ages."

"How," I say, clearly enunciating. "Many. Women."

Resentful silence on the other end.

"And how old?"

Shuffling of papers. "Let's see," she says. "There are five women, four men. Ward is between thirty-six and forty-five," she says, "and, oh, here's Paul, he's fifty-six to sixty-five. And . . . "

"Uh-huh," I say. "Uh-huh. Uh-huh." Maybe I snap the words just a little bit. "What about the women?"

More shuffling of papers. A sigh. "Well, I'm not sure how old Julia is. Or Eileen. And it doesn't say here about Joan. And I don't really know Elaine's age, but she's great."

Is she *serious?* I think this but I say nothing.

"Then there's Lillie," she says. Actually, she chirps. "I think she's in her fifties, but she seems younger. Lillie is a card."

"That's terrific," I say mournfully. "A card."

"You're going to have a great time with her," the marketing person says. "Lillie is just a real kick."

I am not looking for a real kick. I'm looking for exercise, adventure, high-end hotels with private hot tubs, and fancy restaurants where I can gorge on velvety, succulent salmon. But this is a *singles* bike trip, so I'm also looking for something else. Something else in the shape of long-legged, lithe, well-muscled female cyclists between the ages of twenty-eight and forty-two whose smooth flanks ripple with exquisitely sensitive nerve endings, and who possess winsome smiles, above-average hygiene, a hefty trust fund or generous divorce settlement (or both!), a deep and abiding sense of adventure, not too many issues about personal boundaries, the courage to resist the absurd and insulting prohibitions against sexual experimentation promulgated by a patriarchal culture terrified of female power, and a principled readiness to explore the intense and eternal bonds that connect all of humanity, especially in private hot tubs late at night.

I have pored over the brochures of many bicycle outfitters. I have rejected the most expensive companies because, although clients would by definition be loaded, I fear they might also be wrinkled and gray. (Yes, there might be a spoiled and slumming heiress along for the ride but it seems unlikely and I only have one shot, so I'm playing the odds.) I have also passed on the more grueling trips, through deserts and up mountain peaks. The women on these expeditions would no doubt sport the ripply flanks. But I fear I might suffer a heart attack trying to keep up with them. (Speaking of heart attacks, I am forty-seven, overweight, balding, tend to eat packages of cookies and pints of ice cream during times of stress, and move through my days according to an eternally optimistic, carefree and freedom-embracing credo my last girlfriend mistook for "a life as pathetic and self-destructive as it is delusional.")

The marketing person asks whether I'd like a hybrid or road bike. She tells me to measure the distance between my pubic bone and the floor (which I suspect might serve as an apt metaphor for the week ahead, but I'm not exactly sure how).

"You will love Lillie," she says. "She is *such* a kick." The marketing person wishes me well.

Her wishes have not worked. It is the second day of an eight-day Bicycle Adventures trip that will take me through Washington's San Juan Islands to Victoria, British Columbia. My legs ache, my breathing is labored, and my eternal optimism has curdled into a keen, focused resentment. Resentment at Bicycle Adventures in general, whose "gently rolling hills" have turned out to be pitiless mountains. At my hybrid bike, a puke-colored San Rafael DLX, a clunky, unresponsive, ugly heap of metal that keeps me dead last on the hills, and which I have come to call "Missy," after an ineffably treacherous college girlfriend whom I'd rather not discuss. At myself for falling for Missy (both times). At Lorry, the fifty-three-year-old elfin and bearded coleader who says at dinner the first night, "I love the shadows in the morning, the way light plays off the spokes at dusk. I'm happy, seeing life in slow motion," and who refers to bicycles as "vehicles for people to have certain types of life experiences" and who not-so-incidentally saddled me with my piece-of-shit vehicle and who I'm convinced harbors an intense loathing of the world that he tries to conceal with nonstop Baba Ram Dassian biking bunkum along the lines of "I have two speeds: the speed you're looking at, and slower," and which he only truly expresses by lying to us about hills that are mountains then encouraging us until our breathing is labored and our legs ache.

Resentment, too, at all of my fellow riders, because none of them, not a single blessed one except Karen, the apple-cheeked twenty-two-year-old coleader, who even an optimist like myself can see is too young, has ripply flanks and winsome smiles. At Ward, the ex–Boy Scout pharmacist from Illinois, who wears a coat and tie to dinner, won't shut up about the X-Files and beer, and sports a No Whining button on his saddlebag. At Julia (36–45), a New Yorker who complains the first day about horse droppings in Central Park. At Eileen (36–45), Julia's pal, another New Yorker, who considers it her mission to educate the world about the

STEVE FRIEDMAN

wonders of egg creams and who, much, much worse, refers to dinner as "Dindin" and bedtime, "Beddybye." At Paul, a Californian who sings in his church choir and can change a flat tire in 10 minutes. At Joan (36–45), an emergency room physician who spends most of her time discussing, hunting, tasting then describing the various coffees of the San Juan Islands and who, in her relentless search, keeps the rest of us—even hoggish, dull, slothlike, sluggish, perfidious Missy and me—waiting. At Elaine (36–45), a SWAT team member from Florida who packs heat back home and who exclaims to Joan, whenever egg creams or Central Park or anything about New York is mentioned, "You can have it!" and Joan snorts back in agreement, sometimes through a snout full of cappuccino. Resentment at Brad (36–45), a financier from Washington DC, who seems polite and well-mannered, but is slimmer, younger, and makes much more money than I do and who, beneath his kind and helpful exterior, I'm certain is an utter bastard.

But most especially and energetically, my resentment finds Lillie, the putative kick in the pants who has stopped to let me catch up with her and, at this moment, on day two, on San Juan Island, is giving me some serious attitude.

We are near the crest of a torturous, narrow, obscenely steep "gently rolling hill." According to our printed instructions, which we each keep visible beneath the plastic covers of our handlebar bags, we are to turn right at mile 11, onto Federal Road, next to a red and white pole. There's the pole, all right, and Lillie is standing next to it, pointing down the undulating pavement. But according to my odometer we have biked only 10.8 miles. My legs hurt. My feet are cramping. My fellow riders are far, far ahead and young and ripply flanked Karen has been sidling away from me whenever I express friendliness, even though I think it's her job to make all the paying guests feel comfortable and I plan to file a complaint with her corporate masters when I get home. The only thing I can count on is my odometer, and, in the manner that hollow-eyed and psychotic shipwreck survivors cling to rosary beads and faded photographs and other useless artifacts, I cling to my odometer. I point at it, shrug meaningfully, and tell Lillie that I think we're .2 of a mile from the appointed turn.

She sneers at me. No other word will do her expression justice. "I'd rather trust the instructions than your odometer, Steve."

"But . . ."

She points to a hill in the mid-distance. Our fellow bicycle riders are specks upon it. "See you at the hotel," she says, then mounts up and pedals away.

I take it out on Missy, clumsy, unresponsive, ill-chosen, and selfish Missy, whose tires grunt in derision, whose noisy gears mock me, whose treacherous spokes hum ragged ballads of betrayal for the next 14 miles. "C'mon, Missy," I hiss, as Lillie stretches the distance between us. "Work with me, you cow."

Hours later, the group stands at the bottom of a pitch so steep that even the duplicitous and smooth-talking Bicycle Adventures marketer couldn't get away with calling it gentle or rolling. The insipid conversations—are they discussing egg creams or regional espressos?—turn to collective surprise, then shouts of disbelief, then cries of alarm. They are looking at a speck in the distance. The speck, on the top of the rise—the bald, overweight speck wearing scuffed sneakers, with cookie crumbs falling from his mouth, the speck on the pathetic, misshapen piece of puke-green metal—could it be . . . ?

Yes, it is, but in the way he careers and leans, eating up pavement, making love to the murderously steep drops and cruel turns, he is no longer an object of pity and scorn. Now, in his speed, in his headlong descent, he is reminiscent of no one so much as that famous French dead guy whose name the knot of bikers at the bottom of the hill must know—judging from all the spandex they're wearing—but which I can't quite remember. I am almost upon them now, and I can see their surprise turn to terror as I swoop through another curve. The beer-swilling Boy Scout gapes. The coffee lover has turned white. As I pass, the choir boy and Miss Dindin stumble into a ditch. Lillie, caught in my backdraft, crumples into a heap. The others, even universe-loving, homily-spouting Lorry, curse, but I can see (even making love to the murderous pavement, I manage to gracefully turn my head) that they are curses of terror. The only one not cursing is Karen, who regards me with moist-eyed lust.

I wipe cookie crumbs from my mouth. I sneer. Then I shout back to them, in French. *"C'est dommage, mes amis, mais—"*

The alarm clock wakes me. I have a cramp in my left calf.

When we leave our hotel in the morning, and Lorry says to the clerk, "I really hope that life continues to bring you an enormous amount of joy," I roll my eyes at Karen, who still doesn't talk to me much but who I've started to realize is very mature for her age.

When Eileen asks during an afternoon break, "What's for Dindin?" I sigh a little too loudly. And when Joan is late to the van after lunch, I suggest to Karen, whose eyes, I can't help noticing, are the color of the ocean after a cleansing storm, that we drive off without the physician, and that "maybe the coffee will make the good doctor pedal faster." I also snatch chocolate chip cookies from the support van's basket of food four or five times daily, usually when I think no one's looking. I gossip about other group members, too, and even say with a leer before dinner to Karen, whom I have managed to sit next to, "I wonder if Lillie and Paul will be shifting gears together tonight."

Two days later, on day four, I see what a self-centered, bitter, projecting, delusional *shlub* I have become. Or maybe, that I've always been. This awakening is prompted partly by my switch from Missy to a Cannondale R-400 road bike with a tricked-up drivetrain that widens my shifting options; a sea-green machine as slim, elegant, and giving as Missy was portly and spiteful. I love my new bike, whom I think of as Gwyneth, and she loves me back. When I move, Gwyneth responds, immediately and with movement so excited and delighted that it takes my breath away. My improved outlook is also no doubt aided by regular and vigorous riding, about 30 miles a day through the highways and backroads that encircle and slice through the San Juan Islands, nestled in the deep blue Puget Sound, roads that take Gwyneth and me past llama farms, through pumpkin fields, alongside beaches, next to cozy little villages that serve caffe lattes that please Joan immensely and for which I am grateful on her behalf, through brief rain showers and below squawking geese and cormorants and above many banana slugs and up steep inclines straight into a gentle, life-giving, sometimes watery but always warm post–Labor Day sun and back to one of the three high-end hotels on three different islands at the end of the day, where succulent salmon and steamy hot tubs often await.

Surrounded by cormorants and banana slugs, stripped of my normal quotidian worries (Does the guy back in New York City at my corner deli hate me, or is he just part of a sleeper cell? Digital TV vs. high-speed internet porno access? What was my old girlfriend's *problem*? Why am I forty-seven and still single?), epiphanies greet me at the most unlikely times.

Pumping up a gently rolling hill, narrowly avoiding banana slugicide, I realize that being surrounded by people—even ones who often annoy me—and finding deep satisfaction in completing a daily task—no matter how onerous—is what people mean when they refer to "working for a living," and that maybe I should consider getting a job.

Another day, on the ferry from San Juan to Orcas Island, as we're scanning the waters for whales, it hits me that the payoff of this trip is not whether we see a whale or find rich coffee or gorge on velvety, moist salmon. (Actually, *eating* velvety, moist salmon helps me to arrive at this epiphany, but that doesn't detract from its basic truth.) The payoff is the journey itself, the pedaling and shifting, struggling and coasting. And isn't this the secret to life itself? We wake, we move, we arrive. We struggle, we coast. We repeat, on a daily basis, on a deep, cradle-to-grave basis. And what about the word "cycle?" We ride it, but it's the *cycle* of life. When I think of this, rounding a curve between sentinels of emerald old growth, I nearly fall off Gwyneth.

No longer the delusional crank, I begin to feel the love of my fellow bicyclists. The love of Ward the beer-swilling Boy Scout who, on morning five, approaches me at breakfast, just a few minutes after we've dropped our luggage next to the van. Grimacing, staring at the ground, shuffling his feet, he is clearly in pain. "Uh, Steve," he says, *sotto vocce*, "I don't mean to be too personal, but there's something buzzing in your suitcase." (It turns out to be my electric toothbrush, but for all he knows, it's the sex toy popular with *all* bachelor New Yorkers who sign up for singles bike trips." The love of Joan, whom I had suggested leaving to rot with her latte. That evening she asks me to come by her room. I do so, with trepidation.

STEVE FRIEDMAN

Has Karen ratted me out? When I get there, Joan offers me handfuls of Aleve. "I noticed you were limping a little," she says. The love of Julia and Paul who, when I order scallops for dinner one evening, both offer me a taste of their salmon.

I have been so wrong about so many people. Especially Lillie, who is not the spoiled, ditzy, fifty-ish dilettante I took her to be. It turns out she grew up on the harsh plains of the Texas panhandle, a farmer's daughter, and got married as a teenager, then raised a son alone while she worked toward a doctorate in nutrition at UCLA. Sixty-seven years old (sorry, Lillie), she recently retired from a career as a professor of nutrition.

Getting ready for our ride on the morning of the fifth day, Lillie says to me, "Oh, I would love to draft behind you, with your wonderful, big, broad shoulders."

That's when I feel Lillie's love. So what if her flanks don't ripple. Those flanks have tended livestock, raised a child, traveled the world. Those flanks know things. I am seized by an urge to move to the Pacific Palisades. Karen is a mere child. I can see this now. And I can also see that Lillie's eyes are the color of a bruised and saddened sky after a scouring rain. I wonder how Lillie would look in a hot tub.

Am I finally allowing the gentle rhythms of the trip to take root in my long-fallow but now fecund soul, letting go at long last of the idiotic and shallow notions of youth and beauty that a patriarchal culture terrified of female power has promulgated and that have for so tragically many years enslaved me? Is what's happening to me what Lorry was referring to when he said on the first day that "You'll feel different tomorrow and every day, and by the end of the week, you'll feel inspiration, a reawakening"?

Or, to be rational about this, am I merely a lonely bike whore, a pathetic, delusional, opportunistic road slut? I'm not sure of the answer. To calm myself, I sneak into the snack box in the van before the nap that I need to take to clear my head before my velvety salmon dinner. I grab a few fistfuls of peanut-butter cookies to help me think.

At dinner we discuss morbid obesity and body-mass index and the healthy heart (I'm having pasta with lobster and baked cheese), the art of nourishing our dreams, spiritual malaise, how to live in the moment, and why self-love is the greatest love of all.

I'm serene, and the nap and the cookies helped, but I'm still confused. I want clarity. I ask Lillie if she has a boyfriend.

No, she says. She had been dating a guy recently. He was a wonderful man, giving, fun-loving. A serious sailor, too, and rich. "He had a nice boat," she says, "and a nice house. But I can't date a man who doesn't take care of himself. We went out to dinner with a group, and even though I almost never eat dessert, I ordered crème brûlée. He not only finished mine, he also finished the other five that were on the table."

Lillie shakes her head mournfully. "I'm not interested in a man whose stomach precedes him into the room. I won't go out with someone who's not into fitness."

We—the entire table—nod our heads gravely, chat some more, about the next day's ride, and the joys of healthy living and how we will always carry the gifts of this journey, wherever we go.

I'm thinking about some gifts a little sooner. "Lillie," I say, her sentiments about my wonderful shoulders still warming my gut, which, okay, might be kind of oversized but doesn't precede me into any rooms, at least as far as I know. "As long as I'm exercising a lot, and following my dreams and living in the moment and all, is it really so bad if occasionally instead of an orange or a banana, I just go ahead and have a piece of cheesecake before a long ride? Or a couple cookies?"

I want her answer. I need her blessing. I crave her forgiveness.

She looks at me.

The rest of the table looks at her.

Then she sneers. There is no other word for it.

"Well, what do you think, Steve?"

I think I want to stuff myself with chocolate chip cookies and skip the bike (always an option on a Bicycle Adventures trip) and ride in the van, chatting up apple-cheeked, ripply flanked, ocean-eyed Karen, loving, giving, wise Karen, who is driving today. I think I've been a victim of a rigid and patriarchal culture that wants me to mindlessly and robotically embrace the opprobrium directed at the true, deep, meaningful love that can exist between young women and not-quite-so-young men. So what if Karen is twenty-two? She makes no judgments about my cookie-eating. (She's paid not to make such judgments, but that's a detail I choose not to dwell on.) She doesn't make fun of my odometer.

I think I hate Lillie.

But I also think that the talk at dinner last night of crème brûlée and endemic obesity and hapless sailors and imminent death by heart attack has frightened me. Plus, something tells me I might be creeping Karen out a little bit. So today, the last day of the trip, I will try to pedal 20 miles from Port Angeles to the top of Hurricane Ridge. We will climb a mile in elevation.

"Try is a very weak word," Lillie says after breakfast. "Every day is an opportunity to build the life you want."

"Right, Lillie," I spit out. "Thanks a lot for the input. Really appreciate it."

Something strange and wondrous happens on the ride. During my three and a half hours with Gwyneth that blessed Saturday, I forgive Lillie who, after all, doesn't want to take a chance on a glutton who's going to drop dead in front of her, clutching cellophane cookie packages. I forgive Lorry for urging me, as I sweat and grunt and swear, to "be in this moment and enjoy it."

I forgive Karen for sidling away from me at breakfast that day, when I ask what she majored in (landscape architecture, in case you're interested). I forgive the Bicycle Adventures marketer for telling me Lillie was a kick in the pants, and I forgive Bicycle Adventures in general for misleading me about the gently rolling hills. (Had they not lied to me, I would not have come on the trip.) I even forgive Missy, bless her rusty, recalcitrant soul. I see now that she was reliable and stout, a middle-aged companion built for comfort, not speed. The old gal never meant me any harm. She did the best she could; we were just at different places then, and I wish her well. I hope she meets a man who is right for her.

I am so filled with forgiveness and fullness of spirit because, after a couple hours with the sleek and fashionable Gwyneth, I have cycled—yes, *cycled*—through pain and ragged sucking of air and a deep burning in my flanks, which are themselves rippling but with cramps and spasms, and a desperation and fatigue that turns to a suspicion and then a certainty that I can actually *do* this, and there is no room in my heart for anger, or resentment or even any dreams of hot tubs with Lillie or Karen. On the eighth day of an eight-day trip, moving at 4.5 miles an hour (according to my speedometer, which will never betray me and which I will remember forever), with hawks circling above, trees looming over me, the top of Hurricane Ridge just around the next bend, I have finally accepted the greatest gift a singles bicycle trip can bestow. I see that it's not something as transient and meaningless as mere physical coupling that matters, or desperate late-night hot tub gropings, but connections and health and, to quote from a file I now have on my computer, labeled "the wisdom of Lorry," it's about "accepting the universe." I have found delight in the company of others and in my own company. I think I've found happiness.

After a lunch of individually prepared chicken burritos and banana splits on the ridge, I decide to stick with Gwyneth for the ride back to the hotel and the van, which will take us to the ferry, which will chug to Seattle, from where I'll fly back to New York and decisions about high-speed internet access versus digital television and surly foreign deli guys and existential questions about love and companionship and the meaning of life. All that will come, and it will come in its own time. At this moment, though, at this moment I'm thoroughly present in, all I have to do is keep off the brakes and trust Gwyneth and lean into the curves and make love to the pavement and the fragrant firs and the post–Labor Day sun and the cormorants and the screaming wind. I trust it all and it isn't painless but it's easy. It's so easy when I just let go. And it's all downhill.

Here the Bear and the Mafia Roam

Bob Shacochis

In the central Siberian city of Tomsk, children play a game called Dead Telephone, whispering a sentence around a circle until someone fails to repeat the original wording accurately, and for the child who gets the sentence wrong, the penalty is "you must go live in Kamchatka." Meaning that the loser has been imaginatively banished from the relative comforts of Siberia to the very end of the earth. Kamchatka, perhaps Russia's most famous nowhere, the wild east of the Russian and Soviet empires, nine time zones and 10,000 kilometers distant from Moscow.

Tundra. Shimmering twilight. A slow, high-banked river the color of tea, as if it flowed from the spigot of a samovar.

Where I should have been was on a vodka-clear, rock-bottomed river, fast and wild, somewhere to the north and farther inland with a phantom cadre of biologists, fly-fishing for salmon specimens on the Kamchatka peninsula. Where I'd ended up was about three klicks inland from the Sea of Okhotsk, on an estuarine section of another river that I'd been advised, by the self-proclaimed criminals who deposited me here, to forget about, or else.

We had come from the end of the road, 3 hours across tundra and beach, atop my host's—let's call him Misha—GTT, a large, blunt-snouted all-terrain vehicle that came into his possession when the Soviet military began to disintegrate in 1991. Despite Misha's earlier assurances, not only were we not going to the river I'd traveled thousands of miles to fish, in hopes of seeing what I'd never seen before—the phenomenon of a massive salmon run—but we'd be leaving in the morning, a day earlier than I thought had been agreed upon. Misha, who looked like a blond-haired, cornhusking quarterback, had Brandoesque mannerisms; waiting for my tantrum to subside, he tilted his head back and cocked it coolly, peering down the nascent beefiness of his ruddy face, and then chided me in the hushed cadence of the ever-reasonable gangster.

"Robert," he said, "I'm Mafiya, Mafiya, Mafiya—not a tour agent."

Then he wrapped his hands around his throat, as if to strangle himself, and said he would, if I wanted, take care of my inept outfitter back in Petropavlovsk-Kamchatski (P-K), and for a moment I thought, Nice guy!

At the Mafiya's oceanside fish camp, when I explained that, to salvage something out of the trip, I wanted to be ferried across the lagoon to spend the night upriver, Misha considered this desire stupid and pointless, but mostly he considered it dangerous. Bears were as thick as gooseberries over there, he said, and I didn't have a gun, but when I persisted he ordered his boatman to take me across. Rinat, my half-Tatar, half-Russian interpreter/driver, was coming with me. Sergei, our wilderness guide, said he'd rather not.

Now, standing on a tiny tide-swept island in waist-high grass at the end of this remarkably strange day, I cast futilely for silver salmon with my spinning rod, the strong wind sailing the lure within inches of a sandy patch of beach jutting out below the opposite shore. On the steep bank 10 feet above me, Rinat had his nose in the food bag, tossing spoiled provisions out onto the ground.

"Rinat! Are you mad? Throw that food in the river."

Kamchatka is said to have more and larger grizzly bears per square mile than any place on earth, but Rinat was churlishly indifferent to their presence. A city boy, born and raised in P-K, the peninsula's largest metropolis, he was employed by a local tourist company trying to bluff its way into the wilderness biz. His employer—my outfitter—let him come out into the ever-perilous, grizzly-roamed outback without a proper food container, without even a tent (I'd brought my own). Earlier in the summer, we'd done soberingly foolish things together, taken risks that Rinat never seemed to recognize—traversed glaciers where one slip would send you plummeting into oblivion; edged ourselves out onto melting ice bridges; stood on the fragile crater floor of the belching Mutnovsky volcano, our lungs seared by sulfurous gases. How, I often wondered, was this puckish, hardworking fellow ever going to survive his occupation, here in one of the last great wild places left on earth?

"Sushi," Rinat giggled irreverently, pitching stale bread and moldy cheese into the river, making a reference to Michiko Honido, the renowned bear photographer, who was eaten by his Kamchatkan subjects last year.

A minute later I hooked up with a good-size silver salmon, which cheered me deeply, here in the land called the Serengeti of Salmon, where I had been consistently thwarted in my (apparently not) simple quest to savor a fine day of fishing. The fish made its freedom run, keeping me well occupied, and when I looked up again, Rinat, the imp, had set the tundra on fire.

I landed the fish, put my rod down, hopped back to the mainland, and began hauling pots of water while Rinat slapped at the rapidly spreading flames with a fiber sack. Though I'd just reeled in the first salmon of my life, the experience had been akin to losing one's virginity while your little brother's in the room, playing with a loaded pistol.

Later, as I planked one of the filets for smoking, Rinat cut the other into steaks for the cookpot. We lolled around the campfire, uncommonly taciturn, because Rinat had found it politic to give away our last bottle of vodka to the boyos.

"Here we are with the criminals," he said, shaking his head morosely. "Here we are with the bears."

Imagine an Alaska sealed tight for fifty years, suspended in isolation, inaccessible to all outsiders until 1990, when the sanctum's doors ease slowly open to the capitalists on the threshold, the carpetbaggers, the tycoon sportsmen, and, of course, the gangsters. Unworldly Kamchatka, with a not-quite-propitious swing of history's horrible pendulum, is called upon to reinvent itself, and not for the first time.

As gold had once inspired the conquest of the New World, the lust for fur—beaver in North America, sable in Russia—accelerated the exploration of two continents and the spread of two empires. Russia's eastward expansion very much mirrored America's westward expansion—the genocidal subjugation of native peoples in the pursuit of natural riches and trade routes. White guys on the move.

Annexed for the czars by a Cossack expedition in 1697, Kamchatka provided Peter the Great with a global monopoly on the fabulously valuable sable. Within forty years, the ruthless, plundering Cossacks had decimated the coastal-oriented Itelmen and reindeer-herding Koryaks—the likely descendants of indigenous people who had crossed the Bering Strait to North America. A native rebellion in 1731 resulted in a mass suicide, and before long 150,000 tribal people had been reduced to 10,000, their number today, barely 2.5 percent of Kamchatka's population. Racially and culturally, Kamchatka is as Eurocentric as a bottle of Perrier.

In 1725, Peter the Great sent Captain Vitus Bering on an unsuccessful mission to determine the relation of eastern Siberia to the American continent. Bering was recommissioned by Peter's successor, and his Great Northern Expedition, which took years to plan and execute and eventually involved 3,000 people, is rightfully remembered as one of the greatest voyages of discovery. Bering sailed his two packets, the St. *Peter* and the St. *Paul*, into Avachinsky Bay in 1740 and founded the town of Petropavlovsk, named after his ships. The following spring he set sail for the coast of North America, sighting land in July—Kayak Island off the Alaskan coast—and throughout the summer and fall he mapped the Aleutians, charted the Alaskan shoreline, and then turned back toward Kamchatka, discovering the Commander Islands. His efforts had irrevocably opened the Russian Far East and Russian America for development and trade—in particular, the fur trade, which continued to dominate the peninsula's economy until 1912, the year St. Petersburg banned the trapping of sable for three years to restore the species' population.

Surprisingly, no one showed much interest in the more available resource—salmon—until 1896, when the first fish processing plant, sponsored by the Japanese, was established at the mouth of the Kamchatka River, once the site of the peninsula's most prolific run. By the time the last Japanese left the peninsula thirty-one years later, Kamchatka had been thoroughly incorporated into the Soviet system, and both the salmon fishery and the sable trade were transformed into state monopolies. Kamchatkans were free to harvest as much salmon as they wanted until 1930, when the state's imposition of limits radically affected subsistence fishing, and by 1960 the official allowance, 60 kilos a year, was barely sufficient to keep a sled dog from starving. Meanwhile the commercial fishery was booming, and by 1990 Kamchatka's total annual salmon catch had increased from 30,000 tons to 1.5 million tons. As in Alaska, the fishery began to develop dry holes—a river here, a bay there, under severe pressure.

As Kamchatka receded behind the curtain of official xenophobia after World War II, Moscow rapidly developed the area's defenses—a submarine base in Avachinsky Bay; ICBM launch sites, satellite tracking stations, military outposts up and down its coastlines—and expected in return "gross output." Not just salmon and sable; now everything was up for grabs. By the late eighties, central Kamchatka's primary forests, 60 percent old-growth larch, were decimated; the Soviets had managed to annihilate Kamchatka's herring spawning grounds as well. Today, in a debauchery of joint ventures with foreign companies, Moscow has taken aim at the crab and pollock fisheries, at risk to suffer the same fate as the larch, the sable, the herring. Nor has the end of Communism spelled anything but crisis for Kamchatka's legendary brown bears. By 1997, the peninsula's Cold War population of grizzlies, an estimated 20,000 bears, had been halved by poachers and trophy hunters. At the rate things are going, says Boris Kopylov, the vice-director of Kamchatka's State Environmental Protection Committee, the most powerful federal agency mandated to preserve the peninsula's natural resources, "In the next five years all the endangered species will be at a critical level, the sea otters and bears especially." This year, the agency's staff was halved: Conservation law enforcement in remote areas vanished as helicopter patrols were reduced from 300 flying hours to zero, and the system, as Kopylov lamented, didn't work anymore. "If you want to save Kamchatka," said Robert Moiseev, one of the peninsula's leading environmental scientists, "You're welcome to pay for it."

Shortly after dawn, the criminals returned to collect us, a humorless sense of urgency in their manner. The chiefs were mightily vexed, they told us, having last night discovered that thieves had spirited away 1,200 kilos—one ton—of caviar the gang had cached on the beach.

"Check Rinat's knapsack," I said. The criminals smiled uneasily—heh-heh—and we loaded our gear into the skiff. I'd come to Kamchatka, twice, to fish, and so far I'd been allowed to do damn little of it. In July, a rafting trip on the Kamchatka River quickly devolved into some awful hybrid of absurdity—Samuel Beckett meets Jack London. The rafts were dry-rotted, the river had been dead for ten years, the mosquitoes were nightmarish, our fishing "guide" was actually a hawk-eyed *tayozhnik*, a taiga woodsman, who had given his stern heart to hunting and horses but had probably never seen a sportfisherman in his life.

On my second expedition to Kamchatka, the day I arrived in P-K from Anchorage an MI–2 helicopter crashed, killing everyone aboard, and I no longer had a ride to the mythical river up north. My local outfitter hadn't considered a Plan B. The only alternative, untested, that the outfitter could offer was for Rinat and me to head out to the coast and try to beg a lift across the tundra with anybody we could find in possession of a GTT—the acronym translated as "Tracks Vehicle: Heavy."

First we drove in Rinat's truck to a village south of P-K to collect Sergei, the wilderness guide, a Russian version of Bubba, attired in camouflage fatigues, who was an erstwhile law-enforcement officer for RIVOD, the peninsula's Fish Regulatory Board. He was now employed as a field worker by TINRO—the Pacific Scientific Research Institute of Fisheries and Oceanography, a state agency operating in association with the Russian Academy of Science but in cahoots with commercial interests. From 1990 to 1996, hard currency gushed in as TINRO became a clearinghouse for the avaricious flow of foreign investment into Kamchatka's fisheries. "Everybody in the institute got very rich. There was so much money they didn't know what to do with it," a TINRO scientist had told me. "The bosses built big dachas, bought expensive cars." The institute's sudden wealth finally attracted the attention of Moscow, which began sucking up 90 percent of the institute's revenues and controlling quotas.

Sergei, as a quasi-scientific government employee, was our insurance, along for the ride not only to steer us clear of official trouble, but to legitimize whatever it was we might end up doing that was a bit too *diki*—wild, independent—for the apparatchiks.

At the last town before the windswept barrenness of the coast, we turned down a dirt road toward a pre-Soviet Dogpatch, a cluster of clapboard and tar-papered houses, stopping in front of the first one we saw with a GTT in its yard. There on the wooden stoop was Misha, barefoot, wearing camouflage bib overalls, one of his forearms intricately tattooed. He could have been any midwestern hayseed waiting for the glory of team sport. Sergei hopped out, explained our mission, and offered to hire Misha and his machine.

"*Nyet*," insisted Misha. Money, he explained, was nothing to him; therefore, yes, he would take us up the coast, but as his guests. I had no way of measuring the offer and began to ask predictable questions, anticipating predictable answers. The house wasn't his, he said; he came here on the weekends from P-K with his friends to relax.

"What do you do in the city?"

"We are criminals," he replied. "Even the FBI knows about us."

"What'd you do," I joked naively, "sell missiles to Iran?"

Misha narrowed his eyes and demanded to know why I asked such a question. I swore I was only kidding around, and he studied me hard for a good long minute before his demeanor changed and, clapping me on the back, he decided, I suppose, that I was good entertainment out here in the hinterlands—an American writer dropped into his lap.

"Robert, you will write your story about me, you will put me on the cover of your magazine, you will tell the truth," he declared matter-of-factly, an extravagant display of hubris.

The truth, as I understood it, went something like this: Years ago Misha had committed a crime, the nature of which he refused to explain except obscurely. The old system—the commies, I suppose—threw him in jail in

Siberia for "not fitting in," where he fell in with like-minded troublemakers sharing grandiose, if not exactly morally based, ambitions for a better life. Most significantly, he connected with his fierce partner—let's call him Viktor, and then let's forget that we ever called him anything.

Gorbachev, perestroika, freedom, the implosion of the USSR, crony economics, the democracy scam—Misha and his Siberian Mafiya crew moved to Kamchatka and became underworld oligarchs. These were the days, the early nineties, of the *diki* Mafiya: no rules, every man for himself, and bodies in the streets. As best I could determine, Misha and friends privatized—seized—a huge tract of state property on the coast, an expansive fiefdom containing four or five rivers plus a processing plant, and went into the caviar business. Eventually the Mafiya and the government realized they had to coexist, so now, after massive greasing, the Mafiya had all the requisite documents and licenses they needed in order to legally do what they were doing—harvesting and processing an astonishing 30 tons of caviar a season to ship to their associates in Moscow.

"The Mafiya," explained Misha, "is a state within a state," and perhaps it was destined to morph into the state itself, because if the government ever tries to recover the properties and companies and concerns the Mafiya had sunk its claws into, "there will be a coup d'état," said Misha emphatically, "and there will be a civil war." Which was exactly the sort of dire prediction I'd been hearing from every upright citizen in Kamchatka throughout the week.

We went inside the austere little house, where Misha sat me down at the kitchen table and smothered me in hospitality, happily watching me shovel down the grub he set out—pasta with minced pork and silver salmon dumplings. Someone appeared with a large bowl of fresh curds and whey. Bonbons? asked Misha, sticking a box of chocolates in my face. Out came a bottle of Armenian brandy. The cross-cultural we-are-all-brothers stuff proceeded splendidly until I made the mistake of cussing.

"Blyat," I said—shit. I can't even remember about what.

"Robert," Misha objected, "don't hurt my ears with bad words. Real men," he admonished in his lullaby voice, "don't need to talk to each other this way."

In the morning, Misha double-checked the tide chart he carried folded in his wallet. "Robert, let's have one for the road," he said. What he meant was, Let's have one *bottle* for the *beginning* of the road. Aspirin and vodka, the breakfast of criminals. Afterward we mounted the GTT and crawled headfirst through the hatch covers into the cavernous interior. We bucked and roared out of town, across the east-west highway and onto the much-scarred tundra, stopping long enough for Misha, Rinat, and myself to climb up on the roof, where we each wrapped a hand around safety ropes and held on as the driver slammed the beast into gear and we slopped our way forward through the bogs.

An hour later we arrived at the coast, littered with the shabby sprawl of a government fish operation. We churned onward through the pebbly sand, the blue Sea of Okhotsk to our left, huge slabs of tundra peat eroding from coastal bluffs on our right. Misha, surveying his kingdom, took delight in pointing out the sights—white-tailed eagles swooping down out of the moody heavens, flocks of berry-fat ptarmigans tumbling clumsily out of the scrub, a pod of all-white beluga whales, scores of sea otters bobbing in the waves off a river mouth. We crossed another without a hitch and Misha happily announced that we were entering private property—his.

We saluted the first brigade of his workers, a motley crew of caviar cowboys. They looked like—and perhaps might someday soon be—partisan rebels in their black rubber waders, filthy overcoats, stubbled faces. We cracked open another bottle of vodka, ate lunch, and Misha wanted pictures, group pictures, buddy pictures, and I took out my camera. We went on, conferring with another survivalist cell of workers farther up the coast, always a guy with a rifle or shotgun standing nearby.

Misha had become a bit nervous, his bonhomie turned brittle. Somewhere up ahead was his jack-booted partner Viktor, who had outlawed alcohol in the camps. If you signed onto a brigade, if you were lucky enough to be asked, you came to work, worked yourself to numbing exhaustion, but after a 12-day cycle of setting nets, pulling nets, tearing the roe out of thousands of now-worthless salmon and processing the eggs into caviar, you went home with a small fortune—$1,500 a man. Then, and only then, you could drink your Russian self blind, for all Viktor cared.

Twenty minutes later, we came to a pair of Ural trucks ahead on the beach. "No pictures!" Misha warned as I followed him to the dune line, toward a storm-built village of wooden-hulled shipwrecks. At this moment I had to be honest with myself about Misha's character flaws relevant specifically to my presence there on the beach: His pride—he wanted to boast. His gregariousness—he wanted to be liked and appreciated. His generosity—he wanted everyone to understand he was a big man who looked after his own. Viktor, Misha's partner but apparently the first among equals, had no such flaws.

"Here is Viktor," said Misha. It wasn't an introduction. I glanced toward Viktor, who looked at me steadily, his round face icy with menace, and I immediately turned and walked away, careful not to acknowledge him, as he was so clearly offended by my existence. Misha had erred in bringing me here with my retinue, playing games when there was serious work to be done, caviar to salt, traitors to whack, and now he vied for Viktor's forbearance of this cardinal sin. When we rendezvoused with Misha back at the GTT, he was singing the same tune of camaraderie, but in a different key.

"Robert," he said, gazing meaningfully into my eyes, "don't write about us . . . or I will lose all respect for you," which I suppose is how a real man says I will have your ass.

Which brings everything back to this lagoon behind the Mafiya's northernmost outpost, where I stood that morning after my night out on the tundra with Rinat, not caring so much about how the treachery of the stolen caviar might somehow come crashing down on us when we reunited with Misha and Viktor at low tide, but instead far more concerned with my new belief that I was destined never to have a solid day of good fishing here in the angler's paradise of Kamchatka.

When Misha had dropped us here the previous afternoon, we'd spent a moment discussing the nature of things, fishwise. His men had gawked at me, the sportfisherman. Not a one had ever brought in a fish unless he had gaffed, gigged, netted, snagged, or somehow scooped it out of the water like a bear. When Misha finally understood the style of fishing I was intent on doing, he frowned.

"Nyet, nyet, nyet," he said. "Don't bring that here. We don't want catch-and-release here." We argued: If he kept harvesting the roe at such a pace, where would the fish be for his children, his grandchildren? "Robert,"—Misha smiled—"you and I alone are not going to solve this problem."

And then, too quick, always too quick, it was time to go. Back in Misha's orbit, the criminals actually were in high spirits. It had been a good season so far, the silvers were starting to arrive, and the interior of the GTT was packed solid with wooden casks of precious caviar.

"I don't like to catch fish," Misha said breezily. "I like to catch money."

Kamchatka's exploitation was both an old and a new story, but so was the campaign to preserve its wealth of resources. In 1996 Russia bequeathed more than one-fourth of Kamchatkan territory to the UN Development Programme. A stunning gift to mankind—a World Heritage site that includes the Kronotsky Biosphere Nature Preserve, 2.5 million acres of some of the most spectacular landscape on earth. The Kronotsky Preserve contains a geyser field that is second only to Yellowstone's, and the Uzon Caldera, filled with steam vents, smoking lakes, mud cauldrons, and dozens of hot springs. It also is home to three times as many grizzlies as in the entire Yellowstone ecosystem, plus the greatest known populations of Pacific and white-tailed eagles. The park has twenty-two volcanoes, including the Fuji-like Klyuchevskaya, 15,584 feet of elegant cone, the tallest active volcano in Asia or Europe.

Many Kamchatkans fear that, as the economy plummets and the country opens itself to the unchecked appetites of the free market, the peninsula's natural resources will be raided and areas like Kronotsky overrun by tourists. When I spoke with Boris Sinchenko, vice-governor of the Kamchatka region administration and one of the men at the helm of Kamchatka's future, he told me, "In five to ten years, we expect to host 5 to 10 million tourists annually and to have built the infrastructure to accommodate them. The territory is so large, we can easily lose 10 million people in its vastness."

Many Kamchatkans also harbor a corollary fear. The peninsula's total population is less than 500,000, three-quarters of which lives in or around

P-K. An environmental scientist told me with a shrug, "When's there's no electricity, the people say, 'We don't care about nature, give us heat!'" One day, Rinat had slapped an orange sticker on the front of my notebook, given to him by his ex-wife, who worked for a Canadian gold mining conglomerate: Hungry, Homeless, Need a Job? Call the Sierra Club, Ask About Their No Growth Policy. Only the most arrogant conservationist would demand that Kamchatkans remain impoverished in order to preserve their wonderland for a future less hopeless and bleak than the present. Talking with Sinchenko, however, I sensed there was something a bit cynical about signing over a quarter of the peninsula to the enviros at the UN, as if now that it had proved its enlightenment, the state had earned carte blanche to do what it pleased with the rest of its resources.

There were precedents for such cynicism. Twice, in the sixties and the eighties, the Soviets began to erect power plants on swift-flowing rivers inside or near the reserve, destroying spawning grounds and wasting millions of rubles. Nevertheless, a large hydroelectric project is under construction on the Tolmachevo River, and the gorgeous, fish-rich Bystraya River flowing through the village of Esso was stuck with a dam and power station. Sitting below the areas around Esso are some of the richest unmined gold deposits in the world. When I spoke with Boris Kopylov of the State Environmental Protection Committee, he mentioned that his agency had been successful in stopping exploratory drilling on west coast oil deposits and halting placer mining for gold near the mouth of the Kamchatka River, but it was clear that sooner or later the oil was going to be drilled and the Esso gold deposits were going to be extracted, ultimately endangering spawning grounds in central Kamchatka. "In previous years all the [environmental] agencies were completely against all exploration for gas, oil, and gold," said Kopylov. "Now our position is to change a little."

In the salmon fishery, the magnitude of greed, multiplied in many instances by a struggle for survival, was mind-boggling. "Illegal fishing out of Kamchatka yields $2 billion a year," David La Roche, a consultant for the UN's environmental mission to Kamchatka, told me over beers in a P-K café as we talked about the local flowchart for corruption. "The legal fisheries are yielding not as much."

The economic pressures that confront the ordinary Kamchatkan were made viscerally clear to me in July when I met Vladimir Anisimov, the headman of Apacha, a sprawling collective farm about 150 kilometers due west of P-K. A prosperous dairy farm until Gorbachev presided over the nation's demise, Apacha's ability to survive had seriously corroded, its herds whittled away by the state from four thousand to four hundred head, its buildings in sad disrepair. In desperation, the Apacha villagers had signed an experimental one-year contract with the Japanese to collect mushrooms, herbs, and fiddlehead ferns from the surrounding forest. And then, like almost every other collective in Kamchatka, Apacha had gone into the fishing business.

Everyone was waiting, waiting, for the fish to start their run, but when I returned to Apacha in September, I learned that, as in much of Alaska this summer, it never happened—the July run of salmon never really came in from the sea. Nobody in the village had been paid a wage in recent memory. Vladimir was at a loss; the collective hadn't netted half its quota of 1,200 tons when, if truth be told, it had counted on netting its legal quota and then doubling it with another thousand tons off the books, as is the common practice. Apacha was rotting on the hoof, the central government gnawing away at the resources that the people had struggled fifty years to create. Since the middle of August, the ruble had lost two-thirds of its value, and the last day I saw Vladimir, shops were empty of basic foodstuffs, and Apacha was without electricity because there wasn't any fuel to run its generator. Even in such dire straits, the kindness and generosity that all Kamchatkans had shown me did not abandon Vladimir, and he embarrassed me by siphoning gas out of his own vehicle so that I could go fishing.

Sergei, heretofore simply along for the ride, suddenly awoke to the idea that it was time to take control of our half-baked expedition, now that we had parted with the Mafiya and exhausted every option in our one and only plan to head north to that never-fished river. Pointing for Rinat to take a turnoff up ahead on the east-west road, Sergei allowed that if all I truly wanted to do was fish, then he had an idea that might finally relieve me of my obsession.

Sergei disappeared down a path. I sat in Rinat's diesel truck, praying that something good might come of this. Rinat wouldn't look at me, and I could hardly blame him. His country was falling apart around him, and he was stuck chauffeuring a sport-crazed American, one of the nominal victors in an ugly game we had all been forced to play. All he could do was resign himself to an even uglier truth—foreigners equal money equals hope: Drive on.

Sergei reemerged from the trees, beaming. He had a pal, the local *tayozhnik*, who owned a skiff and was caretaker of a hunting cabin about a half-hour's cruise downriver at the base of the mountains, at the mouth of a tributary as thick with char and *mikisha* (rainbows) as the main river itself was obscenely packed with the season's final run of pink salmon. The *tayozhnik* would be willing to take us there.

"But there's a problem," said Sergei, wincing. "No gasoline for the outboard motor."

Okay, that was a problem—there was only one gas station within 100 kilometers, and it was closed. We drove to a shack atop the bluff above an invisible river and picked up the *tayozhnik*, an unshaven backwoods gnome we might have roused from an Appalachian hollow, and together we traveled a half-hour to Apacha, where Vladimir, the destitute headman of his destitute people, came to our rescue with the siphoned gas. Two hours later, back on the bluff, while I repacked my gear for the boat, Sergei and the woodsman suddenly took off to run unspecified errands.

Rinat and I broke out the medicine and resigned ourselves to further delay. Then began the cirque surreal. First to wander across the clearing was a lugubrious old man who stood gaping at me with wet eyes, as if I were the Statue of Liberty. I passed him the bottle of vodka so that he might cheer up. Then a group of hooligans from Apacha screamed up in their battered sedan, disco blasting, apparently convinced we had come to the river to party. Obligingly, I passed around another bottle. Another hour ticked off the clock.

Sergei and the *tayozhnik* returned, followed in short order by a carload of RIVOD inspectors, blue lights flashing, replaced only a few minutes later by the militia, who sprang from their car patting their sidearms. Again, we passed the bottle.

Night was quickly falling. Just as I bent to hoist my duffel bag, a van rolled into the clearing and out flew a not unattractive woman in a track suit and designer eyeglasses. "I heard there was an American here!" she shouted breathlessly and, zeroing in, almost tackled me in her excitement. She dragged me back to the van and shoved me inside, where her three companions rolled their eyes with chagrin, handed me a plastic cup, and apologetically filled it with vodka. My abductor—Marguerite—knelt in front of me, her hands on my knees, babbling flirtatiously.

"What gives?" I said, utterly bewildered. She slipped a business card into my shirt pocket and pleaded that I allow her to represent me, refusing to hear my explanation that there was nothing to "represent." Okay, she said, let's do joint venture.

"Robert?" I heard Sergei calling me. They were ready to go, no more endless dicking around.

I tried to get up, but Marguerite pushed me back in my seat. I grabbed her hands, looked her in the eyes, and firmly declared, "I have to go fishing."

"Nyet," she cried, "nyet, nyet, nyet," and she kissed me. Her friends looked straight ahead, as if it were none of their business.

I lurched for the door, but she had me wrapped up. This couldn't be more bizarre, I told myself—until Marguerite began stuffing six-ounce cans of caviar into the pockets of my slicker. Okay, I said, if you want to come, fine, but I'm going fishing now. Marguerite relaxed just long enough for me to bolt out of the van, but there she was again, welded to my arm, attached to me in some frightening, unknowable way.

There was a quick, sharp exchange between her and the gnome, and the next I knew I was threading my way, alone and free, down the bluff through the darkening slope of stone birches. The air was warm, but when you inhaled it was the river you breathed, its mountain coldness, and I felt transcendentally refreshed. Then we were all in the boat, sans Marguerite, shoving off into the main current of this perfect river, the Plotnikova, clean and fast and wild enough for any harried soul.

We were carried forward on a swift flow of silver light, stars brightening in the deep blue overhead. Then the light died on the river too, just as the *tayozhnik* beached the bow on the top end of a long gravel bar, bellying out into the stream. It was too late, too dark, to forge on to the hunter's camp, and I said fine. Sergei begged off again, said he'd be back to pick us up tomorrow, and I said fine to that too. Rinat and I threw our gear ashore, and I pushed the skiff back into the current and then stood there, the black cold water swirling around my waders, singing praise on high for the incredible fact of my deliverance. This river made noise; this river sang.

We dug out our flashlights and dragged our packs about a hundred yards up from the water's edge to the trunk of a huge tree ripped from the riverbank and washed onto the bar. Rinat collected wood for a campfire, and soon we squatted in a private dome of firelight, watching a pot of water boil for tea. I hadn't eaten all day, and my stomach growled.

"Rinat, where's the food?"

He cleared his throat and confessed he'd given everything to the Mafiya, mumbling some ridiculous explanation about the code of the wilderness.

"Where's my candy?"

"I gave it to the criminals."

"You gave the Mafiya my candy! They had their own candy."

"It was the least we could do," said Rinat, "since, you know, they didn't kill us when you hurt their ears with bad words."

We rocked into each other with laughter, howling at the absurdities we had endured together. Our assorted adventures, supernaturally screwed up and filled with hazard, were over but for one true and honest day of fishing, out on the sheer edge of a magnificent world, in a nation going to hell. I patted my pocket for cigarettes and discovered a tin of Marguerite's caviar, Rinat produced a hunk of brown bread, and we ate. He rolled out his sleeping mat and bag and tucked himself into the tree trunk. "Let me apologize in advance," I said, "if the bears come to eat you."

And in the morning, the fish—like the trees and the gravel bar, like the screaming birds and humming bottleflies, like the sun and its petticoat of mists and everything else to be found in its rightful place—the fish were there. I had never seen anything remotely like it, the last days of an immense salmon run. What first struck me, as it hadn't last night, was the profound stench. The gravel island was carpeted with the carcasses of pink salmon—humpbacks—from the height of the run, one of the most concentrated runs in recent years, as if so many fish within its banks had made the river overflow. Now the slightest low spot on the island was pooled with rotting eggs where fish had spawned. Maggots were everywhere, a sprinkle of filthy snow across the rocks and mud and weeds, and dead fish everywhere, rimed with a crust of maggots. I slipped into my waders, walked down to the river through shoals of decomposing fish, and entered the water. Humpback salmon nosed my boots as they struggled wearily upstream; like the prows of sinking ships, the gasping jaws of debilitated male humpies poked out of the water as the fish drifted by, their milt spent, their energy spent, the last glimmer of life fading into the sweep of current. In the shallows, gulls sat atop spawned but still-living fish, tearing holes into the rosy flesh. Fish still fresh with purpose threw themselves into the air, I don't know why, but what I did know was that the salmon were bringing the infinite energy of the sea upriver, an intravenous delivery of nutrients funneling into the land, the animals, the insects and birdlife and the very trees.

Here, in a salmon, nature compressed the full breath of its expression, the terrible magnificence of its assault, and I stood in the current, mesmerized. On the far bank at the mouth of a tributary there were poachers. At first glance it seemed that they had built low bonfires on the opposite shore, the red flames licking and twisting, but where was the smoke? I wondered, and as I looked more deliberately I saw my mistake: The writhing flames were actually fish. One poacher worked at the base of the tall bank, poised like a heron above the stream, using a long staff to gaff salmon—females, hens—as they swam past and then flipping the fish overhead to a pile on the top of the bank, where his partner crouched, gutting out the roe.

When the spell broke, I sat down on a log and finally accomplished the one thing I had passionately desired to do for days, months, all my life: I rigged my fly rod for salmon fishing.

I decided to head down the bar to where the currents rejoined at the rapids below its downstream point, an eddy splitting off to create slack water. The island was probed by wayward, dead-end channels, trickling into basins where the sand had flooded out, and as I waded through the biggest pool scores of humpback salmon, coalesced into orgies of spawning, scurried before me in the foot-deep shallows like finned rats. In the deeper holes the season's last reds cruised lethargically in their scarlet and olive-green "wedding dresses," as the Kamchatkans call a fish's spawning colors. I sloshed onward to dry land, the fish gasping, the birds screaming, and everywhere the reek of creation.

On the tail of the bar I planted my feet in the muck and cast into a deep turquoise body of water that resembled nothing so much as an aquarium, waiting for the connection, that singular, ineffable tug that hooks a fisherman's hungry heart into whatever you want to call it—the spirit of the fish, the bigness of life or even the smallness, the euphoric, crazed brutality of existence, or simply a fight: the drama of the battle between man and his world. Not every cast, but most, ended with a fish on my hook, a glorious humpback, three to five pounds each, the hens painted in swaths of mulberry, green, and rose, the males beautifully grotesque with keel-like dorsal humps and hooked jaws like the beak of a raptor.

A day of humpies landed on flies here on this grand river was enough to quench my deepest craving for the sport, but then my rod bent from the pressure, the reel sang its lovely shrill song as the line escaped, and here came the silvers, big and angry, like bolts of electricity, filled with the power of the sea. Rinat finally joined me in this dance, and by the late afternoon, when Sergei and the *tayozhnik* returned, we had two fish apiece, the limit, silvers as long and fat as our thighs.

We gathered more wood, Rinat started the fire, and Sergei brought his cookpot from the boat. "I'm going to show you how to make a poachers' *ukhá*" [Russian fish soup], said Sergei, cutting off the salmon heads and tails and sliding them into the boiling pot with diced potatoes and onion and dill. I had caught dozens of pinks but kept only one, a female, and Sergei slit her belly to make instant caviar, unsacking the eggs into a bowl of heavily salted water.

We sat in the gravel with our backs propped against the fallen tree and gazed lazily out at the fast blue dazzle of the river, slurping our fish soup. A raft floated down from around the bend, paddled by two RIVOD officers. The poachers on the opposite shore vanished into the forest, the wardens paddled furiously into the tributary, and we listened as the crack of gunshots resonated over the river, here in the Wild East.

Sergei, waxing philosophical, quoted a poet: "It's impossible to understand Russia, only to believe in it." Then he lifted a spoon of caviar to my lips, and I recalled the last fish I had caught that day, a hen, which had no business hitting my fly, ripe as she was. When I brought her from the water she sprayed a stream of roe, an arc in the air like a chain of ruby moons, splashing over my feet onto this most eternal, unsettled world of the river.

Words Fail Me

James Kaplan

I would like to propose a theory. Recreational players of my vintage—those of us who came up in the great times between the beginning of the Open era and the end of the wood racquet days—have always had an active fantasy life when it comes to tennis. This, I believe, is because we grew into the sport at the last moment when it was possible to imagine (and I stress the word *imagine*) some points of connection between what professional players did on the court and what we did.

I have no idea what young recreational players fantasize about today. How can you even begin to think that what you're doing is in any way similar to what Andy Roddick or Taylor Dent do? Maybe this why my local public courts are so much emptier than they were twenty years ago.

I got a vivid sense of the stark divide between tennis's big-power present and the old days while working with John McEnroe on his autobiography, *You Cannot Be Serious*. John spoke almost wistfully of his stunning first encounters with Boris Becker in the mid-1980s, as John's days of greatness were starting to draw to a close, and Boris's were just beginning.

The young German's size and strength and athleticism, the hugeness of his serve—all were a harbinger of the game's future. And though McEnroe, genius that he was, found a few ways to counter Becker's game before hanging it up, the Brave New World had announced itself. Tennis had changed irrevocably.

Perhaps it was my well-preserved fantasy life from those wood-racquet days that gave me the temerity to ask John if he would play tennis with me—for the book, I hastened to add. My reasoning, and it made sense on the face of it, was that only by actually hitting balls with him could I get a true feeling for what made McEnroe uniquely McEnroe. My dreams of sort of, kind of, holding my own on a court with him—well, those were my own business.

Let me state my credentials. I am a good club player, a 4.0 most days, with flashes of 4.5 if the wind is right and the planets are aligned. Many of you are in precisely the same boat: You know what it feels like to hit the ball with power on both sides, and you can do all the other things, too— hit smashes and drop shots and kick serves and slice serves. Sometimes you can even do all these things on the same day. You might get a couple of games off the pro at your club, maybe even make him a little nervous. To use a mountaineering analogy, players like us walk the snowfields in the foothills of the Himalayas. Now and then we get up a few thousand feet. The rocky escarpments and icy peaks tower far overhead.

I had seen John play, up close, on a number of occasions. I knew that while there was power in his game, it wasn't the essence of his tennis—and that in any case it wasn't the kind of blistering, incomprehensible power of the young pros today. Between his scrawny torso and gray, receding hair, he certainly wasn't physically intimidating, though his presence was always edgy and challenging. Still, I talked myself into feeling like I could hit balls with him and not totally embarrass myself.

John happened to be in a good mood the day I made my modest proposal, and he surprised me by agreeing with a smile.

"Can you play?" he asked.

"A little," I said.

The venue was an indoor practice facility; the surface was red clay. I remember having the absurd thought that the slowness of the dirt would help me against John.

Please understand—I had to figure out a way to deal mentally with this occasion. *Try to have fun,* I told myself. *This will never happen again in your lifetime. Nervous? It's just John McEnroe . . . one of the greatest tennis players of all time.*

We suited up and walked into the court. Despite my strategizing, my heart was knocking. I tried to calm myself by remembering how nervous John told me he'd been the first time he played Jimmy Connors at Wimbledon, in 1977. He'd barely been able to breathe, he'd said. The thought didn't help me.

But as we began to rally, I realized in about 5 seconds that just as there is a world of difference between watching the pros play on TV and seeing them perform in person, there is a chasm between watching a pro play in person and actually playing with him. John hit the ball much harder and with more stinging spin than I had expected, and more consistently deep than anyone I'd ever hit against.

Even in the warm-up, every shot he hit landed within a foot of the baseline. As a result, I was immediately off-balance and sailing about 1 of every 3 balls long.

It didn't matter to John. Wherever I put it, he was there, more than ready. I began to see and maybe even comprehend his uncanny command of space, pace, spin, and speed. No matter how long or wide my errant shots went, he would find ways to return them beautifully and then effortlessly scurry back into position with those little cat steps of his.

It was when we began to play points, of course, that the juggernaut pulled away. Whatever John was playing that day—his A, B, or C game—was more than enough for me. "He can put the ball on a quarter," another former touring pro once told me, and now I could see that that was almost literally true. John aced me at will, in either corner of both boxes. As for my own serve—well, I was very proud not to have double-faulted away the entire match. The only way I can explain it is that in short order I simply ceased to imagine I could win a point.

Nor was John about to give me anything, either. He was all business that afternoon—beautiful to watch, but utterly methodical, efficient, and unsmiling. In fact, I'd never seen a less playful person on a tennis court. I suddenly remembered that one day I had asked him an odd question: Did he like playing tennis? He had thought about it for a second, and then, to my astonishment, told me that he'd never loved playing the game. Genius is strange. No matter who was on the other side of the net, John only knew one way to play—with total seriousness—and that tunnel vision was part of the reason for his success.

Still, I had my moment of glory, although I'm still not sure exactly how it happened. Late in the match, I aced him with a ball that may have skidded off the tape. But there was John McEnroe, whiffing—whiffing!—and giving me—me!—one of his looks. You know the one I mean. For just a second, fantasy and reality had met.

The ace was a lucky accident. But I'll treasure that look till the end of my days.

Tournament-Tough

Barbara Beckwith

The fifteen of us huddle under the dome of Terminal A at Boston's Logan Airport, swapping rumors. Rackets slung over our shoulders, we're sharing what we know about the teams we're up against. Portland's team from the West Coast looks like the strongest, with players mostly in their twenties or thirties. We're at least a decade older.

My squash buddy, Trish Johnston, is forty-one, and I am old enough to be her mother—sixty. We're both past the age when people tend to give up strenuous sports. Yet here we are, en route to the national women's squash team championships in Minneapolis.

"Attention, ladies and gentlemen," announces Eve, Trish's eight-year-old daughter, to the all-women crowd. She grips her mother's hairbrush like a microphone. "We're taking bets," she proclaims, "on who gets here next."

Eve's broadcast is the only media coverage our Massachusetts team's departure gets. Squash is not a high-profile sport in the United States. Until fairly recently, it was played almost exclusively by men in prep schools and private clubs. Few Americans have played the game or even watched it. I myself did not see squash played until after Title IX widened opportunities for women in school and college sports, and women joined clubs where they could learn traditionally male sports.

Trish and I did not go to prep school. We've played squash for only four years. This is our first national tournament. We'll be up against the best amateur players in the United States. I tell myself that I'm going to learn, but I'm as eager as any other player to win. I want Trish to win, too. And I want Eve to see her do it.

Staying cool is my goal. Squash is a head game as well as a body game. Power and speed count. But strategy and placement count more. That's why I managed to take up this sport at midlife and do well. I have beaten players half my age. When I place the ball strategically, my shots are un-gettable and I win the game.

Trish wins, too, especially when she's in the right mindset. But competition has not come easy to either of us. We women over thirty-five did not grow up competing. To win, we must get tournament-tough.

"I'll play—but only if we don't keep score," Trish declared when we first played squash four years ago. I, too, wanted to play "just for fun." I'd just learned the game but, like Trish, was leery of competition. We both assumed it would spoil our pleasure. Side by side on adjacent courts, we played solo squash, ignoring each other's presence.

Our club's pro urged us to play together. I liked Trish's Aussie accent, her flyaway hair, her graceful strokes. Her daughter, Eve, watched us play and called me "Gramma." Still, we refused to count points. We didn't want winners and losers.

The pro pressed us to play "real games." Once we dared keep score, we discovered that we liked it. Counting points made us want to win, which made us run faster, leap farther, and hit deeper. We focused more. We started to hit balls *away from* instead of *to* each other—the point, after all, in squash. We learned and then perfected strategic shots—high cross-courts, tricky boasts, and feathery drop shots. We realized that scoring improved our game.

Warming to competition, we challenged other players. But we soon noticed an odd gender difference. Women players at our club—at least those of us over thirty-five—tended to play the sport differently from men. Male players vied to dominate the game by playing in the center of the court. We women gave our opponents too wide a berth, placing ourselves at a disadvantage for the next shot. We let the loser of one game start the next, defying the rule that gives the service advantage to the winner. We replayed the shot if a player got hit; protocol says the struck player is at fault and must give up a point. We rarely called "let"—interference—and lost points as a result.

When we played "soft" like this, our game suffered. So, Trish and I vowed to play the sport tough and right.

We started to play male players to give us experience in returning hard fast balls. We challenged women players rated at higher levels. We jock-eyed for center court. We lifted weights. We cross-trained. We played to exhaustion and then said, "Let's do 2 more games for stamina."

Trish eventually pulled ahead of me. But I stayed close at her heels. I fought her speed with my wits. We stayed squash buddies. Each of us wanted to win; each of us wanted the other to win as well.

When a poster announced a round robin—with prizes for the winners— we signed up. It was our first official competition. Trish's stomach churned before her first game, but she managed to calm down and win a trophy. I reached the semifinals—no trophy but a slot on the winner's roster. The next fall, we organized a women's team. We played against six other clubs around the state. By the second season, our team won the tournament.

Statewide contests are one thing. The national competition we're en route to is another. In addition, Trish will play a step above the level at which she usually competes. Just before the trip, a more advanced player dropped out. The state captain asked for someone from Trish's level to fill the slot. One by one, the players refused to be "bumped up." Trish, ever obliging— she's a mother, after all—volunteered to bump herself up.

When she's at her best, Trish plays a fluid and strategic game. She re-laxes and moves with ease. She lobs balls so high that they kiss the wall and die in a corner. She feints impressively, setting up for long drives, then switching to tricky corner shots.

And she outsmarts other players. "I never know what she's going to do," her opponents say. When Trish is "on," she's graceful, unpredict-able, and elusive.

BARBARA BECKWITH

Trish wants to inspire Eve. She hopes her daughter will see her win—or at least play her best. The idea of being trounced bothers Trish. But the competition she and I face in Minneapolis—players both younger and more experienced that we are—will be tough.

Our first morning in Minneapolis, Trish and Eve join us for a pretournament breakfast. Trish had a bad night. The rest of us are bunked together, but because Trish brought Eve, they'd been shunted off to a private room. Trish had looked forward to gossipy swapping of training tips and shampoos. She needed that banter to lighten the tension building inside her.

What's more, Eve's "gigapet" electronic toy started beeping in the middle of the night. Trish pushed the "feed me" button to turn it off, then lay awake the rest of the night. She pictured high lobs leading her to victory, then feeble serves leaving her scoreless.

Bagels and banter at breakfast revive Trish. We all trade aches and pains. "My foot is killing me," I moan. "I'm glad they don't do blood tests," says a player on medication for shin pain and asthma. "I'd flunk."

Our talk is an odd reversal of male locker-room bravado. Each of us vies for underdog. "I'm going to be the fodder," says a top-seeded player. "I'll get my butt kicked," says Wendy. It's as if talk of defeat will free us to give our all. Eve licks frosting off a Pop-Tart and listens. I wonder what she's learning.

As girls, Trish and I both loved sports but didn't take competition seriously. Trish grew up in Australia, where every town had public squash courts. Squash looked sweaty and male to her. She never bothered to learn. Instead she played field hockey just for fun.

Growing up in New Jersey, I thought of squash as an almost mythical sport, like polo, that rich guys played. I, too, played hockey, and won "good sportsmanship" awards because I didn't care if I won or lost. As an adult, I hiked, biked, rock-climbed, skiied, and jogged—always for fun. In my forties, back pain slowed me to a walk. At fifty-six, I joined a sports club, determined to recover my athletic self.

Trish, meanwhile, spent her twenties traveling, carrying her hockey stick with her although her only exercise was waitressing. In her thirties, she settled down in Boston, and found herself driving her two kids to after-school sports but playing none of her own. At age thirty-six, Trish joined a sports club. Doctor's orders—her blood pressure was far too high. She planned to swim a few laps, then soak in the hot tub.

On the way to the pool, Trish and I, about a week apart, spotted the row of glassed-in squash courts. For Trish, it was a familiar sight. Except that now she saw women playing the game. Yes, they were sweaty, but sweat was "in"—this was the nineties. Trish was intrigued.

To me, squash was a revelation. I had never seen such an exciting sport. The play was fast and fierce, delicate and graceful. I wanted that grace. I asked the squash pro to teach me the basics. Trish did, too. We both declared we were playing "just for fun."

Trish heads out early for her first match. I come along to support her. Eve skips ahead, swinging a backpack loaded with games. The other Massachusetts players are warming up. Trish checks out the international courts: they're three feet wider than the older and narrower American-sized courts we play on back East.

Our first opponents, the Pittsburgh team, appear with their trainer. Trish and I have no professional backing. Our club dropped its squash pro a year ago. We've been winging it ever since, coaching each other, and training together.

Eve stares at the Pittsburgh players. Their muscular thighs attest to constant lunging after balls. Her mother and I stare, too: their training clearly surpasses ours. Eve pops gum in her mouth and sits on the floor by Trish's court. Taking Crayolas from her backpack, she sketches the scene.

Trish grips the terrycloth binding of the quality-brand racket she bought when she committed herself to playing competitive squash. She fastens her hair with a pink plastic comb, then slams a series of hard shots to warm up the ball. The hollow rubber sphere speeds up as it heats. A squash ball can travel over 100 mph in top matches.

"I love this sport," says Trish in a loud voice, as if to encourage herself. A woman in neon-green tights steps onto the court and warms up as well. Her hair is wild and red. Her stroke is controlled and strong.

The game begins. Trish's mouth is open and relaxed at first. It soon clamps shut. The redhead delivers a wicked serve. Trish returns it, but weakly. Her opponent slams a winning shot. Trish panics. She retreats to the backcourt. She hits defensive shots. She forgets her winning kiss-the-wall-and-die lob.

Games between equally matched players can last up to 35 minutes. Trish loses hers in under 5. "Is it *over?*" asks Eve.

"Think of it as a warm-up," I say. "You have 3 matches to go." I want Trish to stay positive. A few minutes later, I lose my first match, too. "Ohmygod, they're *good*," I say. So this is what great squash looks like, I think. Discipline, that's what we'll get from this weekend. When we get home, we'll train harder. I tell myself that I did well for a sixty-year-old. For Trish, who is younger, it's tougher to lose.

I remind her that if we're outmatched in muscle power, we can still win by using our wits. Squash is a kind of chess—at high speed. The player who decides in a microsecond where to strategically place a shot can win any rally.

Trish's second opponent trounces her and so does mine. "I was blown away," gasps Trish, red-faced and teary-eyed. Eve looks at her mother's face, then looks away. Her shoulders droop. She blows her gum bigger and bigger until it collapses onto her cheeks.

Our team gathers at each break to swap tournament tips. "Play each shot as if it's the first." "Play hard, stay calm." Players traditionally use these sayings like mantras, and they often work. Trish doesn't seem to hear them.

Opponents as well as teammates offer advice. A Texan in her forties tells us she plays only men to prepare for the hardest-hitting women at tournaments. She starts her training sessions with 100 sprints up and down the court. I'm impressed. "We can do that," I say to Trish. But she remains glum. "It's humiliating," she says.

Trish considers skipping tomorrow's matches and flying home tonight.

Instead, we join our teammates to load up on carbohydrates—and more team talk. "I've had a disastrous day," says one top player, who'd lost her first match, "but outside of that, I'm fine." Trish does not get it—how can you lose and laugh? She's focused on regret: Why had she agreed to be bumped up to higher level of play? "I was a jerk to play nicey-nice," she says.

The next day, at breakfast, Trish's usually bouncy hair hangs lank—she hasn't bothered to wash it. Her mood has plummeted. She doesn't take her allotted 5 minutes to warm up on the court. "Why kill myself?" she says.

At the courts, Eve joins a mix of players from different teams as they go through their exercise routine. She copies their movements: 10 sit-ups, 10 push-ups. To get through the last 5, she cheats a little, propping her knees on the floor. "Push-ups are hard," she says.

Eve swims and can dive, she's tried squash and she's starting hockey this year. She may decide to work hard at a sport, hard enough to excel, or she may not. This weekend, she's seeing more women exert themselves more fully than she's ever seen before. She's watching her mother as well. Trish could be a model for Eve—or not.

To let Trish focus on her upcoming match, I say to Eve, "Let's hit a few." She leaps from the floor, grabs a racket, and skips onto an empty court. I feed her balls. She misses the first but returns most others. I'm impressed by her strong forehand, her careful preparation for each stroke, and her easy movements around the court.

"You're good!" I tell Eve. "I can tell you've had lessons." But she suddenly hesitates, her pleasure compromised. "I feel sorry for the guy that teaches me," she says. "He must be bored, just feeding me balls, feeding me balls."

Trish checks the tournament lineup and finds something new to worry about. Her next game is scheduled for a court opposite the bleachers, which means it will draw the largest number of spectators. She now frets about being watched as she is beaten.

I'm getting fed up. "Forget the onlookers," I tell her. "Forget your opponent. The game is between you and the ball." The Texan finishes my rap. "Losing is what you do on the way to winning. Get used to it, Trish," she scolds. "I've played tournaments where I won no points." Trish looks stunned.

Trish's third game unfolds like the first two. Her opponent wins but is gracious, shaking Trish's hand and chatting before they leave the court. Still, Trish exits red-faced and distraught. That evening, she meets up with our state coach in the cramped space of the ladies' room between toilets and sink. "I'm being blown away!" Trish blurts out. "And this was supposed to be fun!"

Word gets out: Trish is demoralized. One player offers to take Eve swimming so Trish can be with her teammates. The next and final day of the tournament, the Massachusetts players find time, between their own matches, to shower Trish with encouragement. "If you're outmatched," says the most experienced competitor, "try to win 1 game. If you can't win a game, go for 1 point. If you can't get a point, try to keep the ball in play."

Trish is thinking about everything and everyone but her own game. She now worries that she may not even give her final opponent the workout she expects. She's haunted by the memory of a player at a Boston match who, after trouncing a lesser player, griped loudly to onlookers: "I never even worked up a sweat."

One minute till game time. Trish's final match. Eve sits up front but buries her head in a book. I don't think she wants to watch.

Trish slumps on the bench outside the court, brooding. She stares at the terrycloth binding of her racket handle. "My binding's too fat," she announces. Grasping a corner of her binding she jerks hard. The fuzzy strip falls to the floor.

"What are you *doing?*" I cry, aghast. Trish's handle, shiny with glue, is down to the basics. It's time to play.

Trish grins as she jogs toward the court, hand and racket fused for this one match. "It's a job that's got to be done," she declares to no one in particular. She's found words that work for her.

Five minutes into the final match, Trish is sweating. But so is her opponent. Each rally lasts several minutes. Trish plays her lovely lob—the one she's famous for back home—and wins points. From the bleachers, her teammates yell, "Good shot!" and when she misses, "Good try!" Eve looks up from her thriller.

During each break in the 3-game match, a cluster of teammates surrounds Trish, whispering suggestions.

Trish leaps back onto the court. She manages to keep the ball away from her opponent's backhand. She forces the play over to her own stronger side.

Trish loses her final match. But she doesn't mind. She'd returned the ball well. She'd won the serve often. She'd earned—with her tricky corner shots and loops lobs—almost half the number of points her opponent won. Trish had played her best. "Finally," she tells me, "I was in the game."

"The last 3 points were awesome," Eve yells.

The next day, we Massachusetts players sprawl across the hotel lobby sofas as we wait for the airport van. Our shoes are off, our feet propped on sports bags, our bodies limp.

Eve, however, has energy to spare. One of Trish's teammates heaves herself off the sofa, shoves a pile of sports bags into a row, and says, "Let's do hurdles." She and Eve leap over them. We cheer, Trish's teammate moves the bags farther apart. "Now let's try this!" she says. And the two leap over the barriers as far as they can go.

Race a Memorable First for 17th Man

Ron C. Judd

Onboard *USA-67*

They told me where not to put my hands. If I could only figure out where not to put the rest of me.

Out here on the angry waters where the America's Cup will be won, a strong nor'westerly has kicked up, bringing with it swells of 6 to 10 feet. We are powering upwind through a 17-knot breeze in USA-67, the sleek blue-and-black boat representing Seattle's hopes for sailing's greatest prize.

An Aussie is at the wheel. Kiwis are at the grinders. About $100,000 worth of sails are snapping and popping overhead. I'm sprawled spread-eagle astern, flat on my back, arms clutching a rail overhead, feet against the other side. Hanging on for dear life. Wishing, like a freshly gaffed ling cod, for that sweet, final bonk on the head.

On upwind legs in heavy seas, riding as the "17th man" observer in the back of the OneWorld boat is a little like trying to stay seated in the middle of the bed of a pickup truck careening down a mountain pass. Each time the boat tacks, I spin around on my weather-suited body's stern end and point my bow the other way, struggling to stay on the uphill side of a deck slanting what for all the world seems like 45 degrees.

"Bad wave coming!" yells a gray-jumpsuited crewman.

They don't kid about these things.

Ka-whump! The big, blue boat slams into it, blasting spray and sending a tsunami into the back of the boat, my little nesting place for the most fantastic two-hour ride of my life.

Here's the thing: No matter how wet, windy, turbulent, or tumultuous it would get this day, I kept catching glimpses of myself in crewmen's sunglasses to realize something I couldn't have dreamed: I never stopped grinning.

Which is saying something, considering how this thrill ride came to be, when the phone rang at 8:30 this morning.

"Ron," declared the voice of Bob Ratliffe, OneWorld's executive director. "Your country needs you."

My mind spun.

"The crew has specifically requested you," Ratliffe continued.

They probably wanted some quick-witted repartee to entertain the troops. Or an opportunity to absorb some of my, ahem, extensive sailing knowledge. Or . . .

"It's blowing big today. They need you as ballast."

He was serious.

I hesitated. See, I can get seasick staring into a chai tea latte whipped up by a light westerly breeze off the coast of Lake Sammamish. And given this day's blustery forecast, lunch could be lost.

But Ratliffe was persistent: OneWorld was up against Prada of Italy, the defending Louis Vuitton Cup champion. And the forecast called for breezes of 25 to 30 knots.

In sailboat racing, extra weight on the deck is actually a good thing in heavy winds. And it just so happened that I had trained extra hard all week for this gig, with a rigorous ballast-boosting training regimen that included ordering extra hollandaise sauce on my daily Eggs Benedict.

I felt rested. Ready. Bulky. Needed. I swallowed hard. "I'll be there," I blurted.

Two hours later, after signing release forms I am fairly certain included the words "last rites" and "not our bloody fault," we were racing toward

RON C. JUDD

New Zealand's Hauraki Gulf in an inflatable chase boat, careening off green, wind-whipped waves bigger than Range Rovers.

Before I had a chance to rethink things, I was being transferred, along with other cargo, onto another inflatable, which caught up with One-World just outside the race course. In rolling seas, connecting with the big sailboat is not unlike an aerial refueling operation: A delicate dance in which the heaving chase boat makes contact with a heaving race yacht, then presses hard at midship while the transfer is made.

Skipper Peter Gilmour greeted me with a firm handshake, and quickly showed me the ropes. Namely, the halyards and lines to avoid.

"We've already lost one finger on this boat," he pointed out, matter-of-factly, tapping on a block. Say no more, captain.

With the start rapidly approaching, crewman Brian Ledbetter of Seattle popped back to offer some valuable advice. He outlined a 3-by-4-foot area where, essentially, nothing can kill you, and you can't screw anything up. At the start, he said, get in it, crouch on all fours like an animal, and hang on.

Ninety seconds later, I saw what he meant. Prada's *Luna Rossa* and our boat circled each other like 25-ton house cats in a shoebox, their crewmen shouting in Italian, our crewmen shouting in Aussie, Kiwi, Japanese, and Ballard American English.*

The start is the one part of the race when the other boat is in close quarters, its reactions completely unpredictable. It is a total, undeniable rush.

At one point, our boat was bearing away from the start area and I completely lost track of the *Luna Rossa*—only to turn and see the gray bow headed dead for my head, less than a dozen yards away. "Stern! Watch the stern!" someone shouted. They veered off, barely, and our young Aussie helmsman, James Spithill, made a smart tack and bee-lined for the start, with another crewman counting down the seconds to another trademark OneWorld clean start.

Life gets a little more normal when the race is on. I scrunched up into

Ballard is a neighborhood in the America's Cup host city of Seattle.

position against the uphill side of the boat, watching the crew work its magic as we tacked upwind on a hard sideways slant.

It's clear that too much credit is given to the boat design; too little to the crew. Their clean, athletic movements in this precarious, upwind dance/slugfest—throughout which the boat's carbon-fiber hull and titanium rigging moan and screech in protest over high tensions and heavy loads—is a sight to behold.

Everyone is doing at least two things at once, monitoring their own equipment—and every single perceived movement of the opposing boat. After each tack is called and flawlessly performed, crewmen shuffle silently back to their posts—heads and bodies low to the deck, anything to reduce drag.

Before you know it, crewman Tatsuya Wakinaga is calling off boat lengths to the first upwind mark: "Four . . . three . . . two . . . one!" Synchronized chaos ensues as the boat tacks gracefully around the mark. Every man aboard, it seems, grabs on to a grinder and cranks furiously, at the same time keeping a careful eye on *Luna Rossa*, at this point still clinging within shouting distance to our port side.

At times like these, communication is constant. Some crewmen wear wireless headsets to receive commands from the helm. But most striking is the way they seem to read each other's minds, communicating through smooth movements honed by months of practice. When a small mistake is made on this boat, nobody yells to point it out. Everybody feels it, files it away—and goes on. It's the stuff for dissection later, on the tow in, not blame games in the middle of a race.

Magically and instantly, the spinnaker billows and we're running with the wind. Downwind runs, by comparison, are pure serenity—a chance to catch your breath. Seated cross-legged, facing astern on the deck, I watch in wonder as the big boat, under full sail, surfs down those big, whitecapped Hauraki Gulf waves with graceful, almost silent, ease.

On these runs, Aussies Gilmour, facing astern, and Spithill, steering forward, seem to have a unique language of navigation and wind. Gilmour, the coach/general manager of this team, constantly scans the horizon to the rear, watching for puffs of wind, or, on this day, particularly strong swells to steer into and ride like a body surfer.

"Big puff coming in five, Jimmy," he says calmly to Spithill. The grinders roll, the sail is trimmed—and, like magic, you feel the boat surge with that puff, pushing forward like a revved-up car with the parking brake removed.

"Nice gain on that one," Gilmour says calmly, then adds, "Big wave on the side, Jimmy." Spithill turns slightly into it, and again, you feel the boat rise almost imperceptibly, riding the crest downwind with a perceptible forward surge.

It's pure magic.

It was so transfixing downwind and so tumultuous upwind that, 90 minutes into the race, it occurred to me I'd been riding on such sensory overload, I'd never even had time to think about getting seasick. I felt good—and lucky.

At the finish line, the crew is subdued. A handshake here, a "nice race" there. If you weren't listening closely, you'd never know we'd crossed the line.

By the time Luna Rossa gets there, OneWorld's chase boat is pulling alongside with lunch and fresh water. Everyone dresses down and relaxes. On the hour-long tow into port, Gilmour and the crew casually discuss what went well, and what needs work. They swap tales about life in Auckland, life in Seattle and the next opponent.

It's just another day at the office for Seattle's America's Cup syndicate. And a lifetime memory for me. At the dock, I thank Gilmour and crew for the ride, telling the skipper if he needs the big ballast, he knows where to call.

As I climb off the boat, I tell one crewman a part of USA-67 will always stay with me—and a part of me will always stay with it.

He thought I was waxing philosophic. But I really meant it. Years from now, when USA-67 is decommissioned, having fought and won many a battle at sea, I'm fairly certain of one thing: They'll still find traces of my fingernails on that black nonslip deck.

Cry Me a River

Zachary Michael Jack

> Shall I part my hair behind? Do I dare to eat a peach?
> I shall wear white flannel trousers, and walk upon the beach.
> I have heard the mermaids singing, each to each.
> I do not think that they will sing to me.
> —From "The Love Song of J. Alfred Prufrock"

My Best Gal and I arrive at the low-slung, windowless affair billing itself as "the state's largest home-owned discount store," Paul's Discount, in the Mississippi River town of Clinton, Iowa.

We are boat shopping for a sporty afternoon cum Indian summer fling. Our budget is $30, our mission, impossible: to secure an inflatable watercraft worthy of the log-jammed, crooked neck, 10-mile slither of the Wapsipinicon River between the unincorporated "towns" of Oxford Mills and Toronto in far eastern Iowa. A has-been sports editor and a lover too long on the disabled list, I have vowed to redress both problem reps in one fell swoop.

During my university days, fueled by alter ego, I boated, floated, and toasted parts of Britain, Ireland, and Europe. I soloed many of the world's most romantic rivers: Dublin's Liffey, London's Thames, France's Seine, and Italy's Adige, along whose banks the world's most famous doomed lovers, Romeo and Juliet, tragically soliloquized. After college, predictably drifting, I rafted whitewater and from the Adirondacks to the Ozarks. Once, in my late twenties, I even made pilgrimage to the sacred waters of Mexico's Lake Patzcuaro, believed by its people to be the very center of the world, the *axis mundi*.

But I'm no water baby, baby. I set myself adrift, over and over, for the same, twisted reason Superman juggles Kryptonite. I measure my self-worth via sick antithesis. Any legit yardstick must be a world of wind and weather, of unanticipated calamity—not my pencil-pushing existence but the milieu of my Iowa farm father who doubled as a sailor and a scuba diver. In such patriarchal waters, I am blissfully, tragically beset—a poor swimmer though an otherwise good athlete. I am out of my element, the equivalent of a point guard working his weak hand, going to his left, haunting the gym until he exercises, exorcises, the weakness.

In my thirties now, I wade through seas more mundane—a flood of bills, a "three-hour tour" commute, a rising tide of other erosive domesticities. More than ever I seek waters deep enough to drown in.

And so, this fall, wishing for more dramatic stuff, I turn to my own backyard, to Iowa's fabled Wapsipinicon, to the river named in the Ojibwe for the homely wild artichoke. This time I plan to surrender the oars but take a first mate. I plan to divest myself of paddle, rudder, and sail—make it *sporting*. I'll nix the power-trip, eshew all instruments of control with the same, giddy reluctance my fellow Gen Xers surrender their Blackberries and G.P.S.es. I will give myself to her, the Wapsi. I will *go with the flow*.

She may not serve up epic chop and spume, but she is untamed, unwieldy—totally uncouth. She'll have to undo.

An hour's worth of quasi-journalistic phone calling earlier in the morning had established Paul's Discount as the only store in hard luck Clinton-on-the-Mississippi still audacious enough, in this late season, to stock inflatable rafts of the kind typically reserved for sinking ships.

In the summer, clean-up hitters for the Texas Rangers Class A farm club, the Clinton Lumber Kings, go yard to the Ol' Miss. Today, the Midwest League season more than a month in the books, it still feels like July. The asphalt parking lot at Paul's Discount positively bakes, sending blacktop mirages shimmering toward the heavens. The flies celebrate their Indian summer luck with one last round of catch-as-catch-can sex. Inside, the air-conditioning is on. Strangely, it is mid October out.

My Best Gal's a Southside Chicago girl, though she spent summers at her family's vacation place up in the Northwoods. I'm a rock-solid, farm-bred, land-loving Sagittarius; she's a water-loving, belly-laughing, good-timey Gemini. After just a few months of dating, I have learned defer to her on the vagaries of watersport and the inscrutable managerial tactics of Ozzie Guillen.

Today, in Paul's cramped aisles, we snag a couple of cheap, Day-Glo orange life vests. We pass on the Bullfrog, Deep Woods Off, and Mag-Lite.

What about paddles, Best Gal wants to know.

"Nay," I say, playing Parliamentarian. "This is a float down the Wapsi," I remind her, "not a row down the Charles." She wrinkles her nose. "This is the Big Ten, Sister, not the Ivy League."

Life vests in tow, we navigate toward the till where we're given the "do you kids know what you're doing" look perfected by late-season hardware marms in paint aisles.

Per our phone call, the good folks at Paul's Discount have set the Super Carvelle, three-person boat by Sevylor, aside for us at check-out. It's as good as drive-up liquor: we leave with the goods in a brown paper bag, no questions asked.

The box features a handsome couple floating tropical waters. The man, a dead ringer for *Dukes of Hazzard* co-hunk John Synder (that's Bo Duke to you and me) oars shirtless while his bikini-clad mate leans back, arms comfortably at her side like she's chilling poolside in an inflatable lazy-boy.

"See there," I tell Best Gal—B.G. for short—once we've wrestled the inflatable dinghy into the backseat of her big-ass, late Reagan era Thunderbird. "Piece of cake. The box has instructions in six languages, including Greek. Clearly this Super Carvelle by Sevylor is a boat that gets around." In the lower left-hand corner of the box, the safety-minded people at Sevylor

U.S.A. Inc., Los Angeles, California, remind: *This is not a life-saving device. Do not leave child unattended while in use.*

"Looks like I'll have to go with you after all," B.G. quips.

We land-locked Americans seem forever flummoxed by this simple fact: the majority of our countrymen boast Big Water right out their back door. More than half live in counties along the Coasts or Great Lakes. Curiously, however, the call of water lapping doesn't extend, at least not in the agrarian Midwest, to riverfront property. In farm-grounded Iowa, where dams lay low rather than large, rivers pose perennial problems: "Trouble, Right here in River City!" as Harold barks it out in that staple of Iowa camp, Meredith Willson's *The Music Man.*

On the ground in Iowa, trouble with a capital "T" means one year in ten you can't farm river bottomland. If you live in a flood plane, you're on your own, bub. The insurance man in town crosses to the other side of the street when he sees you coming.

In late winter, the National Weather Service warns of ice floes as the untamed Wapsi wakes up, breaks up, starting in Minnesota. In late spring, the same fickle meteorologists issue flood warnings up and down the ungovernable stretch. In drought-prone summers, would-be recreators face a different predicament—low water—leaving the river rats no choice but a pathetic, bottom-scraping doggie paddle in lieu of proper submersion. In July silted-in shallows thwart even the leanest of lean-back baptisms, while the river depths birth unseen whirlpools. Bait. And switch.

As any self-respecting Hawkeye knows, Iowa means "Land between Two Rivers"—the Missouri on the left bank and the Mississippi on the right. It's a state where decisions come bundled in convenient twos: International or John Deere, Hawkeye or Cyclone, Paper or Plastic? Meanwhile, Iowa's "lesser" tributaries lurk just out of sight, subversive streaks of gray.

Here I am, a thirty-something-year-old man-child testing the waters of a serious courtship for the first time in almost half a decade. I am, as the saying goes, getting my feet wet. Years ago, I hung up my pica ruler and waded into the swirling, piranha-infested waters of academe, giving up the title sports editor for one that featured a built-in slight, the diminutive *junior professor*. Sadly, the shoe seemed to fit. I realize now, with chagrin, that I have not floated a river, any river, since ordering my regalia.

This fall base camp is Lost Nation, Iowa, a woebegone agrarian town where the grain elevator and redbrick schoolhouse dominate the skyline and the inky Wapsipinicon River greases the woody sloughs south of town. I moved here to be closer to my father and the rest of the family barely hanging on to our farm in nearby Mechanicsville. I moved here because of a name, *Lost Nation*—wistfulness personified, like naming a town *Last Stand* or *WouldaCouldaShoulda*.

When midwestern writer Carol Bly first moved to Madison, Minnesota, a town like mine, in the early 1970s, she dubbed it, quoting F. Scott Fitzgerald, a "Lost Swede Town." In the dispatches to Minnesota Public Radio that followed, she commented on the "sexual chill" of the place, a physical and emotional remoteness.

Lost Nation, Iowa, I am learning, makes stoical Madison, Minnesota, look like the Haight-Ashbury. I have not joined in a playful, collaborative romp beneath the Pleasure Dome, inclusive of sex and pick-up basketball, in many moons.

The *Lost Nation Quasquicentennial, 1872–1997* chapter entitled "How Did It Get Its Name?" posits several, conflicting legends for the appellation *Lost Nation*—first that a German named Baum hunted for long-gone relatives here and, when asked where on god's green earth he was going, said he was looking for his "lost nation." Other possible explanations involve wayfaring Canucks and poetically inclined sportsmen struck dumb by the beauty of the open prairie before them, a dreamy lost nation. Without so much as a whiff of irony, *Quasquicentennial* sums up the competing theories thusly: "There are other stories, all concerning someone or something being lost."

I have become a metaphor incarnate, a *lost nation* made flesh.

Like the forgotten towns through which it passes, the Wapsipinicon River has fallen into profound, glorious neglect. Rising in Mower County, Minnesota, it enters Iowa in Mitchell County on a 225-mile romp to the Mississippi

River. Roughly 98 percent of the land along its banks amounts to row crops, forest, or grasslands—a solid, nearly undeveloped green corridor stretching across two states. The Wapsi, bless its soul, is a rogue.

Populated by low-minded loafers, cockfighters, rattlesnake rustlers, and ginseng thieves, Cedar Rapids, Iowa, writer Jay Sigmund's 1927 story collection, *Wapsipinicon Tales*, proves the point. The based-on-real-life Iowa towns of Sigmund's yarns are described, respectively, as "dilapidated" and "dead holes." Even the farms are "poor Wapsipinicon hill farms."

I've drawn up our sports adventure to follow a trail still warm from the pages of *Wapsipinicon Tales*, taking my Best Gal and me between burgs still looking for a little R-E-S-P-E-C-T—or at least a P.O.—seventy-five years later.

We will shove off from unincorporated Oxford Mills astern the old, crumbling mill, pass under the bridge in unincorporated Masillon, our halfway point, and float to unincorporated Toronto—a trinity of Iowa towns making up the Hawkeye State's own Bermuda Triangle. The backwaters on our Land of the Lost tour boast a Max Spookiness Factor. Chances are good we'll see no one en route.

Then as now, the hauntingly beautiful Wapsipinicon doubles as illicit watering hole and dumping ground, a depository for a farm state's secret shame: unwanted litters, chemical run-off, bloated livestock, flotillas of Bud. In a single weekend in 2006, volunteers removed six tons of trash from the lower Wapsi. A partial list of recovered items included 1 wheelchair, 4 toilet seats, 1 rubber ducky, 28 metal fence posts, 1 porch swing, 1 clevis hitch, 1 hog waterer, 1 sickle blade, 6 lawn chairs, 2 television sets, and 1 Jimmy Hoffa—okay, everything but Hoffa. Every so often a disconsolate farmer adds to the tonnage by driving his Chevy down into the muck.

But the Waspi and its ilk also host miracles, beget jewels. In Sigmund's *Wapsipinicon Tales*, as in real life, river pearls gleam. Mussels abound. Glow worms fantastically phosphoresce. Though Sigmund's river rats live in a despoiled Eden, it is an Eden all the same. So I imagine the wheelchairs yearly dredged from the Wapsi are jettisoned because their owners raise their hands toward the Iowa heavens, and—*Praise Jesus!*—walk for the first time in years.

By contrast, the Mississippi crowds out the miraculous. From Iowa south it buzzes with grain barges, floating casinos, and Joe Blow powerboats. As rivers go, it is a buxom, platinum blond with too many nips and tucks. It is locked up, metered out.

I'll take the Wapsi. A river barely dammed. A river a man can travel for miles and not see a soul save his own.

Now, watching the air pump bring the Super Carvelle by Sevylor to life beside the muddy Wapsi, I am beset by deeply symbolic, borderline Freudian anxieties: *My skills have grown rusty . . . It is too late to put-in . . . the boat's too small for two.* The raft bobs amiably in the slow current, wanting our shoes and socks to come off. Bare-footed, we take Crocs, baseball caps, and long-sleeves in case the sun gets too hot.

We are a Jimmy Buffet song playing in the Tall Corn State.

When we shove off, the river is a picture of autumnal mildness. Paddle-free, we let it take us, side to side and in circles, so that half the time one of us faces backward, looking west, watching the afternoon sun burn mid-sky. We are flip sides of a coin, my Best Gal and I, two sides of an argument, and head over heels. Like a tandem Halloween costume, I am the ass-end. Then we hit an eddy and I am swung around to become head honcho again.

And we are alone—so perfectly, pacifically alone I wonder whether I've already failed in my quest to recover my masculine mojo, to get my Hemingwayesque blood up. Considering the Wapsi's slower than expected trickle as it floats our boat, I worry that our sporty river run might turn leisure cruise. Rafting's a real enough sport, I assure myself. It boasts all the bona fides: national competitions and a governing body. But where, pray tell, are the Jack Nicholsons in the stands, the Paula Abduls on the sidelines, the John 3:16s beyond the gallery ropes?

Trailblazing, that's what Best Gal and I are doing, taking the sport back to its roots, jettisoning the PowerBars and paddles, racing daylight rather than rivals. Golf, after all, doesn't cease to be a sport when Jim and Judy hack it around in the couples night twilight. Take Jim and Judy's ho-hum round and add a delicious twist—swapping out a driver for a Coke bottle, say, as a young Lee Trevino used to do—and, voila, you've

ZACHARY MICHAEL JACK

created a subsport, by Zeus, more challenging, more difficult, and more miscegenatingly wicked than its starched collar parent. Ergo, remote river rafting sans guide, map, oars . . . common sense.

Here's how we roll: The person facing downriver assumes the duties of helmsman and lookout, scanning the surface for snags, eyeing the roiling, chocolate-colored water for signs of submerged limbs akimbo. When, inevitably, the Wapsi shoves us first against one bank and then another, we push off with our legs, scissor kicking off the trunks of trees teetering on the edge. We are forever in danger of puncture, and, by consequence, of shipwreck.

The nearest town offering what motor club's used to quaintly call "services" stands miles behind us now, upriver, well out of sight behind a thick curtain of forest and field. The river slips between black dirt banks and the beige, vegetative wall that is an Iowa cornfield aching for harvest.

If you float it, they will come.

A guy in his early thirties is a paradox, especially so if he's a sports fan. A decade or so removed from college, he becomes a dues payer, a boatswain, a deck-swabber. By day, he entertains the siren song of his still-limitless potential. By night, he double checks his charts, scratching his head. His participations mingle curiously with non-participations. Hope flirts with hopelessness, passiveness with aggressiveness,

The athletes he admires on TV *negotiate* defenses, *respond* to pressure, *overcome* obstacles—the action verbs perfect bullet points in somebody else's slam-dunk resumé. The consummate sportsman *goes with the flow*, managing, paradoxically, to *direct traffic*. The language of successful performance at office, stadium, boardroom or bedroom strikes him, egad, as navigational.

It is in these treacherous waters, where powerfulness swirls with powerlessness, that I have been swimming this fall. For these and other reasons, I've come to float the Wild Artichoke.

Moooooo. Best Gal apes the Holsteins chewing their cud on the south bank. She takes her shirt off, crumpling the bra starboard. She is not bronzed or well endowed but she is beautiful somehow, a bob-haired, sunshiny mix two parts Gidget and one part Elizabeth Swann.

I have the Wapsi to thank for B.G's unexpected toplessness. In a state with more land under cultivation than anywhere else in America, Iowa makes it exceedingly difficult to go native, to get naked. Farmhouses, standing sentry, chaperone virtually every square mile, party pooping. The corn has ears.

On a warm summer night, supply and demand in my land-locked State says there'll be a run on the precious few swimming holes and farm ponds suitable for skinny-dipping. Merely ordinary Iowa rivers, spanned by bridges every few miles, caution rather than compel the exhibitionist: to float in the nude on a regular river is simply to curve inexorably toward new purview, new perverts. The Wild Artichoke, though, thwarts all killjoys and puritans. It's as secret as sin.

Bare-chested, Best Gal aims to be a pirate. Her occupational fantasies include sea shanties and plenty of yo-ho-ho. She favors a life of few complications and easy pillage. When she speaks of the future, she speaks of obtaining a "pirate ship" or at least a "good sloop."

"What'll we call this 'ere skiff, matie?" she brogues. Every good pirate ship, she insists, needs a name.

"Try me," I say.
"Wapsipiniconator?"
"Muy Schwarzenegger."
"Silent Sloop?"
"Too Dashielle Hammett."
"Belle Weather?"
"Tres Frenchy."
"Hell-bent?"
"Some poor schmuck's attempt at a double entendre."
"Arggh," she says.

Because I can, I squeeze her gooseflesh between my toes. The toes, I discover, are far from the tensile, highly erotic sensors they're rumored to be in late night comedy sketches. The permanent calluses I've built up from years of pick-up basketball numb the feel I'm copping.

"How about USS *Kingfisher*," I say drawing out the aspirate "s" in *Fisher*, like in the old, plosive peanut commercials.

The kingfishers, after all, have Maydayed our muddy river all afternoon, trash talking as they emerge with their catch. Their squat bodies, needle-nose beaks, and jaunty, flaunty aeronautics, make them pathetically comic in a Woody sort of way—Woodpecker, Harrelson, or Allen.

"Yes," she says, rolling it around on her tongue. "King-fissshh-er it tissss."

In *Cratylus*, Plato attributes the Doctrine of Flux and the Identity of Opposites to the Greek philosopher Heraclitus, writing, "Heraclitus, I believe, says that all things go and nothing stays, and comparing existence to the flow of a river, he says you could not step twice into the same river." While the profs dicker about what Heraclitus actually did say, Plato and Aristotle agree wholeheartedly on one thing: Heraclitus sunk the battleship that was the Law of Non-Contradiction.

Was it not a mind-blowing contradiction, after all, that the river could be the same and yet other? If a man could never dip his foot in the same river twice, was it because he was not the same man, because these were not the same waters, or because this was not the same river? Heraclitus, the smarty pants profs maintain, earns a spot on the All-Philosophy team—Heraclitus, expert in waking us up from "dogmatic slumbers," master of breaking down defenses.

Philosopher or no, a guy sleepwalks through his twenties. He maybe marries, gets a job, does or doesn't have kids, depending. And at the end of it all—the mortgaging, the procreating, the joyless maintenancing—he misses the jostling fraternity of the gym.

He abandons the living room, then, for the locker room. He learns to tie flies and stands knee-deep in some dumb river. He sets himself adrift on the shoulders of a stream and lets it take him. He wallows seven years in the bed of a nymph, dreaming of Penelope.

His letting go is not a surrender exactly, but a double dare. If the gods have designs on his hearth and home, he says bring it, and drives the lane, hard.

Either way, life or death, the water promises a quick exit. It runs past his boyhood, to his father, who he remembers as its absolute master. The river inscribes, he learns, operating as both knife and stylus.

In popular psychology, a man's desire still charts a watery course. Man-detractors point to a love of sport as Exhibit A in the dumb sublimation of the male appetite, the not-so-subtle channeling of his animal desire. The language leveled against him suggests some specious, libidinous flow moving subterraneously, ceaselessly, forever threatening to undermine his nobler intentions or wreck him on the rocks, à la Odysseus.

And yet, truth be known, Odysseus was a lover, not a fighter, a farmer and a sailor before he turned reluctant warrior. In life's biggest passages, forsooth, the boatman assumes the rudder as the true man's man, a Cap'n Jack Sparrow capable of embracing flux, cannibalizing contradiction. While the warrior denies his rival by destroying him; the boatman, like the yeoman farmer, barters with god and nature, acknowledging both as givens. The boatman's is not a passive existence, not exactly, but a life in which circum surrounds everything he does; he circumscribes, circumnavigates, circumvents, becomes, at last, circumspect.

In my days as a newspaper sports editor, agitated, middle-aged dads used to spin down before me like tops, typically red-faced, either angry at their inability to help Telemachus sink a free-throw on court, or crowing with pride on nights when the kid was money. Even my own father, a reticent Iowa farmer, suffered the same for me once in a memorable come-to-Jesus speech with my baseball coach. I was being slighted, my pop thought, sure that his rhetoric would cause Coach to have a Homeric epiphany and come up with something like, "No, friends, I would not like to bench Telemachus, it is a fearful thing to bench one of the royal line."

I remember one dad in particular, drifting toward me at halftime of a hotly contested district playoff game. I was sitting alone, striving for omniscience, objectivity, as any young sports journalist would.

"You must be blind," he sniffed, "to be missing my boy."

Telemachus was a sophomore back then, a blond, silky-smooth, six-foot-five with a soft jumper and a Pippen-esque glide. He was a perimeter player, a floating, fitful scorer.

Best Gal wants to know how much further now, but I'm pleading the fifth. "There be squalls ahead," she mutters.

I am making rough calculations. At best we have an hour and a half of sunlight to work with, afterglow included. The current in this log-jammed middle passage of the Wapsi I estimate at 1, maybe 2 miles per hour, tops. We put in shortly before 2:00 p.m. By my reckoning, then, we have rafted four pathetically circumambulatory miles in roughly four hours.

"Massillon must be just around this bend," I tell her, though I am not hopeful. The balloon of our burgeoning romance has begun to burst. Her wet shirt is back on now, though the discarded bra still floats in the bilge water at the bottom of the *Kingfisher*.

Outside the boat, the air is crisp, hug-your-honey high school football weather.

We pass a deserted dirt road, nothing more than a path, really, beneath some ancient cottonwoods. Best Gal recommends we take our chances with the overland route, à la Marco Polo.

"If we walk, we'll have the boat to carry and all of our stuff."

"Doable," she says.

" Do you know where we are?"

"Nope."

"Well then," I say, "we stick to the river."

If we can make it to our halfway point, Massillon, I assure her, we'll bum a ride to Toronto to pick up her T-bird.

"You promise?"

"Promise."

It's a plan. We are the oarless, we are the walrus, coo, coo coo choo.

To be a boy growing up on the banks of a muddy midwestern river is to know both fear and fascination. The great Nebraska Poet Laureate and adventurer-journalist John Neihardt, author of the famous *Black Elks Speaks*, grew up with the Missouri River, and it marked him. In his all-but-forgotten

1911 account of canoeing the Missouri, *The River and I*, Neihardt recalls his first exposure to the river as a six-year-old whippersnapper: "There was a dreadful fascination about it," he writes, "the fascination of all huge and irresistible things. I had caught my first wee glimpse into the infinite."

For Neihardt, the river was an epic, a giant, a sublime terror that made him "reach up to the saving forefinger of my father, lest this insane devil-thing before me should suddenly develop an unreasoning hunger for little boys." Neihardt recalls looking down at his turbulent river from the bluffs overlooking Kansas City: "My father seemed as tall as Alexander—and quite as courageous. He seemed to fear it almost not at all. And I should have felt little surprise had he taken me in his arms and stepped easily over that mile or so of liquid madness. He talked calmly about it—quite calmly. He explained at what angle one should hold one's body in the current, and how one should conduct one's legs and arms in the whirlpools, providing one should swim across . . . . Swim across! Why, it took a giant even to talk that way!"

Three quarters of a century after Niehardt and his small crew plied the Missouri River from Fort Benton, Montana, to Sioux City, Iowa, in a 20-foot oak and cypress canoe dubbed "The Atom," participatory journalist Eddie L. Harris took a page from Neihardt's playbook and canoed the length of the Mighty Miss from its pure, Lutheran source at Lake Ithasca, Minnesota, to its dirty mouth at New Orleans.

A St. Louis native like poet T.S. Eliot, who once called the Mississippi a "strong, brown god," Harris opens his travelogue with a memory of river barges loaded with grain and coal and "sins and salvation, dreams and adventures, and destiny. As a child I feared this river and respected it more than I feared God. As an adult now I fear it even more." Echoing Neihardt and Eliot, sometimes to the letter, Harris concludes, "the river in my memory flows brown and heavy and slow, seemingly lazy but always busy with barges and tugs, always working—like my father—always traveling, always awesome and intimidating."

When I first came toe to toe with a river of my own, I, too, was fatherless. My mother had separated from my dad, temporarily as it would turn out, my sister and I in tow. She rented the cheapest roof over our heads she could find, a dive along the Iowa River on Sand Road, where our backyard plunged directly into the swollen Iowa River.

When times were good, we ate grilled cheese and coleslaw together as a family on the porch at our uncle's business, Sutliff Bar and Grill in Sutliff, Iowa, an unincorporated town hard on the banks of the Cedar River near the family farm. When times were bad, my mom, my sister, and I escaped via the Sutliff Bridge en route to Iowa City and Sand Road, holding our breath as the tires of our oversized Olds 88 thwacked the Sutliff Bridge's loose wood planks like a vibraphone.

My pioneer forebears knew these riverbank communities as bustling places back in the days when river waters powered mills in the summer, and, in winter, froze to ice for harvest. Nowadays, such places have become déclassé. In my home county alone a half dozen unincorporated river outposts hug eroded banks, making Sutliff just one of a type where history's cruel twists are more easily swallowed with beer and sport. The Sutliff Bar and Grill of my youth, I realize, bellwethered economic hard times to come, presciently serving up the twin opiates of hooch and sport before "sports bars" existed.

In my youth, the "Sutliff Open" drew crowds to watch drunken, driver-wielding river-rat patrons tee off across the muddy "water hazard" that was the Cedar River. Anyone could enter, and, in my youth, anyone did. There was no lay-up, no lagging, no hanging on to third prize. Just Bubba-golfer John Daly's gospel: *Grip it and rip it*. In the Sutliff Open, in those days, you were either wet or dry, up or down, in or out. When I was handed, as a young grasshopper, a mud-splattered driver and aimed for the opposite bank, I took my first swing at participatory sports journalism.

Contemplating his own canoe trip down the Mississippi, participatory journalist Eddie Harris wrote: "I stand at that magical age, thirty, when a man stops to take stock of his life and he reflects on all the young man's dreams that won't come true. No climbs up Everest, no try-out with the Yankees, no great American novel."

So Telemachus comes to the water's edge and pauses, wondering how it all came to pass.

In the *Kingfisher* now, Best Gal begins to cry, quietly at first, then in great, gasping kid-sobs. Darkness descends. In the eddy where the river doglegs we wallow, pinballing haplessly between shallows and sandbars.

I pull the becalmed boat by a rope tied to the bow. With the B.G's dead weight and a half a boat full of bilge, it is, as the Sec. Def. would say, a tough slog. Every third step, it seems, I trudge into a hole in the river bottom and sink in up to my chin. Best Gal's teeth have begun to chatter behind me like some chintzy Halloween skeleton's, involuntarily clacking. I am pulling like a Borax mule, but I don't know what toward.

Our participation—my participation—has ceased to be a story. It has become a matter of survival. I am on the edge of hypothermia.

Still the stars overhead effervesce, the silence broken only by the periodic *whoop-whoop-whoop* of a crane tenderfooting the banks. In the half hour since sunset, the water below my chest has begun to feel warm, inviting as a bath. Above the nipple, the chill night air raises goosebumps. We have not seen a house or road for over an hour.

Cruel, self-incriminating man-guilt settles over me, dark as night. *What did I have to prove? I should have known better. I am a jackass. Christ, it's the Wapsi not the goddamn Colorado.*

Self-loathing comes in waves, mixing curiously with the adrenaline whose job it is to tell my body it isn't freezing, hasn't had enough. With the rope cutting my shoulder, I feel like a lusty, low-born Egyptian pulling Cleopatra through the cold night air along the Nile, playing Billy Joel to her Christie Brinkley. Along the bank, the jackals do-wa-diddy.

But I'm no Downtown Man. Instead, I am a shivering wreck for the first time in my adult life. Compared to air, the river seems so invitingly tepid I think seriously of laying down in it.

Somewhere in the far reaches of my brain an alarm sounds.

"I've got to get out of the water," I tell Best Gal. "We've got to get out!"

Wordlessly, we ditch the *Kingfisher* on the left bank, grabbing only the essentials—Crocs, keys—and scramble up into the undergrowth. Dark forest envelopes us. Far off, I think I hear the *slap-slap-slap* of car tires thumping a bridge. I offer my hand to B.G, and together we plunge into the woods. I shudder over and over, so close to the edge of hypothermia now I can't feel the brambles puncturing my skin. Still, I am leading, absorbing the blows.

Our lazy river run has become a sudden-death, moonless bushwhack.

An hour later, we come to a small clearing in the woods and take stock. I am cut like a prizefighter, a trickle of blood oozing from my check and from a gash above my eye.

"We could try to sleep," I hear myself say to Best Gal in a voice that sounds like a reasonable stranger's. "Lay down here and wait for daylight."

"But we'll *freeze*." Best Gal's voice is pleading, forceful. For the first time I am aware that I am in the presence of a strong woman, a woman with the ability to rally.

She guides my hand to the small of her back, to where she has gathered the wet folds of her tee behind her, Daisy Duke style, only in reverse. At another time, the gesture would strike me sexy, but not now. In the forest, we are no longer would-be lovers, but Hansel and Gretel, brother and sister in a hell of a pinch.

For the next hour, we inch forward into the void illuminated by our sole source of light: Best Gal's tiny keychain diode. The banks of the Wapsi offer no footpaths and no clearings, only sinkholes, wash-outs, barbwire, and low limbs. Step by Frankenstein step, we move forward into the breach, take the beating.

I have known this sightlessness before, I realize, as a child, when, for giggles, my cousins and I used to turn off the lights and close our eyes like blind beggars in our grandmother's back hall, creeping forward with our arms out like Karloff's mummy, the rest of us heckling and grabbling like so many ghouls.

"Listen," Best Gal says, cupping her ear to the darkness.

In the distance we hear what sounds like the gunning of a late-night hot rod. It approaches and recedes, an airplane turning lazy circles over a deserted island.

We hear it again, radial tires on grooved concrete, we hope, followed by a change in pitch, then back again to the tonic note.

The bridge!

I begin to run. Best Gal falls in behind me, weaving her ring finger around my belt loop. Hunched over and hustling like two unarmed soldiers in a war zone, we head for the distant, stockade outline of a tallgrass field ahead.

An acres-long trudge later, the tallgrass parts and we emerge, blinkered, in a starlit pasture. Several hundred yards in front of us, a late-night love car traces a sharp curve of blacktop, its headlights banking widely.

At the sight of civilization, we break into a desperate run for the highway and the bridge we recognize now as Massillon, our halfway point.

"I could call someone," I offer, breathlessly, though the words feel hollow. Crossing the bridge and heading toward town, I, not long of Lost Nation, rifle through the Rolodex of people-to-call-in-case-of-an-emergency. There are single friends an hour's drive away in Iowa City, doubtless out on this, a Saturday night smack-dab in the middle of football season. There are married friends, too, likewise an hour away, snuggled up on the couch, probably watching a romantic comedy. Then there is my father, less than a half hour down the road. He would have fallen into wine-dark slumber hours ago, sinking into the fitful, nervous sleep of a lifelong farmer. I imagine how this would appear to him: his half-naked, bloodied son, his half-naked son's would-be girlfriend, and the backwater of Massillon, Iowa, by midnight.

Describing Odysseus's reunion with his son, Telemachus, in *The Odyssey*, Homer doubtless elicits the first universal guy-cry in Western literature, the great Ur-blubber still heard wherever men gather to watch *Hoosiers* or *Field of Dreams*: "Loud were the cries," writes the blind poet, "and more unceasing than those of birds, ospreys, or crook-clawed vultures when farmers take away their young before the wings are grown; so pitifully fell the tears beneath their brows." In answer to Telemachus's awestruck incredulity at the old man's resurrection, Odysseus asks his number one son, "Why liken me to immortals? I am your father, him for whom you have sighed and suffered long, enduring outrage at the hands of men."

I cannot call my dad. I will not call my dad. Sand-caked and bloody under Massillon's only streetlight, I am outraged—first at my cowardice, then at the river, finally at all substitutes and surrogates—plastic, twenty-first century "epics" with disposable rafts where once were oceangoing vessels, divorce-wrecked fathers and sons where once were storm-tossed heroes. I am author again with a vengeance, rewriting the story as if fresh from some Lost Nation's golden age: Odysseus and the Chip Off the Ol' Block lovingly restore the classic Chevy; Senior and Junior work on the give and go out back; Big O. and Little T., partners forever, hoist the *Sloop John B.*

In my adapted *Odyssey*, old Odysseus is omnipresent, supremely competent, bloody confident. Restored, our heroes regain the rep they enjoyed in antiquity: odds-beaters, world-changers, brothers to the last. The slaying of the usurpers and the reclamation of the martial bed, the Big O. declares, will be a strictly father and son affair, all others be damned: "Come tell me the number of the suitors," the Big. O. says, "that I may know how many and what sort of men they are . . . we can meet them quite alone, without allies."

So deep is my revisionist's dream that it takes a minute or two walking the shoulder of the road into town to let the blood drain down, to accept the fact that my cocaptain in tonight's trial is not my father, not anyone's father. She has breasts. Woman breasts. And I am responsible for her, not out of any man-obligation, though there is some of that, but out of respect.

"What're we going to say?" Best Gal asks, desperation once again creeping into her voice. "Look at us!"

"We'll knock on a door . . . . We'll tell them we put in late and had to cut our trip short . . . that our car is in Toronto."

"Won't they ask about a boat?"

"We'll tell them it was an inflatable, that it wasn't worth saving."

We ring the doorbell at the first house with lights on, determined to project two aw-shucks kids in over their heads.

We watch a woman's silhouette approach, wait hopefully as her shadow wrestles with the heavy deadbolt. "Let me do the talking," B.G. whispers as the door creaks open, the light from inside spilling out.

The woman listens to our story, occasionally glancing over her shoulder to where her children have left the television to gawk at what the night dredged up. Best Gal's building up expertly to her coup de grace, floating the idea of a ride to her T-bird downriver.

Her request hangs in the air, then drops, a dead duck.

Have we tried the house down the road, the woman at the door wants to know. We haven't, not yet.

The door closes then, quietly but firmly. No apologies. No good lucks. No come on in and use the phone. No pull up a chair to the fire, you poor, poor dears.

The house down the road turns out to be an old farmhouse and barn cobbled together into a singularly creepy domicile. A weathered sign out front advertises "Dried Goods" and "Specialties." I wonder whether "specialties" include ax murder and frontal lobotomy.

Though the large man who answers our knock bears a frightening resemblance to Sloth's mom, Momma Fratelli, in *The Goonies*, his voice is warm, kindly. Behind him, a white-haired woman, a wife or girlfriend perhaps, hovers in a gossamer nightgown. Her hair, combed Victorian straight, falls at her waist.

The man listens to our story, nods slowly, and disappears again, leaving the door ajar as he consults with the wife-mother-apparition. We see her nod assent, and he reappears with two threadbare beach towels. He says stay put; he'll warm up the station wagon. We wrap the towels around us and shiver, idiot sailors hauled in by the Coast Guard.

The rescue wagon, a woodie, kicks up some serious dust as we fishtail the gravel backroads on our way downriver to Toronto. The ride takes less than ten minutes. I ride shotgun, making man-talk with our savior and leaving a wet circle on his car seat when I get out, minutes later, to shake his hand. Best Gal asks for his address. She'd like to send him a thank you card. He has done something noble, she says, even heroic.

We drive the T-bird back to my Toyota in silence. "This is the worst night of my life," Best Gal informs me. As a would-be boyfriend, sportsman, and sports journalist, it is understood that I am failure, thrice damned.

When we get back to my place in Lost Nation, we layer in earnest—winter coats, wool socks, long underwear, gloves. Still, we shiver. We get as close to the space heater as the laws of flammability allow. We make nachos in the toaster oven, and let the imitation cheese burn our mouths.

Afterward, still frozen, we shower together—the water heater otherwise one and done. We turn the water to scalding and take turns standing under the stream. Every few minutes, we tap one another on the shoulder, politely cutting in. It is a sexless, soapless affair. We dry off in separate rooms and sleep without touching on the carpeted floor by the space heater. Our ears burn.

In the morning, we wake up late, sore and out of sorts. I insist we go back and recover the *Kingfisher*.

"You don't want it to fall into enemy hands, do you?" I ask.

In part, I want to purge last night's nightmare, replace it with the sunnier vision of a lazy, sun-dappled river at noontime. By my accounting, the night before we had walked the woods—freezing, wet, and mostly naked—for almost two hours.

I monitor the mortal coil with a mixture of journalistic interest and maternal devotion. I am waiting for my body to rebel—for some knee-jerk, parasympathetic response to too many hours on the edge of endurance and now to too little sleep. I do not comprehend, as a real athlete would, how the body balances its ledger—what penalty it exacts for redlining.

We park the car on the shoulder at the foot of the Massillon Bridge and weave our way through the underbrush, picking our way through the brambles in a fraction of last night's time. We travel west along the north bank, retracing our steps, half-expecting to see a yellow, deflated dinghy around every river bend. We never do.

In *The River and I*, cub journalist John Neihardt waxes poetic before tackling the mighty Missouri with his mates, writing, "Here is the concrete representation of the earnest desire, the momentarily frustrated purpose, the beating at bars, the breathless fighting, the sobbing of the wind-broken runner, the anger, the madness, the laughter. And in it all, the unwearying urge of a purpose."

The raft, nimble as its namesake, eludes us to the last. Best Gal and I idle a minute at a sandbar, two scavenger hunt dropouts. We bury our feet in the sand, watch a small crab attempt the steep bank, over and over, the fine particles continually giving way under its claws.

We hold hands lightly, and, for the first time in 24 hours, we laugh—deeply

and involuntarily—at the gonzo sports journalism of nocturnal river rafting, at last night's buck nakedness, at my hauling her ass down the Wapsi
by rope. At the *Kingfisher* and the bitch that was our float down the Wild
Artichoke. We laugh until the tears well up and the opposite bank becomes
a platonic blur.

We laugh until it hurts.

Shuffleboard and The Future of the Sport

Rodney Rothman

Shuffleboard

For the last three days Abe hasn't been around, so we've been playing shuffleboard, just the three of us: Jimmy, Vince, and I. God, I miss Abe. He has a stabilizing effect on the rest of us because he's the sweetest man alive—tall, gentle, and with the voice of a 1940s cartoon dog. With Abe gone, Jimmy is less lovable and gets to indulge his cranky side. It's worst when it's sunny and the tennis courts next to us are full of players. Jimmy calls it "a hundred heart attacks waiting to happen." Vince, meanwhile, has become even more of a hard ass. He's been riding me, criticizing my grasp of the rules, mechanics, and strategy of the game. I'm sorry; the sport. It's not a game. Don't say "game" unless you want Vince to yell at you.

I'd been showing up at the clubhouse for two weeks straight, hoping for an opening on the tennis courts. Most retirees I know play tennis, and it seemed like a sport I could dominate more easily than softball. My two athletic advantages—brute force and uncontrolled manic energy—can take you pretty far in a sport like tennis. But breaking in proved impossible. The tennis courts were always packed. In the rare event of a fill-in being needed, it became a who-you-know game, so I always ended up watching. Every day I would look over and see Jimmy, Vince, and Abe playing shuffleboard. They're the only ones playing next to nine empty shuffleboard courts. I was curious, but too many young people, when they heard I was living in Century Village,* had jokingly asked whether I was playing shuffleboard. It's the big retirement community cliché. I'd long ago resolved to move beyond it.

Finally, after days of no tennis, I wandered over to the shuffleboard courts. Vince was smart. He drew back and let Abe and Jimmy engage me in conversation. They asked if I'd ever played shuffleboard and I said, "Not since I was a kid." They spoke about the sport with sincerity and eloquence: how relaxing it is, how strategic it is, how it challenges both the mind and body. It appealed to everything I'd been reading about how you age more slowly if you stay sharp physically and mentally. They made shuffleboard seem like exercise for realists.

Then they adopted a self-deprecating tone. Jimmy said that people erroneously believe that shuffleboard players are foolish and ancient, that they "have one foot in the grave and another foot on a banana peel. Grave, sure. But you see a banana peel around here?" He laughed, and I laughed, although I'm still not sure what the joke meant.

Abe and Jimmy are both in their late eighties, and Vince is in his midsixties. He played tennis until a leg injury forced him into a more low-impact sport. He's kind of like a former N BA player who gets injured and has to go play pro ball in Kazakhstan.

Eventually they got around to asking me if I wanted to join them for a match. I checked the action back on the tennis courts. Still too busy. It hadn't yet occurred to me that Jimmy and Abe were lifelong professional salesmen who had been laying down a sales pitch, and that now they were closing.

Jimmy and Abe spend a few minutes teaching me the rudiments of the game. They keep it simple, at first. You and your opponent take turns pushing eight molded plastic discs down a cement lane with lightweight aluminum cues. At the end of the lane there is an upside-down triangle

A Florida retirement community.

RODNEY ROTHMAN

with numbers written in it: 10, 8, 7, and –10. You're trying to land your discs in the boxes and score as many points as possible while avoiding the –10 box, which is called "the kitchen."

"You don't want to be in the kitchen," says Jimmy.

"Why is it called the kitchen?" I ask.

"I don't know. I guess, 'cause what guy would want to be in the kitchen, right?"

"Lots of fellas cook today," says Abe, looking to me for approval. I nod. "My grandson, he's a great cook. Do you cook?"

"Yeah, I cook," I say.

"You're going to make some guy a great wife," says Vince. Jimmy gives Vince a dirty look.

"We start. I'm teamed with Abe. Jimmy and I compete against each other on the same side of the court. The men are supportive of me, though I push the discs down the court at the same shuffleboard skill level as when I last played at the age of nine.

"Nice shot!"

"Good form!"

"This kid's a natural!"

The adoration takes its toll, I begin to feel like some sort of shuffleboard Tiger Woods, a prodigy with incredible latent talent for the sport, phenomenal "disc sense." I feel this way despite the fact that I'm scoring negative points.

While Jimmy and I wait for the others to finish their round, he curses the tennis club.

"They have, what, two, three hundred members? Everyone wants to play tennis. The shuffleboard club used to have hundreds of members." Jimmy points to an athletic-looking man on a far tennis court. "You know who that is?" he says. "That's Max. The president of the Shuffleboard Club. Even *he* plays tennis. They're all over there now, running around like idiots." Jimmy is right about that. The elderly people are exerting themselves over there on the courts. The men in particular appear to think that they're on the pro tour, although tour tennis players wouldn't, I think, wear black socks with their tennis shoes.

I'm remembering a walk I took with my grandfather. We passed a shuffle-board court and I asked him if he ever played. "No," he said, outraged, "shuffleboard is for old people." I found this a peculiar notion coming from an eighty-one-year-old. It appears that the newest wave of retirees, the young-old, are, at the age of sixty-five, rebelling against their parents, the old-old. One gerontologist, Bernice Neugarten, has written a lot about the conflict. Young-old people don't want to do old-old people things. They won't be caught dead playing shuffleboard, since, to them, shuffleboard is death. So now shuffleboard is dying off. Tennis is king.

"If it doesn't appeal to young people, the sport is kaput," says Jimmy. "It's a shame. You sure have a knack for it, though." At this point what's going on is crystal clear. They have plans for me, these old-old guys. I'm some kind of Baby Shuffleboard Moses. They want to beget me, swaddle me, place me in a bulrush basket, and send me downriver to the Tennis Pharaoh.

To my surprise, I find this idea appealing, in a *Last of the Mohicans* kind of way. I like the gravitas of being responsible for carrying the sport forward. I like the fact that I seem so important to these guys. But most of all, I like the idea of becoming the best in the world at a sport. It seems like an attainable-enough goal, even for me. Even after the softball debacle. Nobody else my age plays shuffleboard. Once the current generation of players passes on, I'll be the best by default. Plus, if old people can be good at shuffleboard, how difficult can the sport be?

"We play every day," says Abe, after we've finished up.

"You should join the club," says Jimmy.

"I can join the club?"

"Sure! We'd be happy to have you."

"Okay," I say. "I'm in."

"Then pay up," says Vince. He extends his hand. "Eight dollars' initia-tion fee."

I turn to Jimmy and Abe. One would think that Baby Shuffleboard Moses gets his initiation fee waived.

"You get four free breakfasts," says Jimmy.

I believe salesmen call that the bait and switch.

Next time I show up for shuffleboard, the fun is over. The men are done coddling me. It's not unlike in *An Officer and a Gentleman*, but I'm the only private and there's three Lou Gossett Jr.'s determined to break my spirit. Needless to say, it turns out that shuffleboard is more than just shoving a disc around with a stick. It is a game with—no, I'm sorry, Vince—a *sport* with a tremendous number of rules. I won't bore you with most of them, but two things you should know are: 1) The regulation shuffleboard court must be exactly 52 feet long, and 2) You don't lean on the shuffleboard cue fork-side-down, because then everyone yells at you.

Most days we scrimmage, and it's frustrating. Vince mutters and yells at me. Jimmy is more patient. His whole thing is you have to keep doing it until you internalize it. The short-left-step-long-right-step, the flick at the end of the push so you get the "finesse." Finesse wins and loses matches. Jimmy played for years before he improved to the point of finesse.

"You gotta stick with it," says Abe. "I didn't hit my peak until I was probably seventy-eight or seventy-nine."

I stick with it and try hard to get better. I take shuffleboard strategy books out of the library, full of black-and-white photographs of 1950s shuffleboarders demonstrating proper form, their slacks way too snug around their abdomens. Sometimes I come back to the courts late in the afternoon and practice on my own. It doesn't seem to have any impact. I continue to get my twenty-eight-year-old ass sent to the kitchen.

Abe leaves for a trip to New York in early November, and then, one morning, a new guy shows up. His name is Sam, he's in his late eighties, and it's the first time he's ever come to the shuffleboard courts.

"My wife told me, 'Get out of the condo—or else!'" says Sam. Vince and Jimmy, spotting a new recruit, immediately start selling the guy on the benefits of regular shuffleboard play. Since Abe isn't around, I wonder if I'm supposed to join in.

"It's a good sport," I tell Sam. "It's got strategy."

We split into two teams. Vince is my teammate, and Sam is my opponent. He says he's played shuffleboard before up North, but he seems to have no idea what he's doing. He lines up the black and yellow discs in a jumble, without alternating them by color. I sort them out and eye him down.

"My wife told me to get out of the condo—or else!" says Sam again. Now that I've had some one-on-one time with Sam, I see that he has an unfocused look in his eyes. "Shuffleboard. Good exercise." he says. "My wife told me to get out of the condo or else."

I'm starting to get the very strong impression that Sam might not be all there. This is always a sad thing, something I've yet to get used to even after several months among elderly people. The doctors behind the MacArthur Study on Aging took pains to point out that loss of mental clarity is not as inevitable as many senior citizens believe. Only 10 percent of senior citizens have Alzheimer's. The rest can expect a little deterioration of their mental abilities and short-term memory, but nothing major. Abe and Jimmy are perfect examples, two men, almost ninety, who are as sharp as they've ever been.

But after I notice that Sam is probably not all there, I'm not thinking about any of those things. What I'm thinking is: Finally, somebody I can beat at shuffleboard.

Sam plays with no strategy. He doesn't utilize "St. Pete's pilots" or try to knock me in the kitchen. Each shot is more random than the last. Consequently, I am annihilating him on the court. I'm making shot after shot. My shuffleboard cue has ceased to feel like a shuffleboard cue and feels instead like some sort of musket or mighty staff. I am merciless. I am destroying. The cool early-morning wind is at my back; the sun, still low on the horizon, creates a warming glow around my body. Despite my bad posture, I know I look like a god to Sam.

This doesn't stop my teammate, Vince, from keeping up a steady stream of criticism of my strategic play. He thinks that I'm shooting my discs from the wrong part of the court, resulting in lousy angles. Just to spite Vince, I continue doing exactly that.

By the third round, I'm starting to feel bad. Sam is spending so much time in the kitchen, he should be getting paid minimum wage. Maybe I should be letting this poor guy win. Perhaps he has been through enough. As if happens, I don't have to let him win. Vince's constant criticism has jangled my nerves and now I'm messing up my shots. Somehow my addled opponent and I begin to tie, and then he begins to pull ahead.

"He's blowing it!" Vince keeps muttering to Jimmy, as if I can't hear him from 52 feet away.

"Geez Louise," says Sam, before putting 8 more unanswered points on the board. "He sure takes this serious. It's just a game."

"It's not a game," I say. "It's a sport."

I try to focus. Cross pilot. St. Pete. Knock his points, block my points. Loosen my grip. Short-left-step-long-right-step. Push with my body. Flick the wrist for finesse. This is how shuffleboard is played.

I land myself in the kitchen. I notice that all of a sudden the air has become humid. Goddamn Florida.

"I told him that was a shitty angle," Vince whispers to Jimmy.

"I can hear you, Vince," I say, the anger rushing out of me. "It doesn't make it any easier when you're criticizing every shot."

"If you listened to me," shouts Vince, "you wouldn't be mucking it up!"

"Hey!" yells Jimmy. "Easy, easy!"

Sam takes a step away from the court. "Great, guys," he says, as if he's oblivious to what's happening. "I think that's it for me."

Vince whips toward Sam. "What? We're in the middle of a match."

"You guys take this too serious," he says.

"They're just playing around," says Jimmy.

"I don't take it so serious," says Sam. "I just do it for fun. It's good exercise. I'm goin' home now."

"I thought your wife told you to get out of the condo or else," Vince says. Sam looks at him like he's crazy. He lays his cue along the bench.

"Okay fellas," he says. "Take care now."

I keep thinking about how Abe says he didn't reach his shuffleboard peak until his late seventies. More and more I am accepting that I won't be able to properly play the sport until forty years from now. I don't think it's possible for a young man to slow down enough to master the sport of shuffleboard. You have to wait till the point where it's just too much energy to try hard, and then the Spirit of Shuffleboard fills you, and you're ready to kick some butt.

Once I realize that, it is a lot harder to drag myself out of bed at 6:45 to slide a piece of plastic around. But for some reason I still show up. The sport has kind of grown on me, and I feel some weird obligation to those guys.

While I am on the court the other day, I get a call on my cell phone from my friend Jenni in Los Angeles. She says she hasn't heard from me in a while, and I realize she is right, I have been calling home a lot less frequently. Jenni complains that she has been working a lot of late nights lately on a television show.

Then she changes the subject, starts asking me what I am up to down in Florida. Does she sound jealous?

It is a funny thing to hear on a workday morning, as I stand on the courts with the shuffleboard guys, watching the rising sea of tennis players in front of us. The shuffleboard tournament is starting soon, and I am going to be there. For the first time in a while, I actually feel useful. I am going to part that sea of tennis players and help save shuffleboard.

The Future of the Sport

I'm walking in the clubhouse parking lot one afternoon, when I run into Abe from the Shuffleboard Club. I didn't recognize him; you put a baseball cap on an old man, and he somehow becomes a different guy.

"Hey! Rodney!" he shouts. "You haven't been by the courts in a while!"

"Yeah, I've been a little busy, Abe."

"The tournament starts next Monday!" says Abe. "We need sixteen players! Are you coming for the tournament?"

I thought I was ready for the shuffleboard tournament, but lately I've been having second thoughts. The Century Village shuffleboard tournament takes four months. It requires you to show up three days a week, Monday-Wednesday-Friday. Colossal time commitment. I've seen how intense these guys can get about shuffleboard practice, so I can only imagine. If I missed a match, Vince might actually beat me to death.

"I don't think I'm coming," I tell Abe. My thinking is that if I lower expectations from the beginning, I'll be able to attend the shuffleboard games at my leisure.

"You're not coming? Why not? Aren't you a club member?"

"Yes."

"You should come, then. It's the big thing we do, the tournament. Everyone comes!"

Abe's lip quivers a bit. It could be from emotion, or just one of those quivers that old men's lips do sometimes. Why did it have to be Abe I ran into? Why not Vince or Jimmy? Jimmy is almost as sweet a guy as Abe, but has a crabbier face, a little easier to say no to. With Abe, it's different. He's such a well-intentioned guy. It would be like having to shoot a St. Bernard in the head as it happily sniffs the muzzle of your rifle.

I sigh. "What time to I have to be there, Abe?" He pats my shoulder a few times and I think, *Oh, great, now I'm the dog.*

I show up to the tournament two minutes late, on purpose, as a very conscientious objection. It doesn't seem to register, though. It's bedlam on the shuffleboard courts, in the relative sense. There are twelve club members gathered there already. When have I ever seen more than three people here? Abe and Vince, meanwhile, strut around, showing me off to the other members. I've never seen Abe and Vince so juiced up; they're acting like the mayors of Shuffletown. "This is the camaraderie of the sport," Jimmy tells me. "This is why we do this."

Twenty minutes later, there are still thirteen of us, which I should have recognized as an omen. Everyone has sat down on the benches lining the courts, silent and glum. That strikes me as another bad omen, like cows lying down in grass before a lightning storm.

"This is terrible," says Jimmy. "This has never happened before."

"I'm sure people are still coming," I offer. But I don't believe this. Elderly people may be slow-moving, but in my experience they are punctual.

On Wednesday, we field ten players. We wait around for half an hour and then we go home. On Friday, there are eight. We wait for 45 minutes and go home. Morale hits a new low. Someone's going to stick a shuffleboard cue in an electrical socket and end it all one of these days.

On Monday, I lie in bed until the last possible minute, then go. That day it's just me, Abe, Vince, and Jimmy again. We wait an hour, not even mentioning the tournament, and then Vince makes me scrimmage and kicks my ass.

"Who are all these people?" I ask Abe.

There are at least one hundred people at the Shuffleboard Club Welcome Back Election Breakfast. "They're members," says Jimmy.

"Yeah, but . . . where have they been for the last two weeks?"

"A lot of people belong to clubs for the free food," says Abe. "It's a good deal for them. They pay eight bucks annual membership, and they get three or four meals out of it."

"That's outrageous," I say. "How can you guys stand for that?"

Jimmy shrugs. It's a basic thing that elderly people don't question. You join clubs to get free food.

A muscular-looking seventy-five-year-old stands up in front of the crowd and begins to speak. It's a few seconds before I realize that it's Max, the Shuffleboard Club president. I've never seen him up close before. He has a wiry, compact body with excellent muscle tone. Max is notorious in the Shuffleboard Club for preferring tennis to shuffleboard. He hasn't come by the courts for months.

"Hey, folks," shouts Max. He has the boozy air of someone who has called thousands of meetings to order. "First, let me just say—welcome back to sunny Florida!"

This garners a big laugh, because it's raining outside. Classic shitty opening joke. I feel my fists beginning to clench.

"The bagels will be out in a minute," announces Max. "Two free bagels for everyone. You want a third, you gotta slide five dollars in my pocket!" Everyone in the crowd laughs. I can't believe how mad this makes me. Here I am, getting up early three days a week and then this guy gets to waltz in at the last minute and be Mr. Funny Guy Bagel Man?

Shuffleboard was founded in the fifteenth century. Back then it was often played on an actual board, using coins as playing pieces. The coins were called groats. The groats were shoved by hand or shovel so that they came to a stop within a marked scoring area. It was called shovel-groat, and sometimes shovel-board. Shuffleboard, the modern term, was popularized aboard cruise ships at the turn of the century. I thought about cruise ships as I sat there at the Shuffleboard Club bagel breakfast. Then I thought about the way the *Titanic* created a vacuum when it went down, sucking everyone underwater.

Then the bagel plate made it to me, Jimmy, and Abe, and all that was left was pumpernickel, which somehow seemed like the perfect bagel for the moment.

Shuffleboard has a public relations problem. That's crystal clear at this point. Has a single shuffleboard championship event been broadcast on any of the twelve thousand ESPN channels? Has a single shuffleboard player been featured on the cover of *Sports Illustrated* or in one of those Gatorade commercials sweating that weird green stuff?

After the shuffleboard breakfast, I find Lenny, the shuffleboard club member in charge of flyers. I'm not sure what this duty entails, exactly, since I've never seen a single shuffleboard flyer.

"Lenny," I say, "how would you like some help with flyers?"

"Some help with what?"

"Shuffleboard flyers. You're in charge of them."

"Oh yeah," he says, as if recalling some long-forgotten fact. "That would be great!"

Every morning, Max, the Shuffleboard Club president shows up at the tennis courts at five to eight. He has three outfits that he seems to alternate, all more or less the same: plain white shorts and a shirt striated with a primary color and hugging his gut. Max plays tennis intensely, but not intensely enough to overcome the fact that he runs like a penguin. I've been watching him for a few mornings, filling a notebook with the corny jokes he shouts out to his fellow players while they hit the ball around.

"Are you trying to test my mettle?" he shouts. "I coulda told you I was made of aluminum!"

After a few days, I conclude my fact-gathering and approach the man. "Hi," I say. "You're Max, right?"

"Yeah," he says warily.

"I'm writing something about the community," I say, hoping to quickly disarm him. "Could I interview you about the Tennis Club?"

"Oh, yeah! Sure!" he says. He motions to the other men. "This fella's gonna interview me. I'm gonna be famous!"

"Tell me about the Tennis Club," I say. "It looks pretty popular."

"Oh sure," he says. "We got three hundred, four hundred members. Very popular."

"Uh-huh." I scribble "400" on my pad. "And you're the president of the Shuffleboard Club too, right?"

Max looks around to see if anybody has overheard, then steps closer to me.

"Yeah," he says, more in a gesture than a word.

"I bet the Shuffleboard Club is really popular too," I say.

"Yeah. Very popular." He nods. I nod. I say nothing. "Maybe not as popular," he adds. "Hundred fifty maybe."

"Boy oh boy," I say, "you must be busy, playing tennis and shuffleboard all the time."

"I like to be active, to exercise," he says, sounding apologetic all of a sudden. "A lot of people today, that's what they want, exercise."

"They've been having a lot of trouble with the shuffleboard tournament," I say. "Not enough players. Or something."

Max takes another step closer to me. "You know . . . tennis, it's more prestigious. It's a prestige sport."

I take notes, saying nothing. He feels compelled to continue. "People change their interests," he says. "I'm sure you know that."

"Right. People change . . . interests. Got it."

I continue scribbling, looking up every once in a while to smile at Max, who is beginning to squirm.

Max shows up for the next tournament day, in his tennis clothes. "Take a look! We got customers today!" Jimmy shouts to me, motioning at Max with obvious pleasure.

We begin to scrimmage. Max is out of practice, and Jimmy is unsparing. Every time he knocks one of Max's shots into the kitchen, Jimmy grins and shouts out, "El Presidente!"

At 9:00 the tennis courts let out and the players begin to file past the shuffleboard courts with amused looks on their sweaty faces.

"Is that you, Max?" one asks.

"You play shuffleboard, Max?" another asks.

"Me? Well . . ." Max looks around at us, then back at them. I'm reminded of a high school lunchroom, of a former geek caught by his football buddies eating lunch with his nerdy old friends. After several false starts, Max manages to stammer out a sentence.

"I play every once in a while . . . 'cause . . . the tennis courts were so full today . . . I didn't want to wait, that's all."

"You fellas interested in playing shuffleboard?" asks Abe, oblivious to it all.

"No," one says, his face scrunching up. "It's not my thing."

They walk on. "See you tomorrow!" shouts Max after them, but they don't answer. Welcome back to the Shuffleboard Club, Max.

I put on a pot of coffee and start writing shuffleboard flyers. Simple, edgy, funny, attention-grabbing. This was my mandate.

DO YOU LIKE FUN?

COME PLAY SHUFFLEBOARD!

This was plainly not good. I'm just warming up.

COME CATCH SHUFFLEBOARD FEVER!

(SHUFFLEBOARD FEVER MAY NOT BE COVERED BY MEDICARE)

That one, I feel, is funny but maybe a little subtle. So I decide to leave subtlety behind and employ one of advertising's oldest tricks: lying outright.

SHUFFLEBOARD! THE FASTEST-GROWING SPORT IN AMERICA!

SHUFFLEBOARD! THE MOST POPULAR SPORT IN THE WORLD!

I print them out and lay them in the "good" stack.

Then I begin to think about celebrity endorsements. My gut feeling is that celebrities won't bother to sue me if I appropriate their names to promote a shuffleboard club in South Florida.

My friend Nicholas hooks me up with Randy Van Cleek, one of New York's top advertising guys. He's responsible for, among many other things, a series of award-winning Sony commercials featuring a little blue alien. Randy seems to be an easygoing, open-minded guy, so I ask him to come on board as an unpaid consultant to help me sell shuffleboard to the Century Village population.

"I've never really targeted anything toward senior citizens," says Randy. "Advertising tends to ignore old people. A buddy of mind once did a campaign for a stool loosener. Explosive bowel syndrome, that kind of thing. That's probably the closest I've gotten to it."

I explain to Randy that it doesn't matter that he has no experience. I want to tap into his hip, edgy style, which might appeal to young-old people who still think they're old-young people. "Oh," says Randy. He thinks for a bit. "Here's the thing," he says. "It's not just strengthening shuffleboard. It's weakening its enemies. You want to go after tennis hard. Super-hard. Take tennis out at the knees."

DID YOU KNOW: TENNIS PLAYERS ARE 450% MORE LIKELY TO HAVE
A HEART ATTACK THAN SHUFFLEBOARD PLAYERS?

SHUFFLEBOARD: IT'S HEART SMART

TENNIS IS GREAT EXERCISE. IF YOU CONSIDER EXERCISE GETTING
LIFTED INTO THE BACK OF AN AMBULANCE WITH ACUTE DEHYDRA-
TION.

SHUFFLEBOARD: THE SAFE SPORT.

November 18: The first day the Shuffleboard Club draws over sixteen people to a tournament day. We begin to play our first official match, and then the clouds roll in and the raindrops begin to fall. It might as well be raining frogs. We all go home. Does God hate shuffleboard?

December 3: It is so strange, Jimmy has to count three times: seventeen shuffleboard players have shown up, for no discernible reason. No phone calls have been made. No new ads have been posted. There are no free bagels.

"Okay, then," says Jimmy, sounding shocked. "Let's make some teams."

As many hours as I've spent here, it is the first time I've ever experienced true shuffleboard in action. When the tournament starts rolling, and the adrenaline is kicking in, you start to feel kind of badass. Kind of like a "pool shark," except you're a "shuffleboard shark." Now that I think about it, that doesn't sound as cool.

I compete against an eighty-year-old woman, Lois, who mops the court with me. That's something I've come to like about shuffleboard: It's one of the only sports I can think of where age and sex has little bearing on ability. That said, I feel it's only fair that I get a small revenge on Lois by mentioning here that she is stout and has short hair, and reminds me, physically, of several female school-bus drivers I've had.

"What did I tell ya!" shouts Jimmy from his court. "It's fun, shuffleboard! You havin' fun?"

"Yeah, yeah," I say. "Fun!"

"Future of the sport," says Jimmy, pointing at me with his cue. "The future!" He will go on to win the whole tournament, or at least its four official playing days.

Many months later, I host a shuffleboard party for people my age in Los Angeles. I send out about forty e-mail invitations, but somehow when the day comes only five people have agreed to show up.

The only public shuffleboard court I can locate in the Los Angeles area is down in El Segundo. This is a corporate and industrial wasteland most famous for its enormous oil refinery, located under LAX's southbound flight zone. A sign next to the refinery says: WARNING: EXPOSURE TO

AIR IN OR NEAR REFINERY MAY BE HAZARDOUS TO YOUR HEALTH. I have to laugh. It's for sure: God hates shuffleboard.

The Parks Department supplies us with shuffleboard equipment that looks like it hasn't been used in decades; the discs look more like chew toys. Two players drop out at the last moment, so there are three of us. That isn't enough to play, so I start accosting the baggy-short-wearing skate kids around us to see if we can find more players.

"Anyone want to play shuffleboard?!" Try saying that to fourteen-year-olds and not feeling like a goober.

"No thanks . . . we're good," they say.

"Come on!" I say. "It's just like skateboarding, but with less skating and more shuffling!"

My companions, to my amazement, seem to like shuffleboard. They love the shuffleboard lingo: "the kitchen," "the Tampa pilot," "sucker bait." At the end of the day, as the odd crimson sunset spreads out over the oil refinery, things feel both hopeful and toxic. Everyone even says they'd like to do it again, and deep down I know that shuffleboard is not going to die and I feel happy about that.

On a side note, although nobody but me has ever played shuffleboard before, I'm still beaten soundly. It's kind of embarrassing after all the trash I talked.

First Person

Davis Lee (Davis Miller)

I first became a serious Muhammad Ali watcher in late 1963. I'm still watching him and now I hear that he's going to try to make a comeback. When he was almost thirty-nine, he thought he could beat Larry Holmes and become the "quadruple greatest of all time." It wasn't a necessary thing to prove. Now he says he'll fight Gerry Cooney for the heavyweight title sometime in 1982, after Cooney has knocked out Holmes and Ali himself has won a couple of tune-up bouts.

All of this makes me remember that first glimpse I had of him and all the things that followed. That year I was a small, somewhat sickly ten-year-old and he was golden and twenty-one and was preparing to meet Sonny Liston for the first time. I recall sitting mesmerized in front of my television and listening to Ali's voice roar tinnily from the three-inch speaker as he told the world how he would "destroy the big ugly bear." "I'm big and fast and pretty and can't possibly be beat," the voice said, and I just had to believe. And I remember standing in front of the mirror in the hall after that for an hour at a time, pushing my worm of a left arm out at the reflection, trying feebly to imitate Ali's cobra of a jab.

From then on, most of the events that have defined my life have, in one way or another, been related to Ali. I've always been pleased with that. In 1968, I began studying karate because I longed to become as fine a fistic artist as Ali. I then moved on to boxing and finally to kickboxing, which combined the leg-work of karate with the hand movements of boxing. I wanted to have the grace I so admired in Ali and I soon found out that I could be good—good enough in fact to begin kickboxing professionally in late 1974, shortly after Ali beat George Foreman in Zaire. My girlfriend Lynn and I eloped in September 1977, and we were married in New York the day after we attended the Ali–Earnie Shavers bout at Madison Square Garden. I began to write a couple of years ago and I am working on my first book, which, in part, is about Muhammad Ali.*

I first met Ali face-to-face in June 1975, when he was training for a fight with Joe Bugner that was to take place in Kuala Lumpur, Malaysia. I was twenty-two years old then, fighting as a lightweight out of Winston-Salem, North Carolina, and I was undefeated in my first seven outings. My friend Bobby, who is Angelo Dundee's nephew, casually asked me if I'd like to drive up to Deer Lake, Pennsylvania, with him to watch Ali train.

"I'll see if I can't get you in the ring with him," Bobby said. He was teasing me, knowing I was one of Ali's biggest fans. He knew that my walls were covered with newspaper clippings of Ali's victories, my closet floor littered with articles written in the aftermaths of his defeats. And though I didn't believe I would even get a chance to shake hands with Ali (after all, what interest could the world's most famous boxer have in me?), Bobby knew I wouldn't be able to resist the invitation and that I'd have to go.

Bobby kept his promise, basically because, in the course of a twenty-year ring career, Ali had sparred with everyone from three-year-old tykes to their eighty-year-plus great-grandpappys. Everyone, that is, except a kickboxer. And he was intrigued by the notion of sparring with a *karateka*— even a small one like me. While I was slipping into my Safe T. Kicks (the equivalent of boxing gloves for the feet) and pulling on a pair of red Everlast trunks, I heard him, through the dressing room walls, exhorting the small crowd of spectators who had paid $1.00 each to watch him train. "I will prove to the whole world that I am not only the greatest boxer of all time," he said, "I am also the greatest martial artist." Yes, Ali had found

"Davis Lee" was a nom de plume for Davis Miller for this story.

a new crusade, and yet another universe to conquer. It was a pleasure to hear the same hyperbole through the walls that I had heard come through the TV speakers.

Ali was already standing in the center of the ring when I parted the ropes and stepped through. He introduced me to the crowd as "Mr. Lee, a great karate master," an accolade I certainly didn't deserve, but this was all part of going in the ring with Ali. Then he pointed his gloved left fist at me and, in a voice directed to no one in particular, only to the planet in general, he shouted, "But he must be a fool to get in the ring with Ali. When I'm through, he gonna think he been whupped by Bruce Lee." I smiled, faked a yawn, then winked at him. He shuffled into his variation of the buck-and-wing and flashed a clown's frown.

Then we began to move around the 20-foot, sweat-stained square of spongy canvas. Staying low, I bounced from side to side and flicked a tentative front-kick to his head, from which he easily pulled away. I flipped a round-kick, the kickboxing equivalent of a hook, toward his left kidney as a fake, saw the opening I was looking for and slid inside his arms three half-steps. Then I exploded out of my crouch and rocketed a back-first (thrown like a jab), left-hook combination, straight into the right side of his jaw.

He stepped back and opened his eyes fried-egg wide in feigned disbelief. He had never thought of me before, would never think of me again, but for two seconds he felt I deserved his serious attention. For two long seconds we were inseparably bound, whirling in a circle of electricity, each seeing nothing but the other. For two week-long seconds I was flying. Then he squashed me with just one flyswatter jab.

I saw the punch coming, and I tried to roll with it and I couldn't—it was that fast. A blaze of white went off behind my eyes. Then I felt a second, heavier thump, and I had the sensation that my legs were beginning to melt out from under me.

Ali knew I was hurt and he backed off. It was obvious that he could have knocked me out with a single punch. Instead, he put his arm around my shoulders, we exchanged hugs and smiles, and it was all over.

But in two seconds I had accomplished the one thing I had longed to do since that day I first saw when I was 10 years old. I had hit The Legend, Muhammad Ali, and as we left the ring he spoke to me from a place deep in his abdomen, in a way no man had ever spoken to me before—softly, gently, almost purring. "Hey, you're not as dumb as you look. You're fast—and you sure can hit to be so little."

He may as well have said he was adopting me.

I began to shake. My insides danced to get out. But I managed to stay composed long enough to say the one thing I hoped would (and which seemed to) impress him most. With the absolute confidence I had learned from watching him on television and hearing him on the radio countless times, I said simply, "I know."

SOURCE ACKNOWLEDGMENTS

THE CONTRIBUTORS

Billy Anderson serves as executive director of the AMICI camping charity based in Toronto, Canada, which has raised over $1,000,000 and provided over one thousand camping experiences for Canadian youth. An amateur boxer, licensed skydiver, and accomplished outdoor guide, Anderson's participatory journalism has been included in *Europe from a Backpack* and *Muskoka Magazine*, among other venues. Anderson lives and works in Toronto.

Barbara Beckwith took up squash belatedly at age fifty-six. A freelance writer based in Cambridge, Massachusetts, Beckwith is active in the National Writers' Union. Her work has appeared in *Whatever It Takes: Women on Women's Sport*, among other publications.

Greg Bishop is a two-time winner of the Associated Press Sports Editors (APSE) award for newspapers with circulation of one hundred to two hundred fifty thousand, a first-place winner for feature sportswriting in the Pacific Northwest Chapter of the Society of Professional Journalists, and a two-time honorable mention in the Best American Sports Writing series. A former sports editor at the *Daily Orange* at Syracuse University, Bishop has freelanced for such venues as *Inside Lacrosse*, the *Cleveland Plain Dealer* and the *Washington Post*. Bishop joined the *Seattle Times* as a staff reporter in in 2002, covering the Seattle Seahawks as part of his beat. In 2007, Bishop joined the staff of the *New York Times*, where he covers the New York Jets.

Grace Butcher writes as a consummate athlete, having participated in motocross and road racing for twenty years and having held the title of U.S. 800-meter/880-yard champion from 1958 to 1961. In 1996 Butcher set a world indoor record for the mile for women age 60 to 64. A former regular columnist for *Rider* magazine and a one-time contributor to *Sports Illustrated*, Butcher teaches at Hiram College and lives in northeastern Ohio, where she has recently rekindled an interest in horse racing and riding. A poet as well as a prose writer, her poems have appeared in three collections and many journals and anthologies.

Tim Cahill, winner of a National Magazine Award in 2003 and a recipient of the Lowell Thomas Gold Award from the Society of American Travel Writers, is the author of many books of sports adventure including *Jaguars Ripped My Flesh*. Cahill lives at the foot of Montana's Crazy Mountains and serves as *Outside* magazine's editor at large, as well as a contributing editor to *Esquire* and *Rolling Stone*. His work has appeared in *National Geographic*, the *Los Angeles Times Magazine*, *Sport Diver*, and many others. Like George Plimpton and Paul Gallico before him, Cahill's star has reached the film industry in the form of his coauthored, Academy Award–nominated documentary, *The Living Sea*.

Betsy Crowfoot, a contributing editor for *Sailing* magazine, describes herself as a "late bloomer" who began sailing at the ripe old age of thirty-two. When she's not sailing on the all-women's team based in Long Beach, California, Crowfoot earns a living from her freelance writing, which she has placed in numerous magazines and newspapers. Her mission is to ensure women sailors the highest possible profile and to encourage future generations to pursue sailing. Crowfoot's adventures with her daughter, Coco, can be followed on her website <adventure-mom.com>.

Michael Finkel is author of *True Story: Murder, Memoir, and Mea Culpa* and *Alpine Circus: A Skier's Exotic Adventure's at the Snowy Edge of the World*. Finkel's many international sports participations include skiing in Iran, golfing in Iceland, mountaineering in Greenland, backpacking through Tanzania, and, in this country, bicycling five thousand miles across the United States, running one hundred miles in northern California, ski jumping at Lake

Placid, and joining the U.S. Marines Mountain Warfare Training Center. He has also skied the country's smallest ski area, bowled the world's largest bowling alley, covered as a journalist two Olympic games, competed at the World Lumberjack Championships, and summitted Kilimanjaro. A contributing editor for *Ski* magazine for more than ten years, Michael Finkel lives in Montana.

Steve Friedman, whose work has been selected a half dozen times and counting for The Best American Sports Writing series, is the author of *The Gentleman's Guide to Life* and the coauthor (with N BA star Jayson Williams) of the *New York Times* bestseller *Loose Balls*, as well as *The Agony of Victory: When Winning Isn't Enough*. A longtime senior editor at GQ and a contributing editor at *Esquire*, Friedman's work has appeared in newspapers and magazines including *Ski, Backpacker, Bicycling, Outside*, the *New York Times*, and the *Washington Post*. A St. Louis native and graduate of Stanford University, Friedman lives in New York City, where he teaches courses at mediabistro .com and serves as a writer at large for the Rodale Sports Group.

Paul Gallico's career as a participatory journalist was launched, ironically, when he was knocked cold sparring with Jack Dempsey. A New York City native, Gallico assumed the post of sports editor at the *New York Daily News* in 1923, writing daily columns while gradually segueing into a career as a fiction writer after placing short stories in such leading magazines as *Vanity Fair* and the *Saturday Evening Post*, the latter of which published his O. Henry Award–winning story, "The Snow Goose." After his fiction writing breakthrough, Gallico quit his sports department gig and moved to Europe, where he wrote *Farewell to Sport*. His essay "The Feel" is considered a manifesto for participatory journalism and a defining influence on George Plimpton. A World War II correspondent and popular novelist and screenwriter, Gallico was also a formidable athlete. Prodigiously versatile and prolific, he helped organize the Golden Gloves amateur boxing competition and pursued fencing and deep-sea fishing with gusto while authoring more than forty books and twenty movies, including *The Poseidon Adventure*, which was made into a feature film in 1972 and again in 2006.

Helga Hengge was the first German woman to successfully summit Mount Everest and the first American woman to do so from the north side. A former New York–based fashion editor for *Miss Vogue*, the dual American-German citizen Hengge has since returned to Germany, where her Everest ascent has resulted in a bestselling book, *Nur der Himmel ist höher* (*Only the Sky Above*) and a successful career as a keynote speaker. She continues to climb, and to write.

Leslie Heywood directs the Nell Jackson Center for the Study of Female Athletes and teaches at the State University of New York, Binghamton. A competitive powerlifter and a former track and cross country standout, she is the author of *Pretty Good for a Girl: A Memoir* and *Bodymakers: A Cultural Anatomy of Women's Bodybuilding*, among others.

John Hildebrand, author of several books of participatory journalism, has had his work selected for the Best American Sports Writing series while placing outdoor, sports, and adventure articles in such magazines as *Harper's, Audubon*, and *Sports Illustrated*. Hildebrand received a BA in Journalism from the University of Michigan in 1971 and an MFA in Creative Writing from the University of Alaska in 1974. In 1977 he joined the English Department at the University of Wisconsin–Eau Claire, where he has since earned the Maxwell Schoenfeld Distinguished Professorship. He has been awarded a Bush Artist Fellowship, a Wisconsin Arts Board Fellowship, the BANTA Award from the Wisconsin Literary Association, and a Friends of American Writers Literary Award.

Zachary Michael Jack, a former Iowa newspaper sports editor, has written or edited more than a half dozen books. A regular reviewer for the *Journal of Sport History* and an active member of the Society for Sport Literature, Jack specializes in writing about baseball, football, golf, and nature sports, while teaching courses in literary journalism and creative writing at North Central College in Naperville, Illinois. A writer of poetry, essay, literary journalism, history, and cultural criticism, Jack's work has been featured in the *Chicago Tribune*, the *Des Moines Register*, and on Chicago Public Radio and Iowa Public Radio. A winner of the Prentice Hall writing award and nominee for a Pushcart (Best of the Small Presses) prize, Jack has been a writer-in-residence at New York's Blue Mountain Center, Ireland's Tyrone Guthrie Centre, and Mexico's Great River Arts Institute. His most recent book is *Letters to a Young Iowan: Good Sense from the Good Folks of Iowa for Young People Everywhere*.

Mark Jenkins is the author of several award-winning sports adventure books, including *The Hardway*, *To Timbuktu*, and *Off the Map*. A winner of the Alpine Club Literary Award and Polartec Explorer's Award, and holder of the McGaw/Hull Endowed Chair of Literature at the University of Wyoming, Jenkins is most widely known for his longstanding and widely read *Outside* magazine column, "The Hard Way." Jenkins's accounts of sports endurance span the globe and encompass many athletic firsts, including the first ascent of the highest peaks in the Arctic Circle, the first descent of the Niger River headwaters in West Africa, and the first coast-to-coast crossing of the former Soviet Union on bicycle, a feat which earned Jenkins a place in the *Guinness Book of Sports Records*. Jenkins's writing and photography have appeared in dozens of national and international publications, including *Bicycling*, *Condé Nast Traveler*, *GQ*, *Playboy*, *Reader's Digest*, *Sierra*, *Sports Afield*, the *Utne Reader*, the *Washington Post*, and *World*. He has been interviewed by *Good Morning America*, CNN, PBS, BBC, and NPR. Jenkins lives with his family in Laramie, Wyoming.

Ron C. Judd's journalism has been selected for the Best American Sports Writing series. His *Seattle Times* column "Trail Mix" explores the outdoors in the Northwest. A Seattle area native and *Seattle Times* writer since 1988, Judd has covered a range of sports from the high jump at the Olympic Games to the high places of Olympic National Park.

James Kaplan's widely read sports journalism includes the coauthored Brad Gilbert book, *I've Got Your Back: Coaching Top Performers from Center Court to the Corner Office*, and the co-written John McEnroe *New York Times* bestselling memoir, *You Cannot Be Serious*. Since the late 1980s he has contributed articles to *Vanity Fair*, *Entertainment Weekly*, *New York Magazine*, *The New York Times Magazine*, *Esquire*, the *New Yorker*, and *Tennis*, among others. A one-time Warner Brothers screenwriter, Kaplan teaches magazine writing at New School University and lives in New York.

Don Kardong, winner of the Fred Lebow Award given by the National Distance Running Hall of Fame, is a senior writer for *Runner's World* magazine, founder of the 50,000-strong Lilac Bloomsday Run in Spokane, Washington, and past president of the Road Runners Club of America (1996–2000). In addition to writing several books, including an American Library Association Editor's Choice, *Thirty Phone Booths to Boston: Tales of a Wayward Runner*, Kardong has written for *Running Times, Runner*, and *Running*. Kardong's penchant for novelty races has led him to race to the top of the Empire State Building and run across the Grand Canyon. Unsurpassed as a writer-athlete, Kardong is a former fourth place Olympic marathoner. An author, speaker, consultant, and online coach, Kardong lives in Spokane, Washington.

Donald Katz, winner of the *Chicago Tribune* Heartland Prize for Nonfiction, and a National Book Critics Circle and National Magazine Award nominee, is the author of many books, the most popular of which anthologize the brand of madcap adventure Katz made famous in *The Valley of the Fallen: And Other Places*. Though Katz's sportswriting is often humorous, his serious nonfiction, namely, *Just Do It: The Nike Spirit in the Corporate World*, for which he spent seventeen months among Nike's senior management, shows the range of his immersion journalism. Katz is a contributing editor for *Rolling Stone* and has been a contributor to the *New Republic, Esquire, Outside, Sports Illustrated*, and *Men's Journal*. He is the founder of the spoken-word audio company Audible, Inc.

Melissa King's work was selected for the Best American Sports Writing series and her first book, *She's Got Next: A Story of Getting In, Staying Open, and Taking a Shot*, has been featured in the *Chicago Tribune, Newsday*, and the *San Francisco Chronicle* in addition to being covered by National Public Radio and ESPN2's "Cold Pizza." Her nonfiction has appeared in the *Chicago Reader, Sports Illustrated*, and *The New York Times Play Magazine*, among others.

Davis Lee (Davis Miller), a finalist for the 1990 National Magazine Award for "My Dinner with Ali," has turned celebrity fetish and participatory journalism into a trailblazing career and two popular participatory sports accounts, The Zen of Muhammad Ali and The Tao of Bruce Lee. His oft-anthologized piece, "My Dinner with Ali," was selected in 1999 by David Halberstam as one of the fifty best pieces of sportswriting of the twentieth century. A related story, "The Zen of Muhammad Ali," was nominated for the 1994 Pulitzer Prize and was later included in the 1994 edition of The Best American Sports Writing. Miller's writing has appeared in the upper echelon of sports and men's magazines, including Men's Journal, Sport, Esquire, and Sports Illustrated. An accomplished kickboxer, Miller lives near Winston-Salem, North Carolina.

Corey Levitan, winner of multiple first place journalism awards from the Greater Los Angeles Press Club for daily/weekly newspapers with circulations under 100,000, writes the popular participatory column, "Fear and Loafing in Las Vegas," for the Las Vegas Review-Journal. His popular website by the same name asks readers to consider his style as a combination of Hunter S. Thompson and Seinfeld's George Costanza. After the fashion of George Plimpton, Levitan's participations are multisport, including playing point guard for the ABA's Las Vegas Venom and standing in as a little league umpire, stock car racer, and balloon pilot. His racier nonsport immersions include working as a nude model, filling in as a mist sprayer at a topless pool, and serving as a sex toys party host, to name just a few. A minor celebrity in Sin City, Levitan has been interviewed about his exploits by the likes of Howard Stern and turned the tables to interview legends Steven Spielberg, Johnny Cash, and Ray Charles. His byline has appeared in magazines such as Rolling Stone, Details, and Entertainment Weekly, and newspapers such as the New York Post, the New York Daily News, and the Los Angeles Times.

Jeff MacGregor is a six-time National Magazine Award nominee whose work has been selected for inclusion in Sports Illustrated's 50 Years of Great Writing and Sports Illustrated: The Anniversary Book, as well as the Best American Sports Writing series. His first major book, Sunday Money: Speed! Lust! Madness! Death! A Hot Lap Around America with NASCAR, was selected as an editor's choice by the *New York Times Book Review*, the *Chicago Tribune*, the *Atlanta Journal-Constitution*, *Sports Illustrated*, Book Lust, and Amazon Best Books of 2005. MacGregor is currently a special contributor at *Sports Illustrated* magazine. He has written for the *New York Times*, the *New Yorker*, *Esquire*, *Men's Journal*, *Details*, and *Los Angeles Magazine*, and has taught both fiction and nonfiction at Yale University.

David Mamet has earned the Pulitzer Prize for playwriting, Oscar and Golden Globe nominations for best screenplay, and a Tony nomination for *Glengarry Glen Ross*. A Chicagoan whose screenwriting and producing credits include *The Untouchables* and *Hoffa*, respectively, Mamet writes often of the masculine psyche, a preoccupation that has made him a contributor to sportswriting magazines such as *Sports Afield*.

Jack McCallum, recipient of the Basketball Hall of Fame's Curt Gowdy Media Award for outstanding writing and a selectee for the Best American Sports Writing series, has been at *Sports Illustrated* since 1981 and the chief NBA writer since 1985. His popular sports journalism participations include *Seven Seconds or Less: My Season on the Bench with the Runnin' and Gunnin'* Phoenix Suns, for which McCallum served as an "assistant coach" for the 2005–2006 season. McCallum has also authored *Unfinished Business: On and Off the Court with the 1990–91 Boston Celtics* and coauthored *Foul Lines: A Pro Basketball Novel*. He lives in Bethlehem, Pennsylvania.

Bill McKibben is a recipient of the Guggenheim and Lyndhurst Fellowship for his engaged and engaging nonfiction on the environment, sport, and community. A former writer for the *New Yorker*, McKibben's books of sports participations include *Long Distance: A Year of Living Strenuously*, which details a grueling year spent training for endurance events, and the more recent *Wandering Home*, an account of his solitary hike from Ripton, Vermont, to his former home in the Adirondack Mountains. A pioneering advocate for climate change awareness, McKibben is a frequent contributor to magazines such as *Outside*, *Mother Jones*, and *Orion*, among many others. He currently teaches as a scholar-in-residence at Middlebury College.

James McManus, a 2001 winner of the Peter Lisagor Award for sports journalism, is best known for his book of participatory journalism, *Positively Fifth Street: Murderers, Cheetahs, and Binion's World Series of Poker*, which tells how McManus gambled his book advance into a fifth place World Series finish. The author of many books, McManus teaches writing at the School of the Art Institute in Chicago.

T. Edward Nickens is a winner of two first place awards in the prestigious Outdoor Writers of Association of America (OWAA) national writing contest. A freelance journalist specializing in outdoor adventure, Eddie Nickens has paddled remote Canadian rivers and tracked Florida panthers to investigate the effects of urban sprawl on large predators, among countless other participations. His award-winning articles and essays have appeared in *Field & Stream, Smithsonian, National Wildlife, National Geographic Adventure, Men's Journal, Backpacker, Audubon,* and *Wildlife Conservation.* He lectures widely and serves as a consultant for a diverse clientele, including The Discovery Channel. He lives in Raleigh, North Carolina.

Nick Paumgarten is an editor for "Talk of the Town" at the *New Yorker*, a former reporter and editor at the *New York Observer*, and a past contributor to Slate.com. Paumgarten's sports participations include a lengthy *New Yorker* account of ski mountaineering, about which he was interviewed by Noah Adams on National Public Radio; a 2005 profile of Roger Federer for *Men's Vogue* entitled "Levels of the Game" and billed as "A Roger Federer Fanatic Follows His Man from TV Set to Center Court"; and a 2005 immersion *New Yorker* experience with Explorers Club President Richard Wiese in a high altitude chamber in preparation for Wiese's ascent of two Mexican volcanoes.

George Plimpton is the dean of participatory sportswriters and a towering figure in international arts and letters. Upon his death in 2003, Plimpton, who was tapped to be the first editor of the legendary *Paris Review* in 1952, was eulogized on both sides of the Atlantic. A September 29, 2003, *Guardian* obituary credited Plimpton with bringing "sports journalism in from the tabloid ghetto." Plimpton's sports participations began with a *Sports Illustrated*–sponsored, 3-round exhibition with light-heavyweight champ Archie Moore, an encounter he described belatedly in his book *Shadow Box*. Plimpton's participatory breakthroughs came with the best-selling *Out of My League* in 1961 and *Paper Lion* in 1965. Though most of Plimpton's bestselling participations came in the 1960s and 1970s, his later work was collected by his second wife, Sarah Whitehead Dudley, in the posthumous collection, *The Man in the Flying Lawn Chair: And Other Excursions and Observations*. A friend of the Kennedys and the man credited with wrestling Sirhan Sirhan to the ground after Bobby Kennedy's assassination, Plimpton achieved celebrity status as a writer and man about town: he was to the New York City of the 1960s and 1970s what Gertrude Stein was to Paris of the 1920s: consummate host, gossip, and provocateur. Like his predecessor Paul Gallico, Plimpton's star drew him to television and film, where he made cameo appearances in films such as *Bonfire of the Vanities* and *Good Will Hunting*, as well as on television shows from *The Simpsons* to *E.R.* Ironically, as he came to define contemporary literary sports journalism, Plimpton wrote in his 1997 introduction to *The Best American Sports Writing*, "Because I only wrote about sports part-time, . . . I never truly felt myself a member of the sportswriting fraternity."

Rodney Rothman's first book, *Early Bird: A Memoir of Premature Retirement*, a participatory account of living in a Boca Raton retirement community and competing against octogenarians at such sports as softball, tennis, gambling, and shuffleboard, was featured on *The Today Show* and CBS *Sunday Morning*. A former head writer for the *Late Show with David Letterman*, Rothman has also written for the *New York Times*, the *New Yorker*, and *Men's Journal*, among others.

Bob Shacochis, winner of the National Book Award and a contributing editor for *Outside* and *Harper's* magazines, is a versatile writer of fiction and literary journalism. A one-time volunteer for the Peace Corps, Shacochis's New Journalism is vested in political justice, a passion that plays out in his books of nonfiction about Caribbean politics: *The Immaculate Invasion* and *Conversations with Cuba*. An amateur gourmand, Shacochis worked as a cooking columnist for GQ and, in the spirit of Ernest Hemingway, edited the volume *Drinking, Smoking, and Screwing: Great Writers on Good Times*.

Rob Story, recipient of the Lowell Thomas Award for print journalism, is the author of *Outside Adventure Travel: Mountain Biking*. An avid skier who averages fifty days on the slopes every winter, Story is an editor-at-large at *Bike* and has written for magazines including *Outside*, *Powder*, and *Skiing*. He is based in Telluride, Colorado.

Robert Twigger, winner of the prestigious William Hill Sports Book of the Year Award and the Somerset Maugham Award for Literature, has devoted his writing life to participatory journalism, adventures captured in several books, including *Angry White Pajamas: A Scrawny Oxford Poet Takes Lessons from the Tokyo Riot Police*, which he has written as a film script for Miramax. In several decades as a participatory writer he has caught the world's longest snake—documented in his Channel 4/National Geographic film *Big Snake*—and was the first person since 1793 to cross Western Canada in a birchbark canoe. He has written many books, made multiple documentary films, and written and lectured extensively in Britain. He divides his time between the Middle East and Europe.

Tom Verducci holds the title of senior writer for *Sports Illustrated*. Before joining SI, Verducci spent ten years as a sports reporter for *Newsday*, serving as its national baseball columnist from 1990 to 1993. Along with colleagues Rick Reilly and Jack McCallum, Verducci is the SI heir apparent to George Plimpton, an ascendance announced by his popular 2005 account of playing left field in a five-day stint with the Toronto Blue Jays titled "I was a Toronto Blue Jay." Born in East Orange, New Jersey, and raised in Glen Ridge, Verducci has always been a standout athlete, having led his high school football team to a state championship. Verducci currently lives, and golfs, in New Jersey.

Sam Walker, winner of the Hopwood and Arthur Miller Awards, serves as senior special writer for the *Wall Street Journal*. Prior to joining the Journal in 1998, he worked for the *Atlanta Journal-Constitution* and spent five years at the *Christian Science Monitor*. He has been a regular guest on both ESPN and CNBC and has appeared on CNN, C-SPAN, NPR, and BBC Radio. Author of the popular book *Fantasyland: A Sportswriter's Obsessive Bid to Win* *the Most Ruthless Fantasy Baseball League*, Walker actually won the American League Tout Wars championship in just his second season playing Rotisserie Baseball. He lives in New York City.

Dan Washburn's columns in the "Sporting Life" newspaper series won him first place in the Sports/Outdoor Writing category in the award series sponsored by Gannett, as well as first place awards from the Georgia Sports Writer's Association, Georgia Press Association, Georgia Associated Press, Best of Gannett, and the National Shooting Sports Federation. In addition to writing for the *Times* of Gainesville, Georgia, Washburn served as the senior sports copy editor for *TV Guide*. In 2002 the native Pennsylvanian took his sports show on the road, moving to Shanghai to kick off his award-winning blog, *Shanghai Dairies*, and to begin work on a participatory book about the Chinese professional golf tour. His sports journalism has appeared in ESPN.com, *Baseball America*, and other top outlets.

Dana White is executive editor of *Golf for Women* and coauthor of two books, *Picabo: Nothing to Hide* and *The Heart of a Soldier: A True Story of Love, War, and Sacrifice with Captain Kate Blaise*. A tireless advocate for women, White was part of the editorial team that launched Condé Nast's *Women's Sports & Fitness* and has freelanced for magazines such as SELF and *Parenting*. She began her career as an editorial assistant at *Skiing* magazine, where she rose through the masthead to become executive editor. White lives in Westchester County.

Randy Wayne White is a contributing editor to *Outside* magazine and a former tackle-fishing guide based in Sanibel Island, Florida. An avid windsurfer and saltwater boater, White has published more than two dozen articles for major magazines, most on sport risk takers and adventurers. His Doc Ford crime novels have been honored by the Mystery Bookseller's Association as one of the "Hundred Favorite Mysteries of the Twentieth Century."